RIN-NE

Story and Art by
Rumiko Takahashi

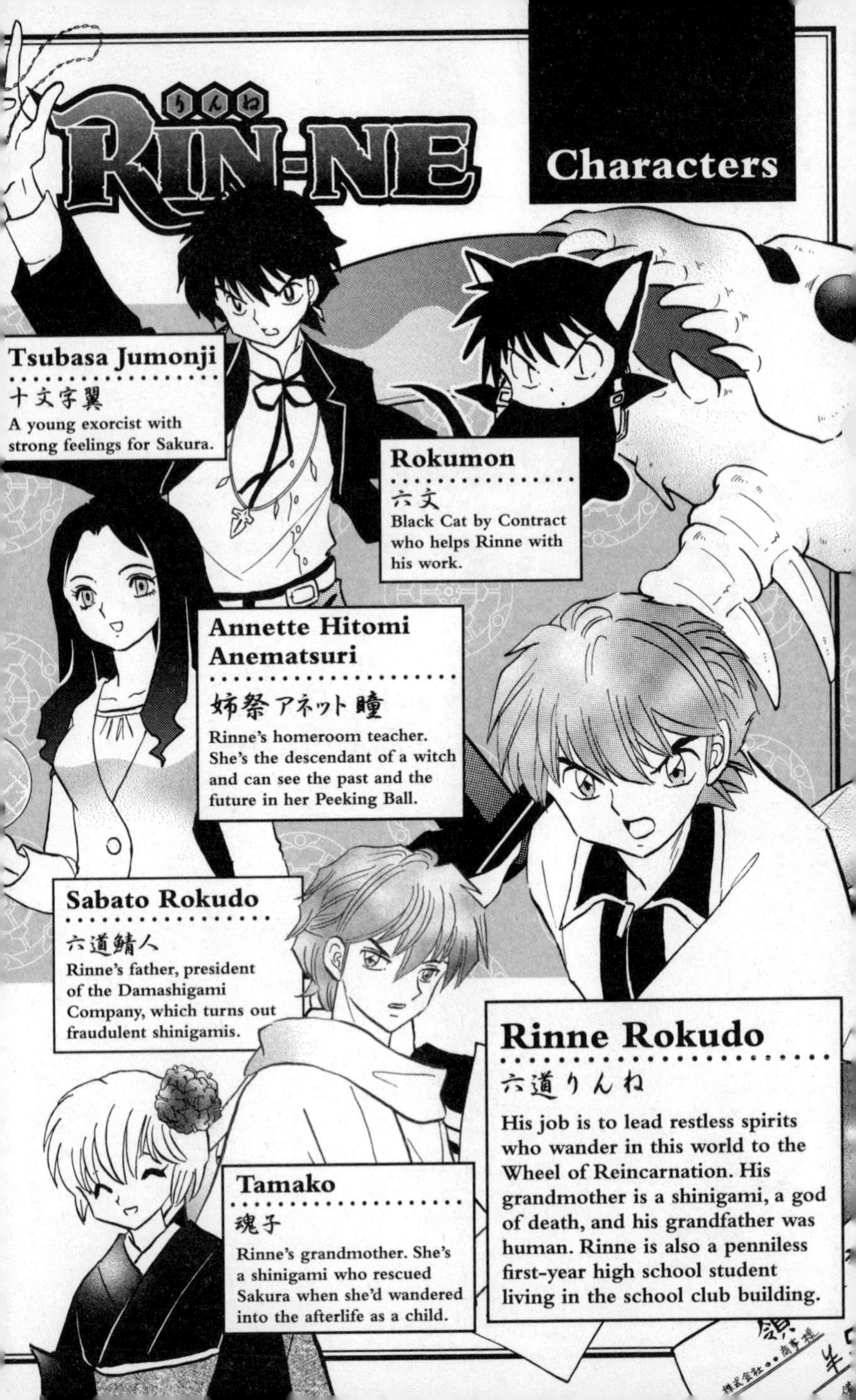
りんね
RIN-NE
Characters
Tsubasa Jumonji
十文字翼
A young exorcist with strong feelings for Sakura.
Rokumon
六文
Black Cat by Contract who helps Rinne with his work.
Annette Hitomi Anematsuri
姉祭アネット瞳
Rinne's homeroom teacher. She's the descendant of a witch and can see the past and the future in her Peeking Ball.
Sabato Rokudo
六道鯖人
Rinne's father, president of the Damashigami Company, which turns out fraudulent shinigamis.
Rinne Rokudo
六道りんね
His job is to lead restless spirits who wander in this world to the Wheel of Reincarnation. His grandmother is a shinigami, a god of death, and his grandfather was human. Rinne is also a penniless first-year high school student living in the school club building.
Tamako
魂子
Rinne's grandmother. She's a shinigami who rescued Sakura when she'd wandered into the afterlife as a child.

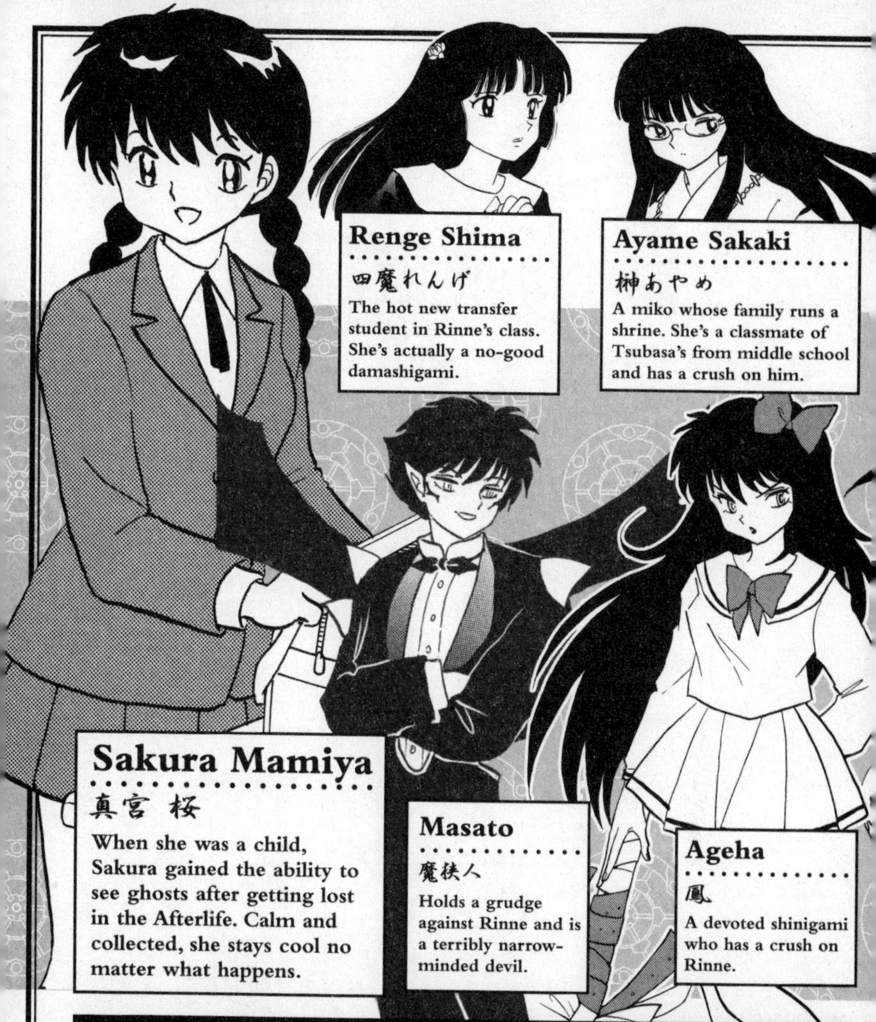
Renge Shima
四魔れんげ
The hot new transfer student in Rinne's class. She's actually a no-good damashigami.
Ayame Sakaki
榊あやめ
A miko whose family runs a shrine. She's a classmate of Tsubasa's from middle school and has a crush on him.
Sakura Mamiya
真宮 桜
When she was a child, Sakura gained the ability to see ghosts after getting lost in the Afterlife. Calm and collected, she stays cool no matter what happens.
Masato
魔狭人
Holds a grudge against Rinne and is a terribly narrow-minded devil.
Ageha
鳳
A devoted shinigami who has a crush on Rinne.

The Story So Far

Sakura, the girl who can see ghosts, and Rinne, the shinigami (sort of), spend their days together, helping spirits that can't pass on reach the Afterlife, and dealing with all kinds of strange phenomena at their school.

Renge forges a shinigami license in her name hoping to catch the attention of her crush, Kain. Rinne knows the truth, but Renge begs him to keep her secret. Meanwhile, the staff at the Lifespan Administration Bureau have already detected the forged license! With the fiasco that ensues, plus a wedding chapel ghost and an enchanted hot water bottle, Rinne's life is a whirlwind of supernatural shenanigans!

Contents

Chapter 309: Beautiful Windows......5

Chapter 310: Christmas Exorcism......23

Chapter 311: The Black Hamaya......41

Chapter 312: I Want to Bite You......59

Chapter 313: Otome's Scythe......77

Chapter 314: Something's Watching......95

Chapter 315: Otome's Memories.......115

Chapter 316: The Details of Her Disappearance.......133

Chapter 317: Truth and Lies!......151

Chapter 318: The White Spirit......169

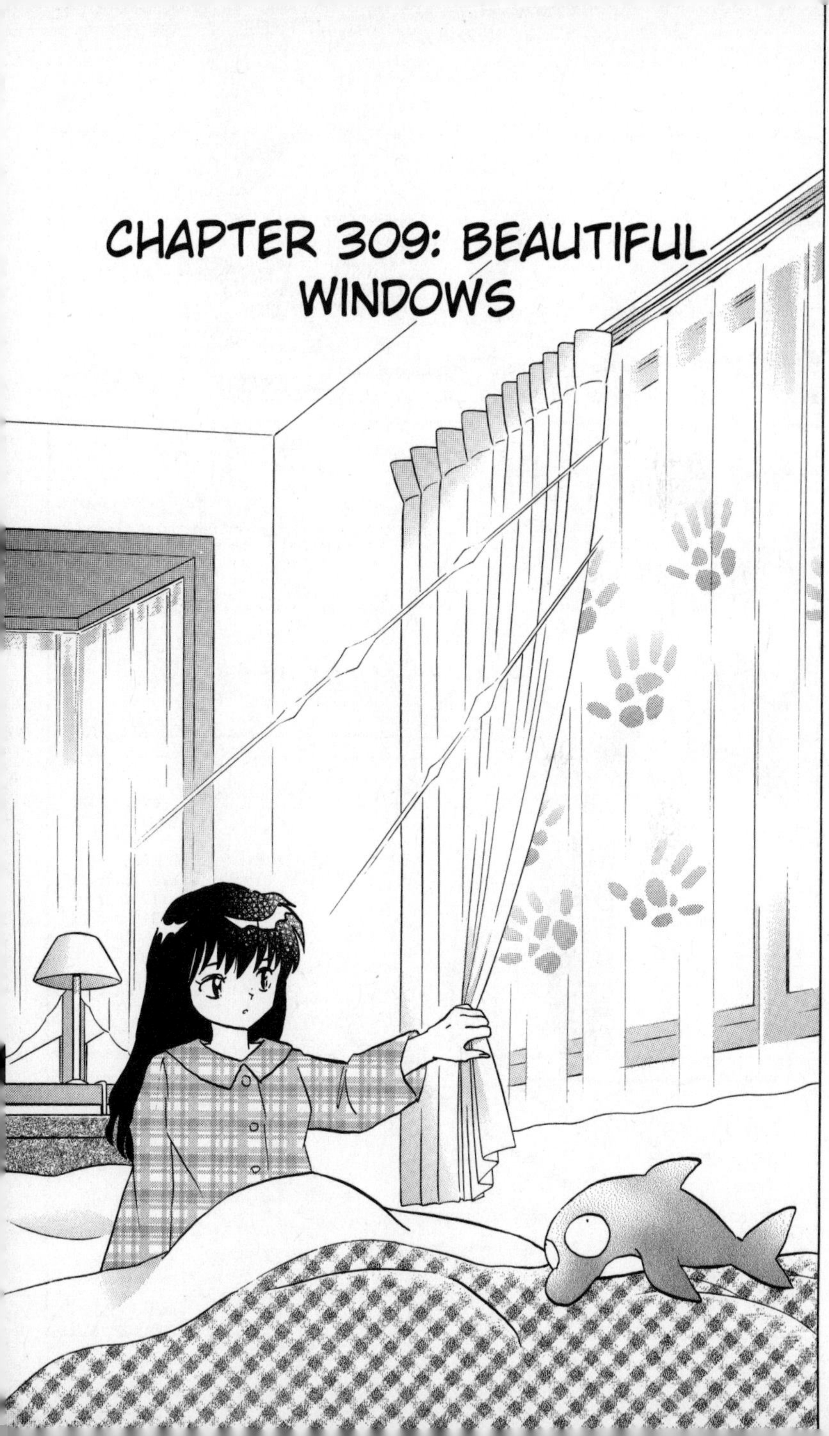
CHAPTER 309: BEAUTIFUL WINDOWS

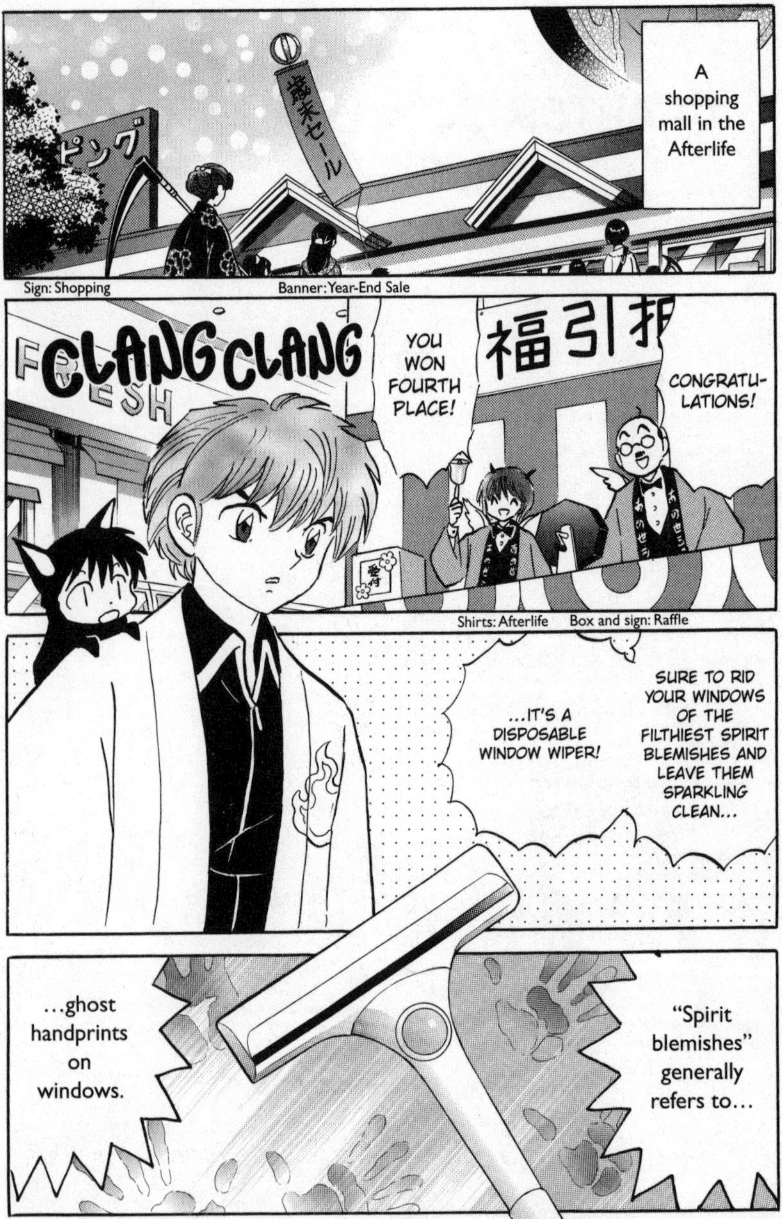
A shopping mall in the Afterlife
Sign: Shopping
Banner: Year-End Sale
CONGRATULATIONS!
YOU WON FOURTH PLACE!
福引
CLANG CLANG
FRESH
Shirts: Afterlife
Box and sign: Raffle
SURE TO RID YOUR WINDOWS OF THE FILTHIEST SPIRIT BLEMISHES AND LEAVE THEM SPARKLING CLEAN...
...IT'S A DISPOSABLE WINDOW WIPER!
"Spirit blemishes" generally refers to...
...ghost handprints on windows.

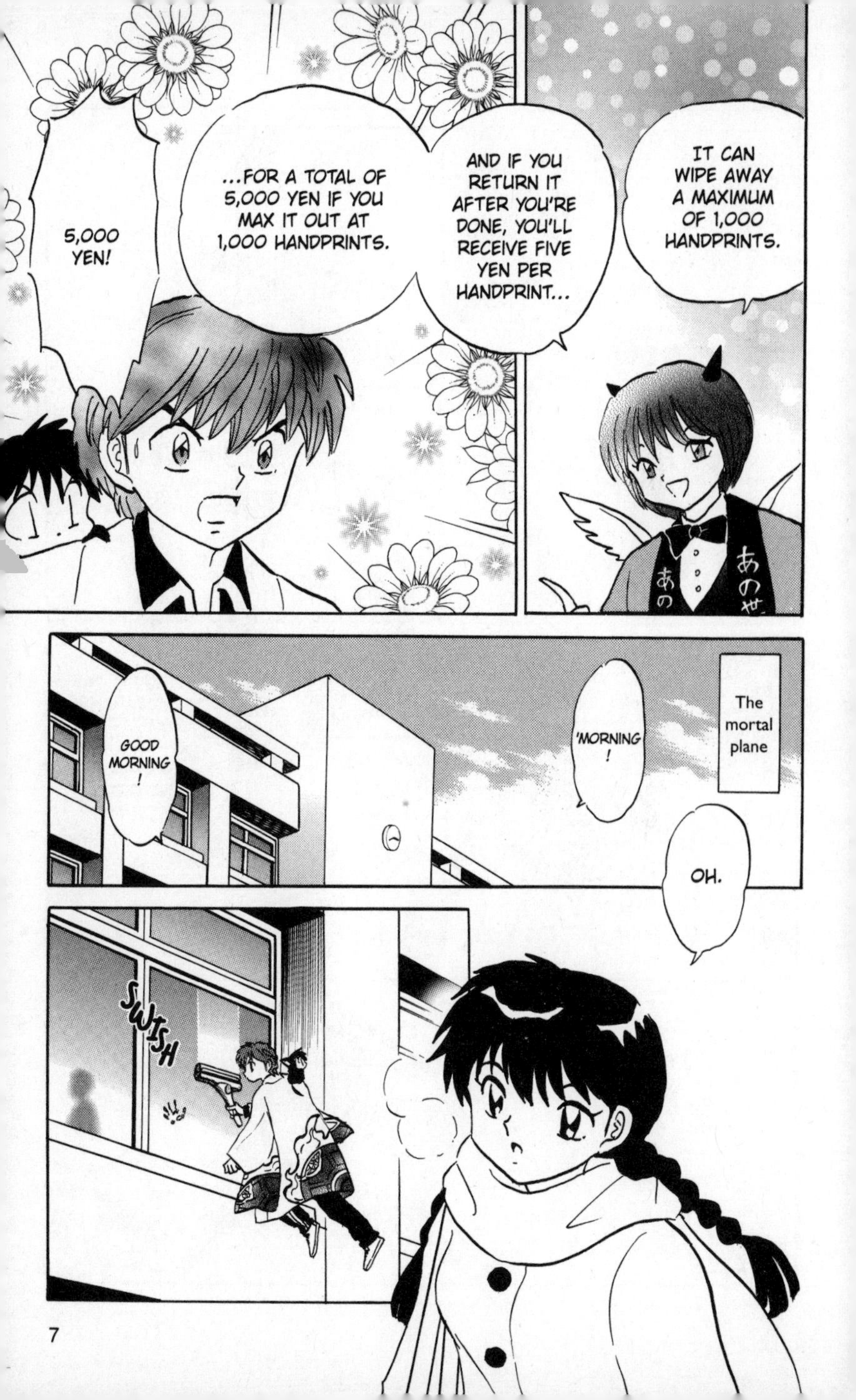
IT CAN WIPE AWAY A MAXIMUM OF 1,000 HANDPRINTS.
AND IF YOU RETURN IT AFTER YOU'RE DONE, YOU'LL RECEIVE FIVE YEN PER HANDPRINT...
...FOR A TOTAL OF 5,000 YEN IF YOU MAX IT OUT AT 1,000 HANDPRINTS.
5,000 YEN!
The mortal plane
'MORNING!
GOOD MORNING!
OH.
SWISH

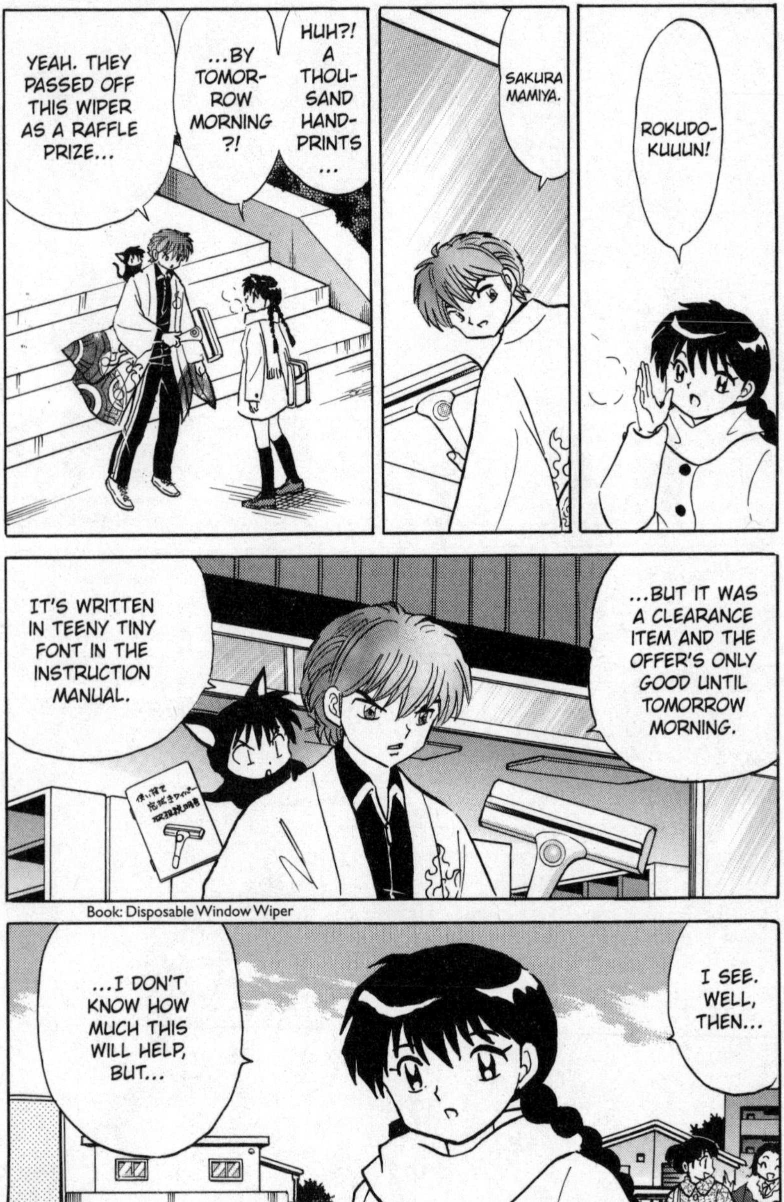
ROKUDO-KUUUN!
SAKURA MAMIYA.
HUH?! A THOUSAND HANDPRINTS...
...BY TOMORROW MORNING?!
YEAH. THEY PASSED OFF THIS WIPER AS A RAFFLE PRIZE...
...BUT IT WAS A CLEARANCE ITEM AND THE OFFER'S ONLY GOOD UNTIL TOMORROW MORNING.
IT'S WRITTEN IN TEENY TINY FONT IN THE INSTRUCTION MANUAL.
Book: Disposable Window Wiper
I SEE. WELL, THEN...
...I DON'T KNOW HOW MUCH THIS WILL HELP, BUT...

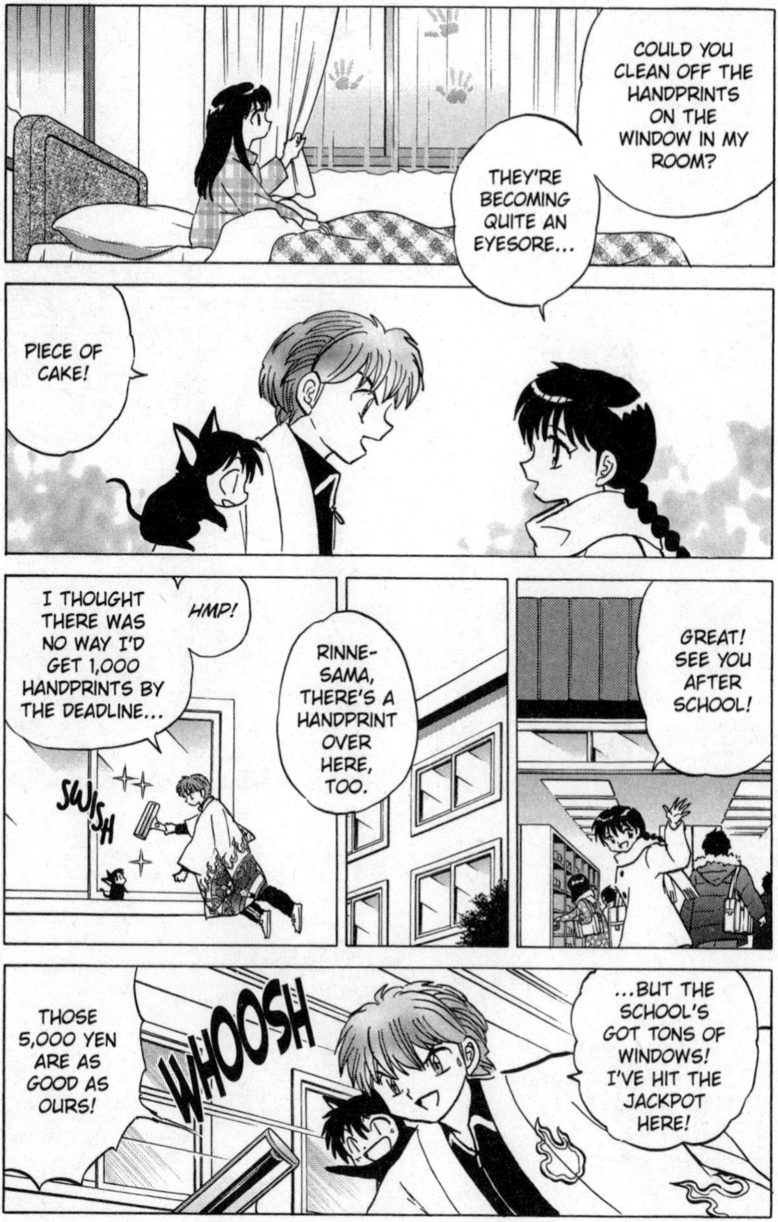
COULD YOU CLEAN OFF THE HANDPRINTS ON THE WINDOW IN MY ROOM?
THEY'RE BECOMING QUITE AN EYESORE...
PIECE OF CAKE!
GREAT! SEE YOU AFTER SCHOOL!
RINNE-SAMA, THERE'S A HANDPRINT OVER HERE, TOO.
HMP!
I THOUGHT THERE WAS NO WAY I'D GET 1,000 HANDPRINTS BY THE DEADLINE...
SWISH
...BUT THE SCHOOL'S GOT TONS OF WINDOWS! I'VE HIT THE JACKPOT HERE!
WHOOSH
THOSE 5,000 YEN ARE AS GOOD AS OURS!

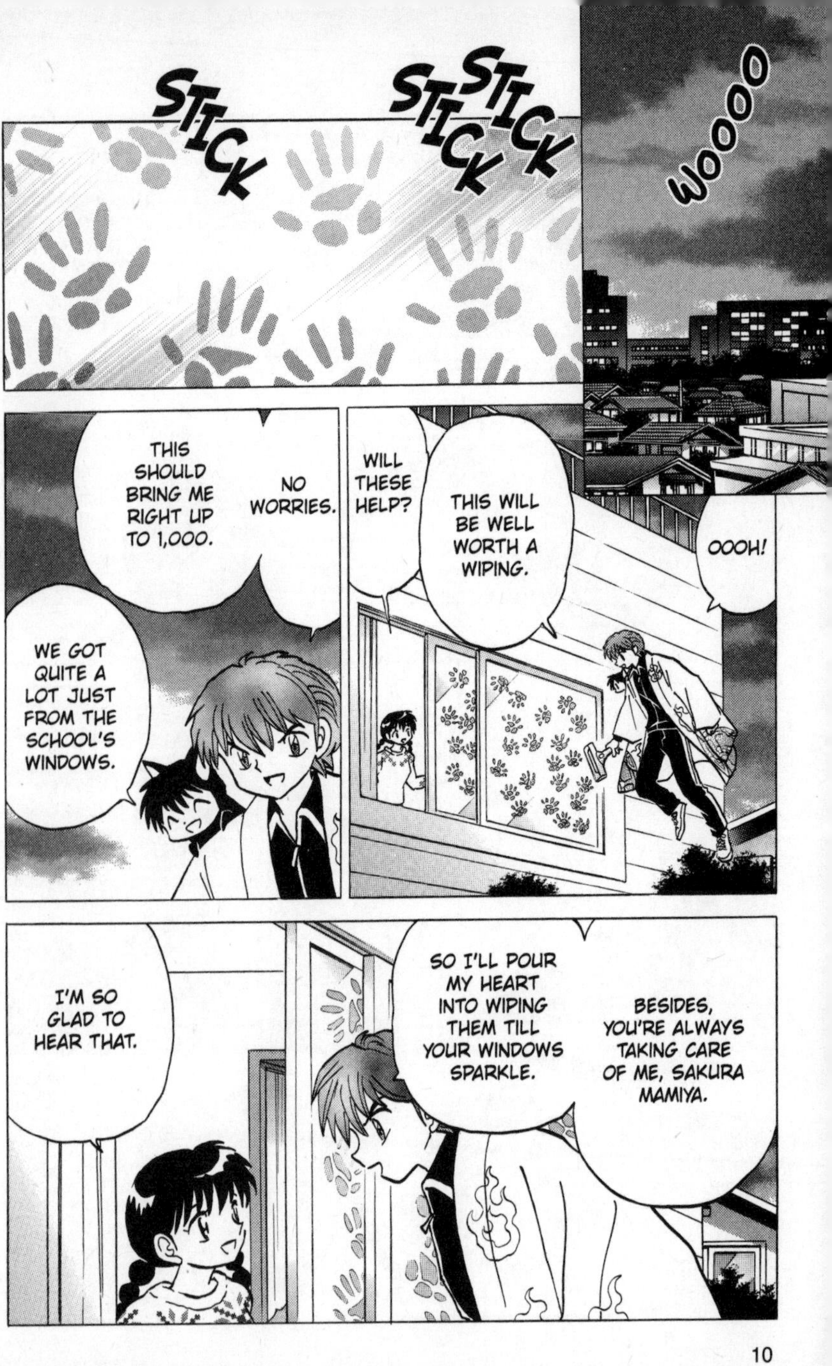
WOOOO
STICK STICK
STICK
OOOH!
THIS WILL BE WELL WORTH A WIPING.
WILL THESE HELP?
NO WORRIES.
THIS SHOULD BRING ME RIGHT UP TO 1,000.
WE GOT QUITE A LOT JUST FROM THE SCHOOL'S WINDOWS.
BESIDES, YOU'RE ALWAYS TAKING CARE OF ME, SAKURA MAMIYA.
SO I'LL POUR MY HEART INTO WIPING THEM TILL YOUR WINDOWS SPARKLE.
I'M SO GLAD TO HEAR THAT.

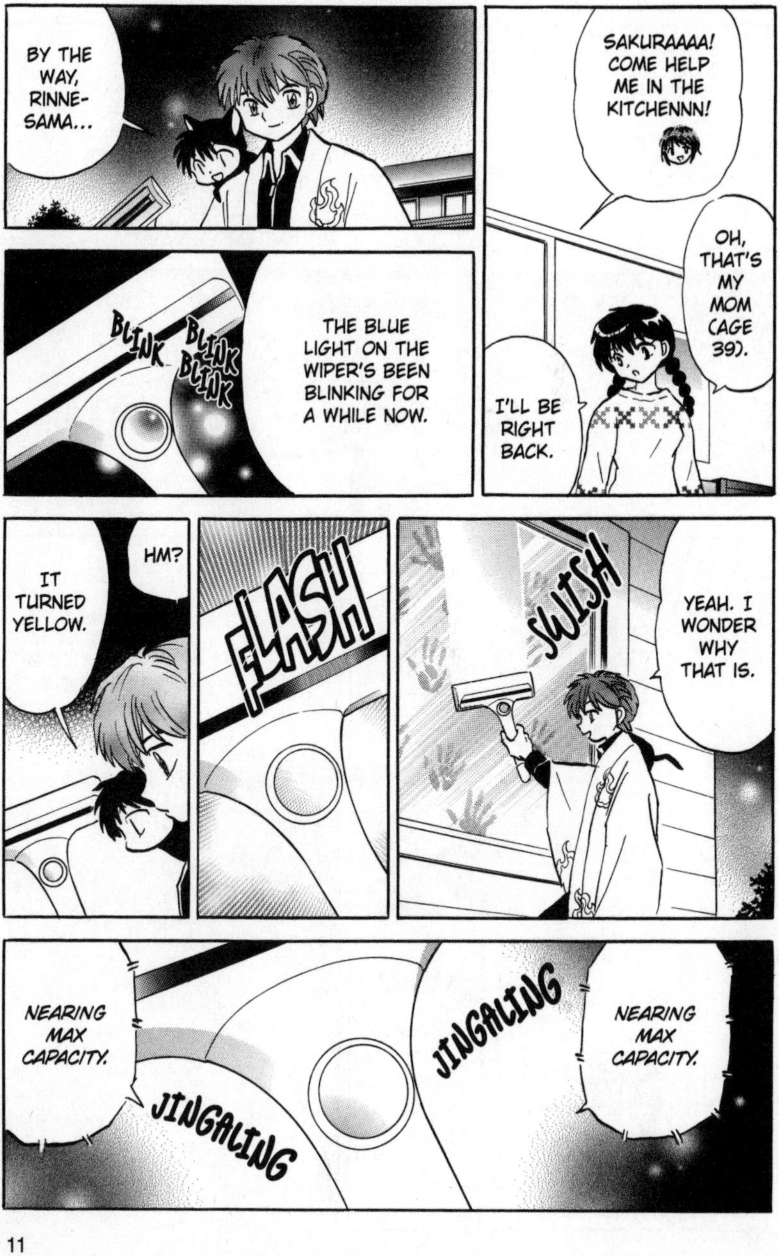
SAKURAAAA! COME HELP ME IN THE KITCHENNN!
OH, THAT'S MY MOM (AGE 39).
I'LL BE RIGHT BACK.
BY THE WAY, RINNE-SAMA...
BLINK BLINK BLINK
THE BLUE LIGHT ON THE WIPER'S BEEN BLINKING FOR A WHILE NOW.
SWISH
YEAH. I WONDER WHY THAT IS.
FLASH
HM?
IT TURNED YELLOW.
NEARING MAX CAPACITY.
JINGALING
NEARING MAX CAPACITY.
JINGALING

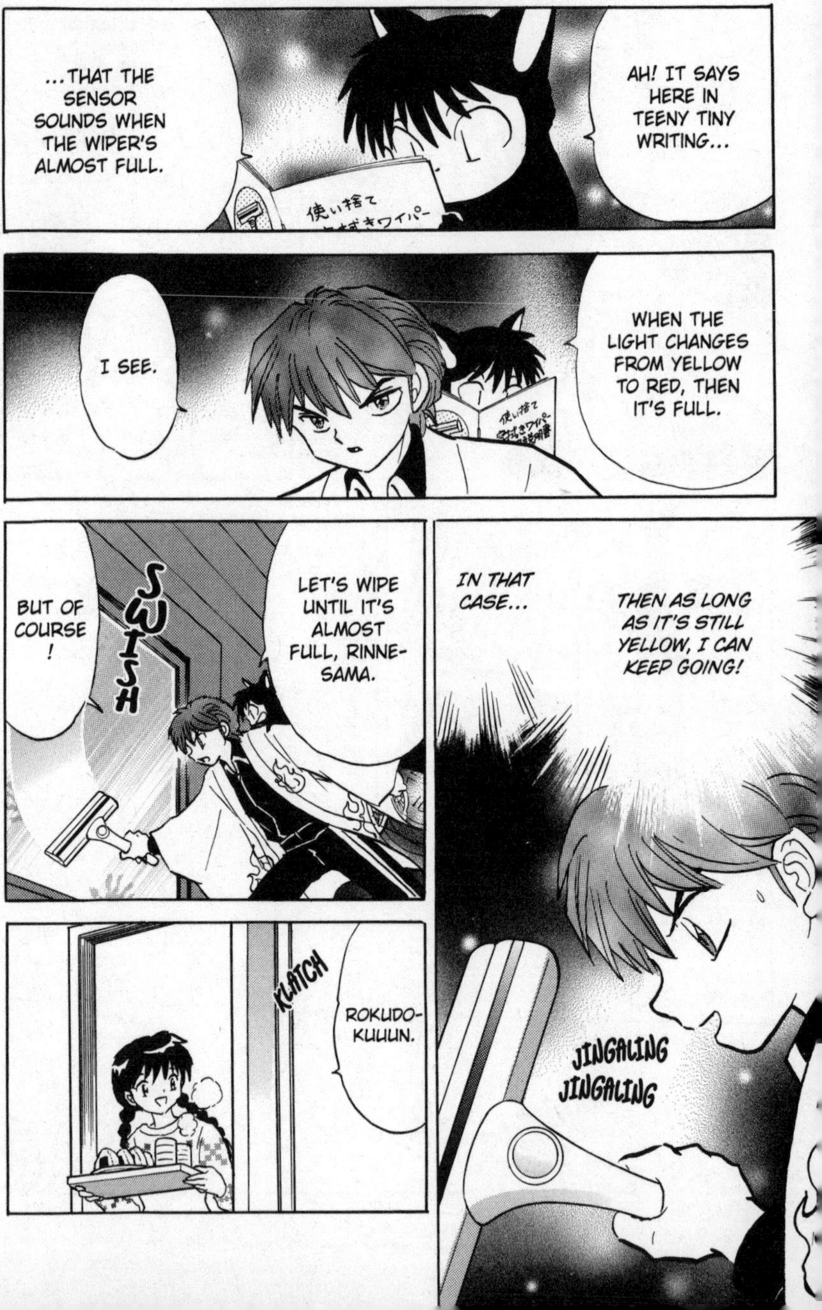
AH! IT SAYS HERE IN TEENY TINY WRITING...
...THAT THE SENSOR SOUNDS WHEN THE WIPER'S ALMOST FULL.
WHEN THE LIGHT CHANGES FROM YELLOW TO RED, THEN IT'S FULL.
I SEE.
THEN AS LONG AS IT'S STILL YELLOW, I CAN KEEP GOING!
IN THAT CASE...
JINGALING
JINGALING
LET'S WIPE UNTIL IT'S ALMOST FULL, RINNE-SAMA.
BUT OF COURSE!
SWISH
ROKUDO-KUUUN.
KLATCH

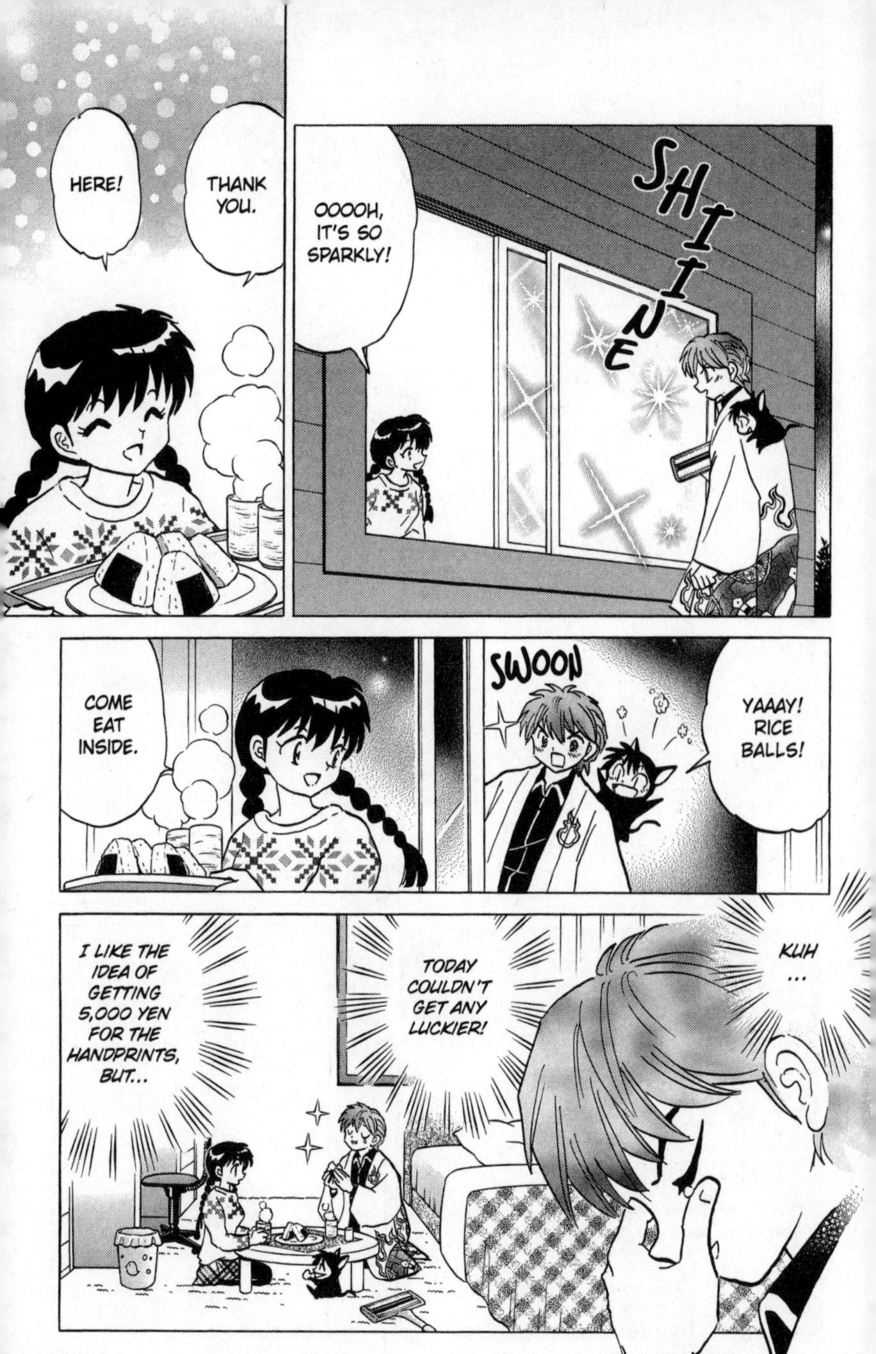
SHIIINE
OOOOH, IT'S SO SPARKLY!
THANK YOU.
HERE!
YAAAY! RICE BALLS!
SWOON
COME EAT INSIDE.
KUH...
TODAY COULDN'T GET ANY LUCKIER!
I LIKE THE IDEA OF GETTING 5,000 YEN FOR THE HANDPRINTS, BUT...

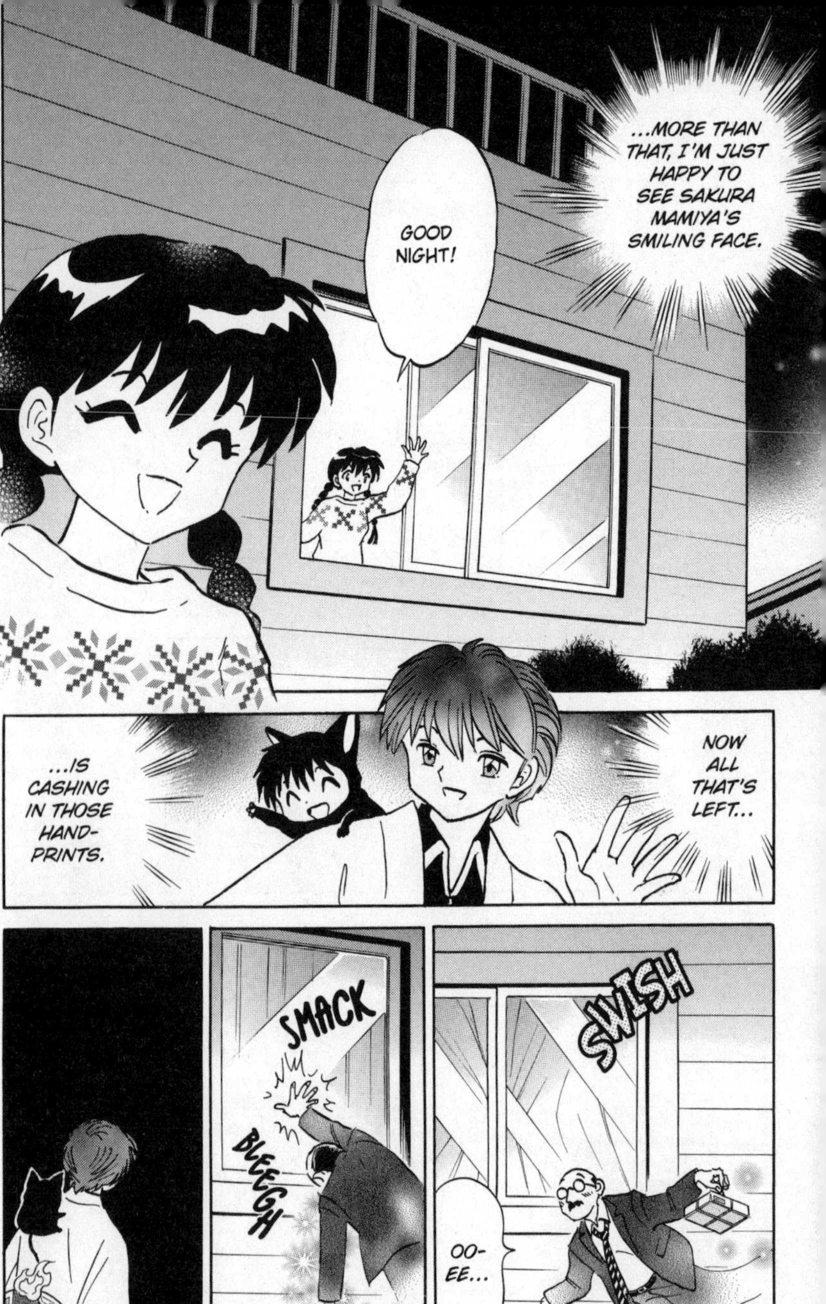
...MORE THAN THAT, I'M JUST HAPPY TO SEE SAKURA MAMIYA'S SMILING FACE.
GOOD NIGHT!
NOW ALL THAT'S LEFT...
...IS CASHING IN THOSE HAND-PRINTS.
SWISH
OO-EE...
SMACK
BLEEGH

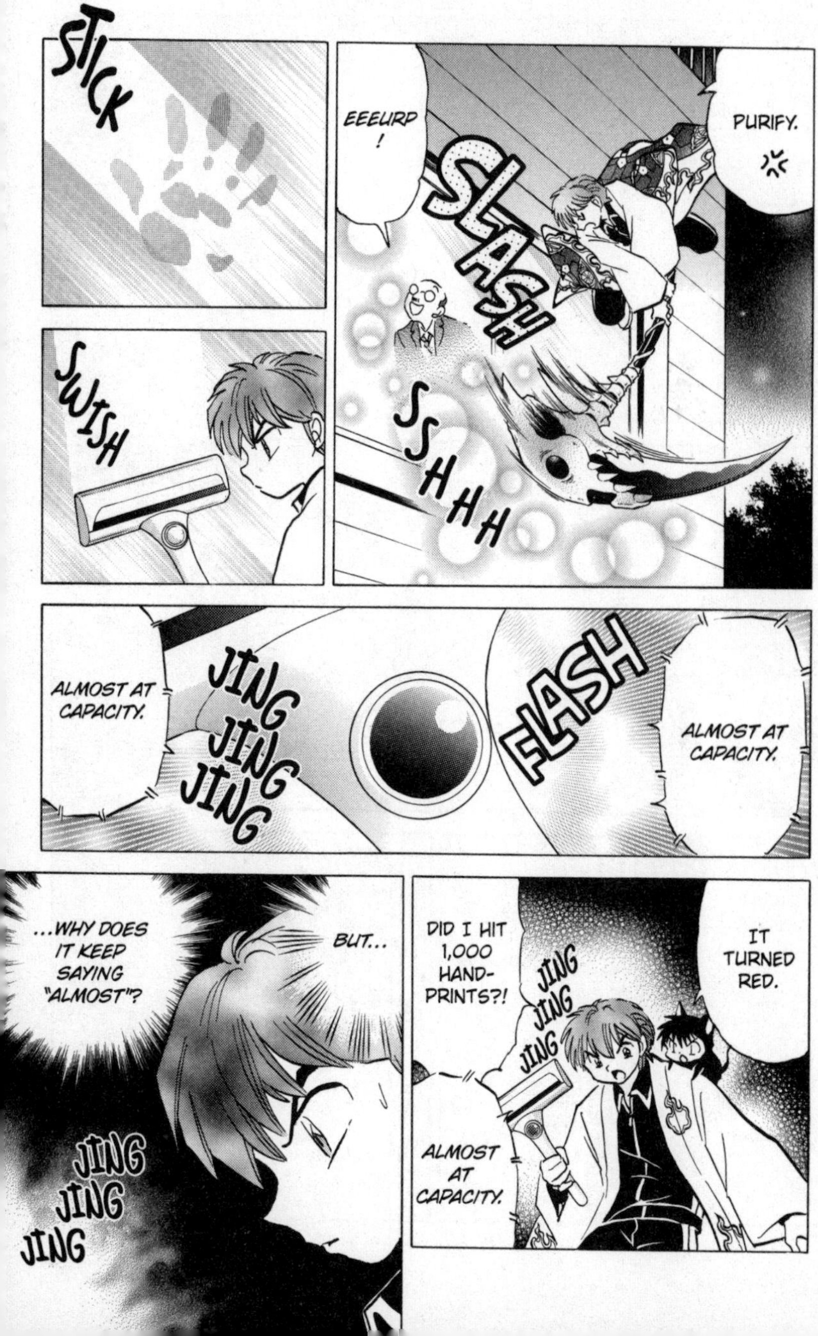
PURIFY.
EEEURP!
SLASH
SSHHHH
STICK
SWISH
ALMOST AT CAPACITY.
FLASH
JING JING JING
ALMOST AT CAPACITY.
IT TURNED RED.
DID I HIT 1,000 HAND-PRINTS?!
JING JING JING
ALMOST AT CAPACITY.
BUT...
...WHY DOES IT KEEP SAYING "ALMOST"?
JING JING JING

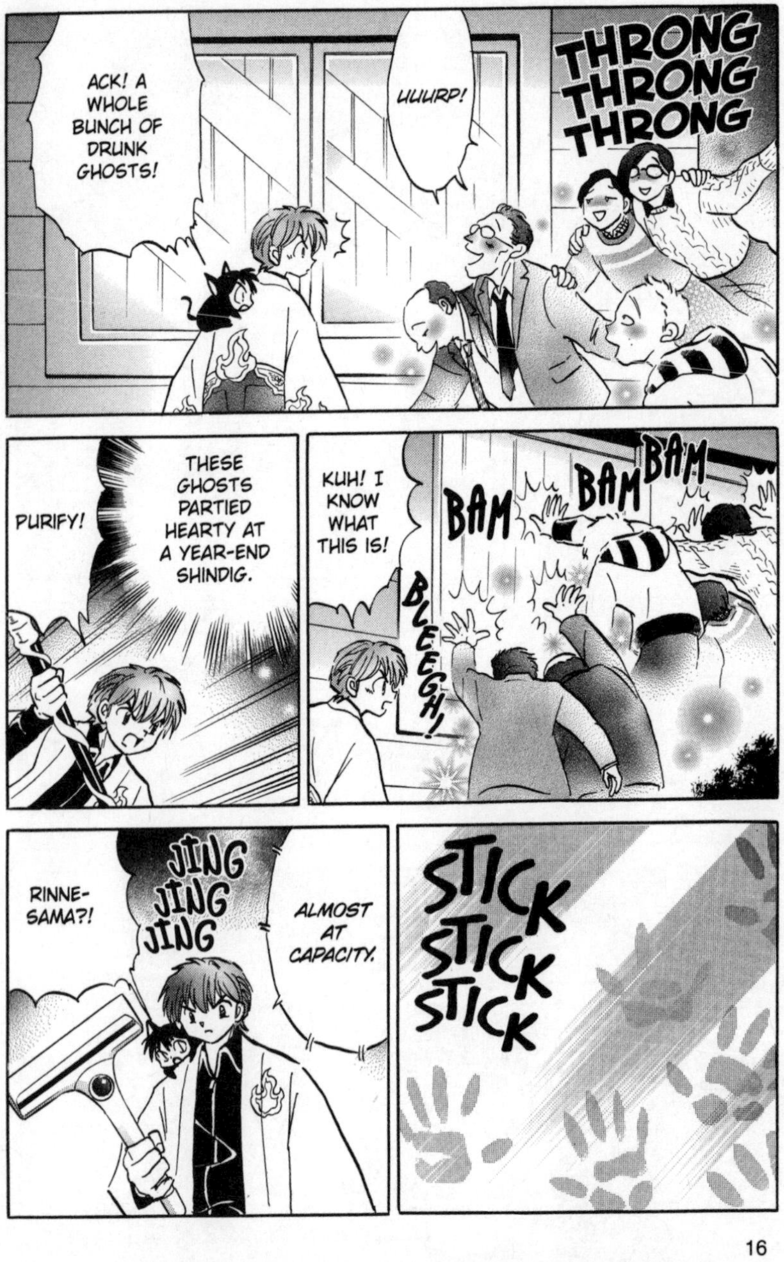
THRONG THRONG THRONG
UUURP!
ACK! A WHOLE BUNCH OF DRUNK GHOSTS!
BAM BAM BAM
KUH! I KNOW WHAT THIS IS!
BLEEGH!
THESE GHOSTS PARTIED HEARTY AT A YEAR-END SHINDIG.
PURIFY!
STICK STICK STICK
ALMOST AT CAPACITY.
JING JING JING
RINNE-SAMA?!

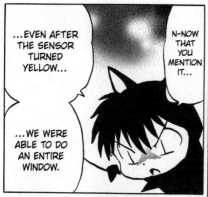

SO I CAN...
...KEEP GOING? IS THAT WHAT THIS MEANS?
JING JING JING
N-NOW THAT YOU MENTION IT...
...EVEN AFTER THE SENSOR TURNED YELLOW...
...WE WERE ABLE TO DO AN ENTIRE WINDOW.
MAYBE...
...WE CAN HARVEST MORE THAN 1,000 HANDPRINTS.
ANYWAY, IF I WERE TO LEAVE ANY HANDPRINTS...
WHAT IN THE...?
AAAW
...SAKURA MAMIYA WOULD BE DISAP-POINTED TOMORROW MORNING.
THIS IS FOR SAKURA-SAMA!
EXACTLY!

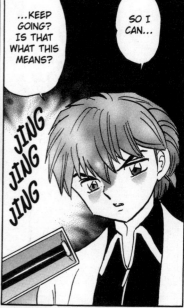

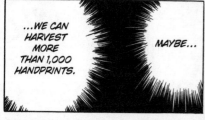

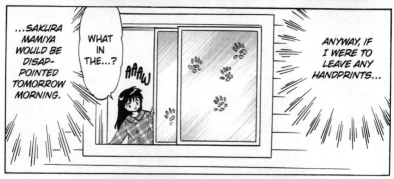

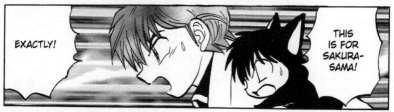

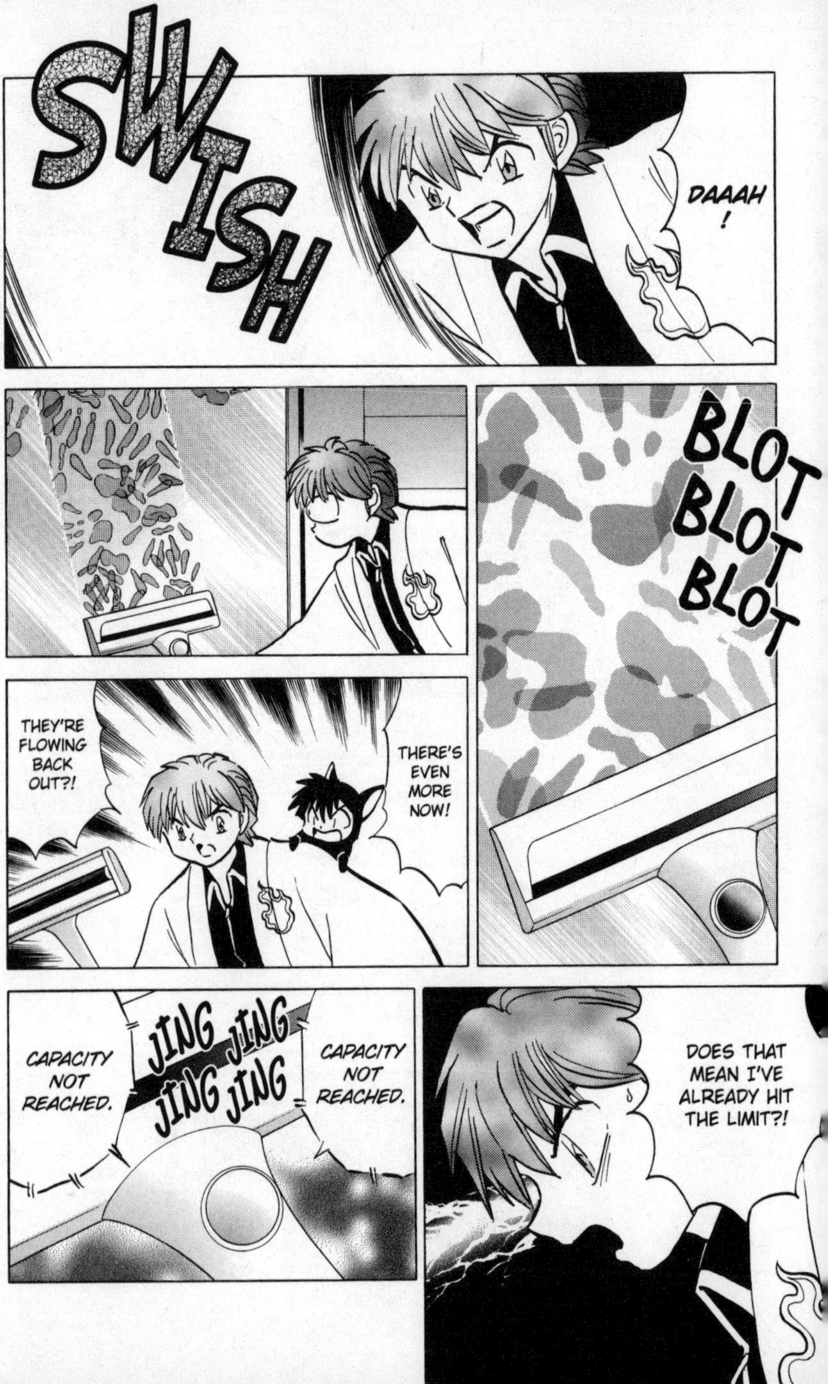
DAAAH!
SWISH
BLOT BLOT BLOT
THERE'S EVEN MORE NOW!
THEY'RE FLOWING BACK OUT?!
DOES THAT MEAN I'VE ALREADY HIT THE LIMIT?!
CAPACITY NOT REACHED.
JING JING JING JING
CAPACITY NOT REACHED.

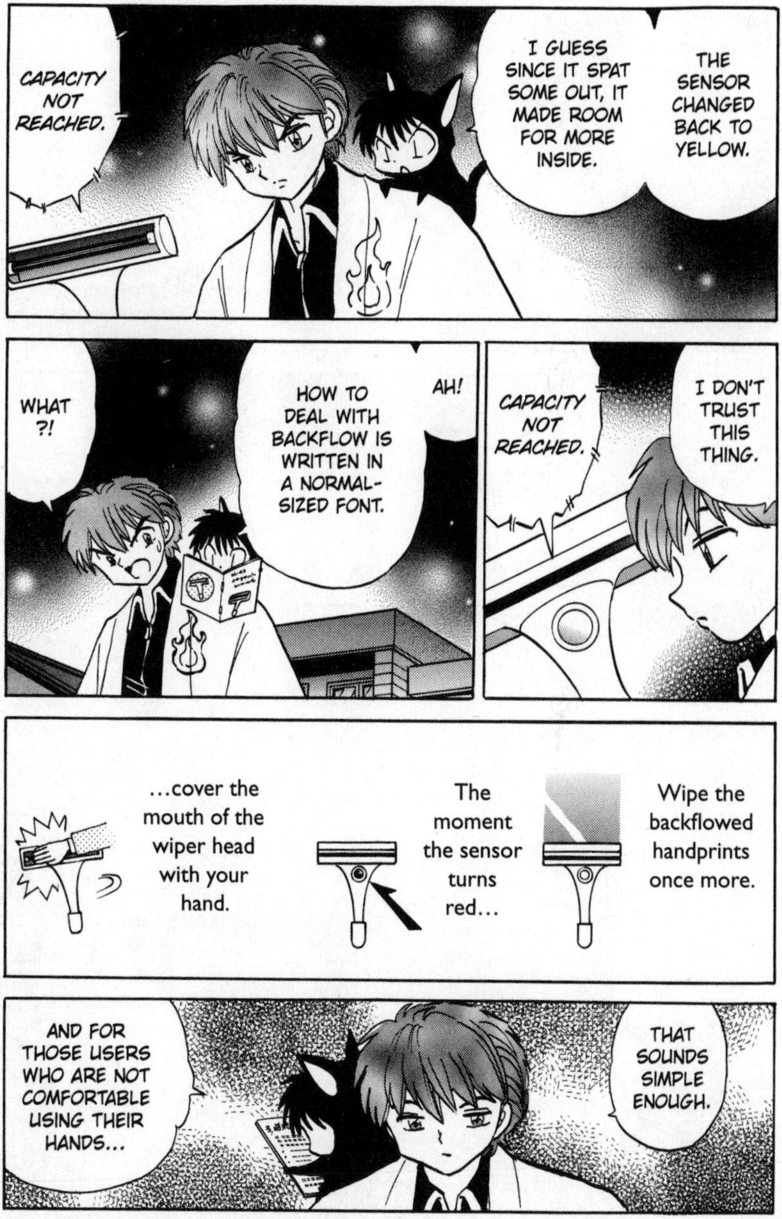

THE SENSOR CHANGED BACK TO YELLOW.
I GUESS SINCE IT SPAT SOME OUT, IT MADE ROOM FOR MORE INSIDE.
CAPACITY NOT REACHED.
I DON'T TRUST THIS THING.
CAPACITY NOT REACHED.
AH!
HOW TO DEAL WITH BACKFLOW IS WRITTEN IN A NORMAL-SIZED FONT.
WHAT ?!
Wipe the backflowed handprints once more.
The moment the sensor turns red…
…cover the mouth of the wiper head with your hand.
THAT SOUNDS SIMPLE ENOUGH.
AND FOR THOSE USERS WHO ARE NOT COMFORTABLE USING THEIR HANDS…

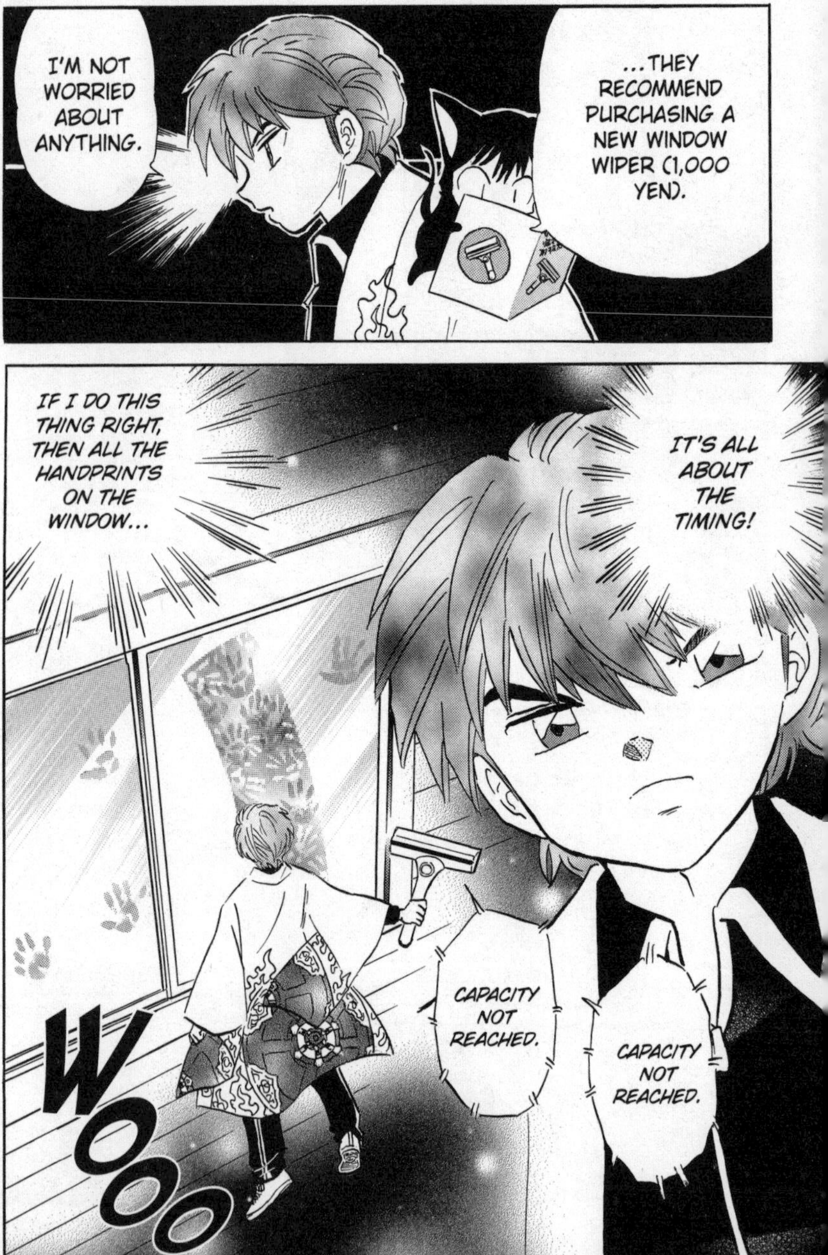
...THEY RECOMMEND PURCHASING A NEW WINDOW WIPER (1,000 YEN).
I'M NOT WORRIED ABOUT ANYTHING.
IT'S ALL ABOUT THE TIMING!
IF I DO THIS THING RIGHT, THEN ALL THE HANDPRINTS ON THE WINDOW...
CAPACITY NOT REACHED.
CAPACITY NOT REACHED.
WOOO

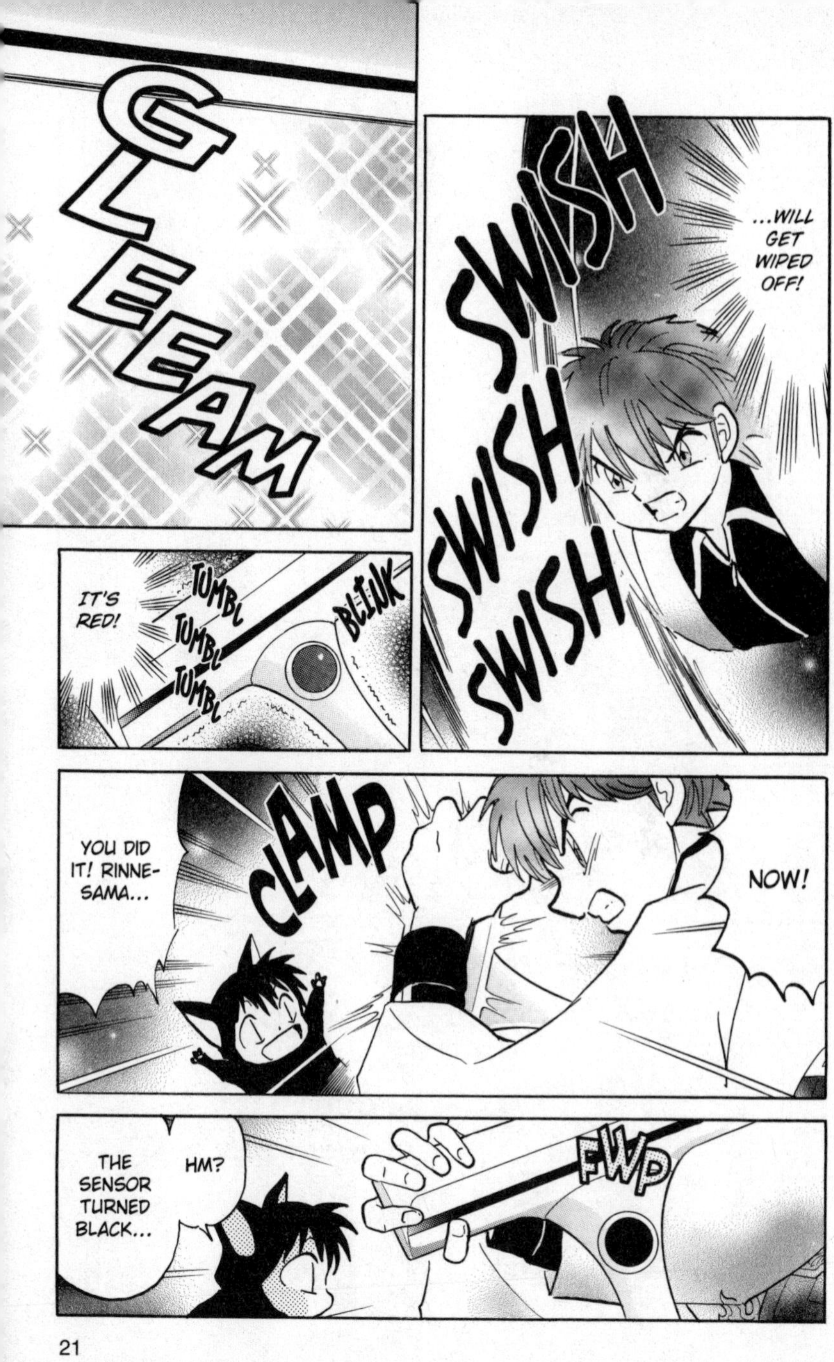
SWISH
SWISH
SWISH
SWISH
...WILL GET WIPED OFF!
GLEEAM
BLINK
TUMBL
TUMBL
TUMBL
IT'S RED!
NOW!
CLAMP
YOU DID IT! RINNE-SAMA...
FWP
HM?
THE SENSOR TURNED BLACK...

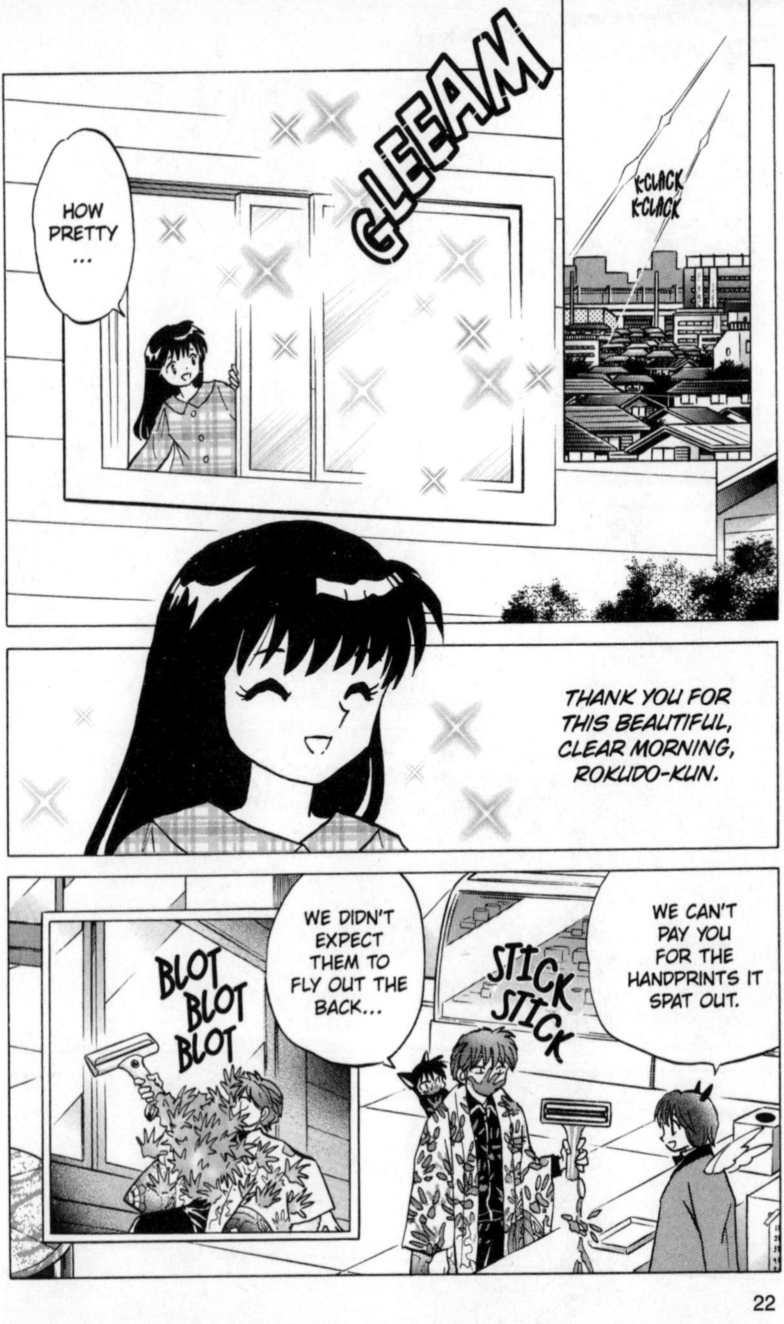
K-CLACK K-CLACK
GLEEAM
HOW PRETTY ...
THANK YOU FOR THIS BEAUTIFUL, CLEAR MORNING, ROKUDO-KUN.
WE CAN'T PAY YOU FOR THE HANDPRINTS IT SPAT OUT.
STICK STICK
WE DIDN'T EXPECT THEM TO FLY OUT THE BACK...
BLOT BLOT BLOT

CHAPTER 310: CHRISTMAS EXORCISM

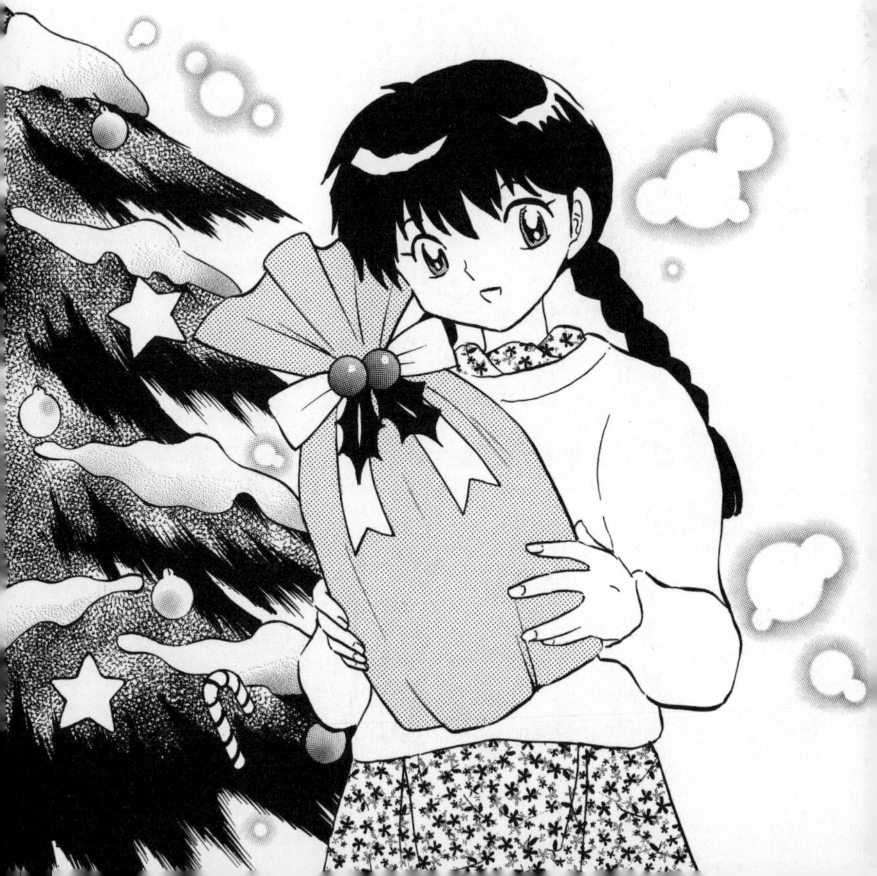

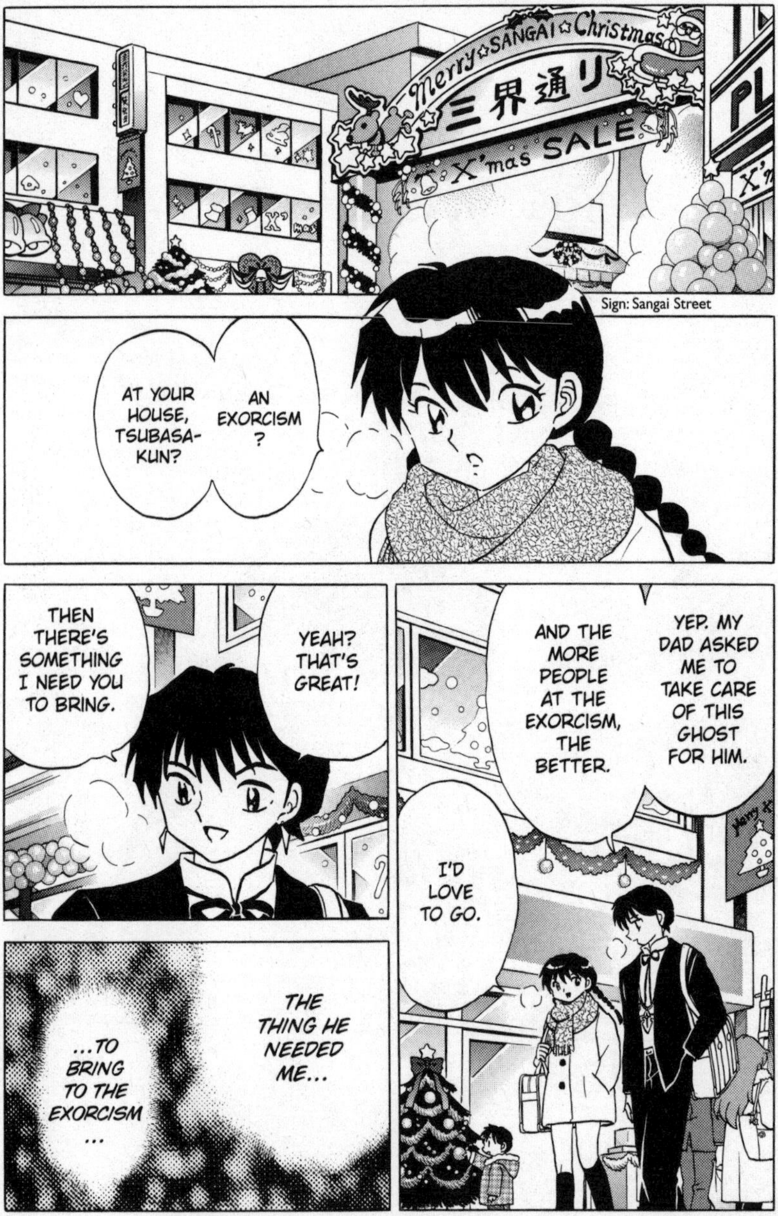
Merry☆SANGAI☆Christmas
三界通り
X'mas SALE
AN EXORCISM?
AT YOUR HOUSE, TSUBASA-KUN?
YEP. MY DAD ASKED ME TO TAKE CARE OF THIS GHOST FOR HIM.
AND THE MORE PEOPLE AT THE EXORCISM, THE BETTER.
I'D LOVE TO GO.
YEAH? THAT'S GREAT!
THEN THERE'S SOMETHING I NEED YOU TO BRING.
THE THING HE NEEDED ME...
...TO BRING TO THE EXORCISM...
Sign: Sangai Street

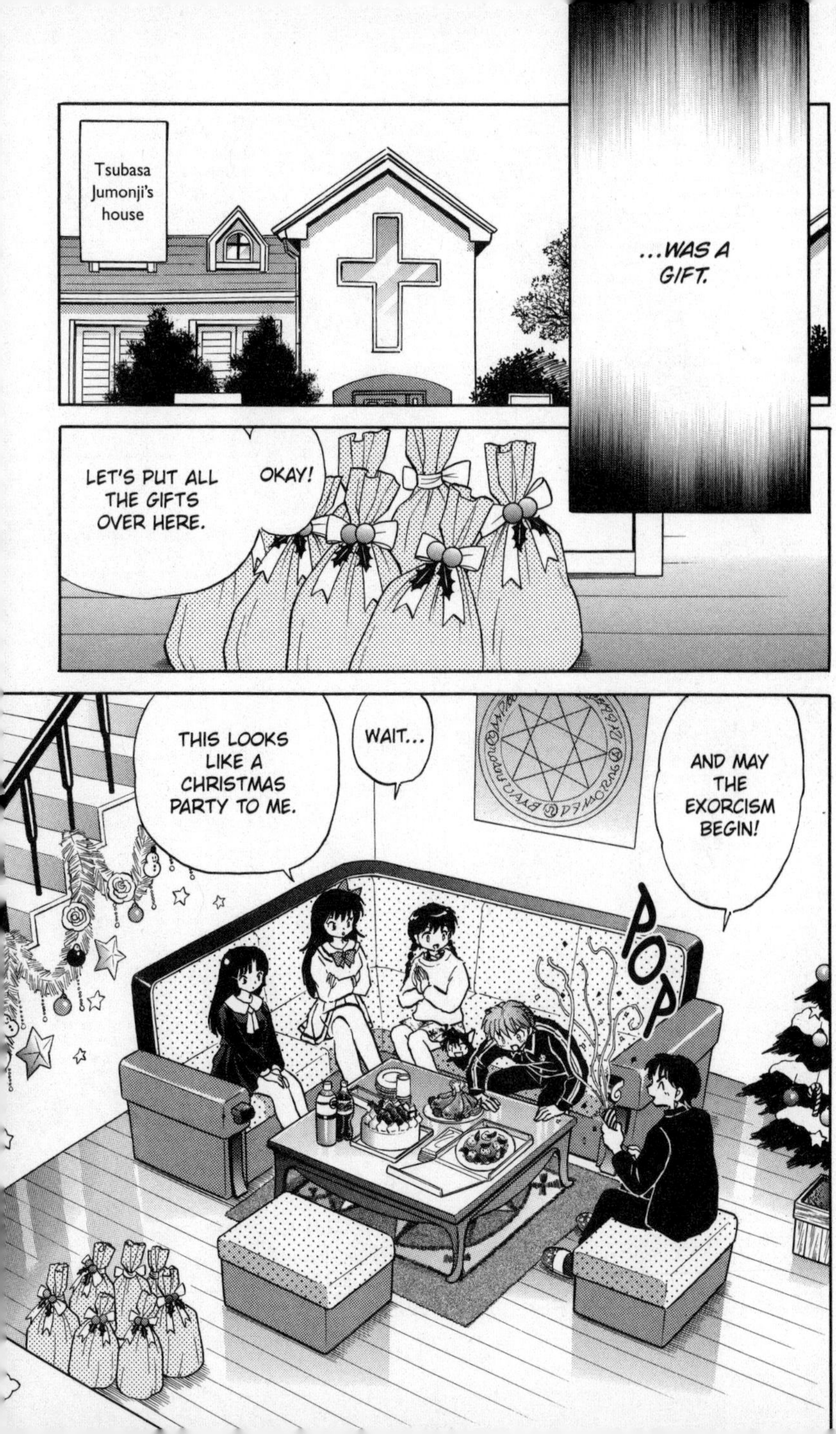
...WAS A GIFT.
Tsubasa Jumonji's house
LET'S PUT ALL THE GIFTS OVER HERE.
OKAY!
AND MAY THE EXORCISM BEGIN!
POP
WAIT...
THIS LOOKS LIKE A CHRISTMAS PARTY TO ME.

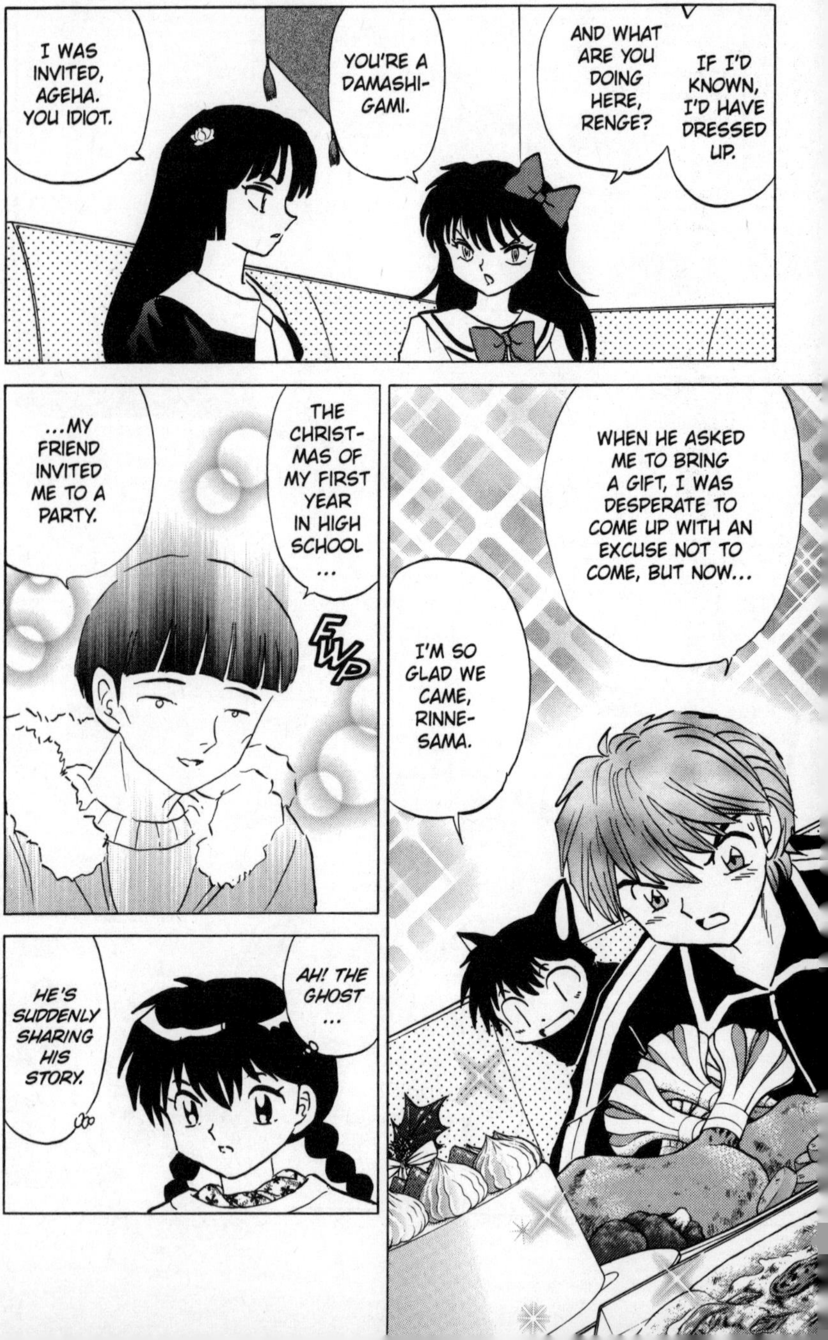
IF I'D KNOWN, I'D HAVE DRESSED UP.
AND WHAT ARE YOU DOING HERE, RENGE?
YOU'RE A DAMASHI-GAMI.
I WAS INVITED, AGEHA. YOU IDIOT.
WHEN HE ASKED ME TO BRING A GIFT, I WAS DESPERATE TO COME UP WITH AN EXCUSE NOT TO COME, BUT NOW...
I'M SO GLAD WE CAME, RINNE-SAMA.
THE CHRISTMAS OF MY FIRST YEAR IN HIGH SCHOOL...
FWP
...MY FRIEND INVITED ME TO A PARTY.
AH! THE GHOST...
HE'S SUDDENLY SHARING HIS STORY.

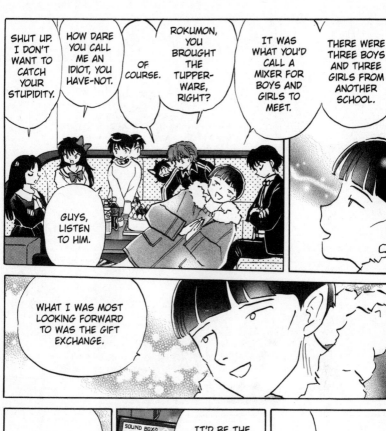

THERE WERE THREE BOYS AND THREE GIRLS FROM ANOTHER SCHOOL.
IT WAS WHAT YOU'D CALL A MIXER FOR BOYS AND GIRLS TO MEET.
ROKUMON, YOU BROUGHT THE TUPPER-WARE, RIGHT?
OF COURSE.
HOW DARE YOU CALL ME AN IDIOT, YOU HAVE-NOT.
SHUT UP. I DON'T WANT TO CATCH YOUR STUPIDITY.
GUYS, LISTEN TO HIM.
WHAT I WAS MOST LOOKING FORWARD TO WAS THE GIFT EXCHANGE.
GIFT...
IT'D BE THE FIRST TIME I'D EVER RECEIVED A GIFT FROM A GIRL.
SOUND BOX
AND IF SHE LIKED MY GIFT...

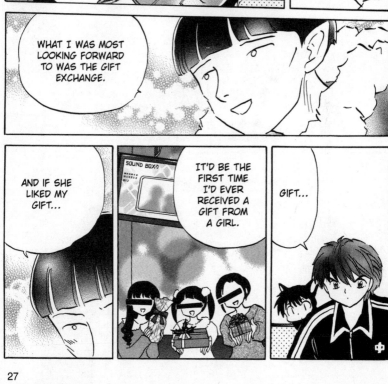

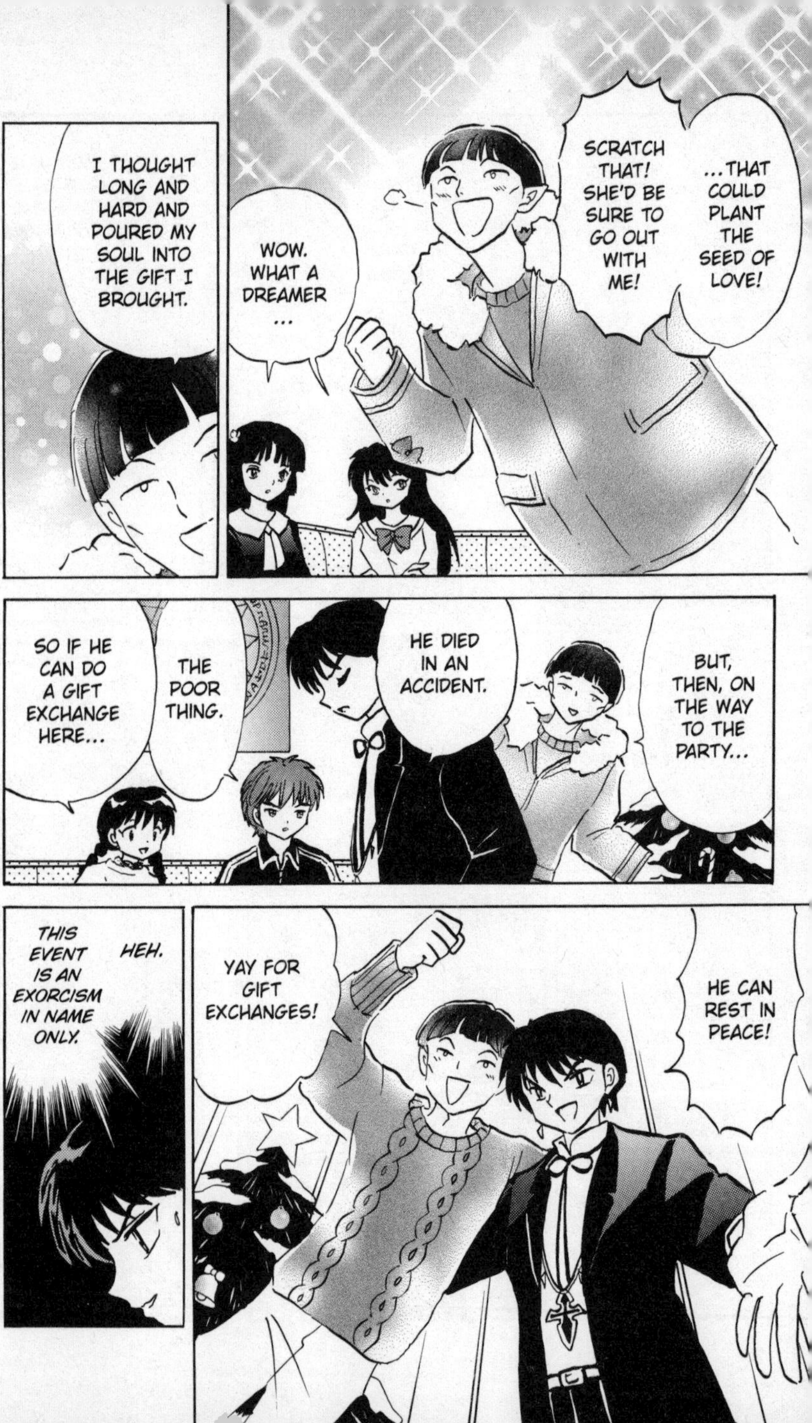

...THAT COULD PLANT THE SEED OF LOVE!
SCRATCH THAT! SHE'D BE SURE TO GO OUT WITH ME!
WOW. WHAT A DREAMER ...
I THOUGHT LONG AND HARD AND POURED MY SOUL INTO THE GIFT I BROUGHT.
BUT, THEN, ON THE WAY TO THE PARTY...
HE DIED IN AN ACCIDENT.
THE POOR THING.
SO IF HE CAN DO A GIFT EXCHANGE HERE...
HE CAN REST IN PEACE!
YAY FOR GIFT EXCHANGES!
HEH.
THIS EVENT IS AN EXORCISM IN NAME ONLY.

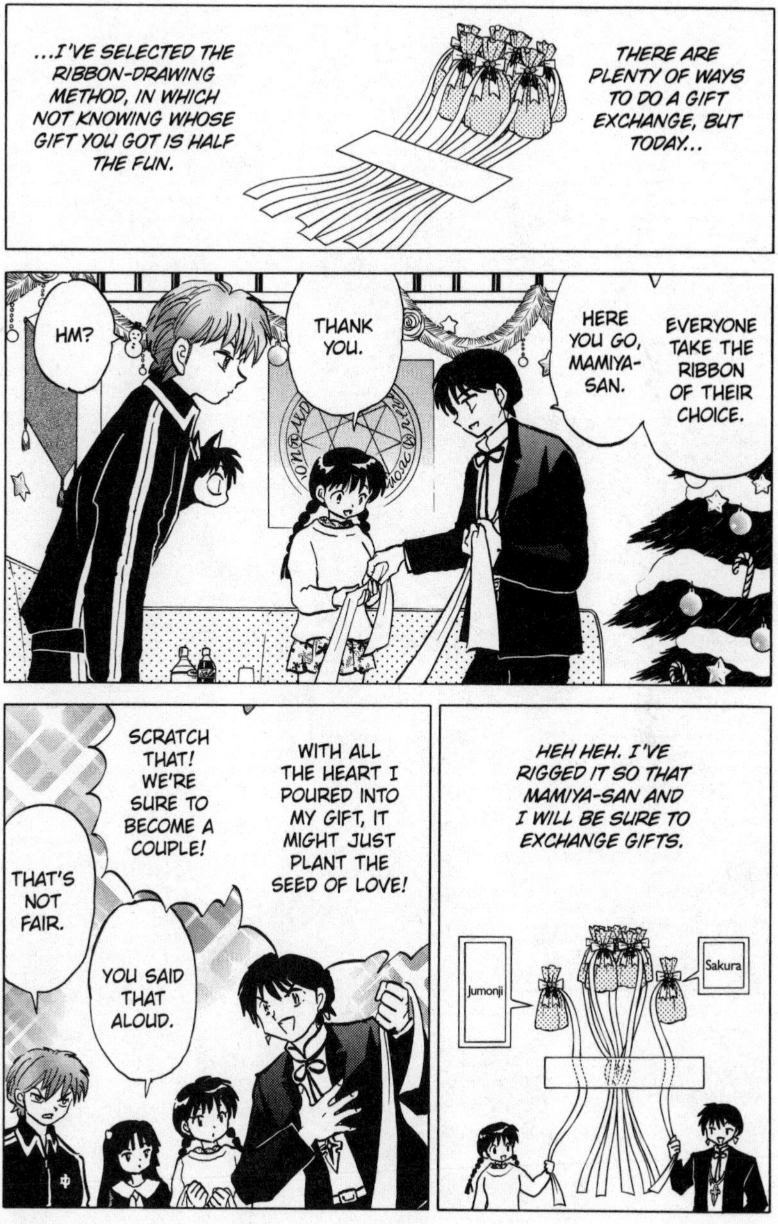
THERE ARE PLENTY OF WAYS TO DO A GIFT EXCHANGE, BUT TODAY...
...I'VE SELECTED THE RIBBON-DRAWING METHOD, IN WHICH NOT KNOWING WHOSE GIFT YOU GOT IS HALF THE FUN.
EVERYONE TAKE THE RIBBON OF THEIR CHOICE.
HERE YOU GO, MAMIYA-SAN.
THANK YOU.
HM?
HEH HEH. I'VE RIGGED IT SO THAT MAMIYA-SAN AND I WILL BE SURE TO EXCHANGE GIFTS.
Sakura
Jumonji
WITH ALL THE HEART I POURED INTO MY GIFT, IT MIGHT JUST PLANT THE SEED OF LOVE!
SCRATCH THAT! WE'RE SURE TO BECOME A COUPLE!
YOU SAID THAT ALOUD.
THAT'S NOT FAIR.

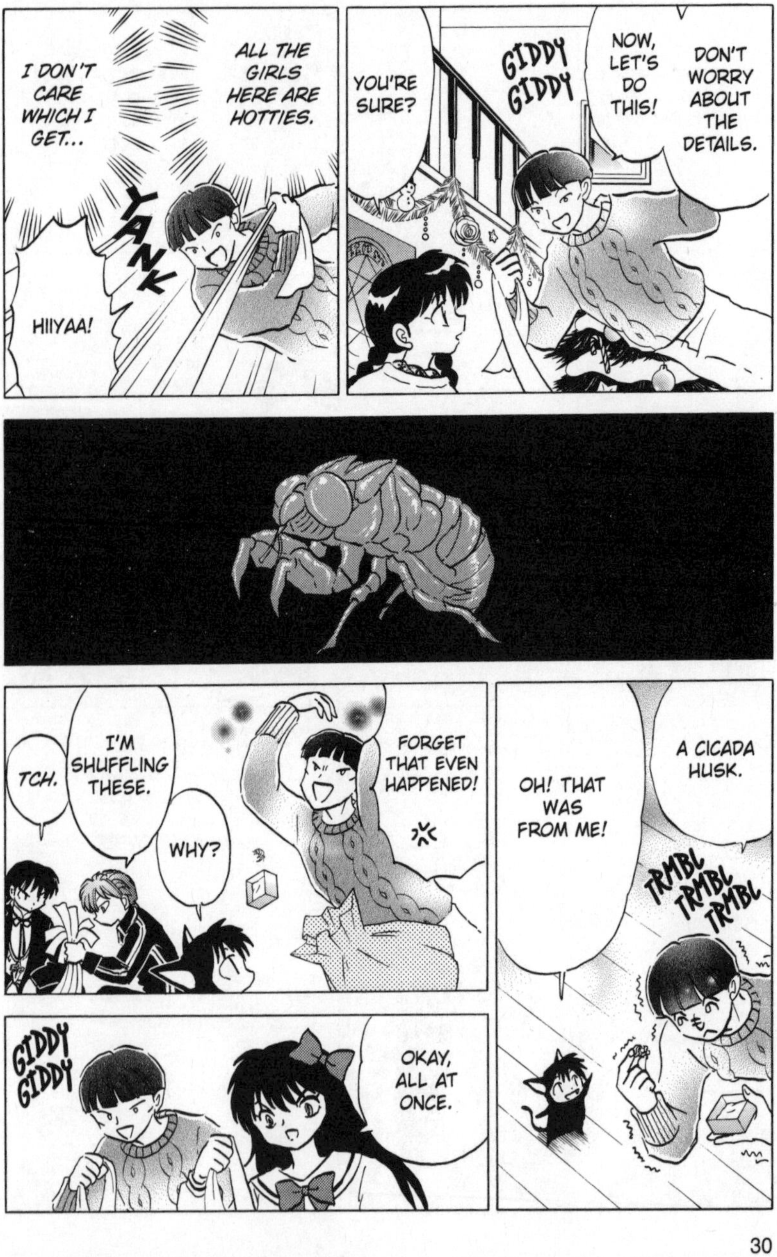
DON'T WORRY ABOUT THE DETAILS.
NOW, LET'S DO THIS!
GIDDY GIDDY
YOU'RE SURE?
ALL THE GIRLS HERE ARE HOTTIES.
I DON'T CARE WHICH I GET...
YANK
HIIYAA!
A CICADA HUSK.
OH! THAT WAS FROM ME!
TRMBL TRMBL TRMBL
FORGET THAT EVEN HAPPENED!
I'M SHUFFLING THESE.
TCH.
WHY?
OKAY, ALL AT ONCE.
GIDDY GIDDY

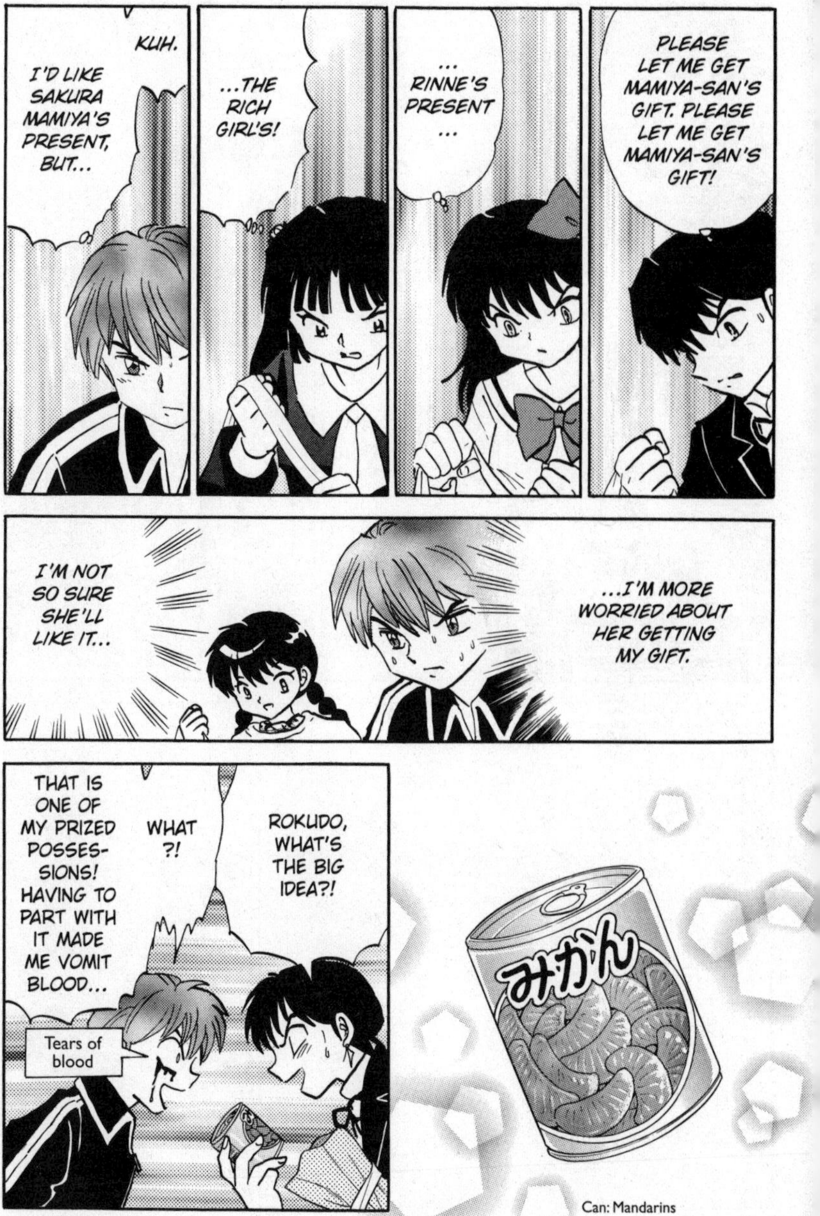
PLEASE LET ME GET MAMIYA-SAN'S GIFT. PLEASE LET ME GET MAMIYA-SAN'S GIFT!
... RINNE'S PRESENT ...
...THE RICH GIRL'S!
KUH.
I'D LIKE SAKURA MAMIYA'S PRESENT, BUT...
...I'M MORE WORRIED ABOUT HER GETTING MY GIFT.
I'M NOT SO SURE SHE'LL LIKE IT...
みかん
ROKUDO, WHAT'S THE BIG IDEA?!
WHAT ?!
THAT IS ONE OF MY PRIZED POSSES-SIONS! HAVING TO PART WITH IT MADE ME VOMIT BLOOD...
Tears of blood

Can: Mandarins

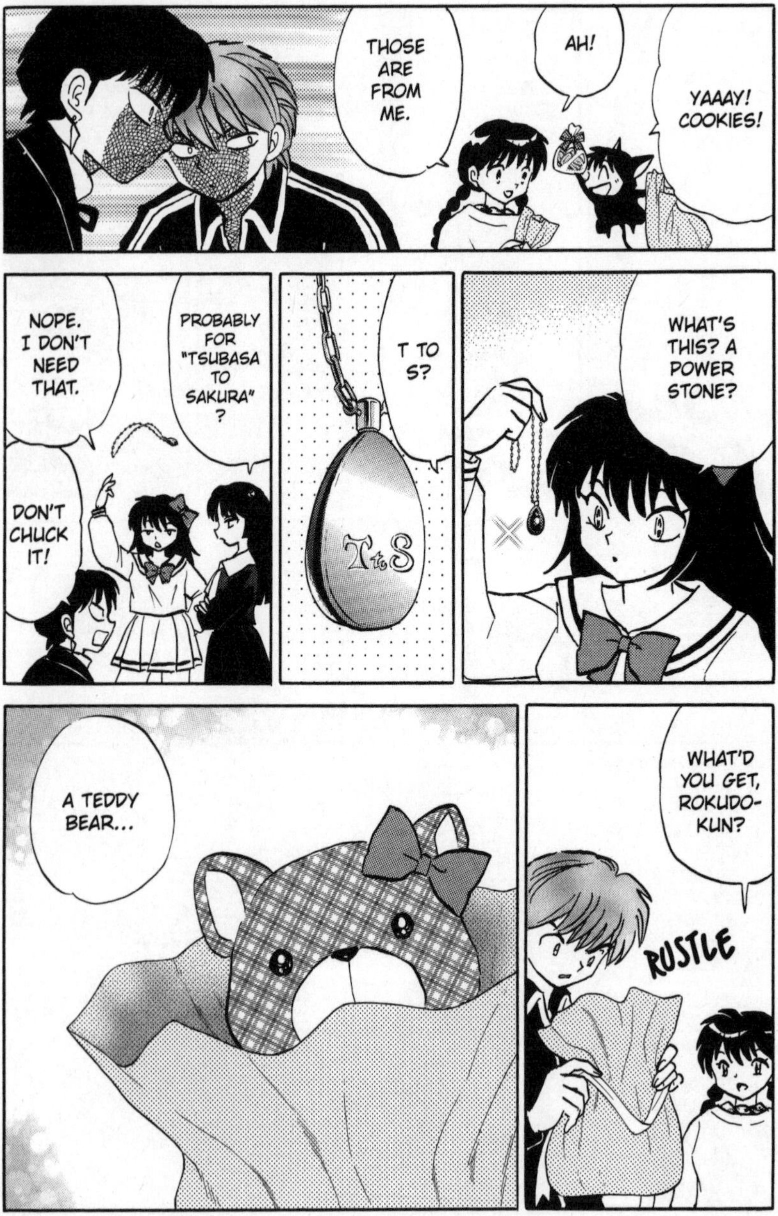
YAAAY! COOKIES!
AH!
THOSE ARE FROM ME.
WHAT'S THIS? A POWER STONE?
T TO S?
PROBABLY FOR "TSUBASA TO SAKURA"?
NOPE. I DON'T NEED THAT.
DON'T CHUCK IT!
WHAT'D YOU GET, ROKUDO-KUN?
RUSTLE
A TEDDY BEAR...

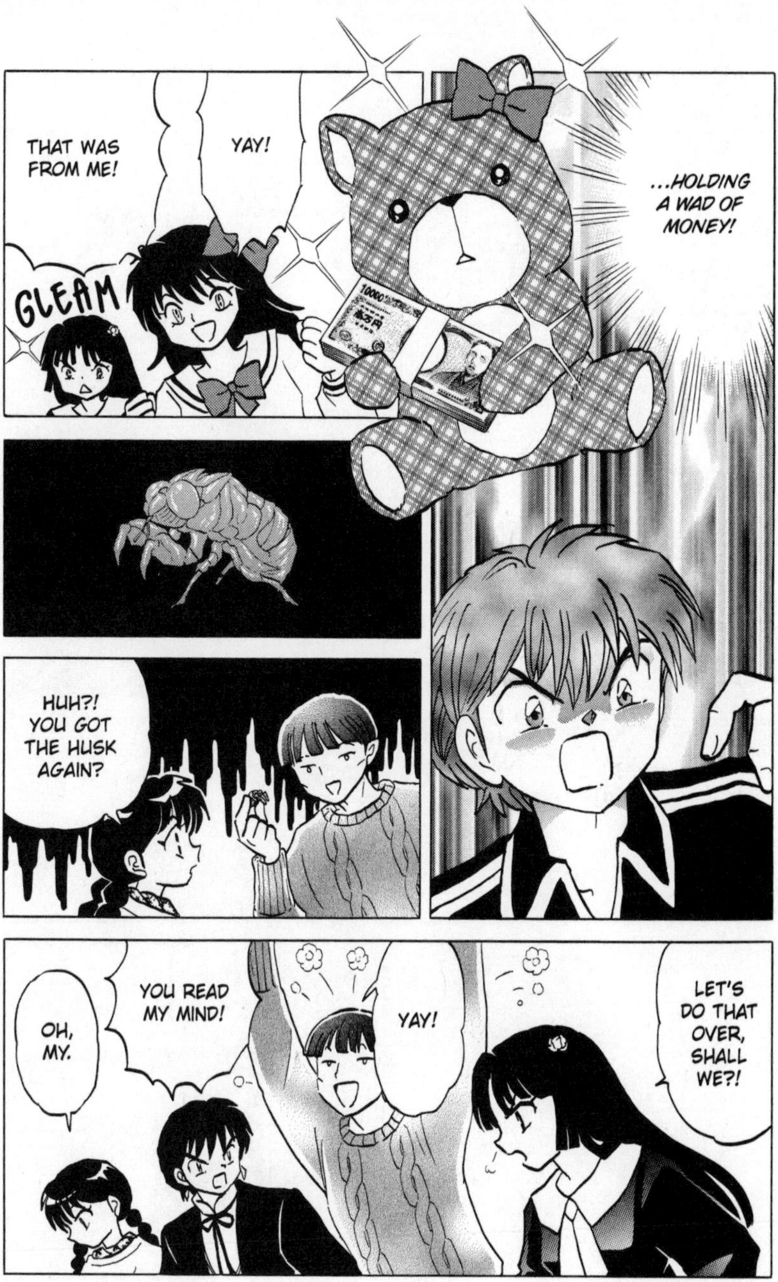
...HOLDING A WAD OF MONEY!
YAY!
THAT WAS FROM ME!
GLEAM
HUH?! YOU GOT THE HUSK AGAIN?
LET'S DO THAT OVER, SHALL WE?!
YAY!
YOU READ MY MIND!
OH, MY.

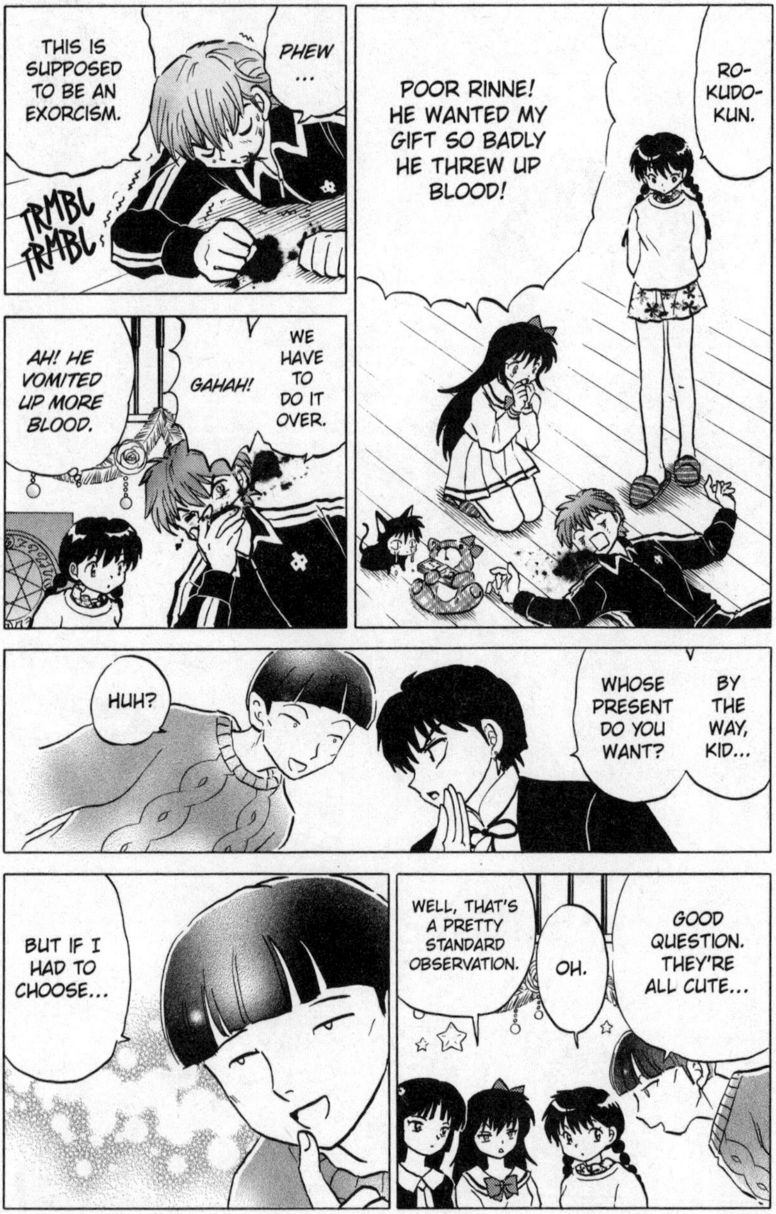
RO-KUDO-KUN.
POOR RINNE! HE WANTED MY GIFT SO BADLY HE THREW UP BLOOD!
PHEW ...
THIS IS SUPPOSED TO BE AN EXORCISM.
TRMBL TRMBL
WE HAVE TO DO IT OVER.
GAHAH!
AH! HE VOMITED UP MORE BLOOD.
BY THE WAY, KID...
WHOSE PRESENT DO YOU WANT?
HUH?
GOOD QUESTION. THEY'RE ALL CUTE...
OH.
WELL, THAT'S A PRETTY STANDARD OBSERVATION.
BUT IF I HAD TO CHOOSE...

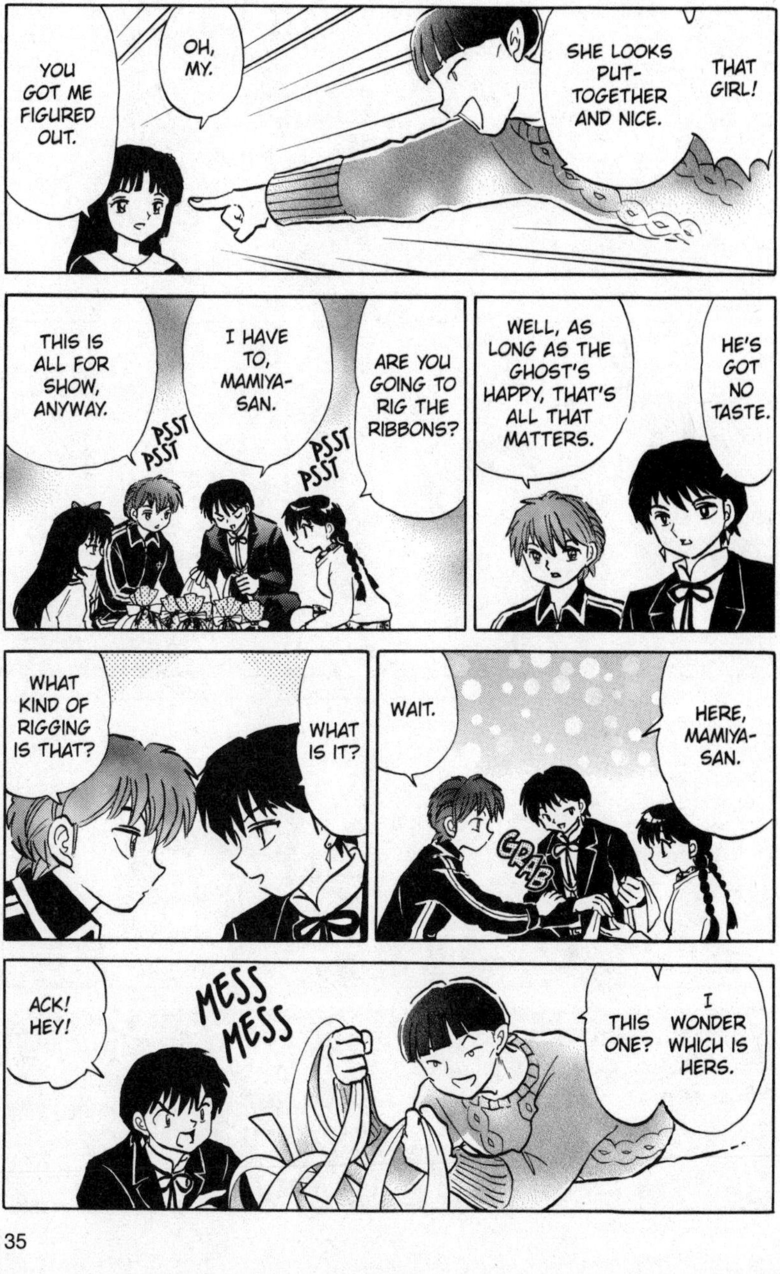

THAT GIRL!
SHE LOOKS PUT-TOGETHER AND NICE.
OH, MY.
YOU GOT ME FIGURED OUT.
HE'S GOT NO TASTE.
WELL, AS LONG AS THE GHOST'S HAPPY, THAT'S ALL THAT MATTERS.
ARE YOU GOING TO RIG THE RIBBONS?
PSST PSST
I HAVE TO, MAMIYA-SAN.
PSST PSST
THIS IS ALL FOR SHOW, ANYWAY.
HERE, MAMIYA-SAN.
WAIT.
GRAB
WHAT IS IT?
WHAT KIND OF RIGGING IS THAT?
I WONDER WHICH IS HERS.
THIS ONE?
MESS MESS
ACK! HEY!

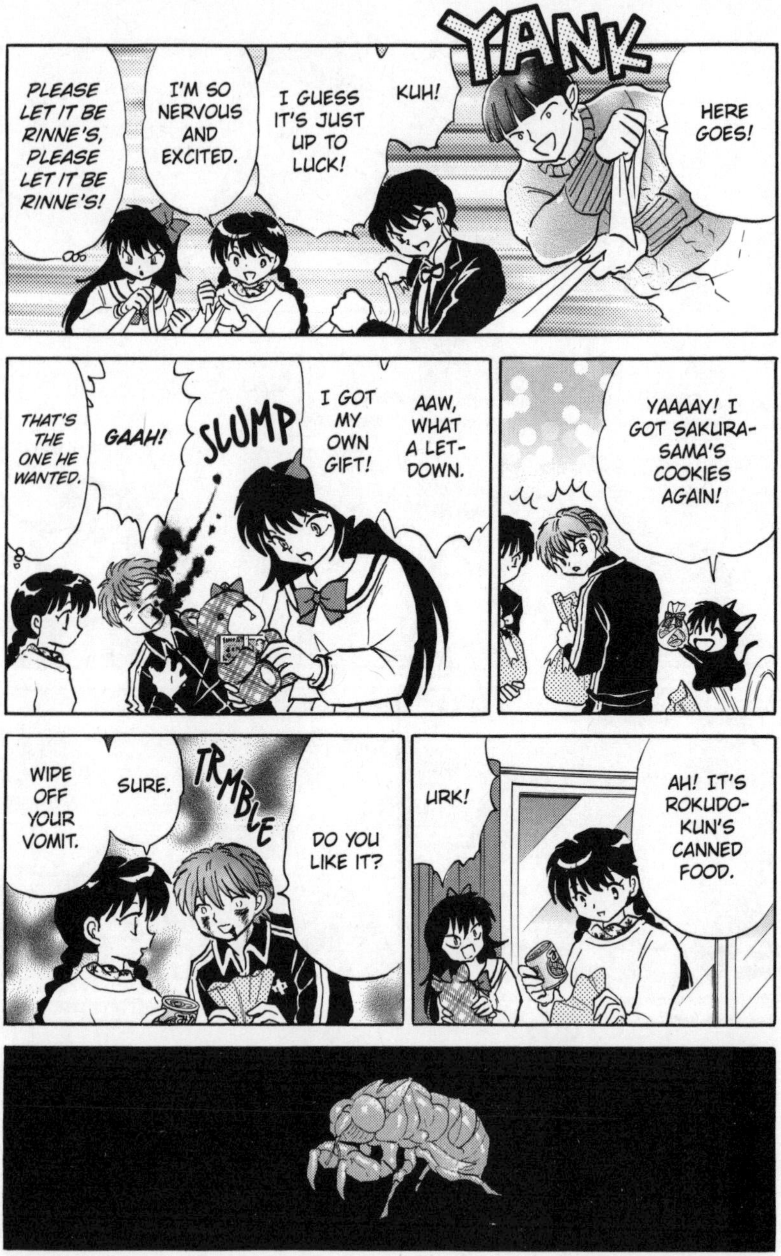
YANK
HERE GOES!
KUH!
I GUESS IT'S JUST UP TO LUCK!
I'M SO NERVOUS AND EXCITED.
PLEASE LET IT BE RINNE'S, PLEASE LET IT BE RINNE'S!
YAAAAY! I GOT SAKURA-SAMA'S COOKIES AGAIN!
AAW, WHAT A LET-DOWN.
I GOT MY OWN GIFT!
SLUMP
GAAH!
THAT'S THE ONE HE WANTED.
AH! IT'S ROKUDO-KUN'S CANNED FOOD.
URK!
DO YOU LIKE IT?
TRMBLE
SURE.
WIPE OFF YOUR VOMIT.

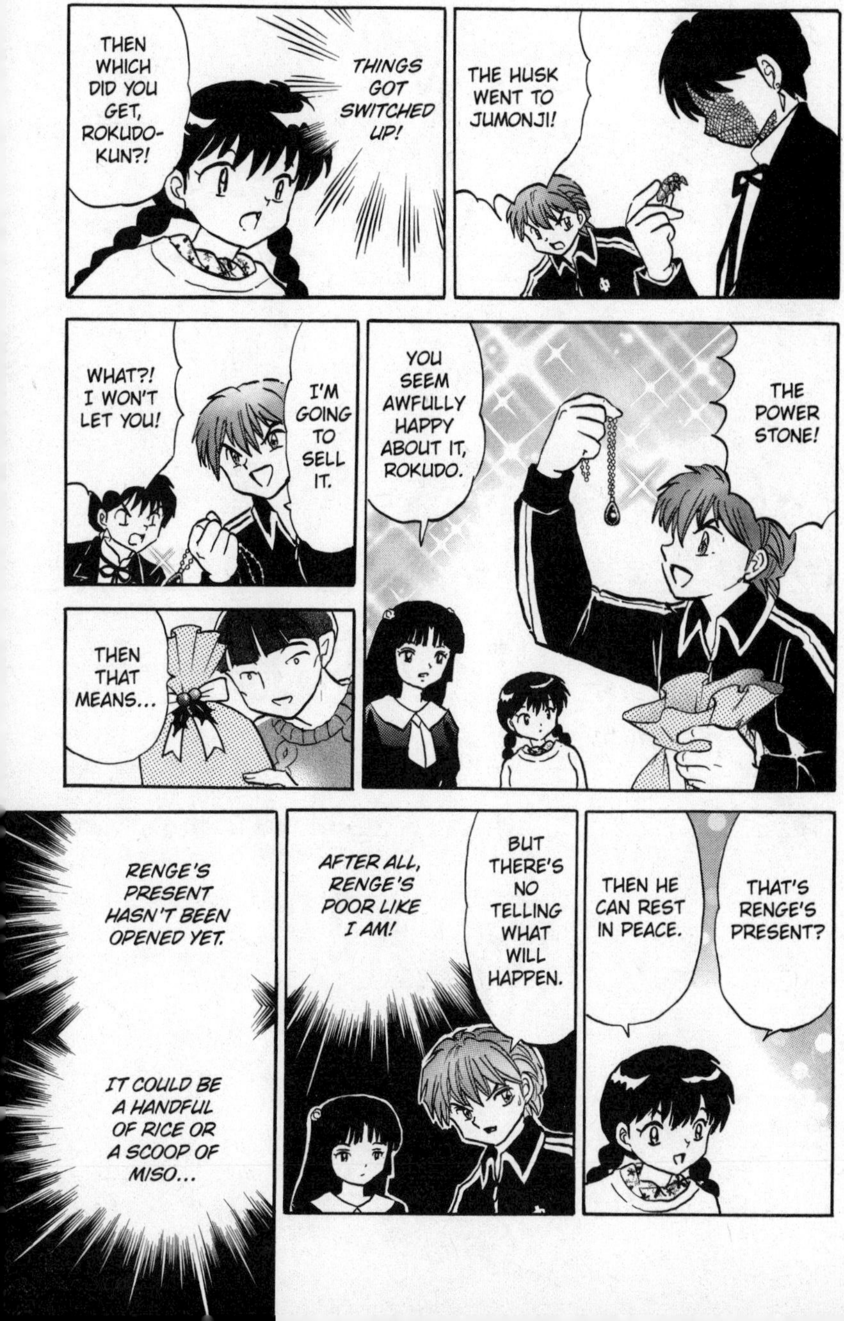
THE HUSK WENT TO JUMONJI!
THINGS GOT SWITCHED UP!
THEN WHICH DID YOU GET, ROKUDO-KUN?!
THE POWER STONE!
YOU SEEM AWFULLY HAPPY ABOUT IT, ROKUDO.
I'M GOING TO SELL IT.
WHAT?! I WON'T LET YOU!
THEN THAT MEANS...
THAT'S RENGE'S PRESENT?
THEN HE CAN REST IN PEACE.
BUT THERE'S NO TELLING WHAT WILL HAPPEN.
AFTER ALL, RENGE'S POOR LIKE I AM!
RENGE'S PRESENT HASN'T BEEN OPENED YET.
IT COULD BE A HANDFUL OF RICE OR A SCOOP OF MISO...

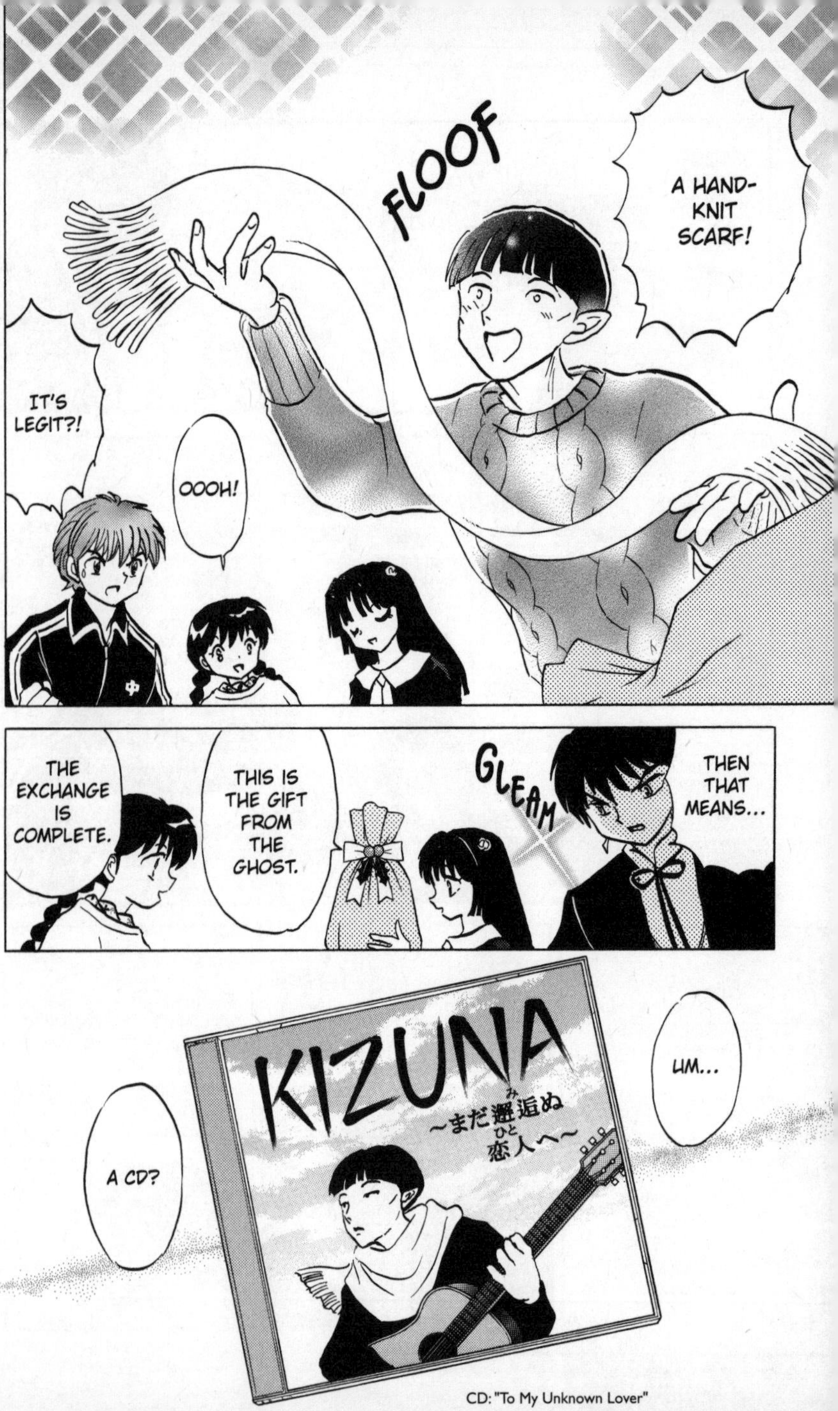
A HAND-KNIT SCARF!
FLOOF
IT'S LEGIT?!
OOOH!
THEN THAT MEANS...
GLEAM
THIS IS THE GIFT FROM THE GHOST.
THE EXCHANGE IS COMPLETE.
UM...
KIZUNA
~まだ邂逅ぬ恋人へ~
A CD?

CD: "To My Unknown Lover"

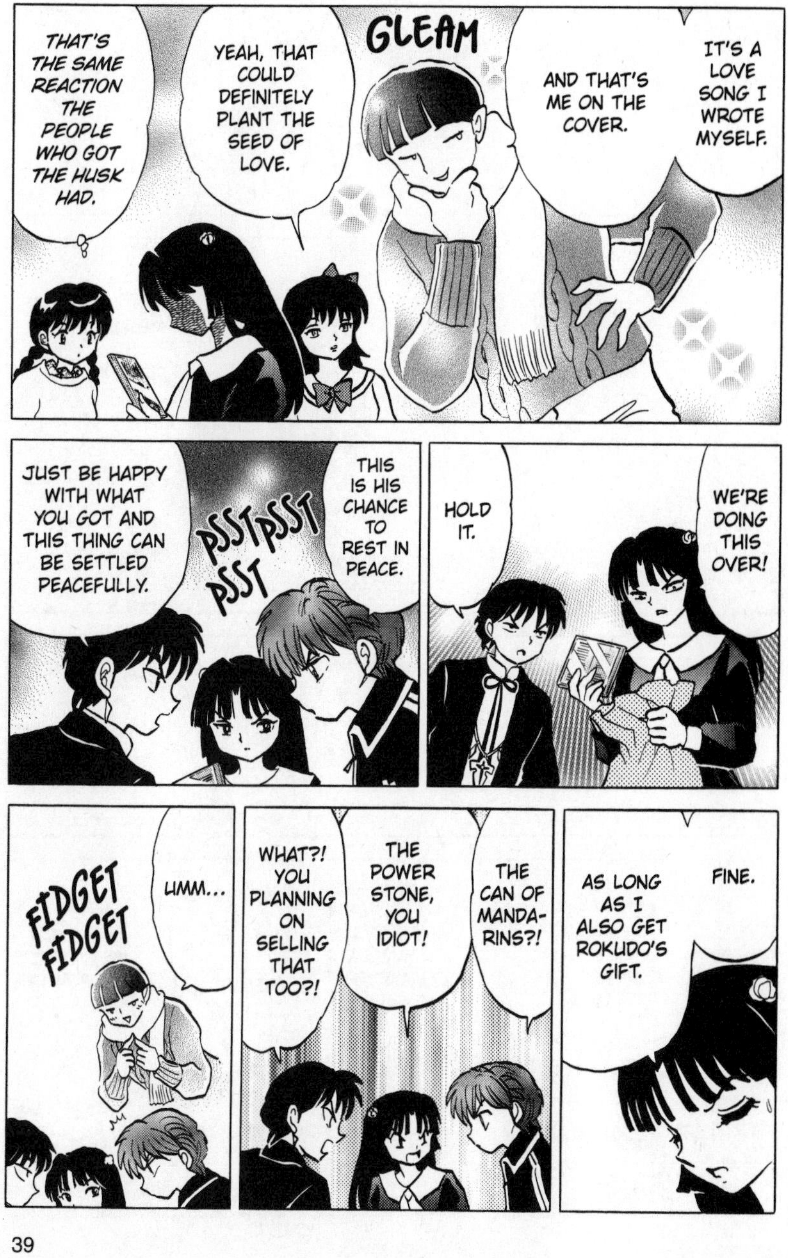
IT'S A LOVE SONG I WROTE MYSELF.
AND THAT'S ME ON THE COVER.
GLEAM
YEAH, THAT COULD DEFINITELY PLANT THE SEED OF LOVE.
THAT'S THE SAME REACTION THE PEOPLE WHO GOT THE HUSK HAD.
WE'RE DOING THIS OVER!
HOLD IT.
THIS IS HIS CHANCE TO REST IN PEACE.
PSST PSST PSST
JUST BE HAPPY WITH WHAT YOU GOT AND THIS THING CAN BE SETTLED PEACEFULLY.
FINE.
AS LONG AS I ALSO GET ROKUDO'S GIFT.
THE CAN OF MANDA-RINS?!
THE POWER STONE, YOU IDIOT!
WHAT?! YOU PLANNING ON SELLING THAT TOO?!
UMM...
FIDGET FIDGET

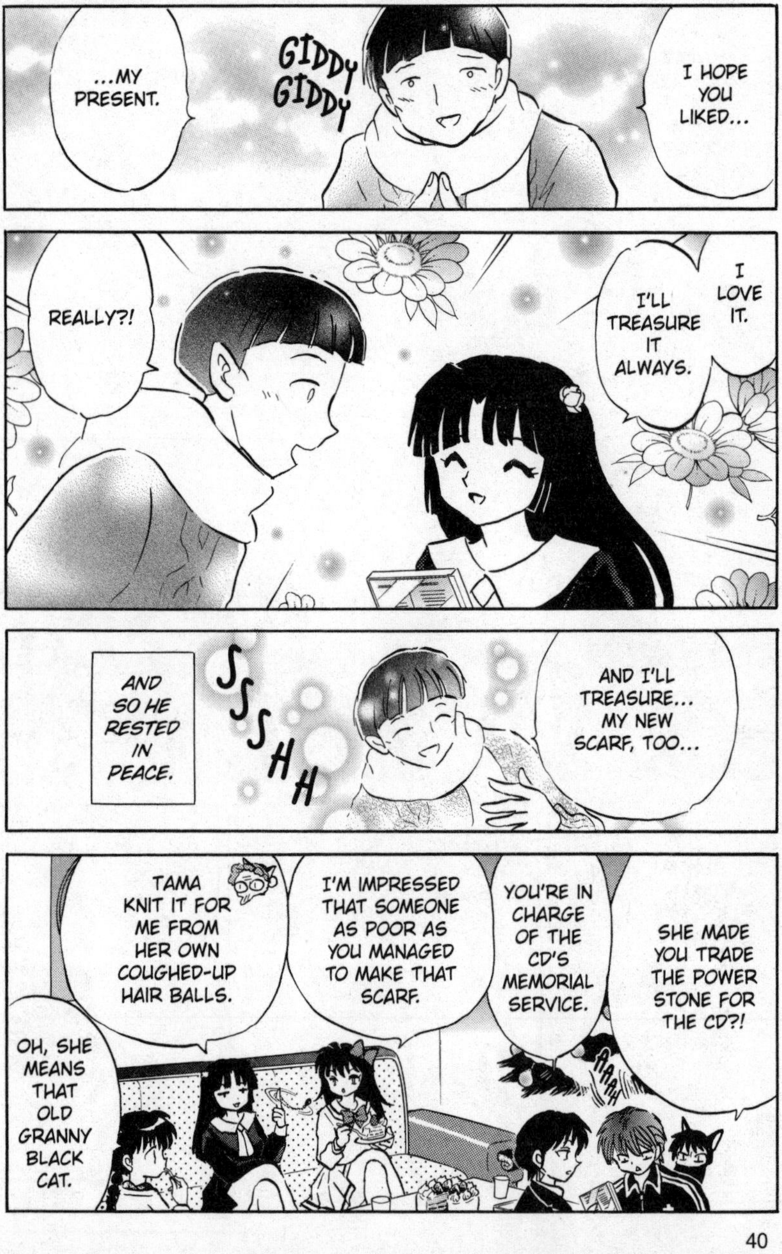
I HOPE YOU LIKED...
GIDDY GIDDY
...MY PRESENT.
I LOVE IT.
I'LL TREASURE IT ALWAYS.
REALLY?!
AND I'LL TREASURE... MY NEW SCARF, TOO...
SSSHH
AND SO HE RESTED IN PEACE.
SHE MADE YOU TRADE THE POWER STONE FOR THE CD?!
AAAH
YOU'RE IN CHARGE OF THE CD'S MEMORIAL SERVICE.
I'M IMPRESSED THAT SOMEONE AS POOR AS YOU MANAGED TO MAKE THAT SCARF.
TAMA KNIT IT FOR ME FROM HER OWN COUGHED-UP HAIR BALLS.
OH, SHE MEANS THAT OLD GRANNY BLACK CAT.

CHAPTER 311: THE BLACK HAMAYA

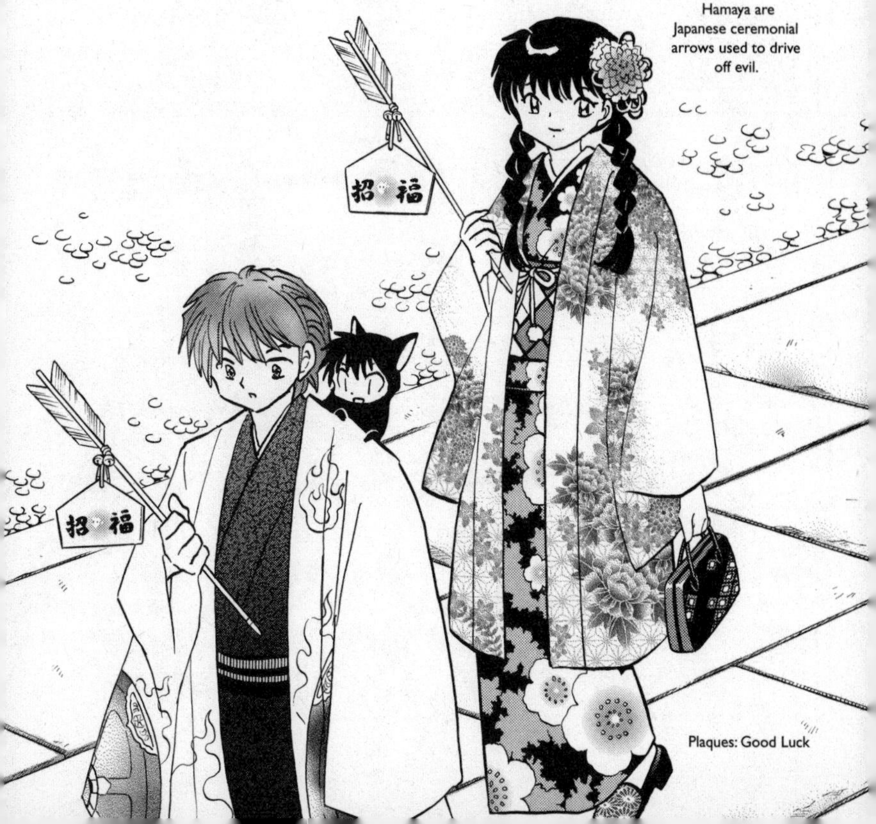
Hamaya are Japanese ceremonial arrows used to drive off evil.
招福
招福
Plaques: Good Luck

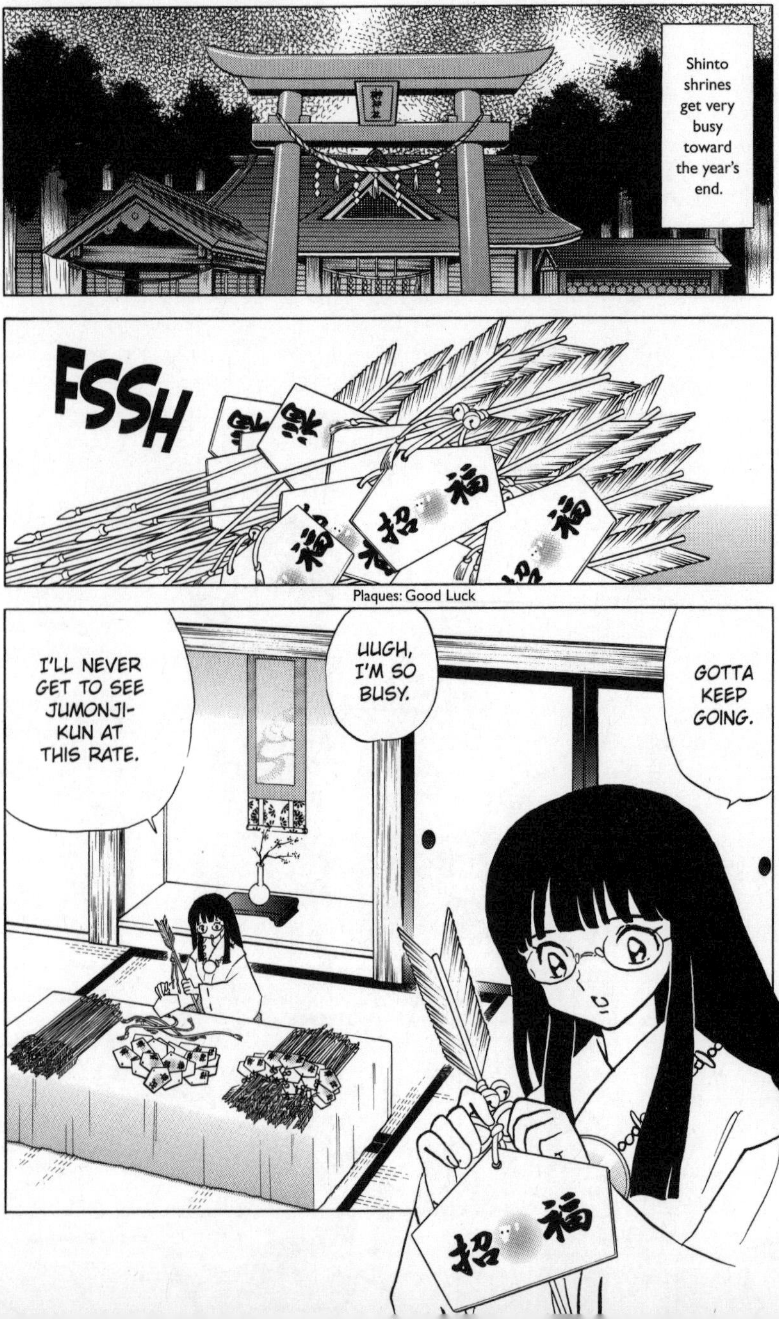
Shinto shrines get very busy toward the year's end.
FSSH
Plaques: Good Luck
GOTTA KEEP GOING.
UUGH, I'M SO BUSY.
I'LL NEVER GET TO SEE JUMONJI-KUN AT THIS RATE.

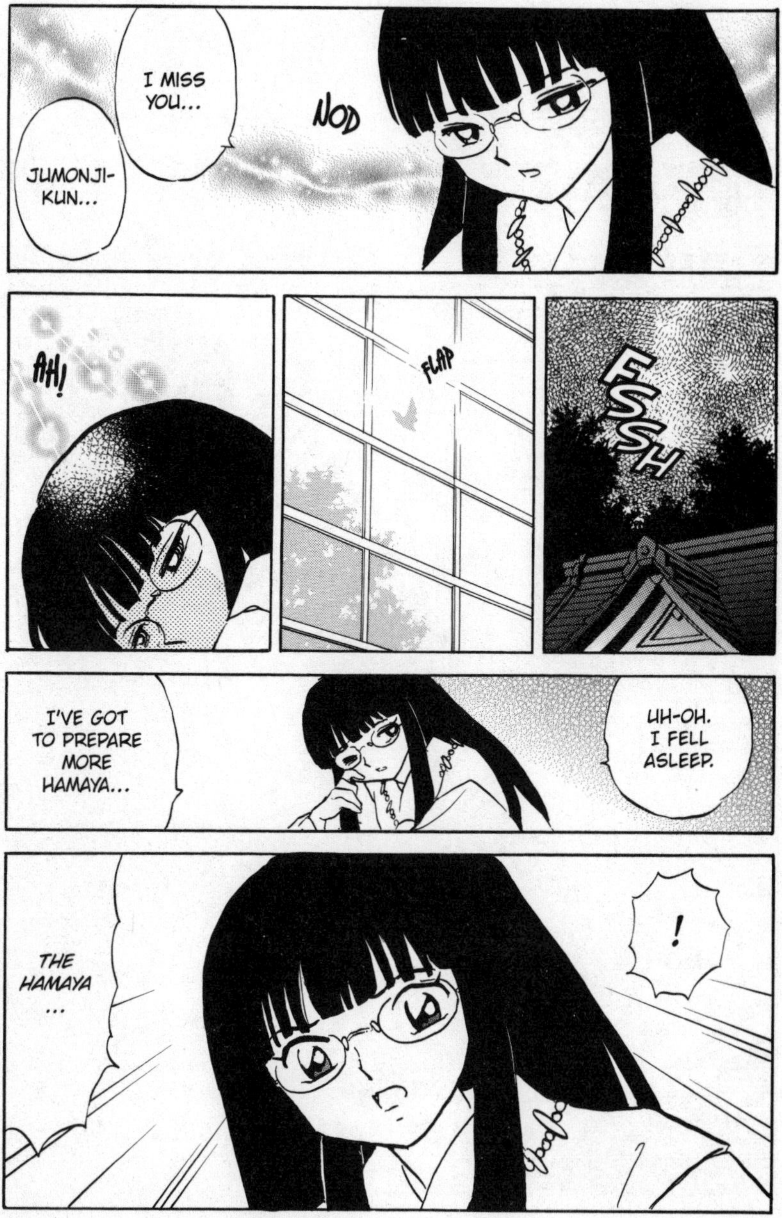
NOD
I MISS YOU...
JUMONJI-KUN...
FSSH
FLAP
AH!
UH-OH. I FELL ASLEEP.
I'VE GOT TO PREPARE MORE HAMAYA...
!
THE HAMAYA ...

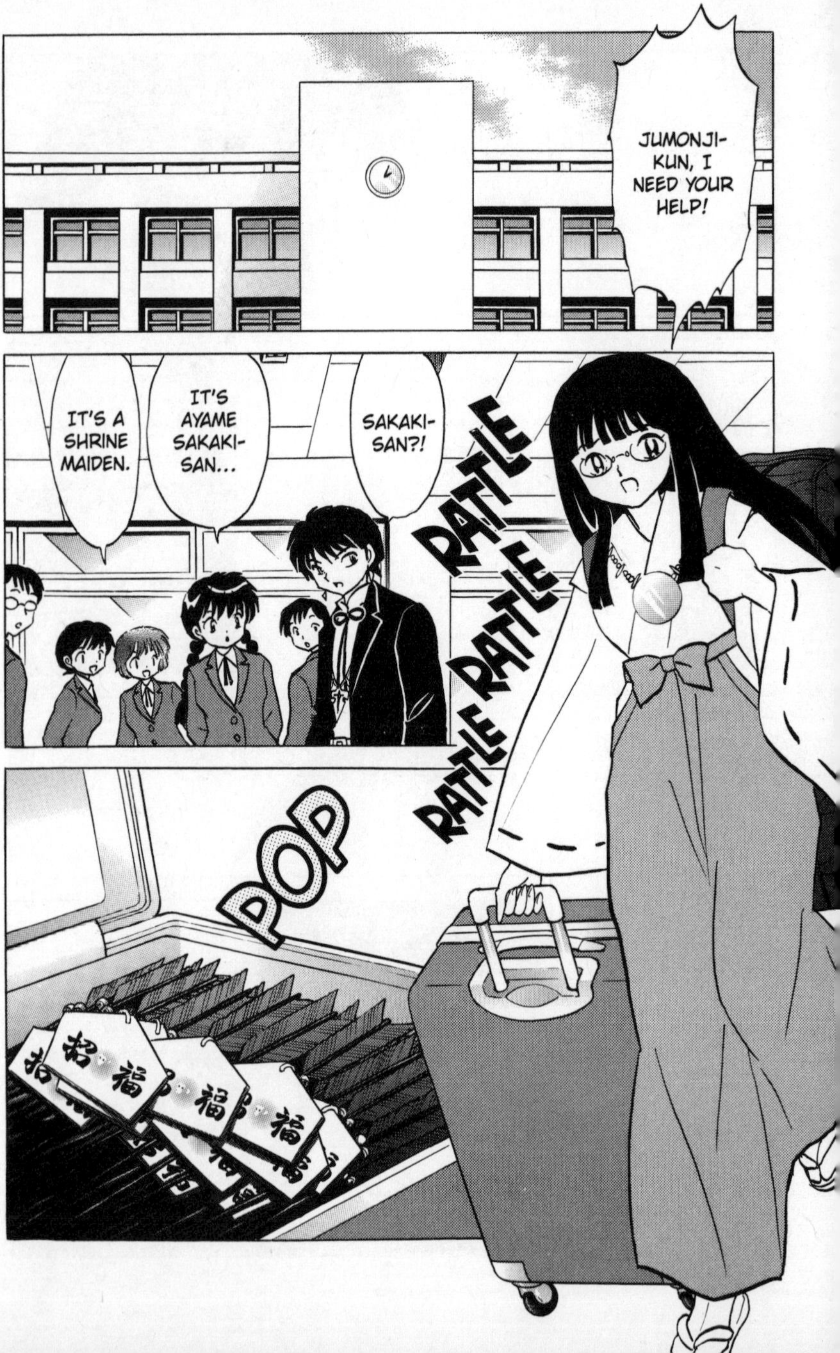
JUMONJI-KUN, I NEED YOUR HELP!
SAKAKI-SAN?!
IT'S AYAME SAKAKI-SAN...
IT'S A SHRINE MAIDEN.
RATTLE RATTLE RATTLE
POP

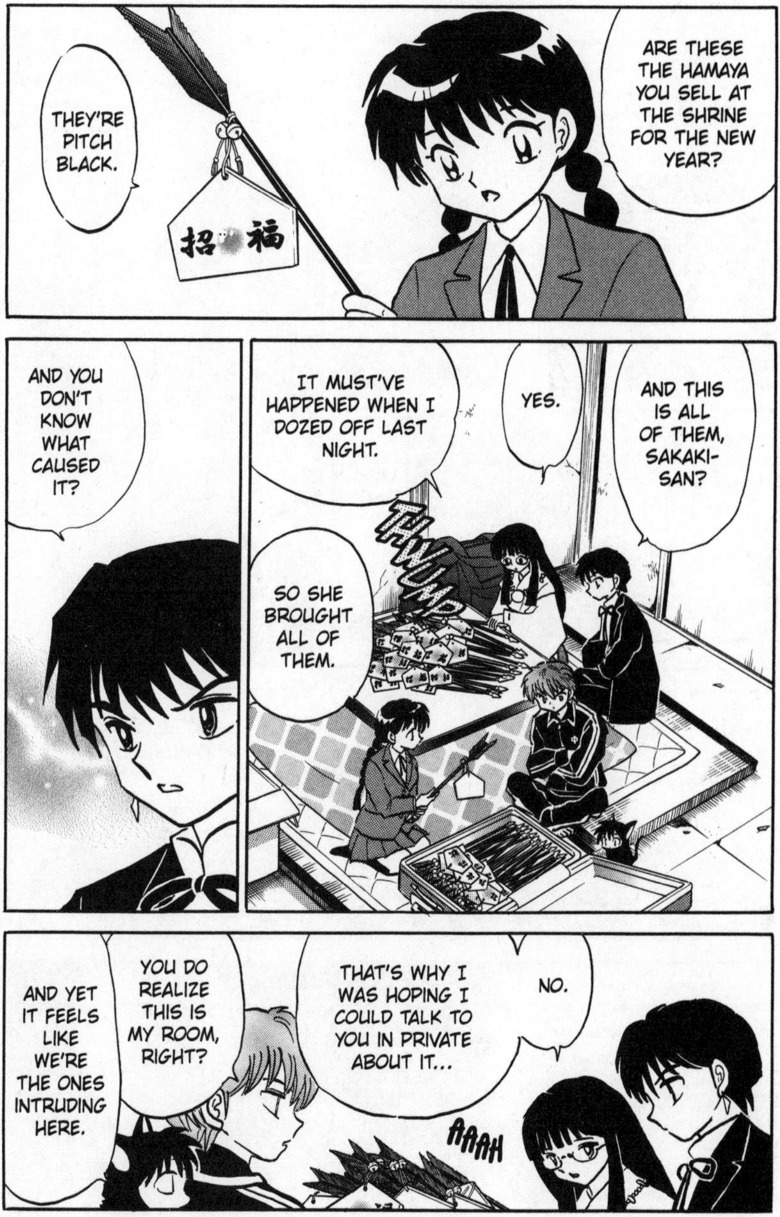
ARE THESE THE HAMAYA YOU SELL AT THE SHRINE FOR THE NEW YEAR?
THEY'RE PITCH BLACK.
AND THIS IS ALL OF THEM, SAKAKI-SAN?
YES.
IT MUST'VE HAPPENED WHEN I DOZED OFF LAST NIGHT.
THUMP
SO SHE BROUGHT ALL OF THEM.
AND YOU DON'T KNOW WHAT CAUSED IT?
NO.
THAT'S WHY I WAS HOPING I COULD TALK TO YOU IN PRIVATE ABOUT IT...
AAAH
YOU DO REALIZE THIS IS MY ROOM, RIGHT?
AND YET IT FEELS LIKE WE'RE THE ONES INTRUDING HERE.

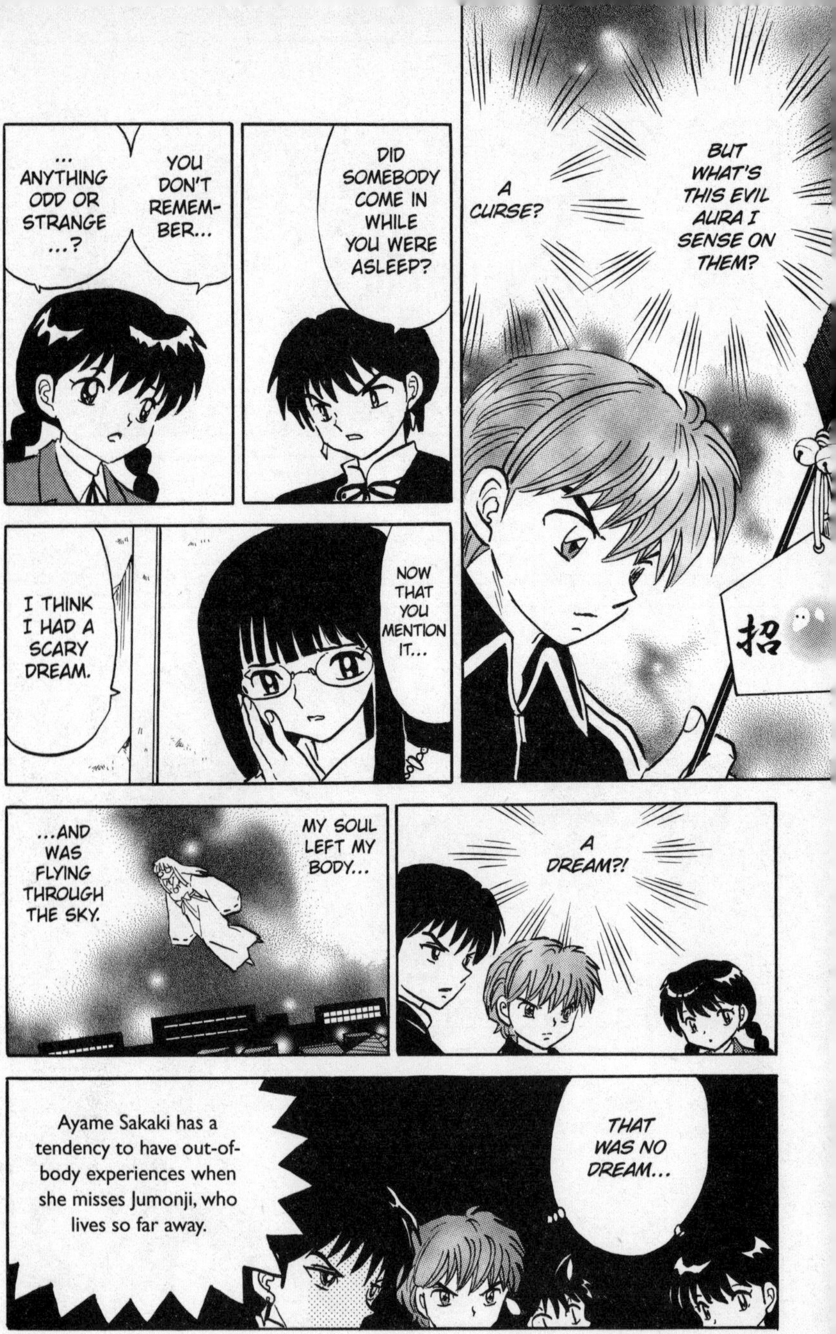

BUT WHAT'S THIS EVIL AURA I SENSE ON THEM?
A CURSE?
DID SOMEBODY COME IN WHILE YOU WERE ASLEEP?
YOU DON'T REMEMBER...
... ANYTHING ODD OR STRANGE ...?
NOW THAT YOU MENTION IT...
I THINK I HAD A SCARY DREAM.
A DREAM?!
MY SOUL LEFT MY BODY...
...AND WAS FLYING THROUGH THE SKY.
THAT WAS NO DREAM...
Ayame Sakaki has a tendency to have out-of-body experiences when she misses Jumonji, who lives so far away.

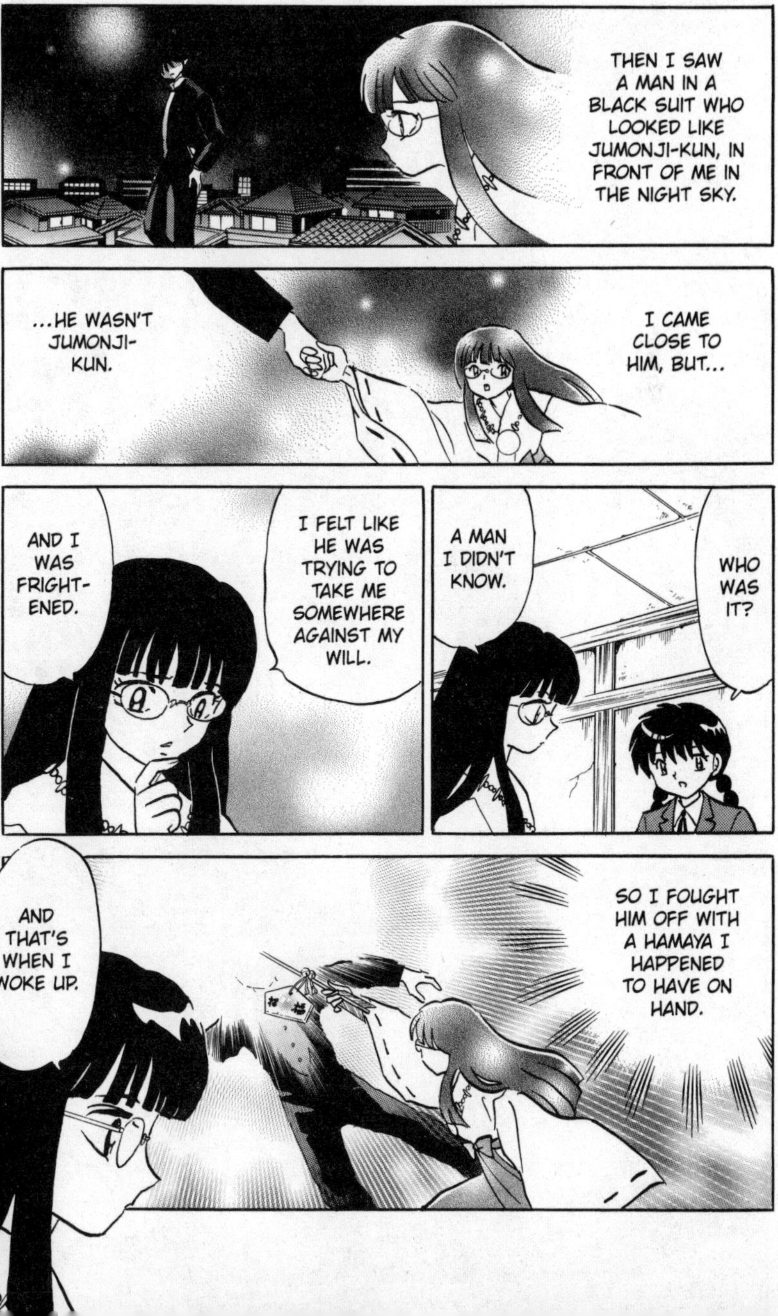
THEN I SAW A MAN IN A BLACK SUIT WHO LOOKED LIKE JUMONJI-KUN, IN FRONT OF ME IN THE NIGHT SKY.
I CAME CLOSE TO HIM, BUT...
...HE WASN'T JUMONJI-KUN.
WHO WAS IT?
A MAN I DIDN'T KNOW.
I FELT LIKE HE WAS TRYING TO TAKE ME SOMEWHERE AGAINST MY WILL.
AND I WAS FRIGHT-ENED.
SO I FOUGHT HIM OFF WITH A HAMAYA I HAPPENED TO HAVE ON HAND.
AND THAT'S WHEN I WOKE UP.

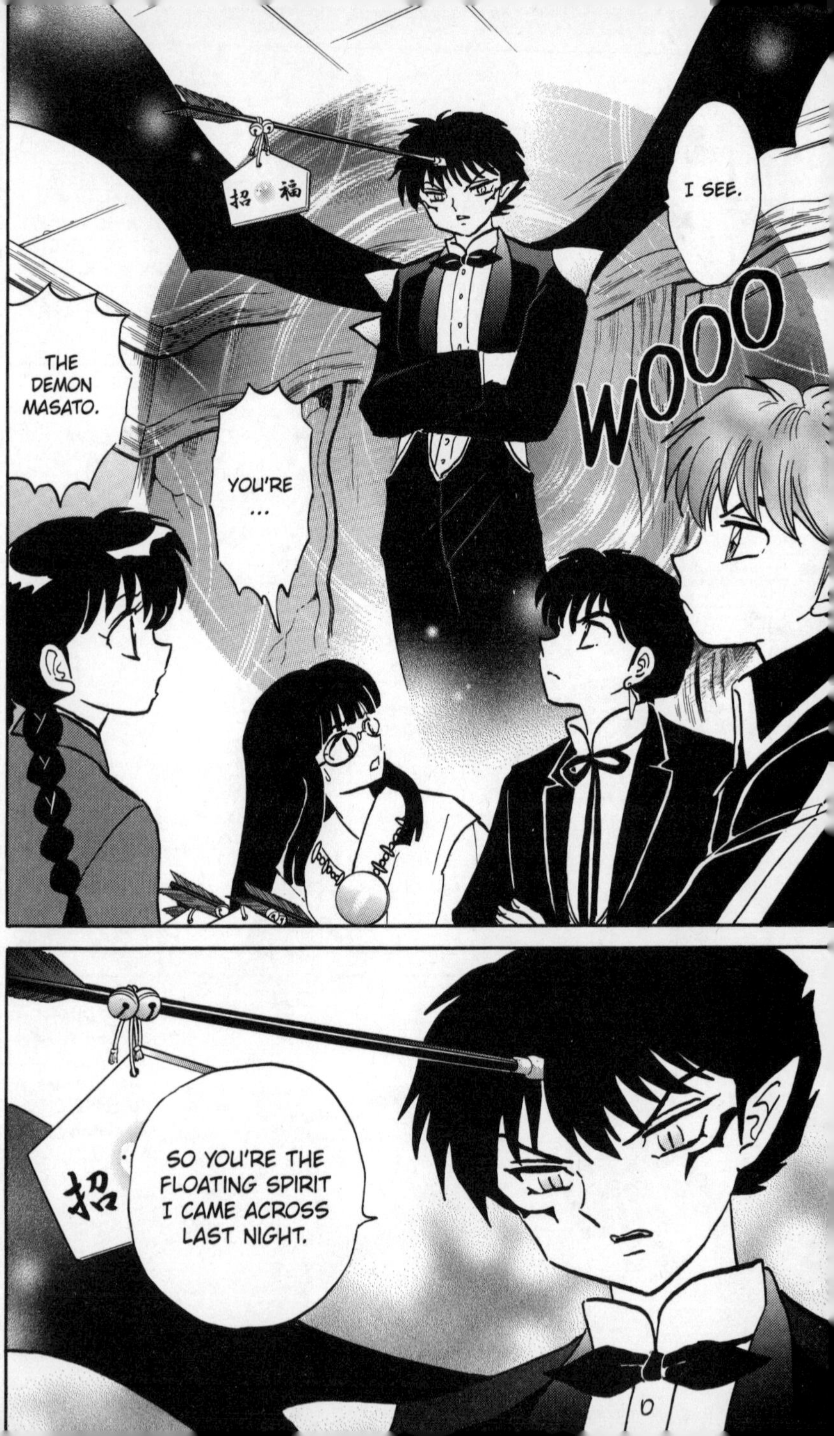
I SEE.
WOOO
YOU'RE ...
THE DEMON MASATO.
招 福
SO YOU'RE THE FLOATING SPIRIT I CAME ACROSS LAST NIGHT.
招

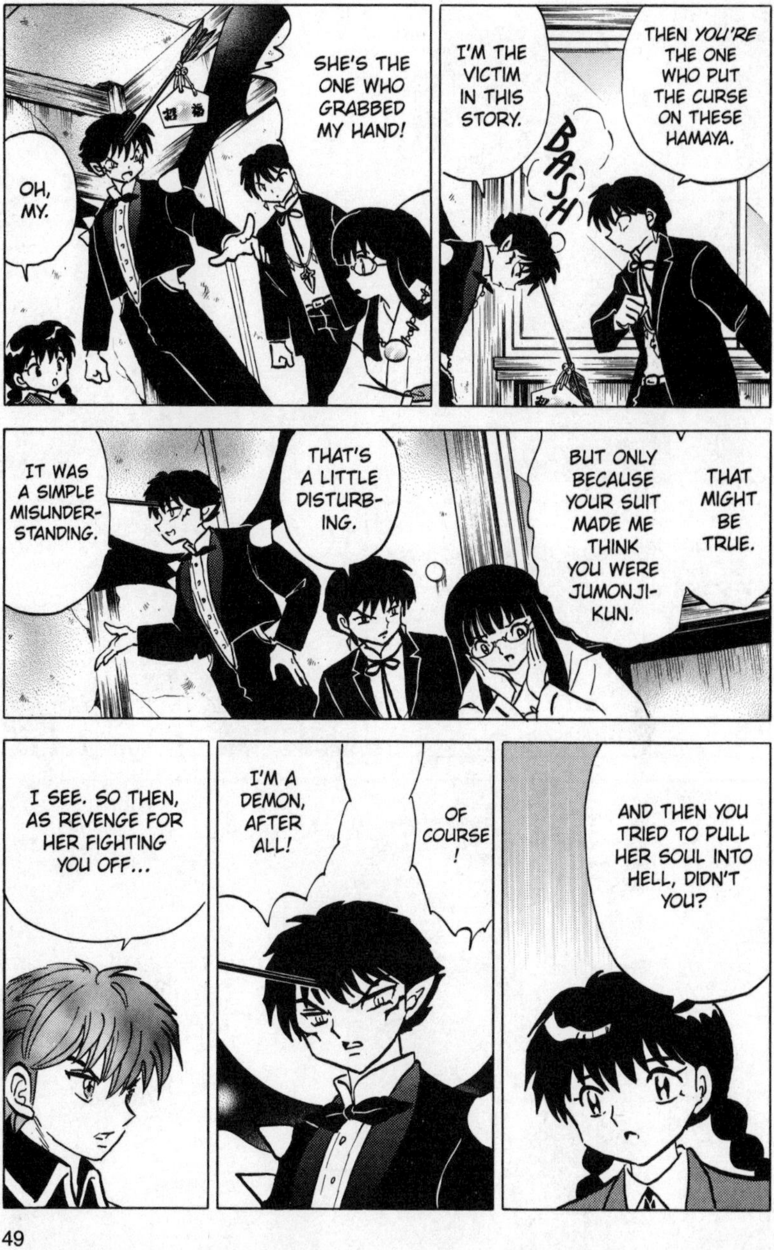
THEN *YOU'RE* THE ONE WHO PUT THE CURSE ON THESE HAMAYA.
I'M THE VICTIM IN THIS STORY.
BASH
SHE'S THE ONE WHO GRABBED MY HAND!
OH, MY.
THAT MIGHT BE TRUE.
BUT ONLY BECAUSE YOUR SUIT MADE ME THINK YOU WERE JUMONJI-KUN.
THAT'S A LITTLE DISTURBING.
IT WAS A SIMPLE MISUNDERSTANDING.
AND THEN YOU TRIED TO PULL HER SOUL INTO HELL, DIDN'T YOU?
OF COURSE!
I'M A DEMON, AFTER ALL!
I SEE. SO THEN, AS REVENGE FOR HER FIGHTING YOU OFF...

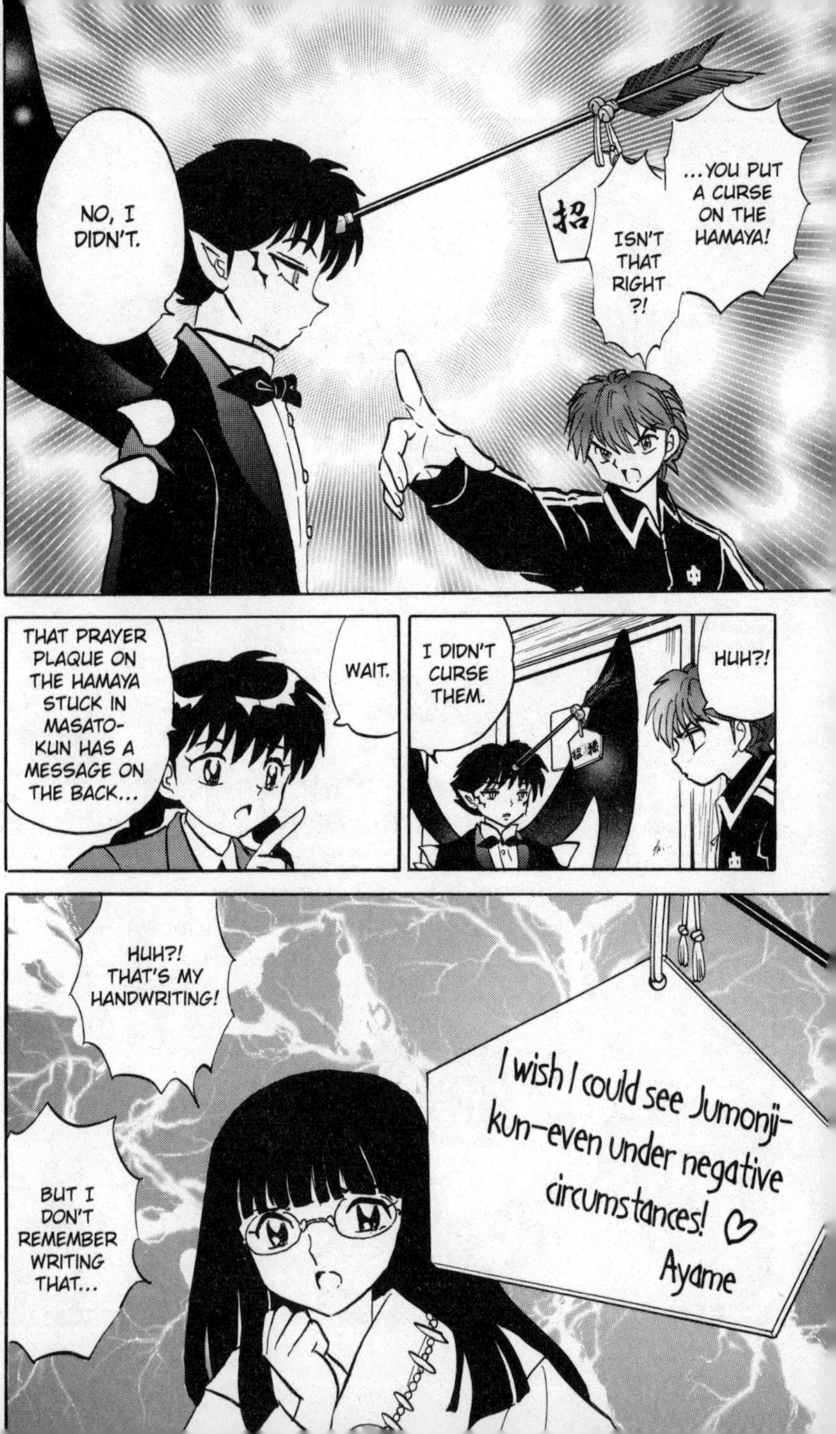
...YOU PUT A CURSE ON THE HAMAYA!
ISN'T THAT RIGHT?!
招
NO, I DIDN'T.
HUH?!
I DIDN'T CURSE THEM.
WAIT.
THAT PRAYER PLAQUE ON THE HAMAYA STUCK IN MASATO-KUN HAS A MESSAGE ON THE BACK...
I wish I could see Jumonji-kun—even under negative circumstances! ♡ Ayame
HUH?! THAT'S MY HANDWRITING!
BUT I DON'T REMEMBER WRITING THAT...

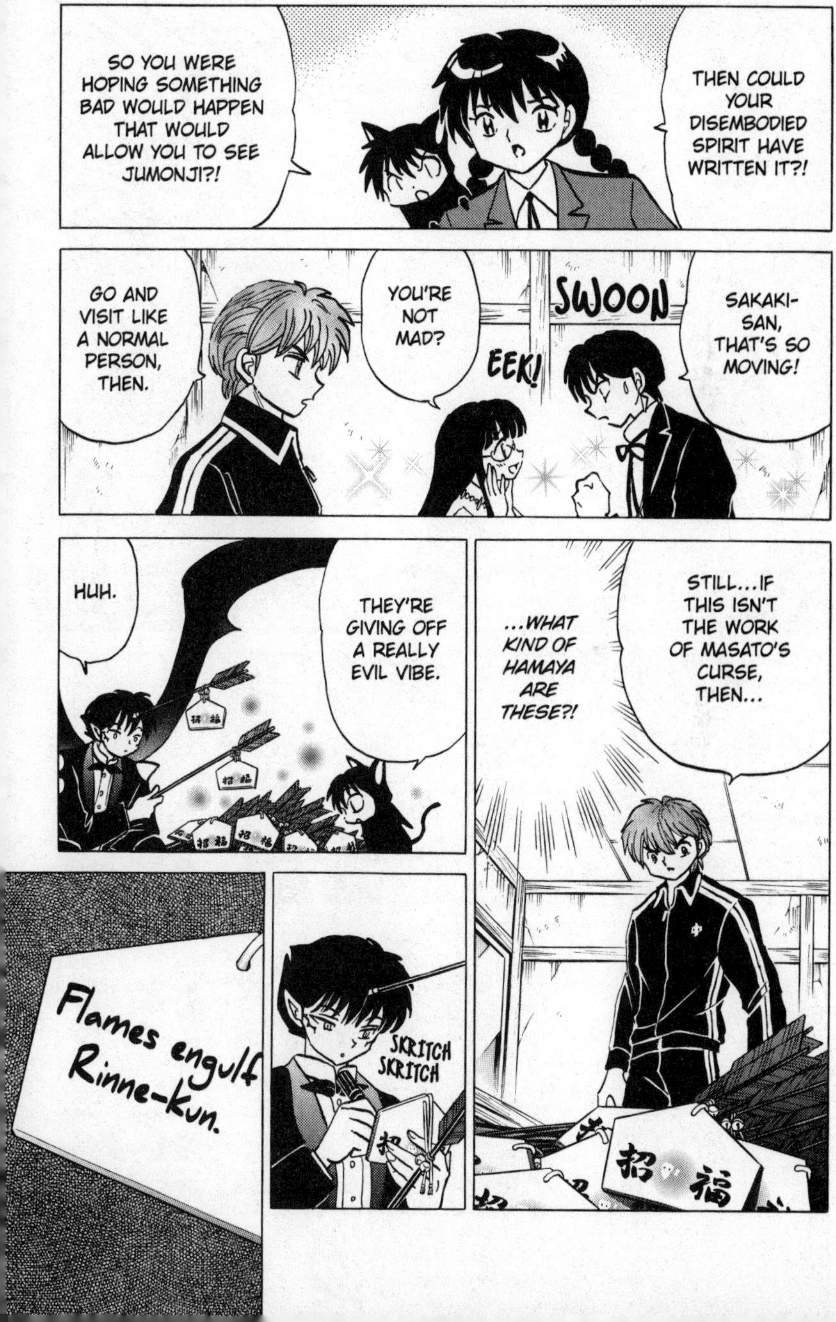
THEN COULD YOUR DISEMBODIED SPIRIT HAVE WRITTEN IT?!
SO YOU WERE HOPING SOMETHING BAD WOULD HAPPEN THAT WOULD ALLOW YOU TO SEE JUMONJI?!
SAKAKI-SAN, THAT'S SO MOVING!
SWOON
EEK!
YOU'RE NOT MAD?
GO AND VISIT LIKE A NORMAL PERSON, THEN.
STILL...IF THIS ISN'T THE WORK OF MASATO'S CURSE, THEN...
...WHAT KIND OF HAMAYA ARE THESE?!
THEY'RE GIVING OFF A REALLY EVIL VIBE.
HUH.
SKRITCH SKRITCH
Flames engulf Rinne-kun.

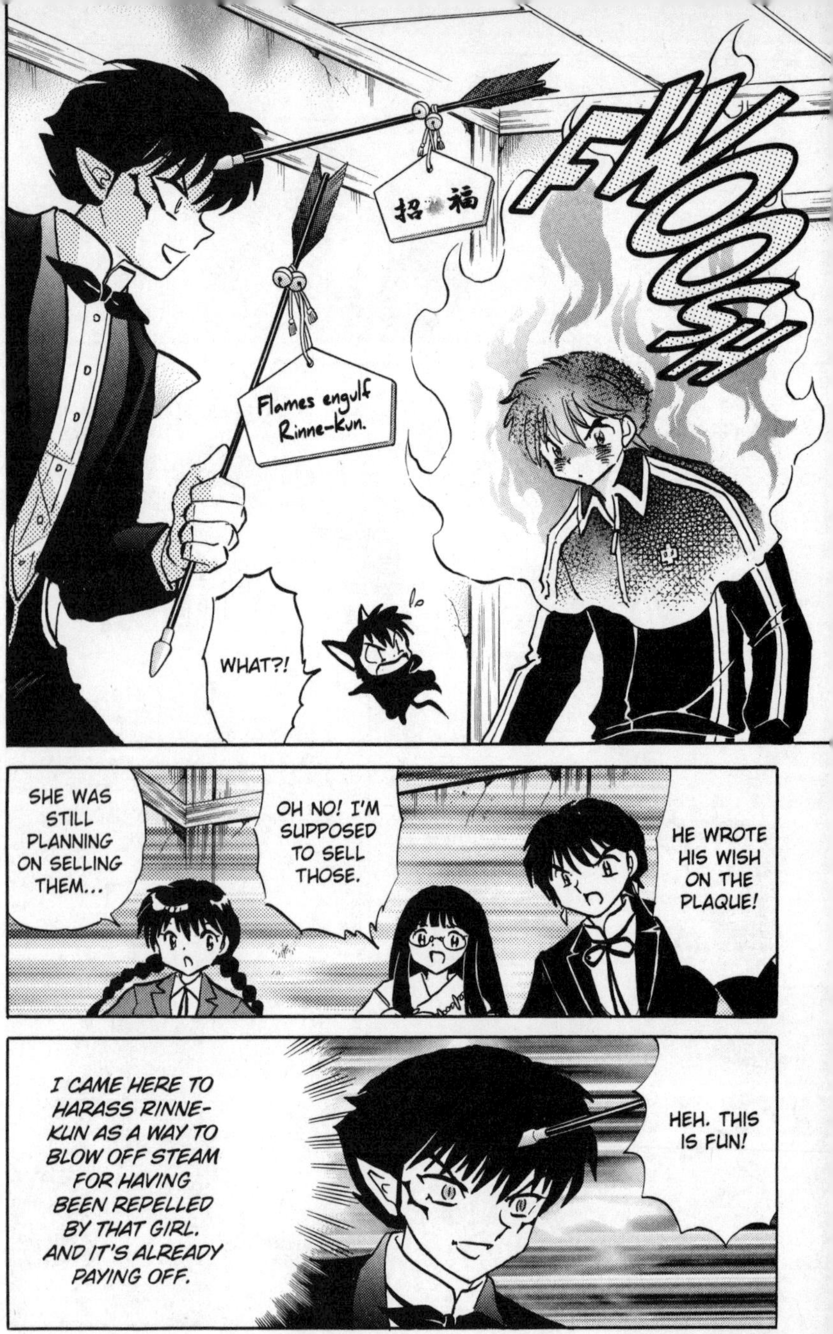
FWOOSH
招福
Flames engulf Rinne-Kun.
WHAT?!
HE WROTE HIS WISH ON THE PLAQUE!
OH NO! I'M SUPPOSED TO SELL THOSE.
SHE WAS STILL PLANNING ON SELLING THEM...
HEH. THIS IS FUN!
I CAME HERE TO HARASS RINNE-KUN AS A WAY TO BLOW OFF STEAM FOR HAVING BEEN REPELLED BY THAT GIRL. AND IT'S ALREADY PAYING OFF.

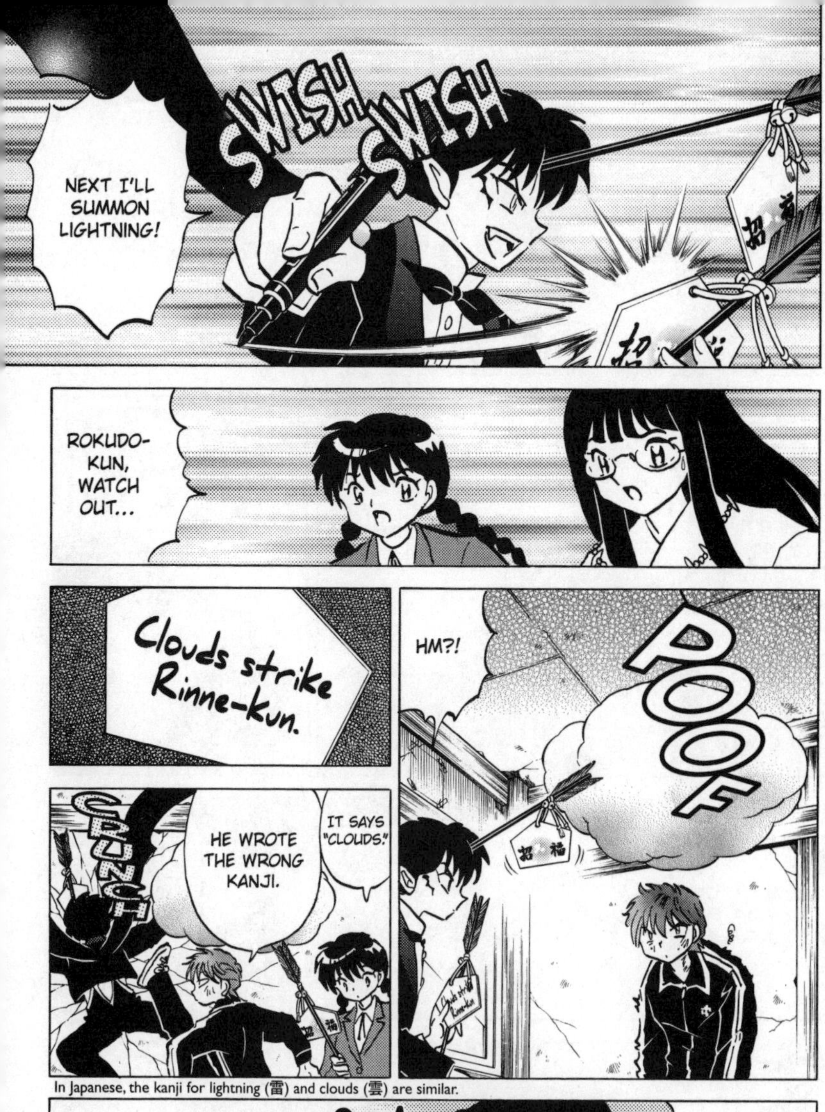
SWISH SWISH
NEXT I'LL SUMMON LIGHTNING!
ROKUDO-KUN, WATCH OUT...
HM?!
POOF
Clouds strike Rinne-kun.
CRUNCH
IT SAYS "CLOUDS."
HE WROTE THE WRONG KANJI.

In Japanese, the kanji for lightning (雷) and clouds (雲) are similar.

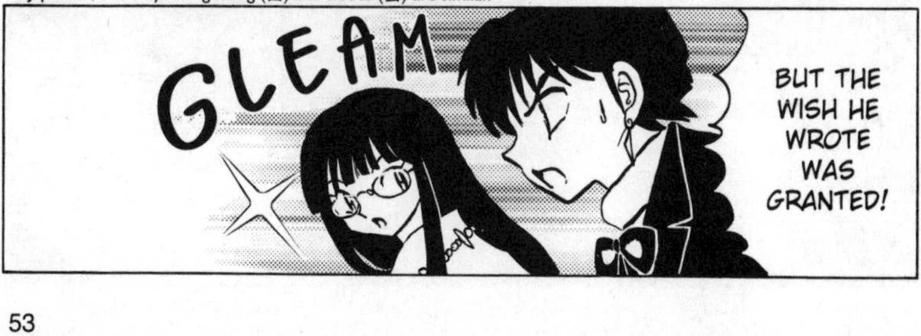
BUT THE WISH HE WROTE WAS GRANTED!
GLEAM

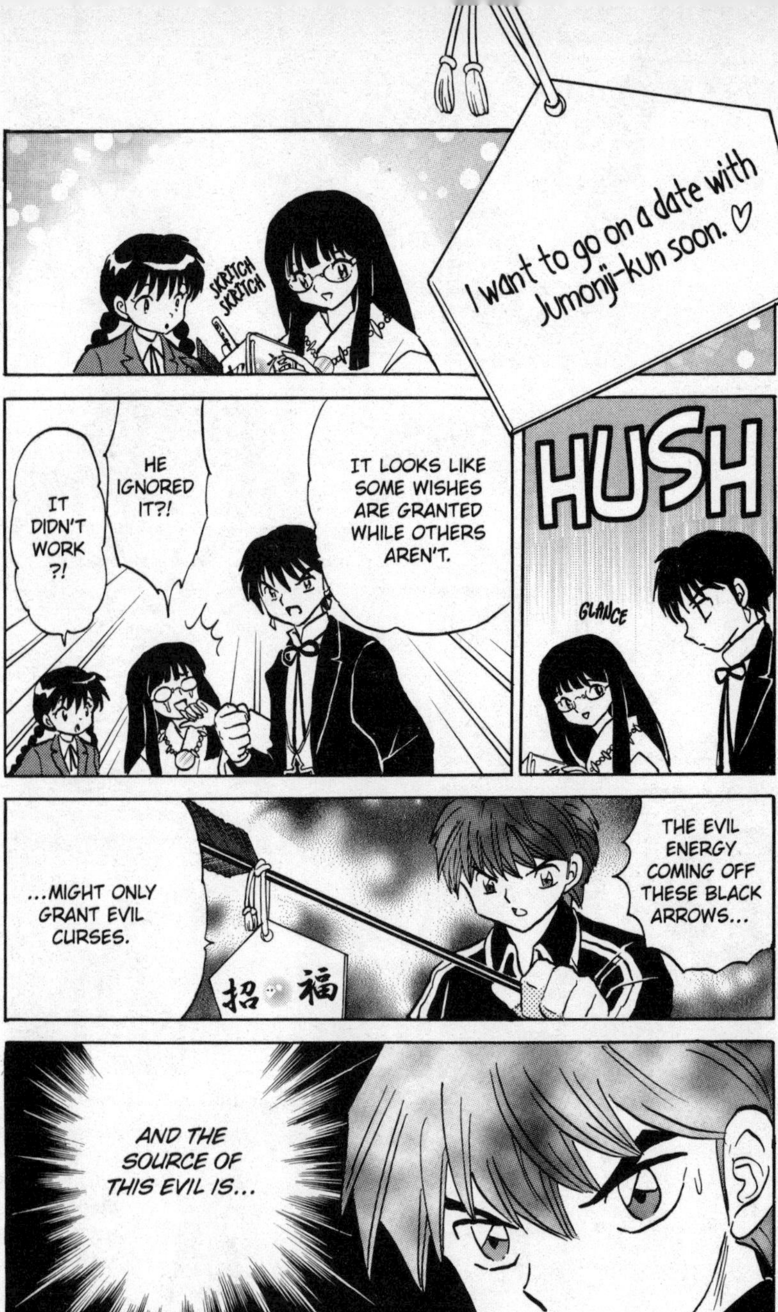
I want to go on a date with Jumonji-kun soon. ♡
SKRITCH SKRITCH
HUSH
GLANCE
IT LOOKS LIKE SOME WISHES ARE GRANTED WHILE OTHERS AREN'T.
HE IGNORED IT?!
IT DIDN'T WORK?!
THE EVIL ENERGY COMING OFF THESE BLACK ARROWS...
...MIGHT ONLY GRANT EVIL CURSES.
招福
AND THE SOURCE OF THIS EVIL IS...

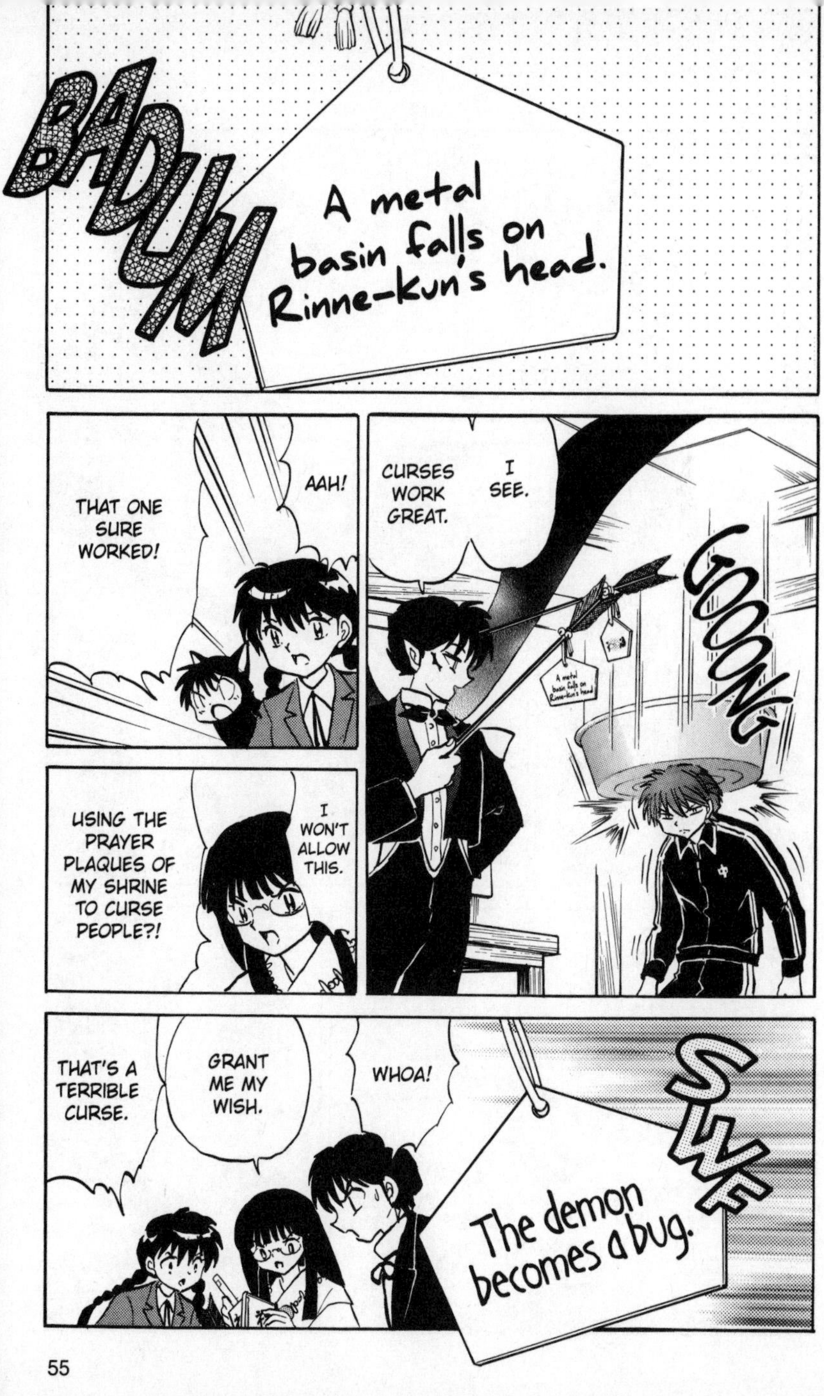
BADUM
A metal basin falls on Rinne-kun's head.
I SEE.
CURSES WORK GREAT.
GOOONG
A metal basin falls on Rinne-kun's head.
AAH!
THAT ONE SURE WORKED!
I WON'T ALLOW THIS.
USING THE PRAYER PLAQUES OF MY SHRINE TO CURSE PEOPLE?!
SWF
The demon becomes a bug.
WHOA!
GRANT ME MY WISH.
THAT'S A TERRIBLE CURSE.

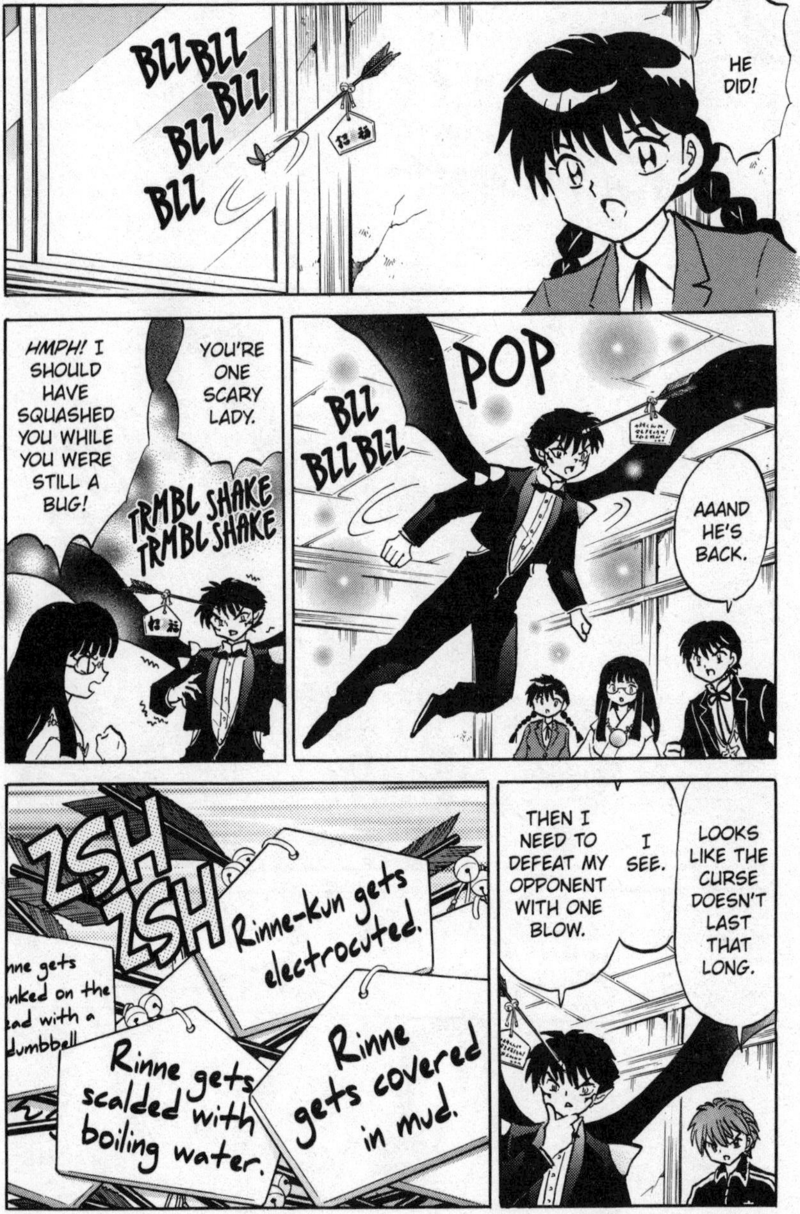
HE DID!
BZZ BZZ BZZ BZZ
POP
BZZ BZZ BZZ
AAAND HE'S BACK.
YOU'RE ONE SCARY LADY.
HMPH! I SHOULD HAVE SQUASHED YOU WHILE YOU WERE STILL A BUG!
TRMBL SHAKE TRMBL SHAKE
LOOKS LIKE THE CURSE DOESN'T LAST THAT LONG.
I SEE.
THEN I NEED TO DEFEAT MY OPPONENT WITH ONE BLOW.
ZSH ZSH
Rinne-kun gets electrocuted.
nne gets nked on the ad with a dumbbell
Rinne gets covered in mud.
Rinne gets scalded with boiling water.

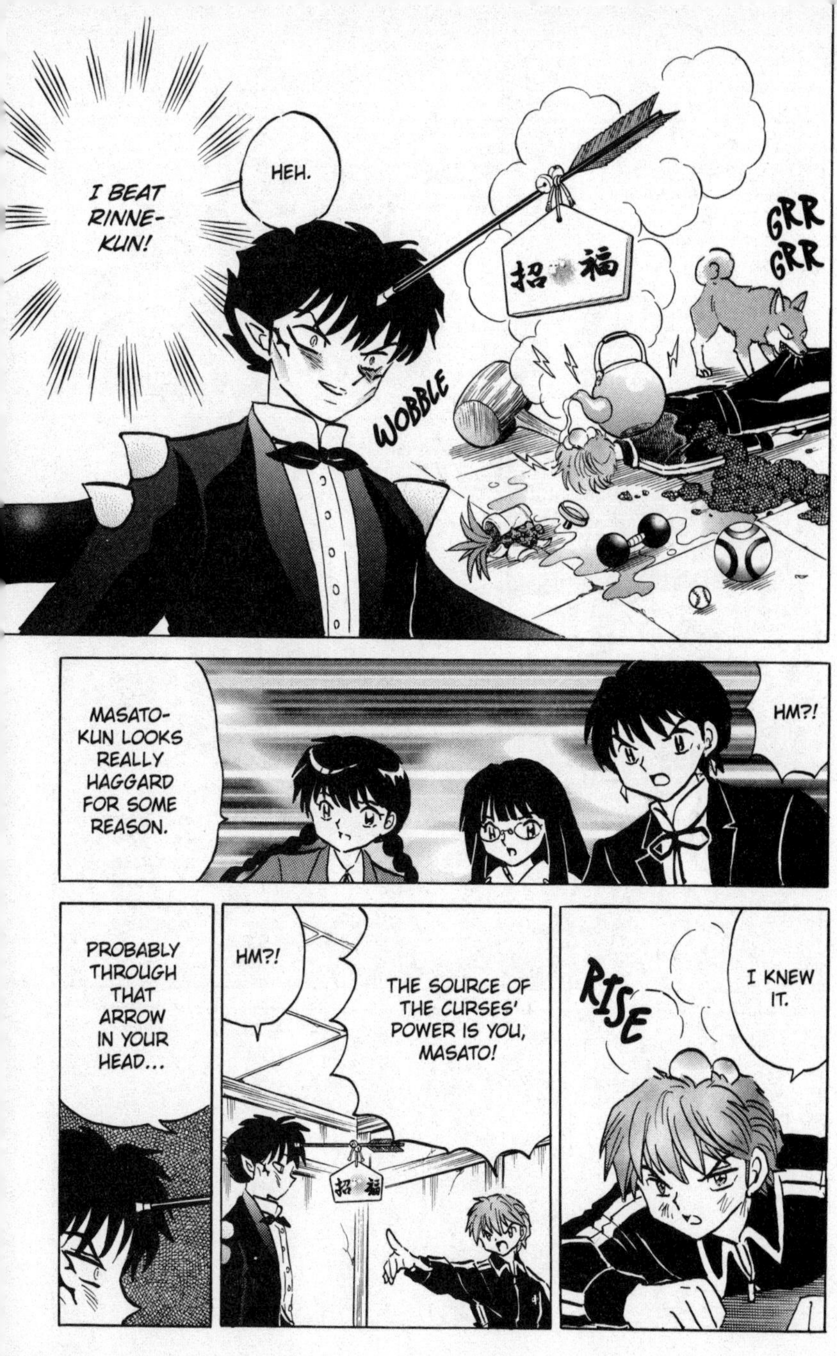
GRR GRR
HEH.
I BEAT RINNE-KUN!
WOBBLE
HM?!
MASATO-KUN LOOKS REALLY HAGGARD FOR SOME REASON.
I KNEW IT.
RISE
THE SOURCE OF THE CURSES' POWER IS YOU, MASATO!
HM?!
PROBABLY THROUGH THAT ARROW IN YOUR HEAD...

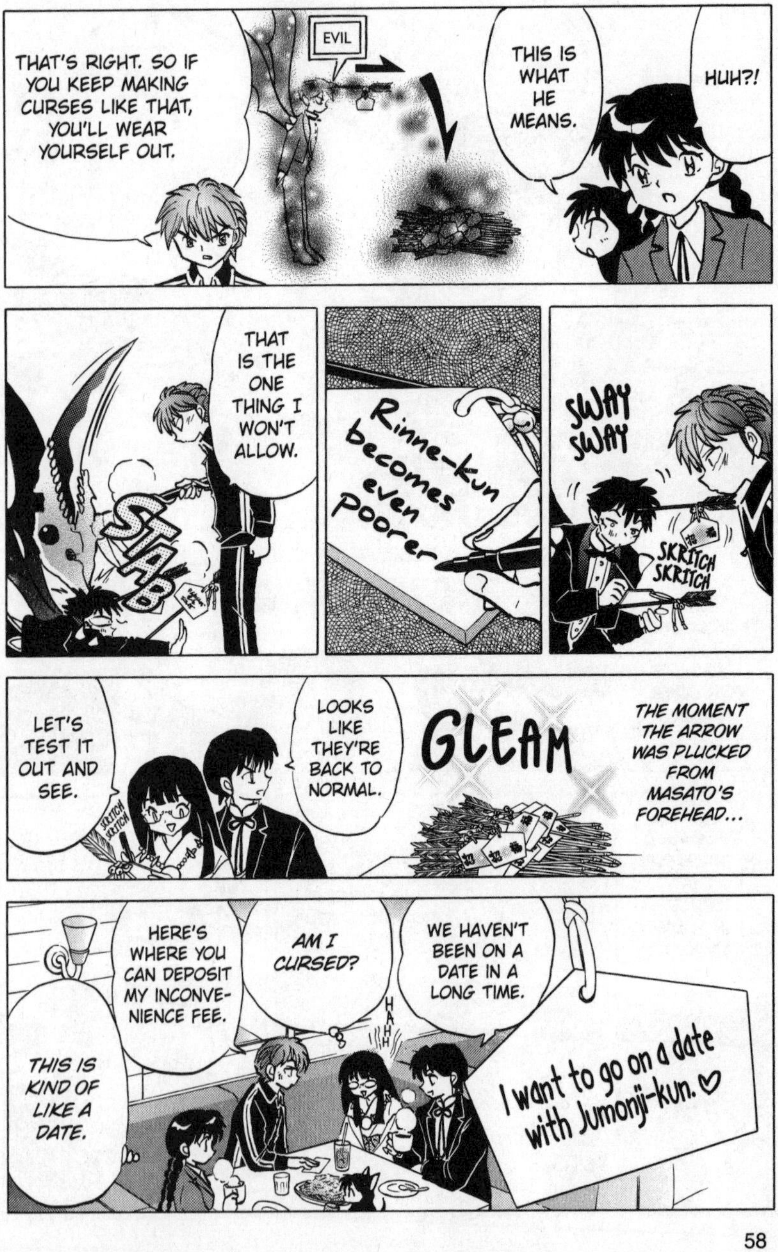
HUH?!
THIS IS WHAT HE MEANS.
EVIL
THAT'S RIGHT. SO IF YOU KEEP MAKING CURSES LIKE THAT, YOU'LL WEAR YOURSELF OUT.
SWAY SWAY
SKRITCH SKRITCH
Rinne-kun becomes even poorer
THAT IS THE ONE THING I WON'T ALLOW.
STAB
THE MOMENT THE ARROW WAS PLUCKED FROM MASATO'S FOREHEAD...
GLEAM
LOOKS LIKE THEY'RE BACK TO NORMAL.
LET'S TEST IT OUT AND SEE.
SKRITCH SKRITCH
I want to go on a date with Jumonji-kun. ♥
WE HAVEN'T BEEN ON A DATE IN A LONG TIME.
HAHH
AM I CURSED?
HERE'S WHERE YOU CAN DEPOSIT MY INCONVENIENCE FEE.
THIS IS KIND OF LIKE A DATE.

CHAPTER 312: I WANT TO BITE YOU

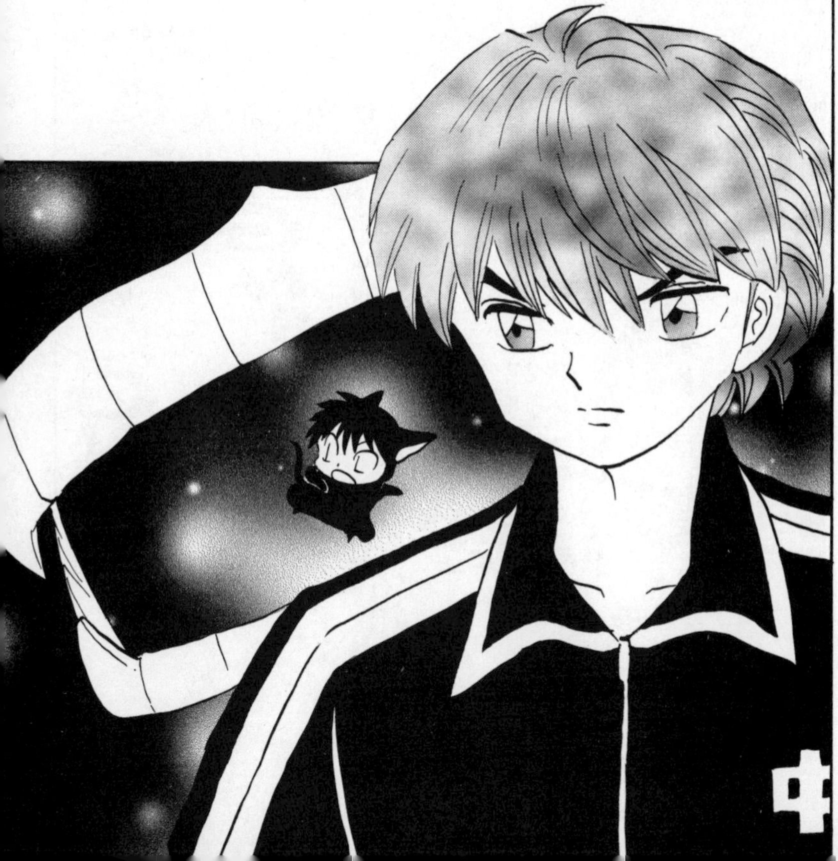

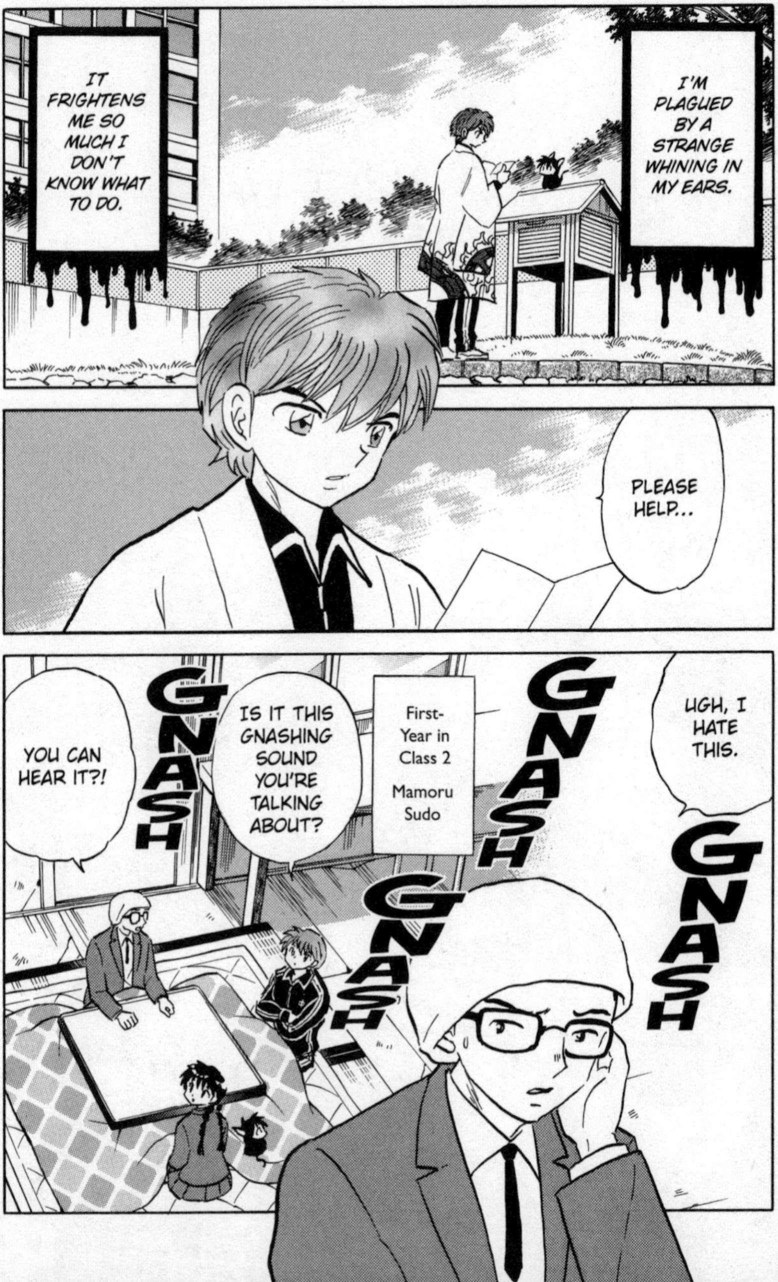
I'M PLAGUED BY A STRANGE WHINING IN MY EARS.
IT FRIGHTENS ME SO MUCH I DON'T KNOW WHAT TO DO.
PLEASE HELP...
UGH, I HATE THIS.
GNASH
GNASH
GNASH
First-Year in Class 2
Mamoru Sudo
IS IT THIS GNASHING SOUND YOU'RE TALKING ABOUT?
GNASH
YOU CAN HEAR IT?!

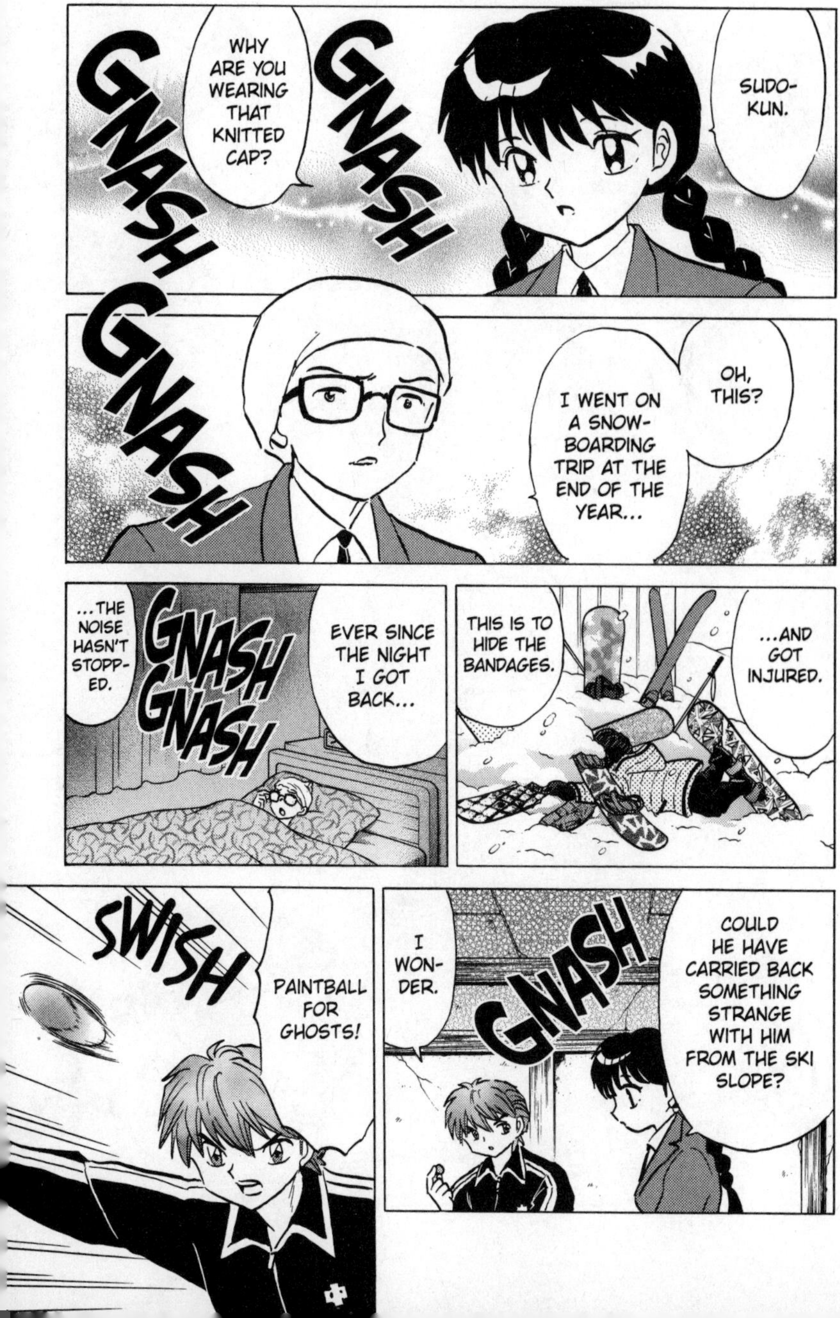
SUDO-KUN.
GNASH
GNASH
WHY ARE YOU WEARING THAT KNITTED CAP?
OH, THIS?
I WENT ON A SNOW-BOARDING TRIP AT THE END OF THE YEAR...
GNASH
...AND GOT INJURED.
THIS IS TO HIDE THE BANDAGES.
EVER SINCE THE NIGHT I GOT BACK...
GNASH GNASH
...THE NOISE HASN'T STOPP-ED.
COULD HE HAVE CARRIED BACK SOMETHING STRANGE WITH HIM FROM THE SKI SLOPE?
GNASH
I WON-DER.
SWISH
PAINTBALL FOR GHOSTS!

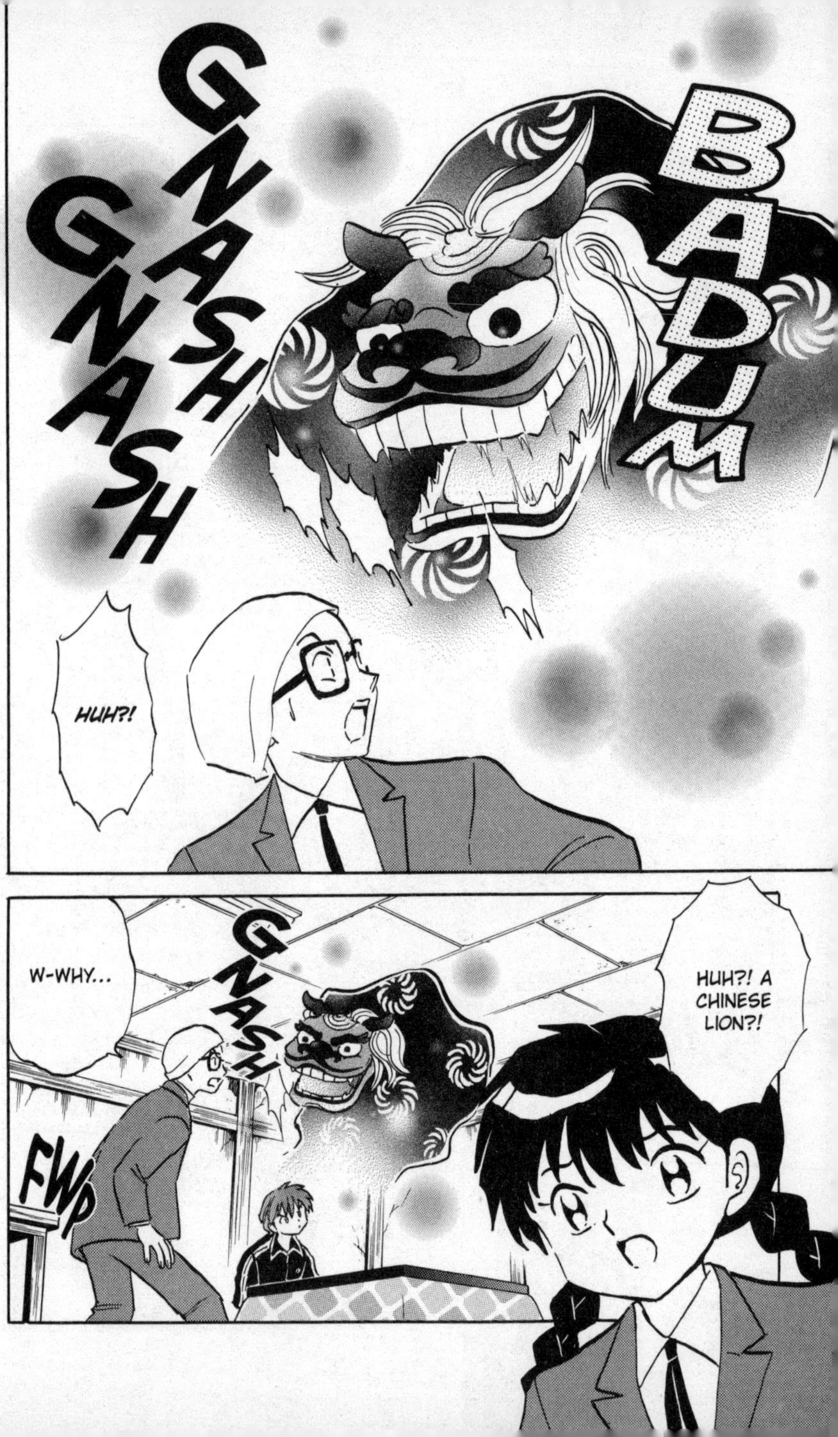
BADUM
GNASH GNASH
HUH?!
HUH?! A CHINESE LION?!
GNASH
W-WHY...
FWP

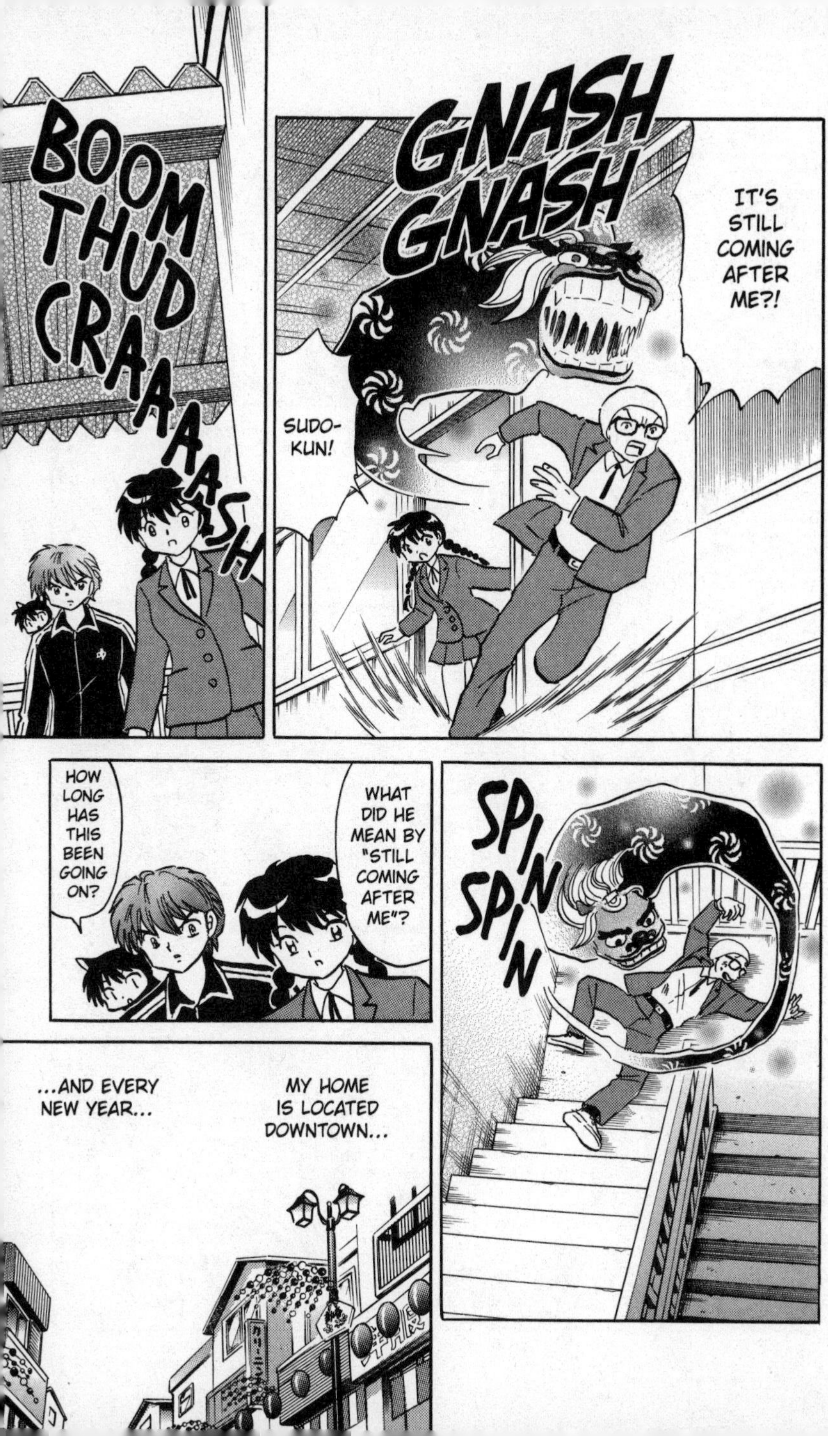

GNASH GNASH
IT'S STILL COMING AFTER ME?!
SUDO-KUN!
BOOM THUD CRAAAASH
SPIN SPIN SPIN
WHAT DID HE MEAN BY "STILL COMING AFTER ME"?
HOW LONG HAS THIS BEEN GOING ON?
MY HOME IS LOCATED DOWNTOWN...
...AND EVERY NEW YEAR...

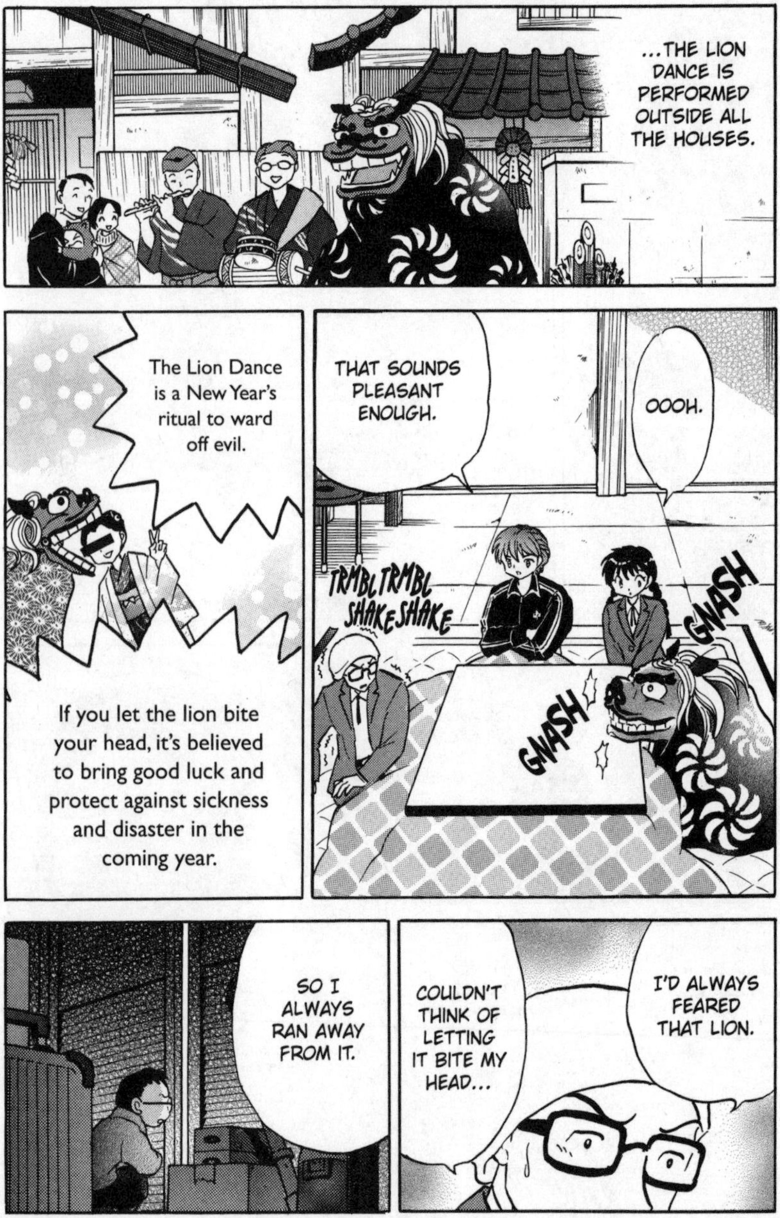
...THE LION DANCE IS PERFORMED OUTSIDE ALL THE HOUSES.
OOOH.
THAT SOUNDS PLEASANT ENOUGH.
GNASH
TRMBL TRMBL SHAKE SHAKE
GNASH
The Lion Dance is a New Year's ritual to ward off evil.
If you let the lion bite your head, it's believed to bring good luck and protect against sickness and disaster in the coming year.
I'D ALWAYS FEARED THAT LION.
COULDN'T THINK OF LETTING IT BITE MY HEAD...
SO I ALWAYS RAN AWAY FROM IT.

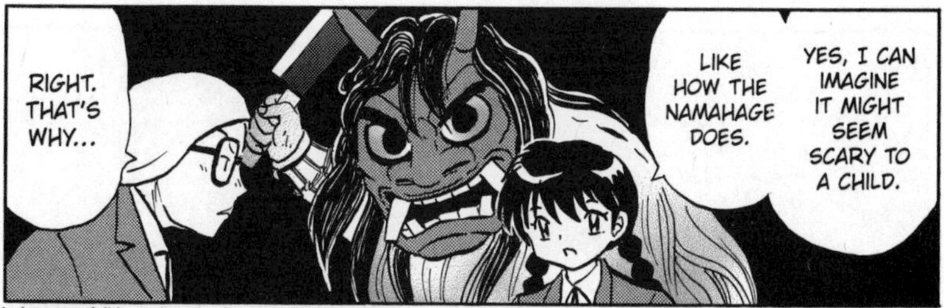
YES, I CAN IMAGINE IT MIGHT SEEM SCARY TO A CHILD.
LIKE HOW THE NAMAHAGE DOES.
RIGHT. THAT'S WHY...
In Japanese folklore, the namahage is a being with an ogre face, a straw cape and a knife.

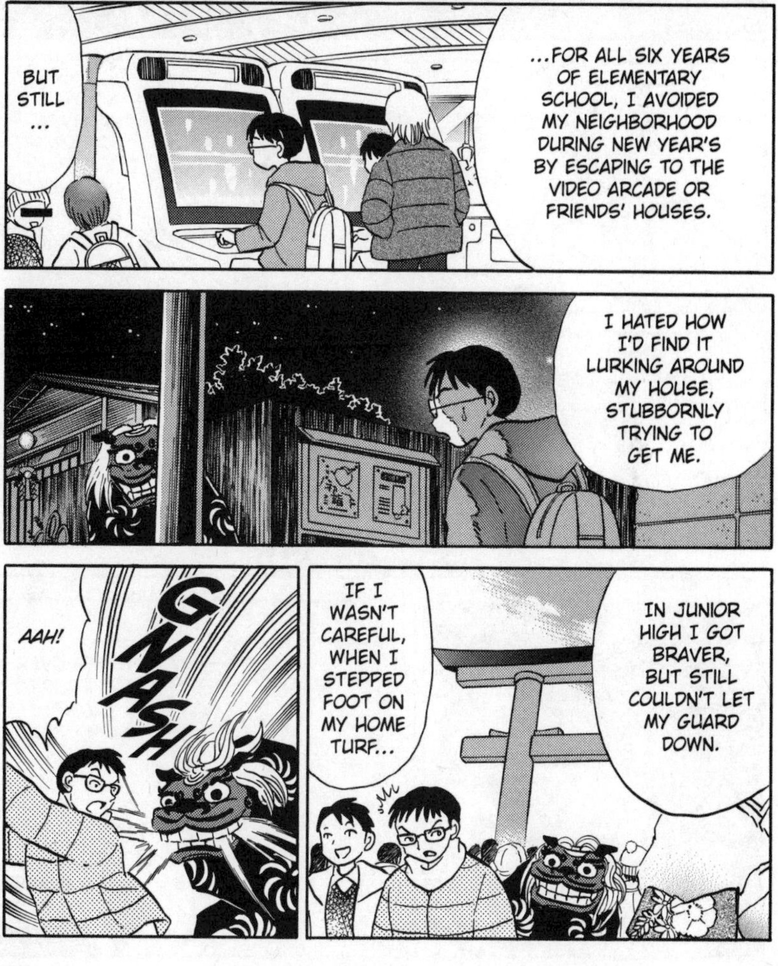
...FOR ALL SIX YEARS OF ELEMENTARY SCHOOL, I AVOIDED MY NEIGHBORHOOD DURING NEW YEAR'S BY ESCAPING TO THE VIDEO ARCADE OR FRIENDS' HOUSES.
BUT STILL...
I HATED HOW I'D FIND IT LURKING AROUND MY HOUSE, STUBBORNLY TRYING TO GET ME.
IN JUNIOR HIGH I GOT BRAVER, BUT STILL COULDN'T LET MY GUARD DOWN.
IF I WASN'T CAREFUL, WHEN I STEPPED FOOT ON MY HOME TURF...
GNASH
AAH!

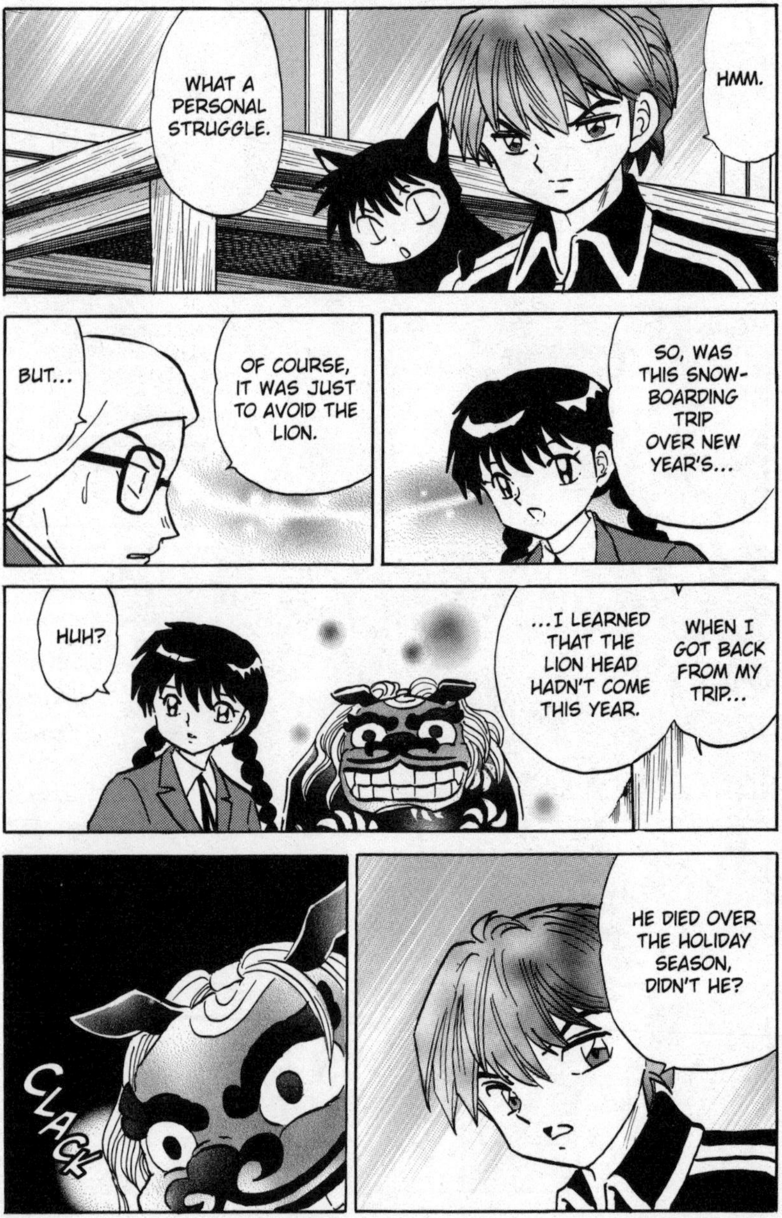
HMM.
WHAT A PERSONAL STRUGGLE.
SO, WAS THIS SNOW-BOARDING TRIP OVER NEW YEAR'S...
OF COURSE, IT WAS JUST TO AVOID THE LION.
BUT...
WHEN I GOT BACK FROM MY TRIP...
...I LEARNED THAT THE LION HEAD HADN'T COME THIS YEAR.
HUH?
HE DIED OVER THE HOLIDAY SEASON, DIDN'T HE?
CLACK

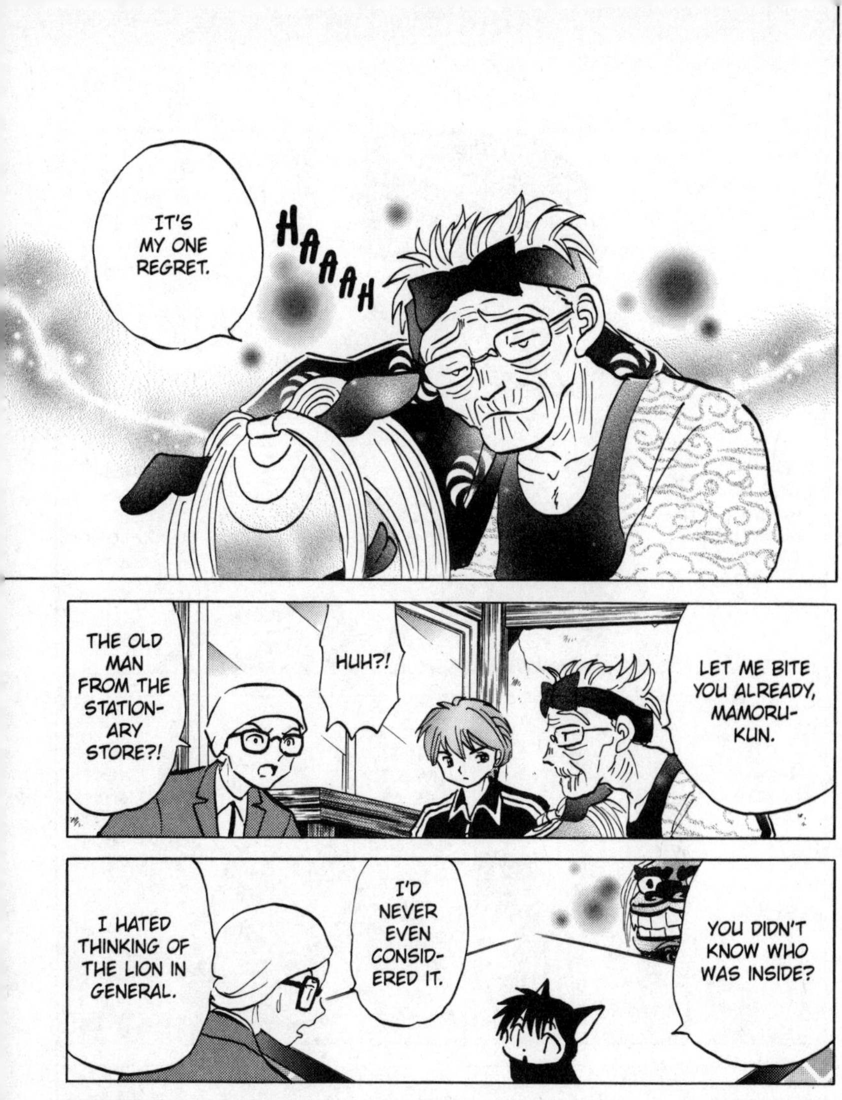
HAAAAH
IT'S MY ONE REGRET.
LET ME BITE YOU ALREADY, MAMORU-KUN.
HUH?!
THE OLD MAN FROM THE STATION-ARY STORE?!
YOU DIDN'T KNOW WHO WAS INSIDE?
I'D NEVER EVEN CONSID-ERED IT.
I HATED THINKING OF THE LION IN GENERAL.
YOU CAME TO MY WAKE.
THANK YOU.
WELL ...
THAT'S BECAUSE I DIDN'T KNOW YOUR TRUE IDENTITY.

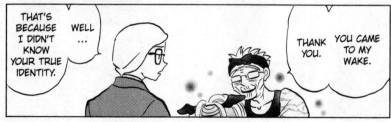

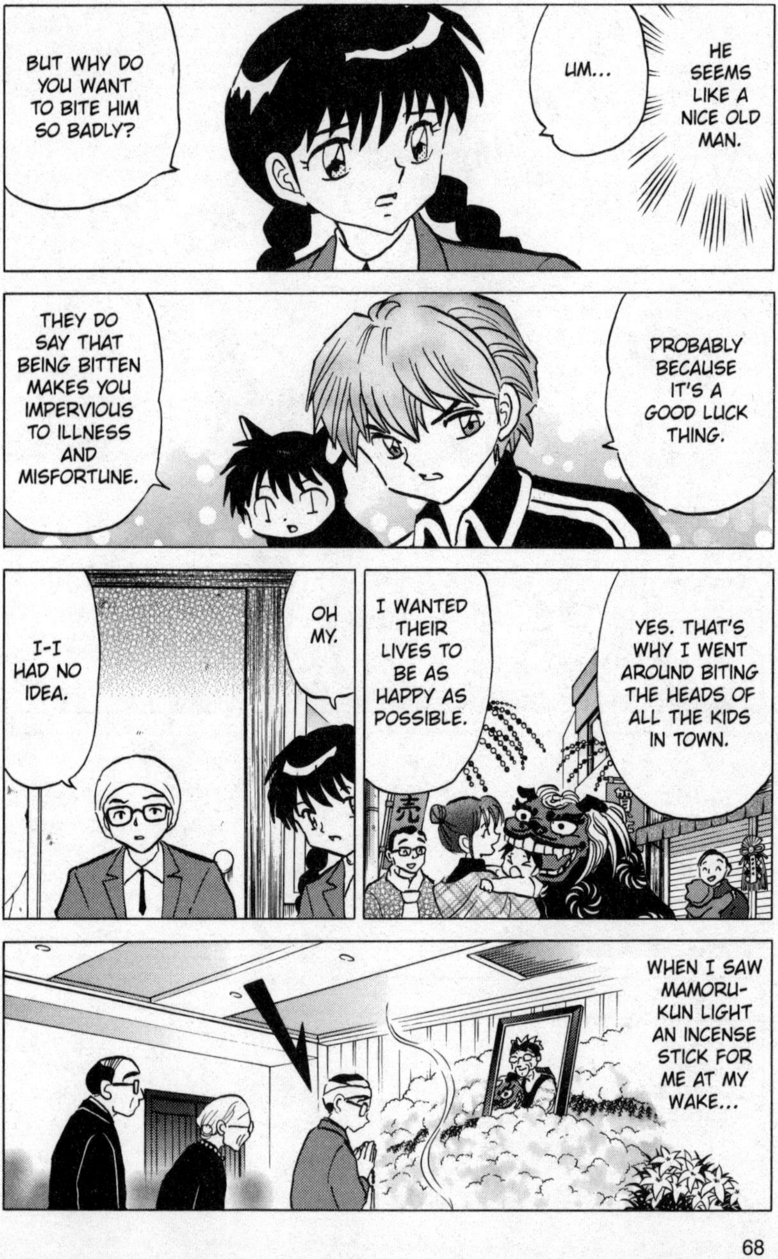
HE SEEMS LIKE A NICE OLD MAN.
UM...
BUT WHY DO YOU WANT TO BITE HIM SO BADLY?
PROBABLY BECAUSE IT'S A GOOD LUCK THING.
THEY DO SAY THAT BEING BITTEN MAKES YOU IMPERVIOUS TO ILLNESS AND MISFORTUNE.
YES. THAT'S WHY I WENT AROUND BITING THE HEADS OF ALL THE KIDS IN TOWN.
I WANTED THEIR LIVES TO BE AS HAPPY AS POSSIBLE.
売
OH MY.
I-I HAD NO IDEA.
WHEN I SAW MAMORU-KUN LIGHT AN INCENSE STICK FOR ME AT MY WAKE...

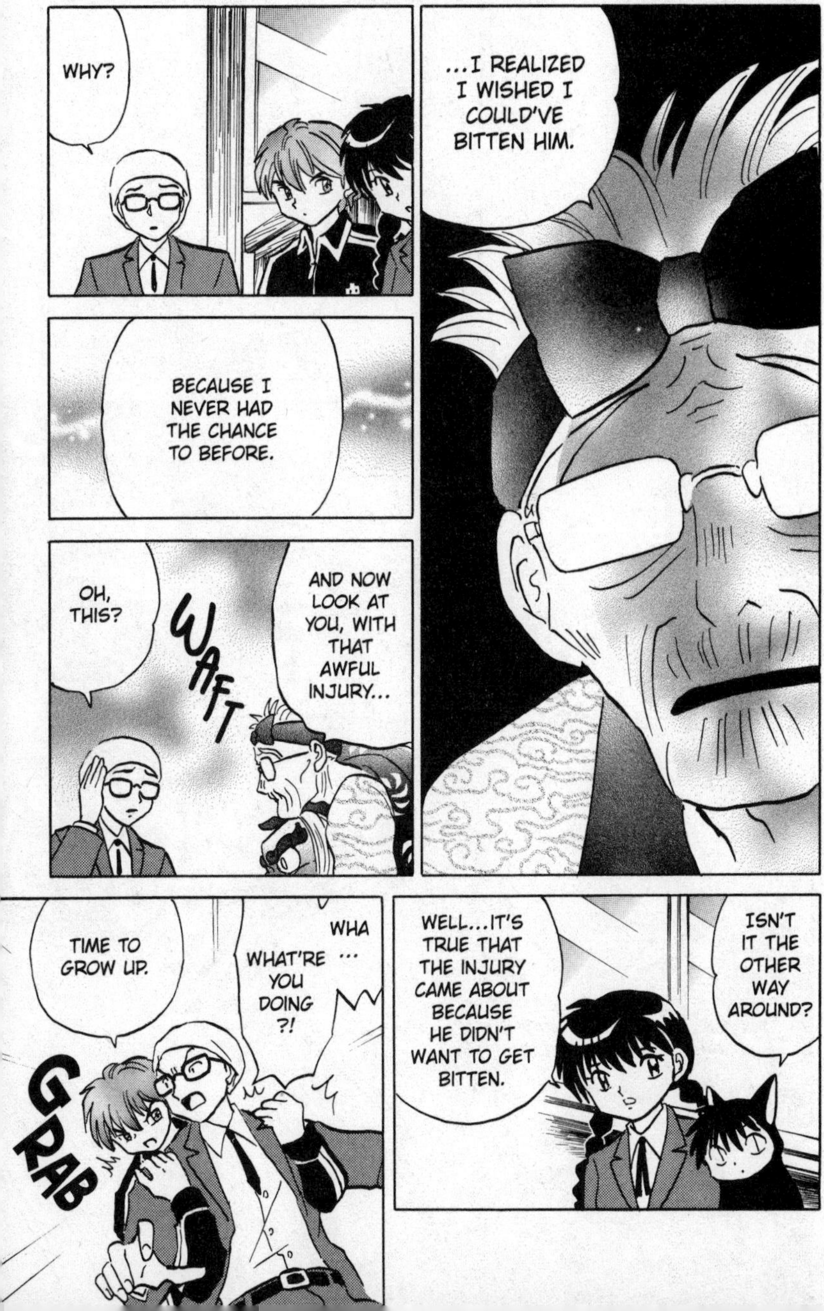
...I REALIZED I WISHED I COULD'VE BITTEN HIM.
WHY?
BECAUSE I NEVER HAD THE CHANCE TO BEFORE.
AND NOW LOOK AT YOU, WITH THAT AWFUL INJURY...
WAFT
OH, THIS?
ISN'T IT THE OTHER WAY AROUND?
WELL...IT'S TRUE THAT THE INJURY CAME ABOUT BECAUSE HE DIDN'T WANT TO GET BITTEN.
WHA...
WHAT'RE YOU DOING ?!
TIME TO GROW UP.
GRAB

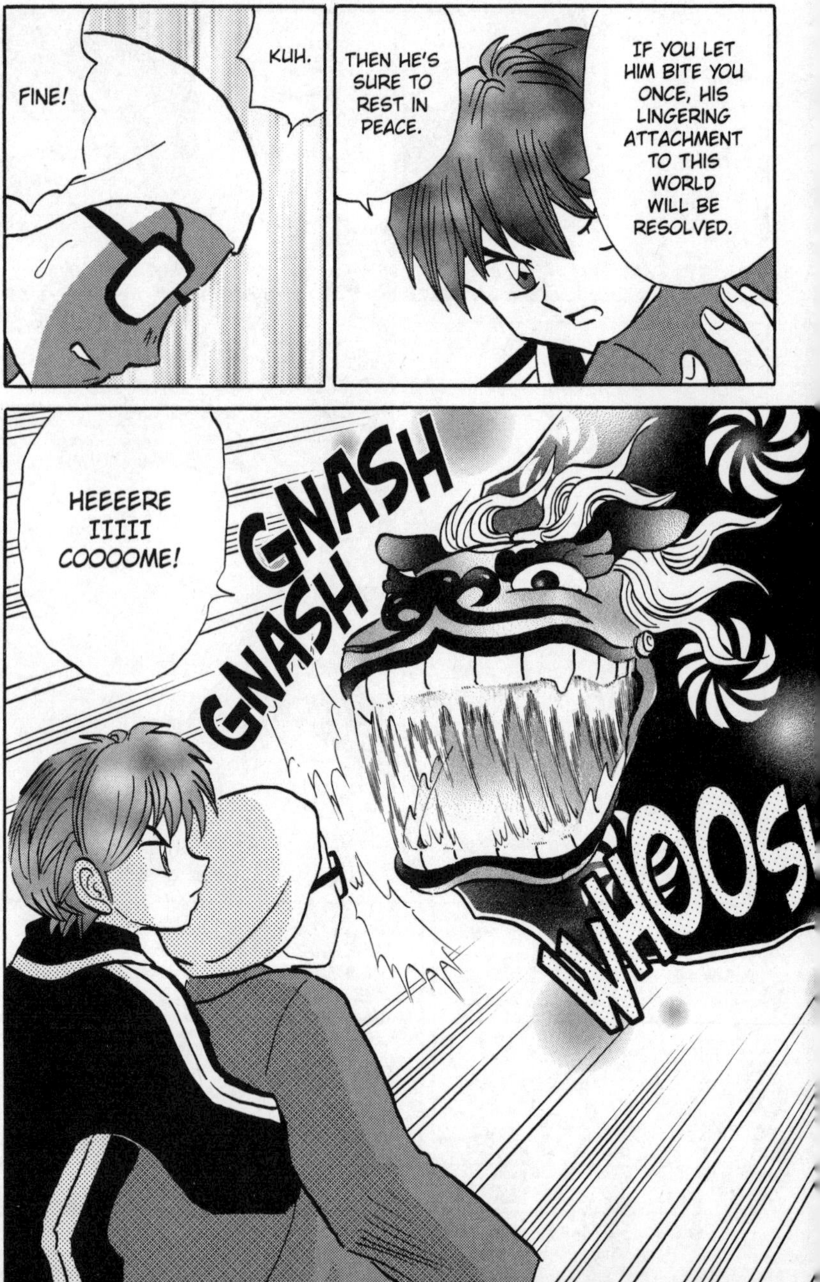
IF YOU LET HIM BITE YOU ONCE, HIS LINGERING ATTACHMENT TO THIS WORLD WILL BE RESOLVED.
THEN HE'S SURE TO REST IN PEACE.
KUH.
FINE!
GNASH
GNASH
HEEEERE IIIII COOOOME!
WHOOS

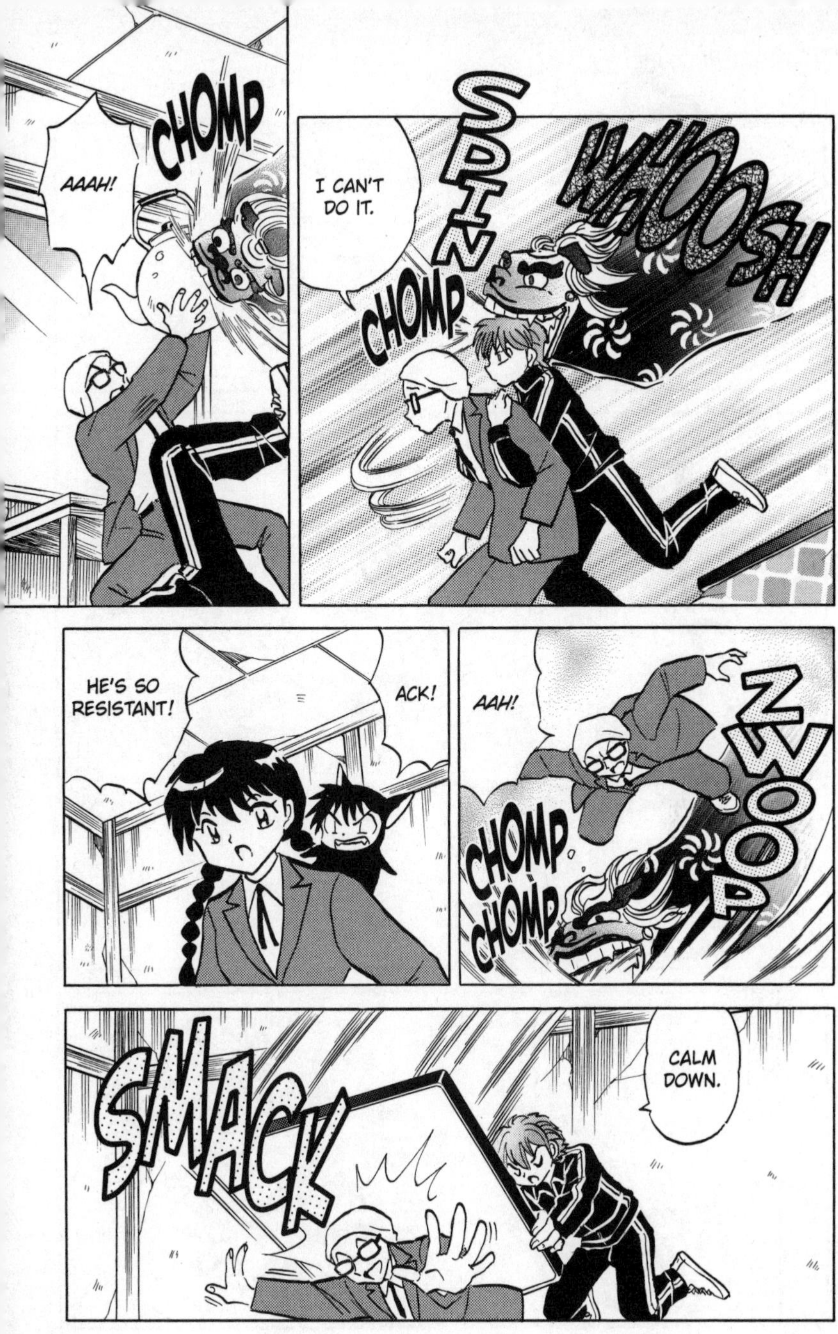
WHOOSH
SPIN
I CAN'T DO IT.
CHOMP
CHOMP
AAAH!
ZWOOP
AAH!
CHOMP CHOMP
ACK!
HE'S SO RESISTANT!
CALM DOWN.
SMACK

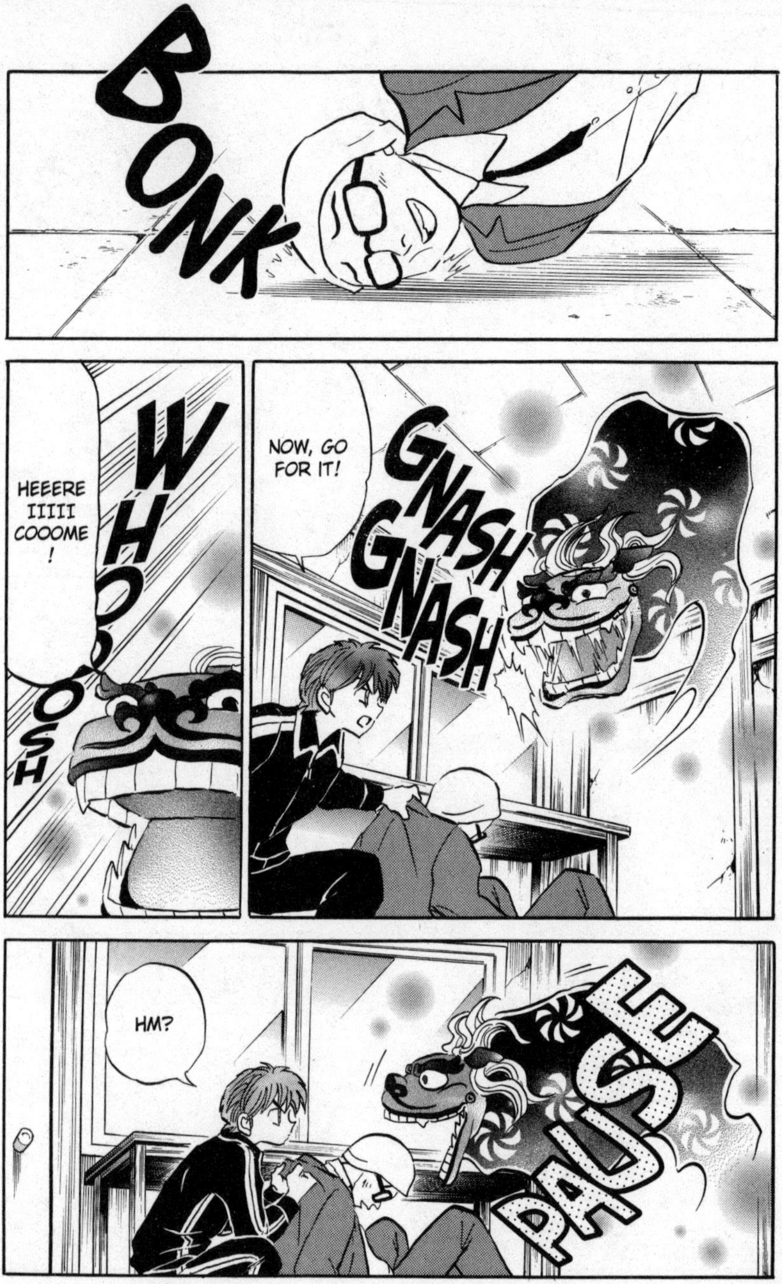
BONK
NOW, GO FOR IT!
GNASH GNASH
HEEERE IIIII COOOME!
WHOOOOOSH
HM?
PAUSE

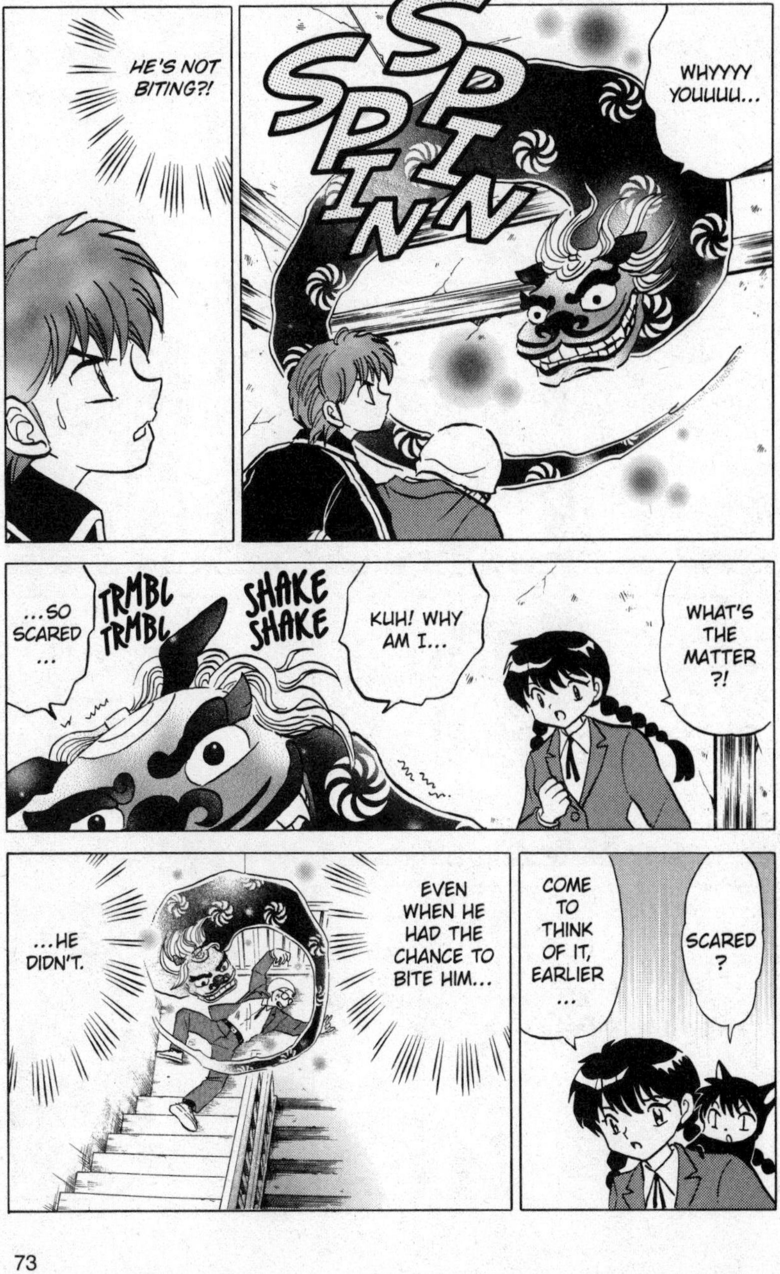
SPIN
SPIN
WHYYYY YOUUUU...
HE'S NOT BITING?!
WHAT'S THE MATTER ?!
KUH! WHY AM I...
SHAKE SHAKE
TRMBL TRMBL
...SO SCARED ...
SCARED ?
COME TO THINK OF IT, EARLIER ...
EVEN WHEN HE HAD THE CHANCE TO BITE HIM...
...HE DIDN'T.

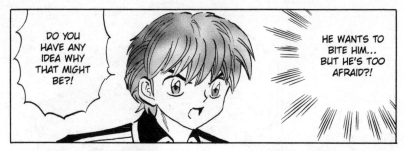

HE WANTS TO BITE HIM... BUT HE'S TOO AFRAID?!
DO YOU HAVE ANY IDEA WHY THAT MIGHT BE?!
I-I DON'T KNOW...
TRMBL TRMBL TRMBL
THINK!
WELL, THE MORNING OF NEW YEAR'S DAY....
OKAY! I'M GOING TO BITE ALL THE LITTLE HEADS I CAN!
AND THEN THE LAST THING I REMEMBER IS TAKING A BIG MOUTHFUL OF OZONI...
OZONI.
IN OTHER WORDS ...
...YOU GOT SOME MOCHI STUCK IN YOUR THROAT AND DIED?
IS THAT WHAT HAPPENED ?
RISE
ACTUALLY, I REMEMBER HEARING THAT AT THE WAKE.

Ozoni is a Japanese New Year's soup with sticky rice cakes (mochi).

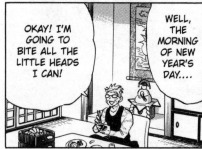

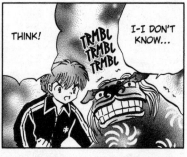

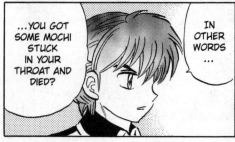

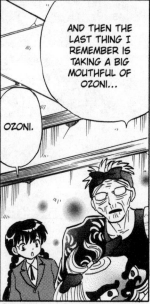

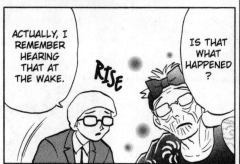

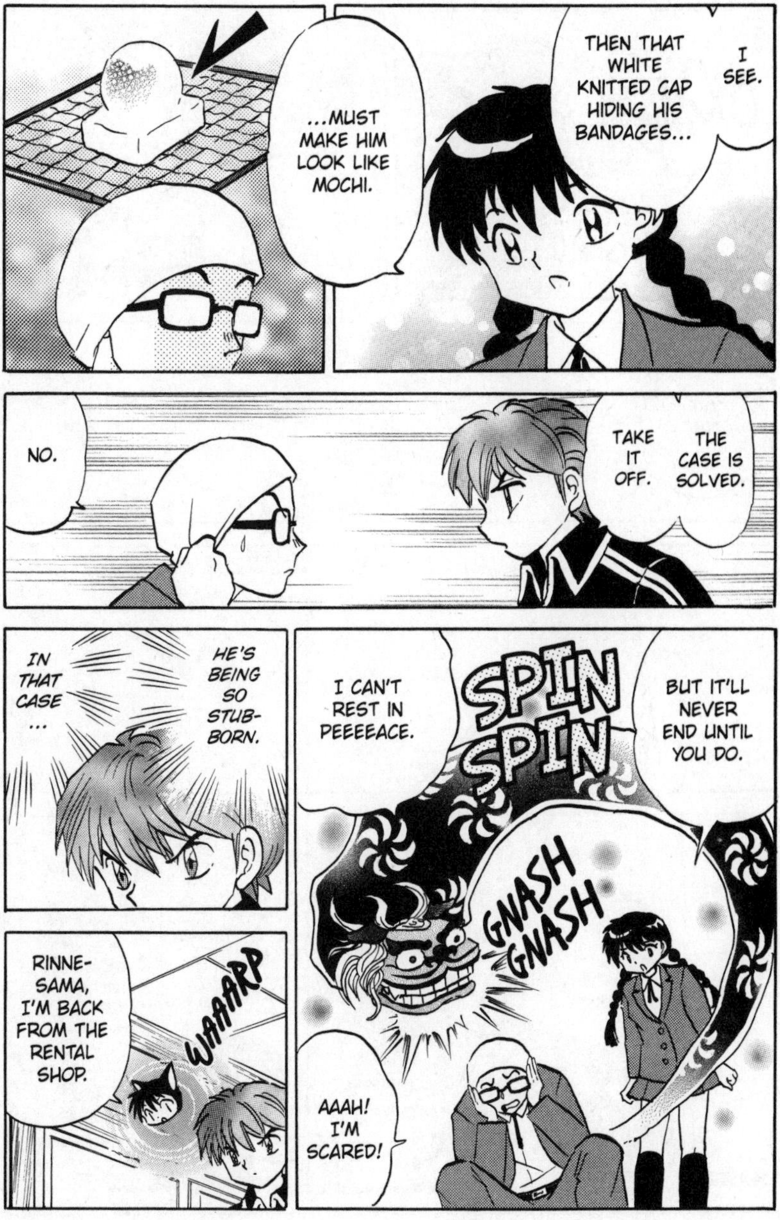
I SEE.
THEN THAT WHITE KNITTED CAP HIDING HIS BANDAGES...
...MUST MAKE HIM LOOK LIKE MOCHI.
THE CASE IS SOLVED.
TAKE IT OFF.
NO.
BUT IT'LL NEVER END UNTIL YOU DO.
SPIN SPIN
I CAN'T REST IN PEEEEACE.
GNASH GNASH
AAAH! I'M SCARED!
HE'S BEING SO STUB-BORN.
IN THAT CASE...
WAAARP
RINNE-SAMA, I'M BACK FROM THE RENTAL SHOP.

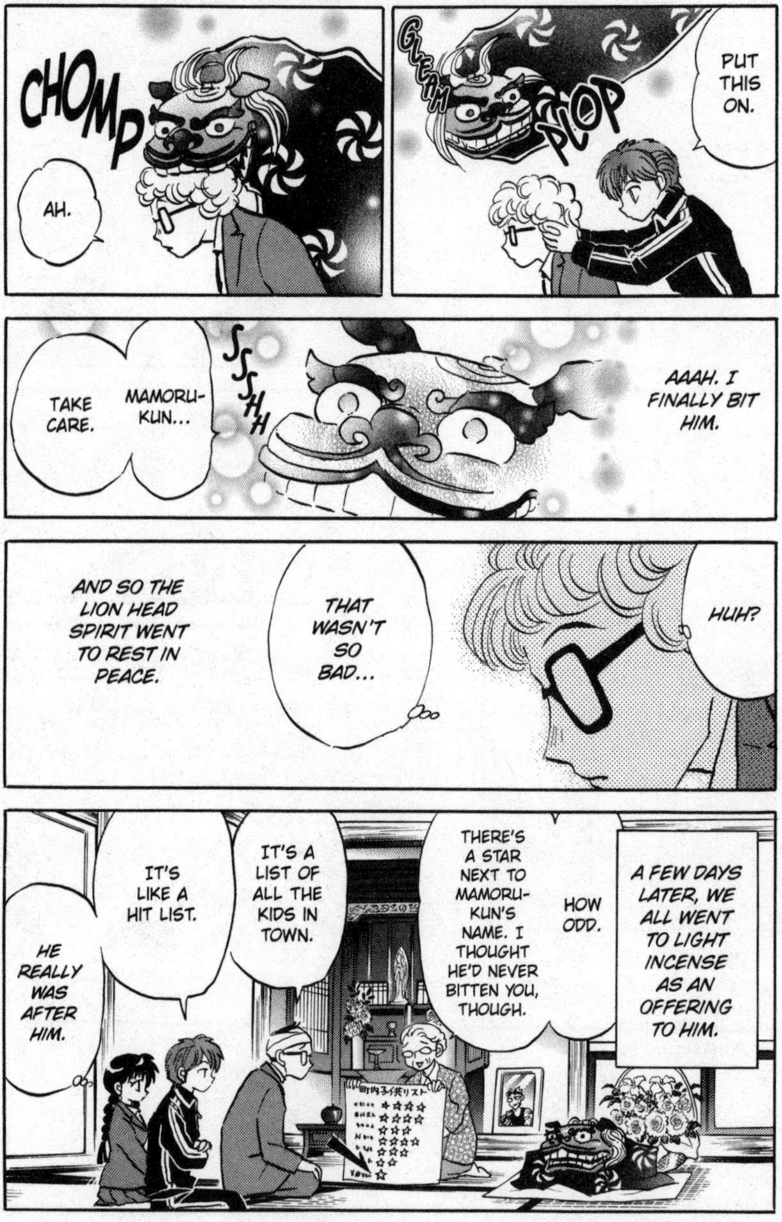
GLEAM
PLOP
PUT THIS ON.
CHOMP
AH.
AAAH. I FINALLY BIT HIM.
SSSHH
MAMORU-KUN...
TAKE CARE.
HUH?
THAT WASN'T SO BAD...
AND SO THE LION HEAD SPIRIT WENT TO REST IN PEACE.
A FEW DAYS LATER, WE ALL WENT TO LIGHT INCENSE AS AN OFFERING TO HIM.
HOW ODD.
THERE'S A STAR NEXT TO MAMORU-KUN'S NAME. I THOUGHT HE'D NEVER BITTEN YOU, THOUGH.
IT'S A LIST OF ALL THE KIDS IN TOWN.
IT'S LIKE A HIT LIST.
HE REALLY WAS AFTER HIM.

CHAPTER 313: OTOME'S SCYTHE

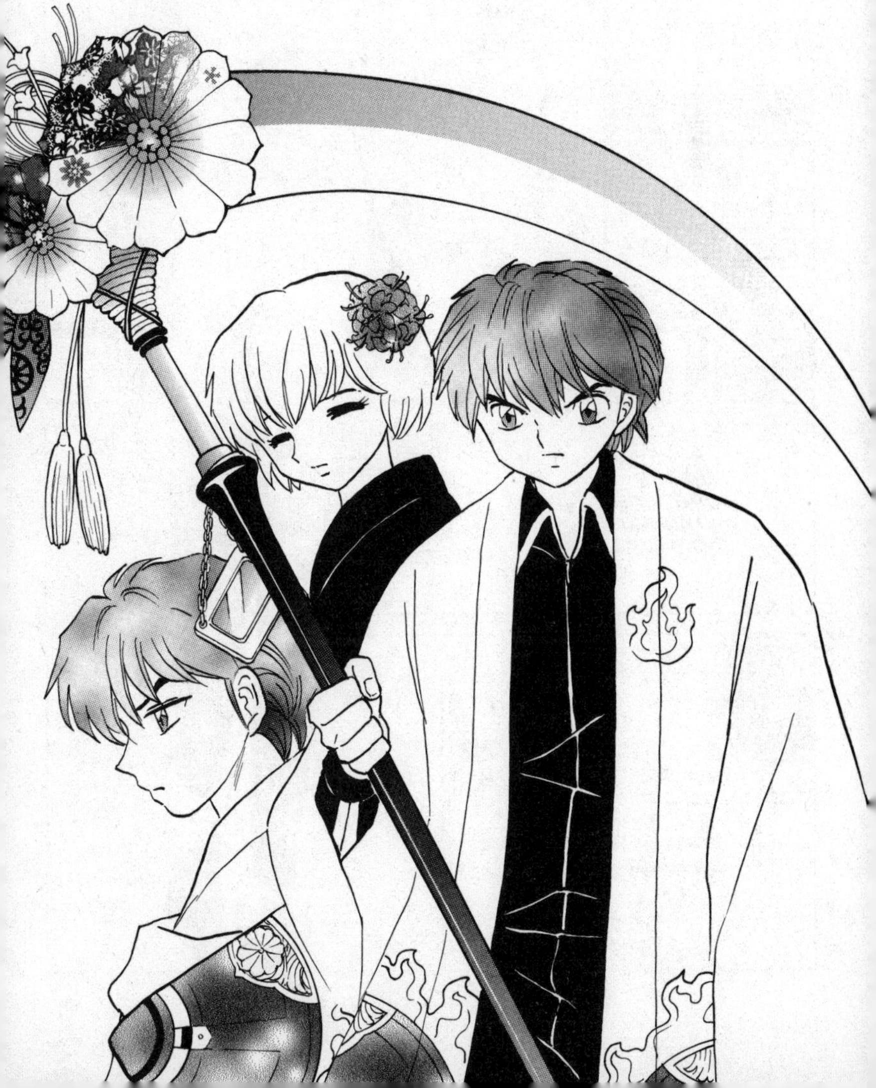

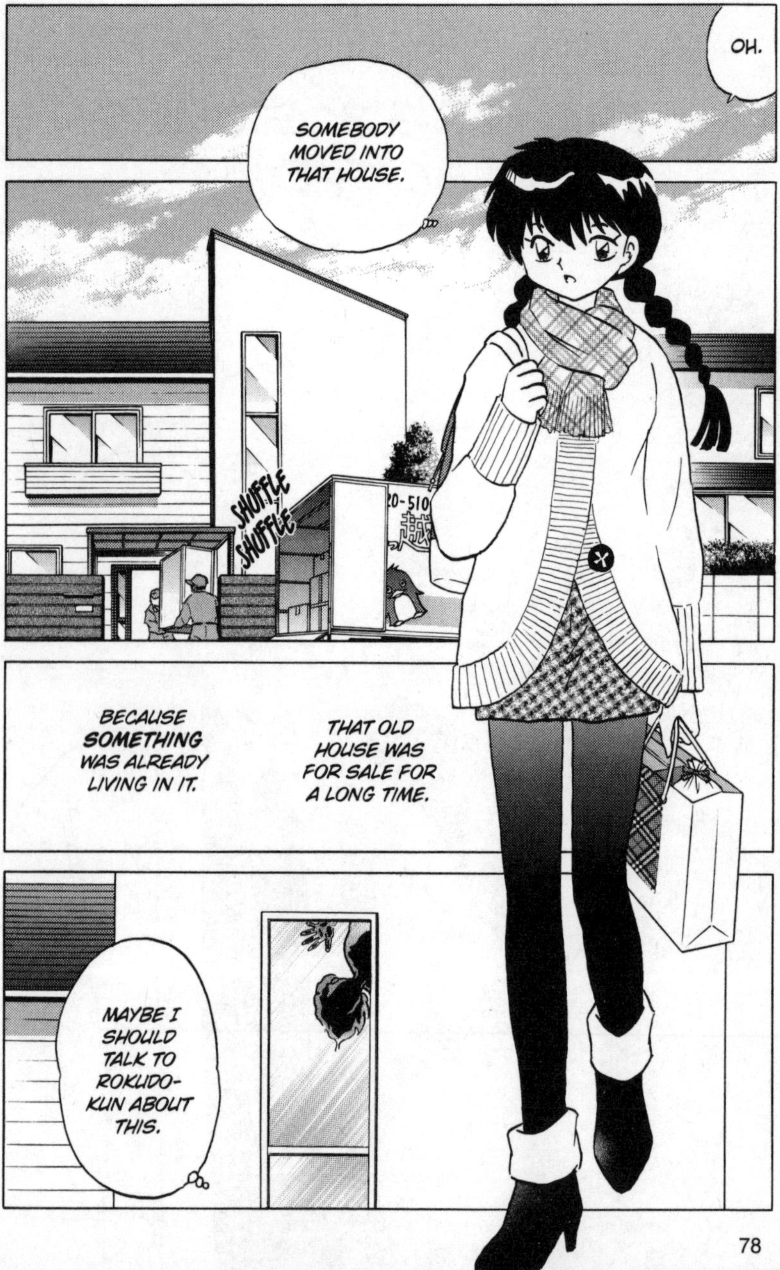
OH.
SOMEBODY MOVED INTO THAT HOUSE.
SHUFFLE SHUFFLE
THAT OLD HOUSE WAS FOR SALE FOR A LONG TIME.
BECAUSE **SOMETHING** WAS ALREADY LIVING IN IT.
MAYBE I SHOULD TALK TO ROKUDO-KUN ABOUT THIS.

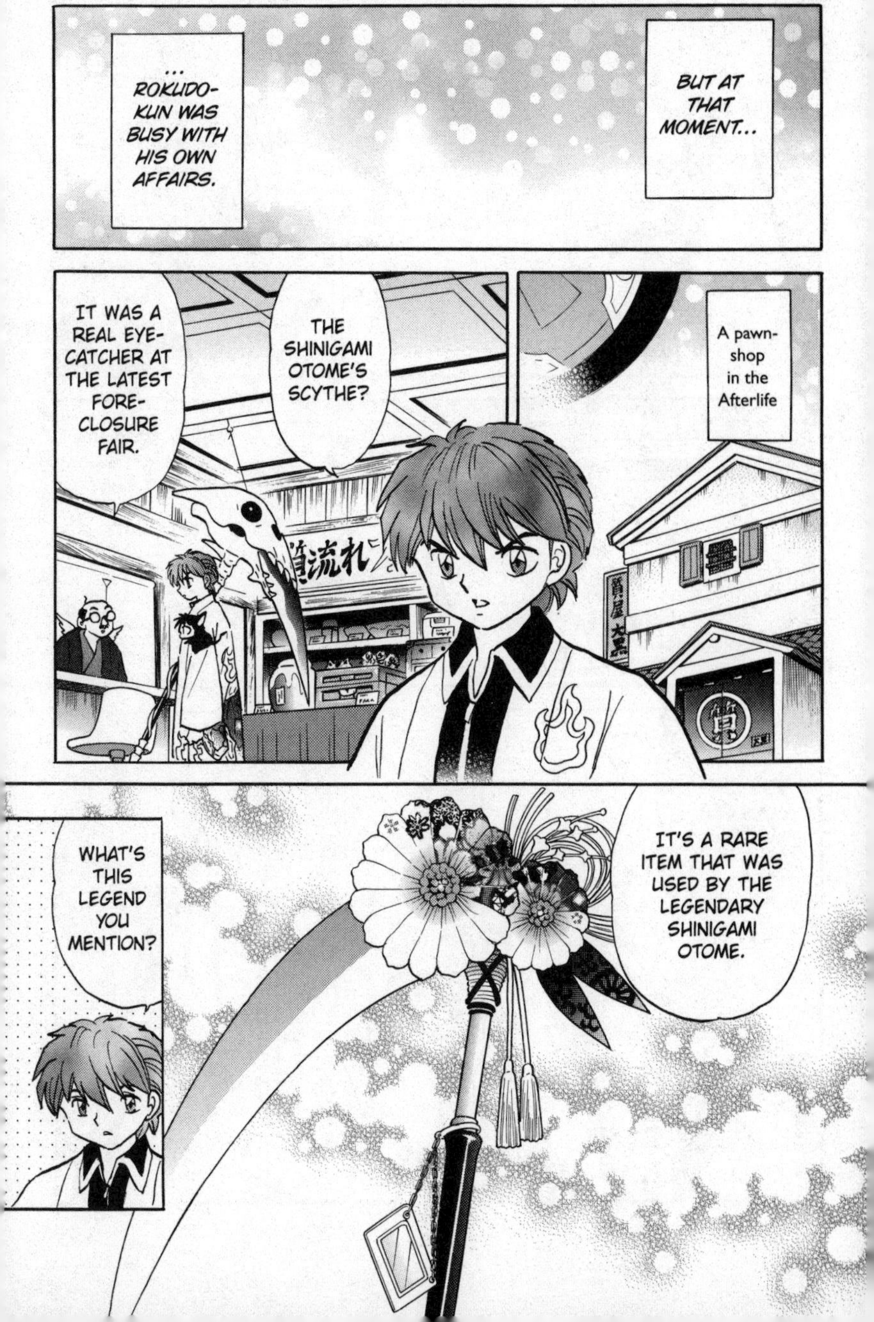
BUT AT THAT MOMENT...
...ROKUDO-KUN WAS BUSY WITH HIS OWN AFFAIRS.
A pawn-shop in the Afterlife
THE SHINIGAMI OTOME'S SCYTHE?
IT WAS A REAL EYE-CATCHER AT THE LATEST FORE-CLOSURE FAIR.
IT'S A RARE ITEM THAT WAS USED BY THE LEGENDARY SHINIGAMI OTOME.
WHAT'S THIS LEGEND YOU MENTION?

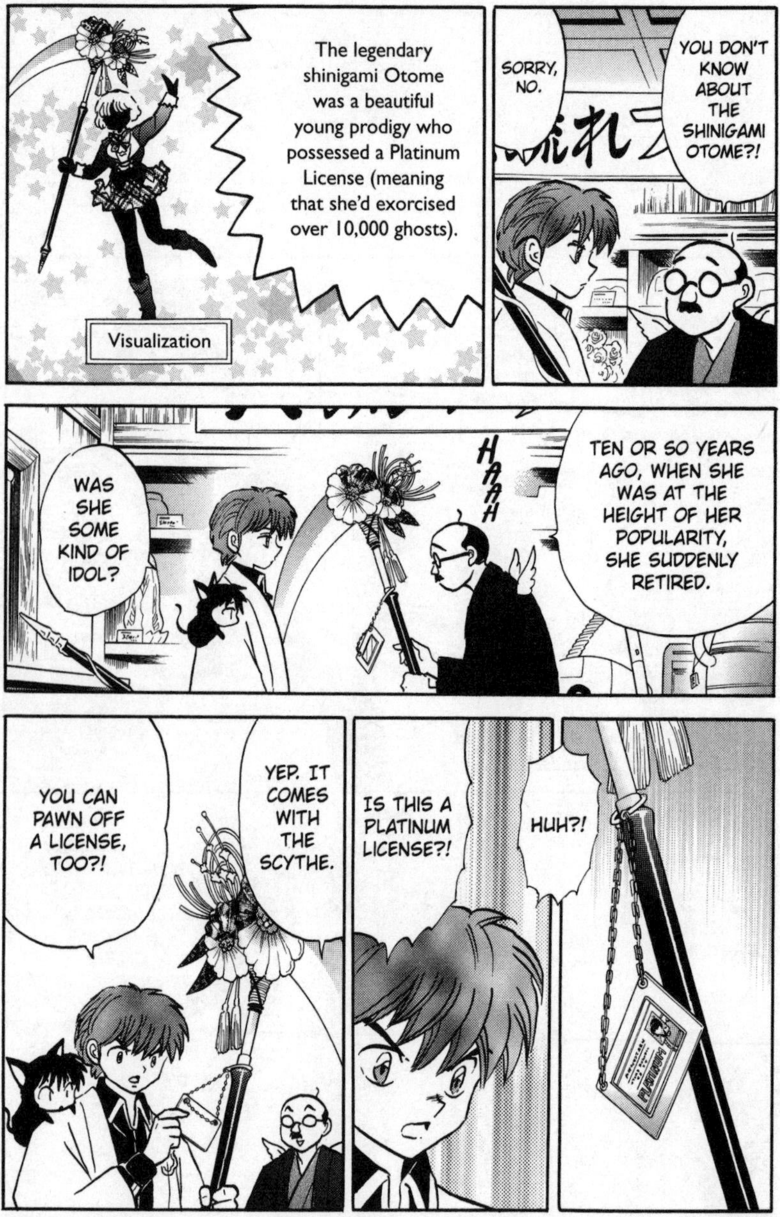
YOU DON'T KNOW ABOUT THE SHINIGAMI OTOME?!
SORRY, NO.
The legendary shinigami Otome was a beautiful young prodigy who possessed a Platinum License (meaning that she'd exorcised over 10,000 ghosts).
Visualization
TEN OR SO YEARS AGO, WHEN SHE WAS AT THE HEIGHT OF HER POPULARITY, SHE SUDDENLY RETIRED.
HAAAH
WAS SHE SOME KIND OF IDOL?
HUH?!
IS THIS A PLATINUM LICENSE?!
YEP. IT COMES WITH THE SCYTHE.
YOU CAN PAWN OFF A LICENSE, TOO?!

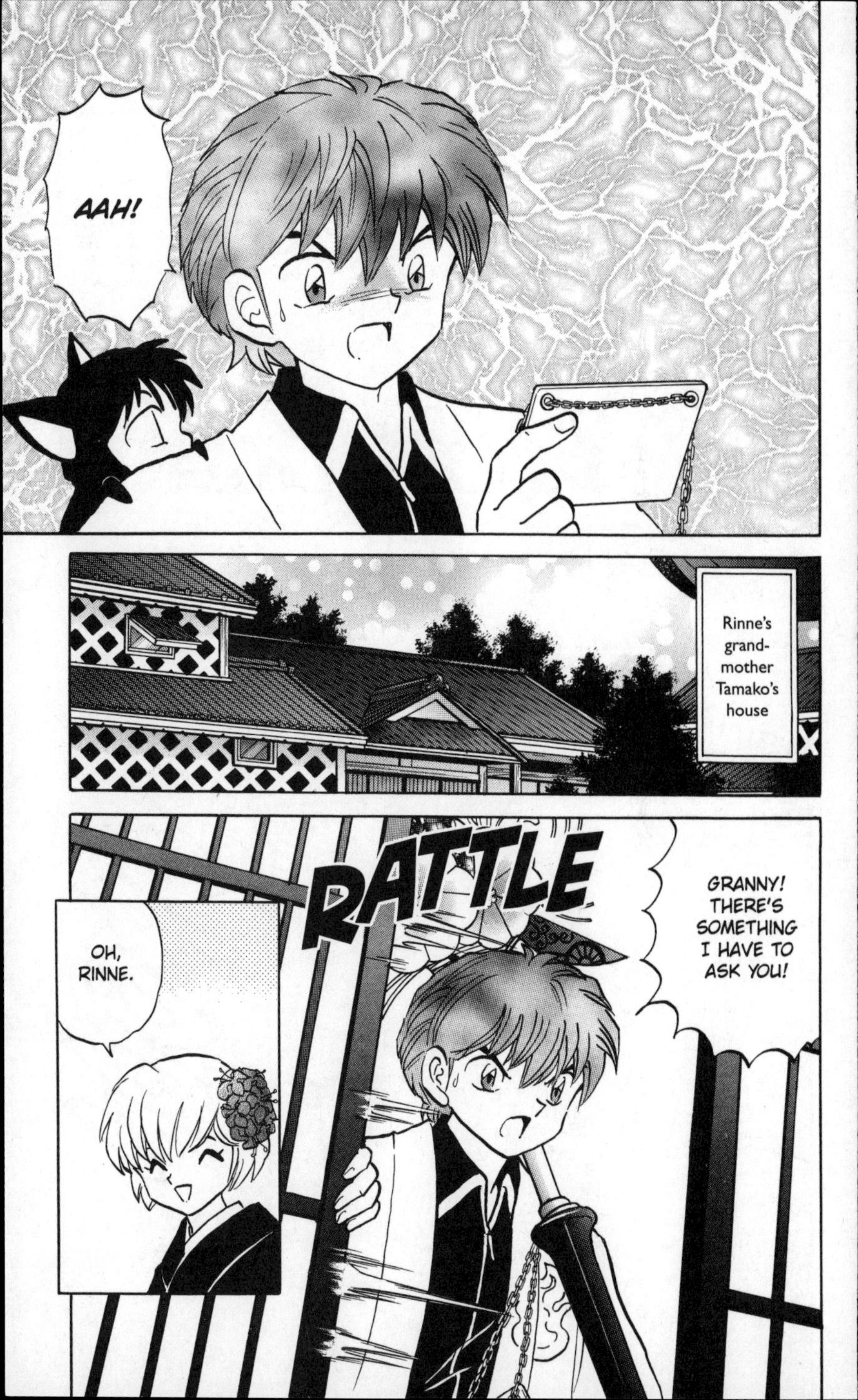
AAH!
Rinne's grand-mother Tamako's house
RATTLE
GRANNY! THERE'S SOMETHING I HAVE TO ASK YOU!
OH, RINNE.

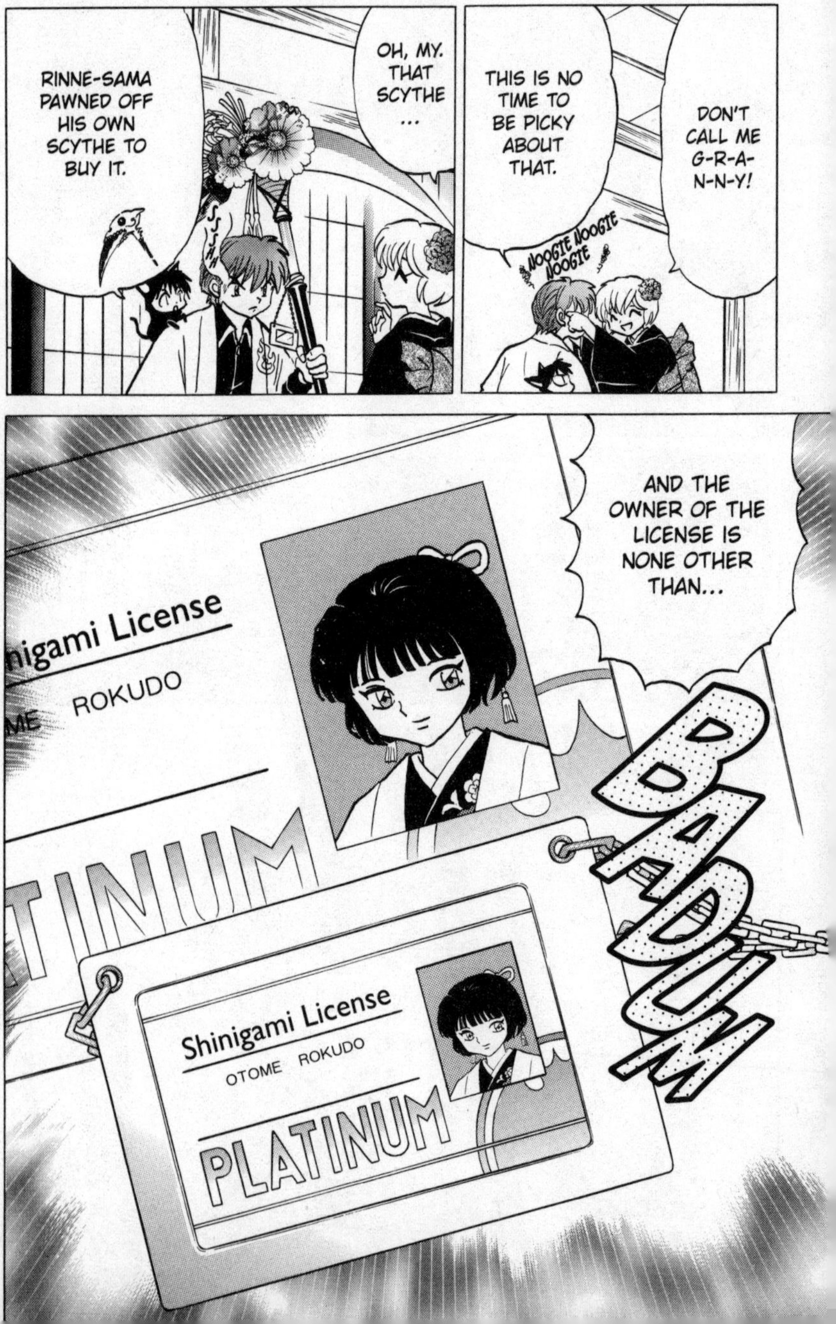
DON'T CALL ME G-R-A-N-N-Y!
THIS IS NO TIME TO BE PICKY ABOUT THAT.
NOOGIE NOOGIE NOOGIE
OH, MY. THAT SCYTHE ...
RINNE-SAMA PAWNED OFF HIS OWN SCYTHE TO BUY IT.
SSSHH
AND THE OWNER OF THE LICENSE IS NONE OTHER THAN...
BADUM
Shinigami License
OTOME ROKUDO
PLATINUM

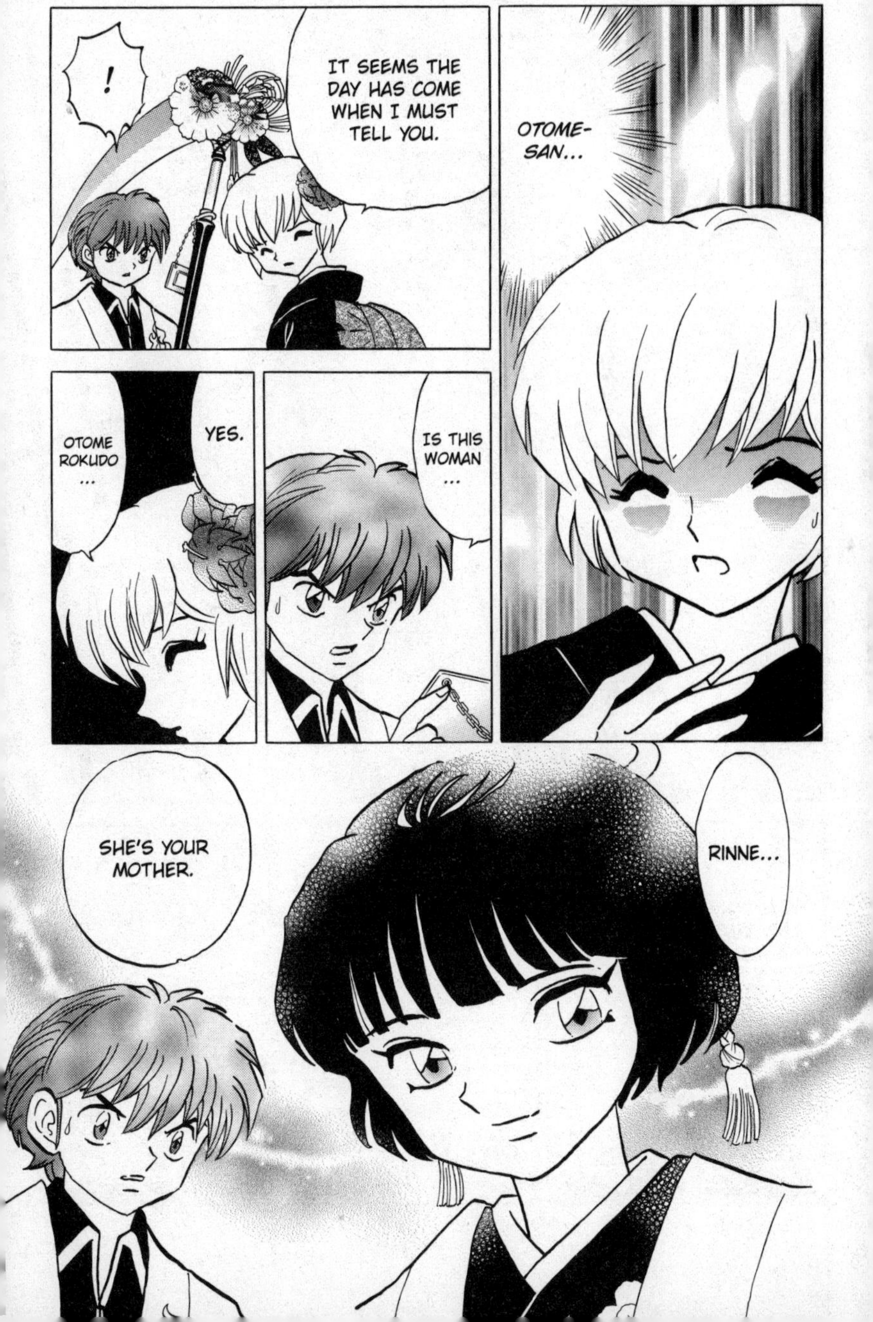
OTOME-SAN...
IT SEEMS THE DAY HAS COME WHEN I MUST TELL YOU.
!
IS THIS WOMAN ...
YES.
OTOME ROKUDO ...
RINNE...
SHE'S YOUR MOTHER.

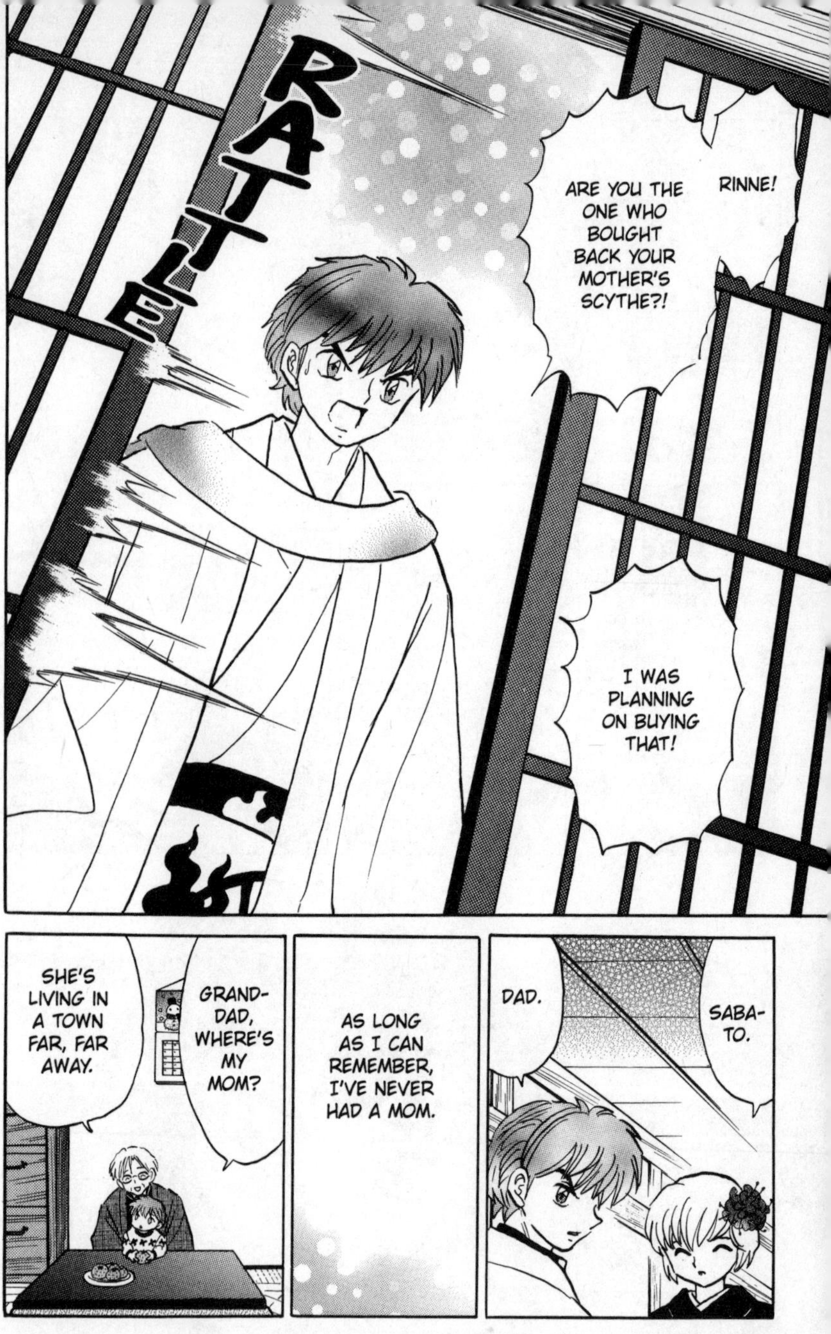
RINNE!
ARE YOU THE ONE WHO BOUGHT BACK YOUR MOTHER'S SCYTHE?!
RATTLE
I WAS PLANNING ON BUYING THAT!
SABA-TO.
DAD.
AS LONG AS I CAN REMEMBER, I'VE NEVER HAD A MOM.
GRAND-DAD, WHERE'S MY MOM?
SHE'S LIVING IN A TOWN FAR, FAR AWAY.

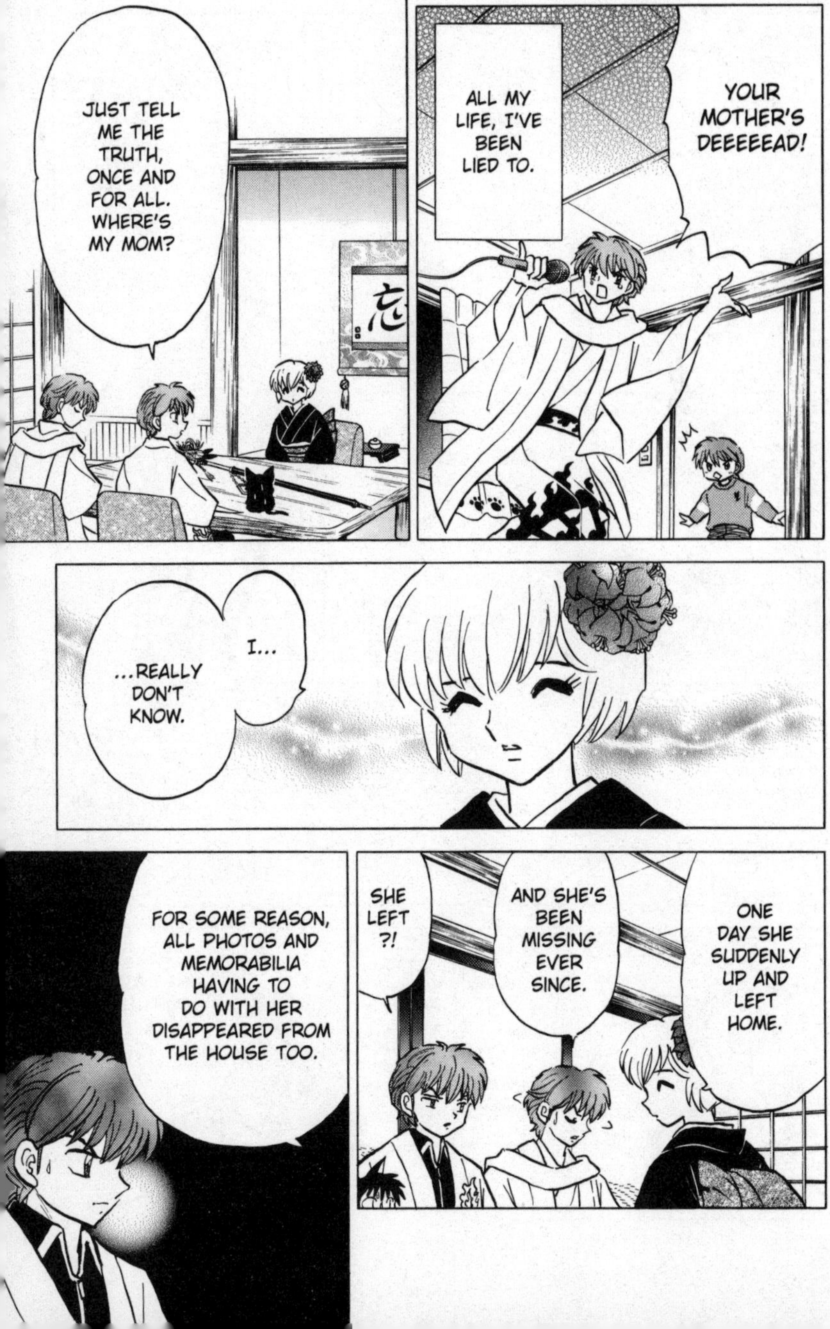
YOUR MOTHER'S DEEEEEAD!
ALL MY LIFE, I'VE BEEN LIED TO.
JUST TELL ME THE TRUTH, ONCE AND FOR ALL. WHERE'S MY MOM?
忘
I...
...REALLY DON'T KNOW.
ONE DAY SHE SUDDENLY UP AND LEFT HOME.
AND SHE'S BEEN MISSING EVER SINCE.
SHE LEFT?!
FOR SOME REASON, ALL PHOTOS AND MEMORABILIA HAVING TO DO WITH HER DISAPPEARED FROM THE HOUSE TOO.

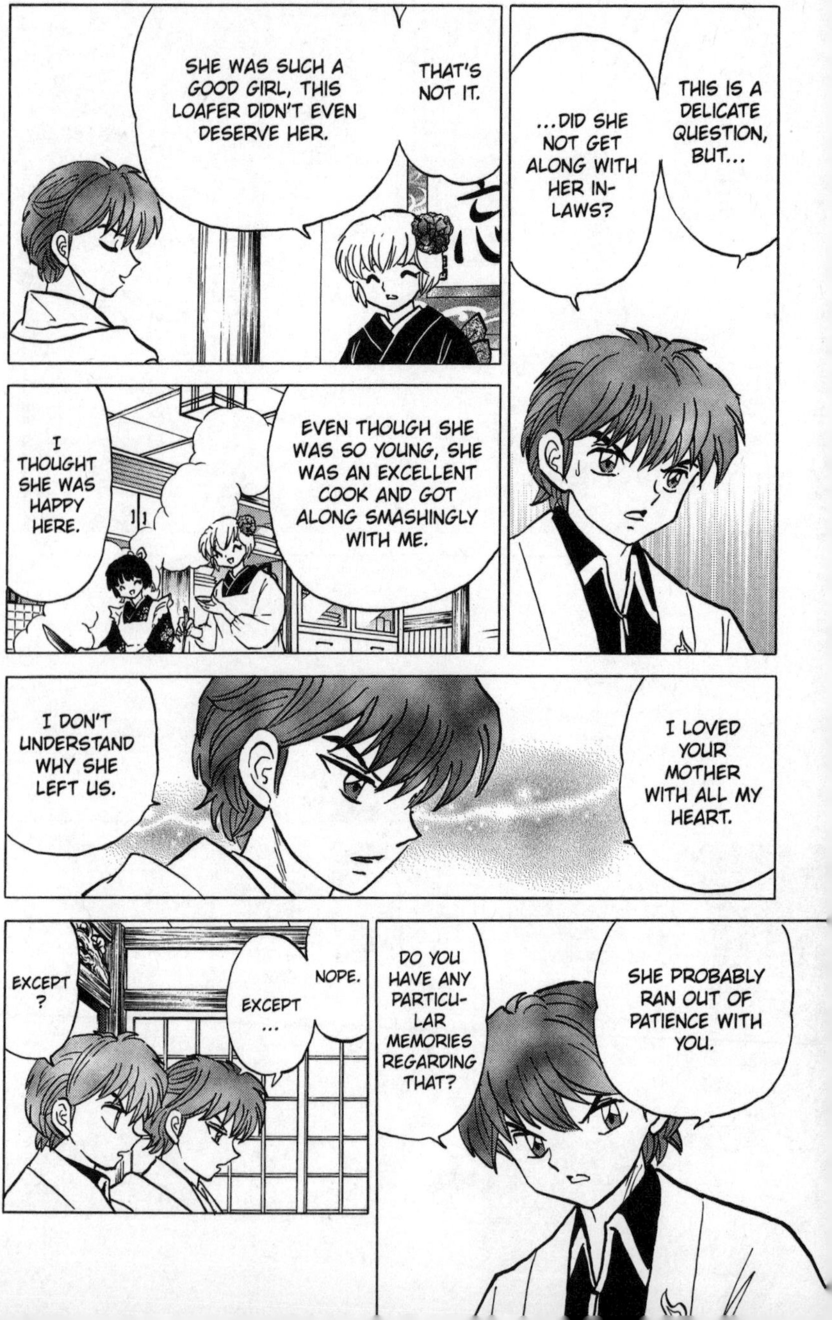
THIS IS A DELICATE QUESTION, BUT...
...DID SHE NOT GET ALONG WITH HER IN-LAWS?
THAT'S NOT IT.
SHE WAS SUCH A GOOD GIRL, THIS LOAFER DIDN'T EVEN DESERVE HER.
EVEN THOUGH SHE WAS SO YOUNG, SHE WAS AN EXCELLENT COOK AND GOT ALONG SMASHINGLY WITH ME.
I THOUGHT SHE WAS HAPPY HERE.
I LOVED YOUR MOTHER WITH ALL MY HEART.
I DON'T UNDERSTAND WHY SHE LEFT US.
SHE PROBABLY RAN OUT OF PATIENCE WITH YOU.
DO YOU HAVE ANY PARTICULAR MEMORIES REGARDING THAT?
NOPE.
EXCEPT ...
EXCEPT ?

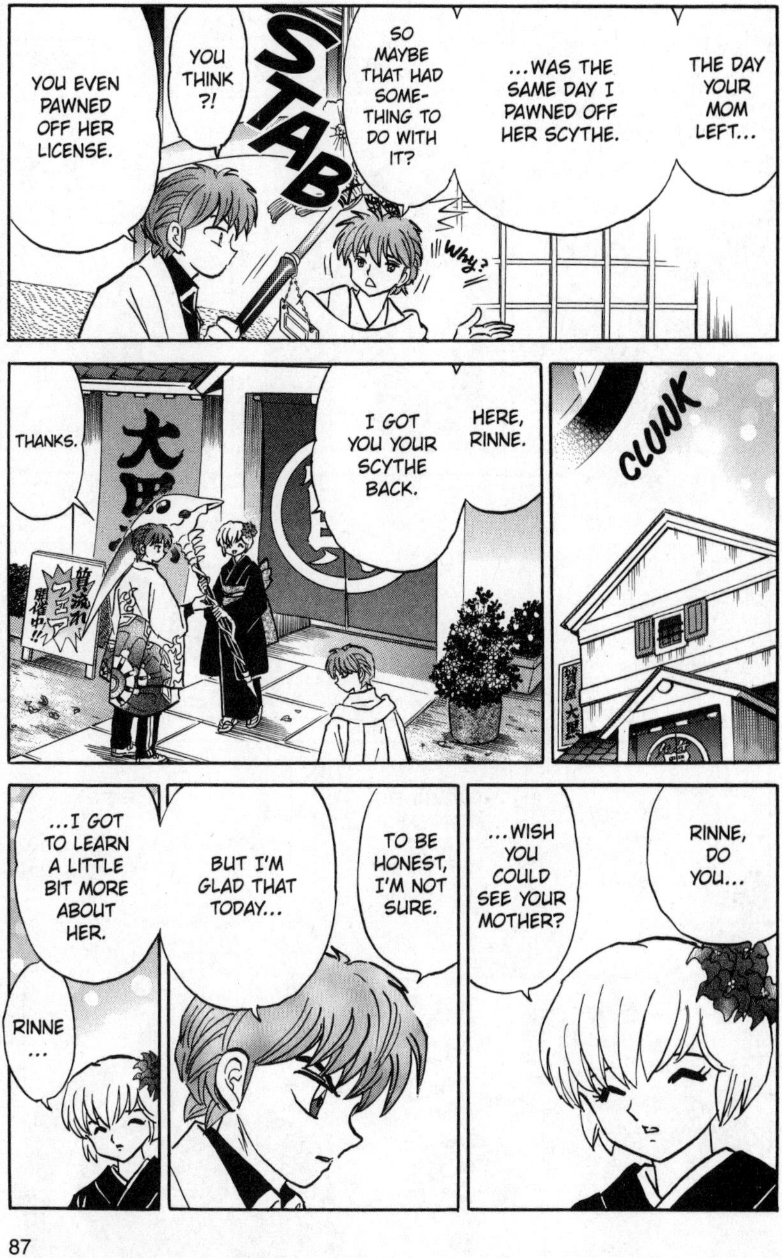
THE DAY YOUR MOM LEFT…
…WAS THE SAME DAY I PAWNED OFF HER SCYTHE.
SO MAYBE THAT HAD SOME-THING TO DO WITH IT?
why?
STAB
YOU THINK?!
YOU EVEN PAWNED OFF HER LICENSE.
CLUNK
HERE, RINNE.
I GOT YOU YOUR SCYTHE BACK.
質流れフェア開催中!!
THANKS.
RINNE, DO YOU…
…WISH YOU COULD SEE YOUR MOTHER?
TO BE HONEST, I'M NOT SURE.
BUT I'M GLAD THAT TODAY…
…I GOT TO LEARN A LITTLE BIT MORE ABOUT HER.
RINNE…

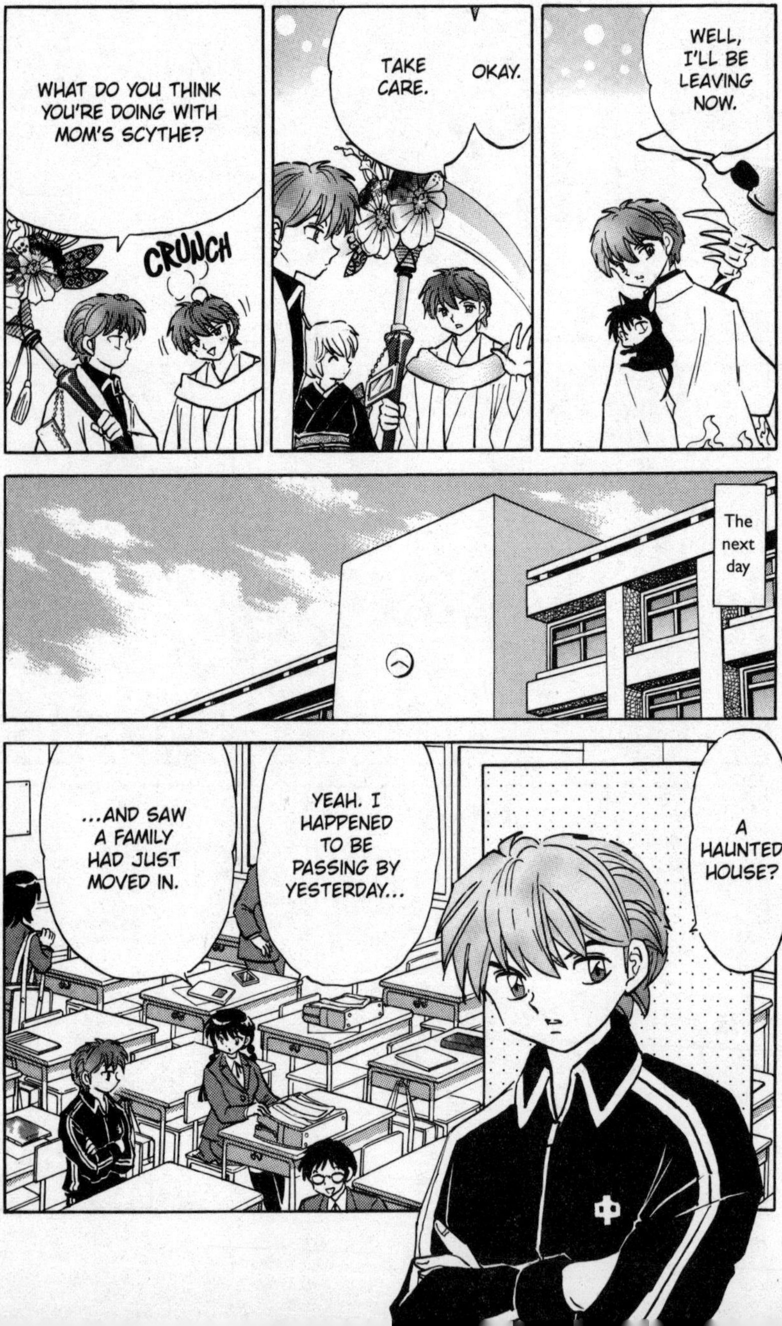
WELL, I'LL BE LEAVING NOW.
OKAY.
TAKE CARE.
WHAT DO YOU THINK YOU'RE DOING WITH MOM'S SCYTHE?
CRUNCH
The next day
A HAUNTED HOUSE?
YEAH. I HAPPENED TO BE PASSING BY YESTERDAY...
...AND SAW A FAMILY HAD JUST MOVED IN.

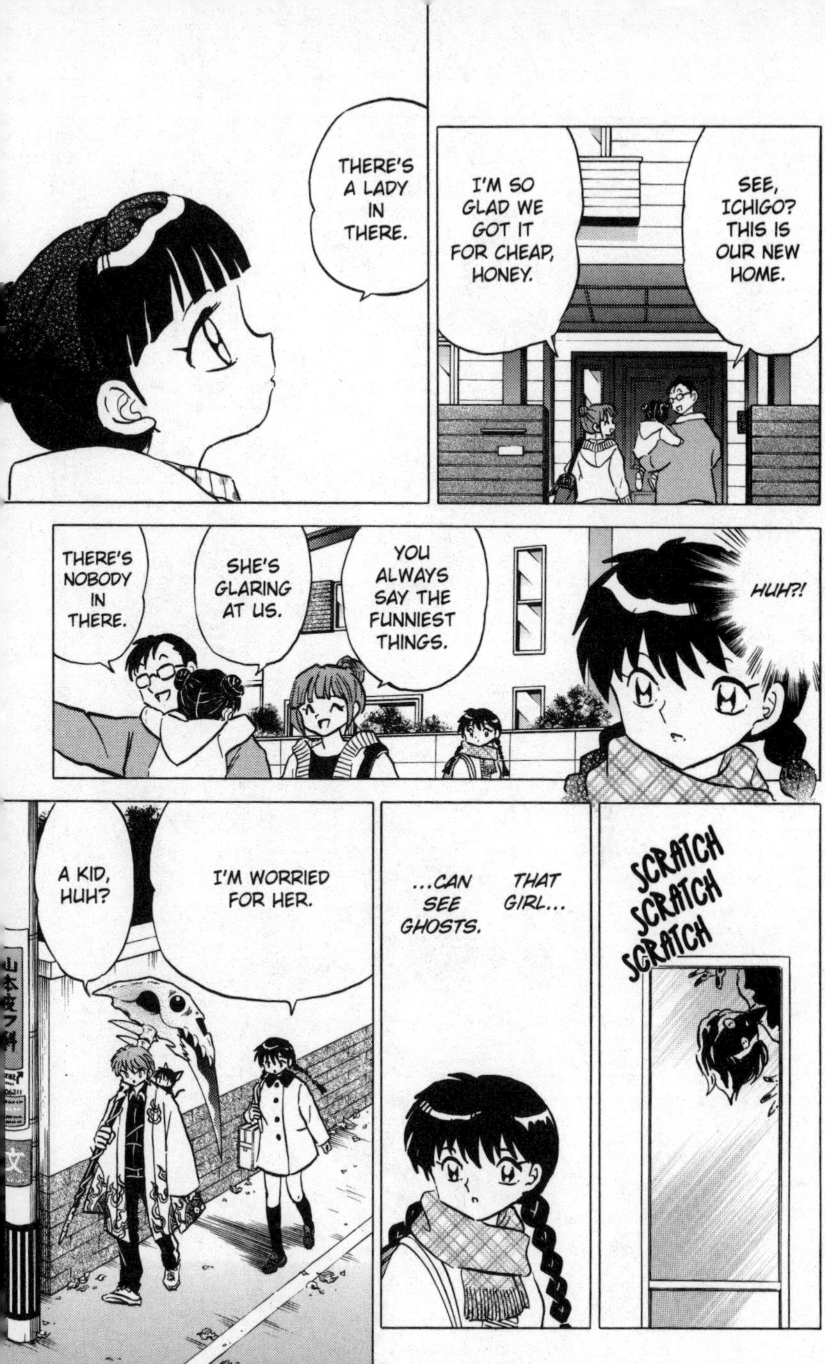
SEE, ICHIGO? THIS IS OUR NEW HOME.
I'M SO GLAD WE GOT IT FOR CHEAP, HONEY.
THERE'S A LADY IN THERE.
HUH?!
YOU ALWAYS SAY THE FUNNIEST THINGS.
SHE'S GLARING AT US.
THERE'S NOBODY IN THERE.
SCRATCH
SCRATCH
SCRATCH
THAT GIRL...
...CAN SEE GHOSTS.
I'M WORRIED FOR HER.
A KID, HUH?

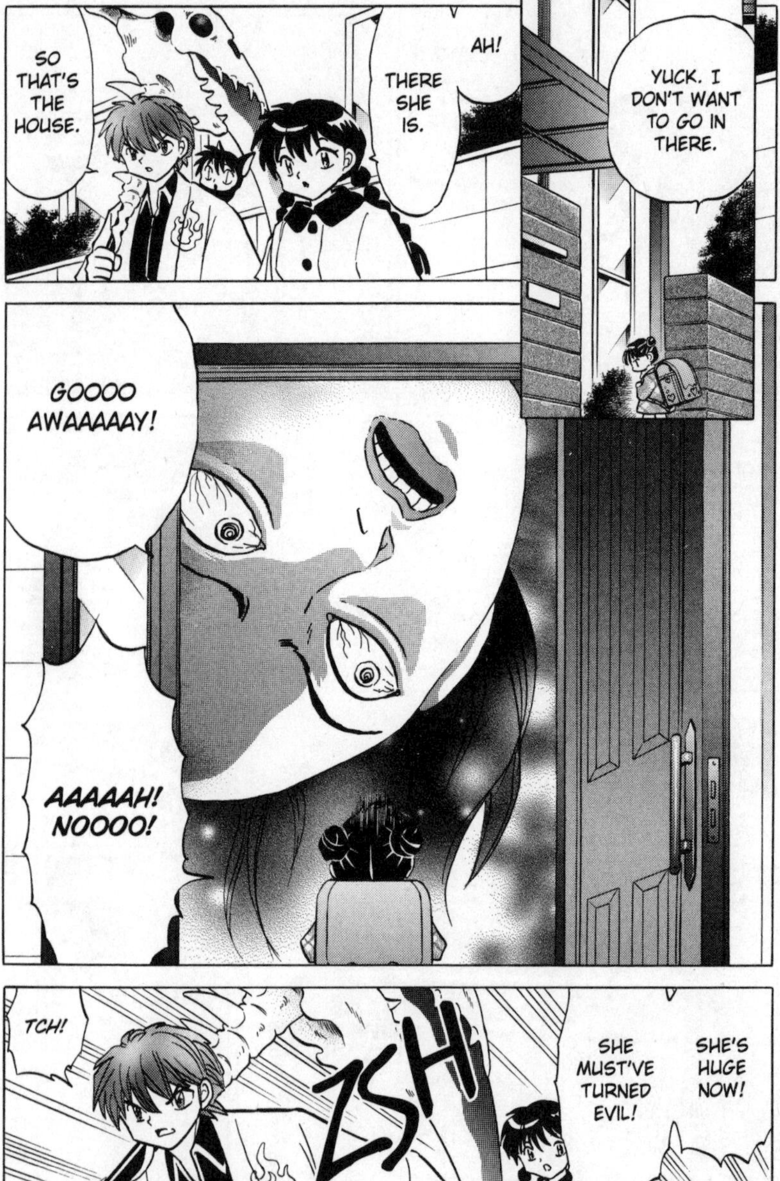
YUCK. I DON'T WANT TO GO IN THERE.
AH!
THERE SHE IS.
SO THAT'S THE HOUSE.
GOOOO AWAAAAAY!
AAAAAH! NOOOO!
SHE'S HUGE NOW!
SHE MUST'VE TURNED EVIL!
ZSH
TCH!

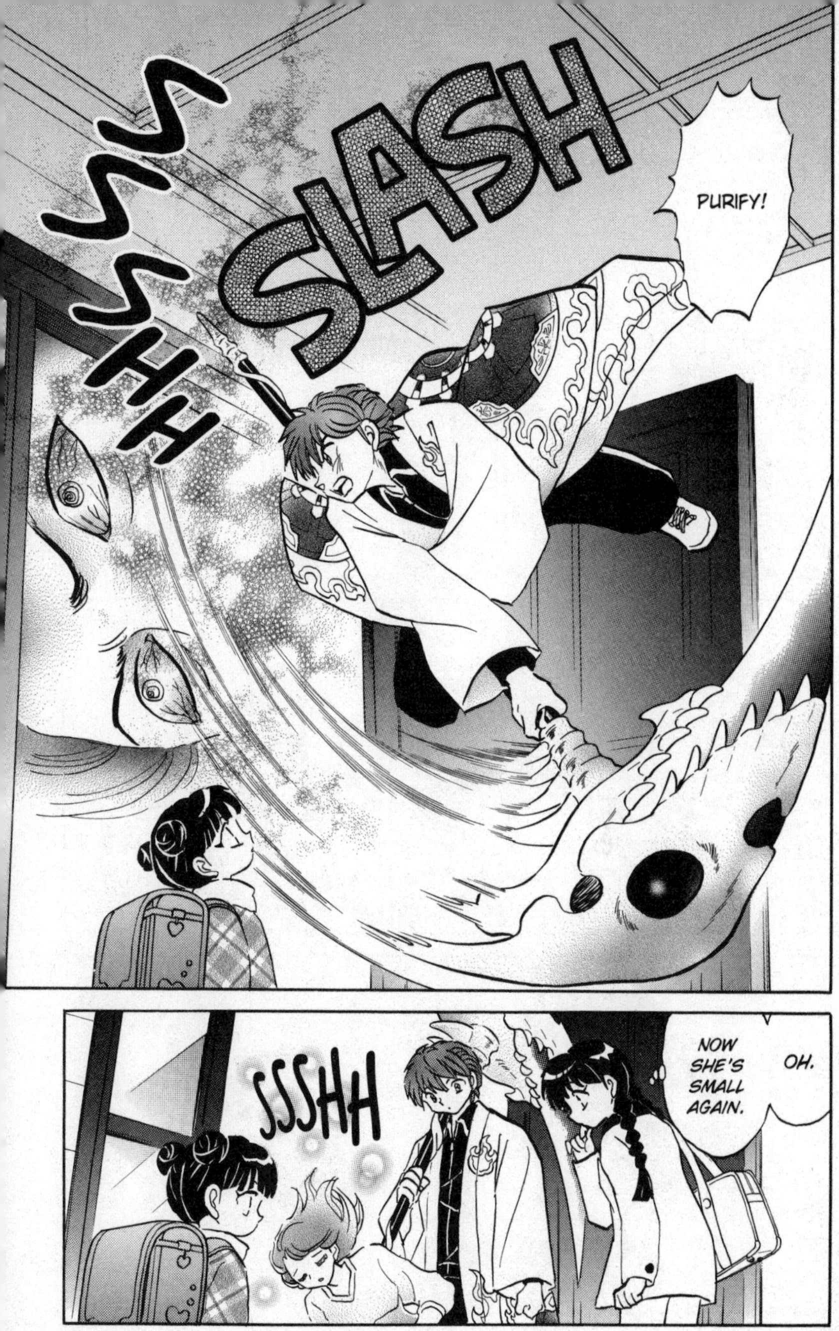
PURIFY!
SLASH
SSSHH
OH.
NOW SHE'S SMALL AGAIN.
SSSHH

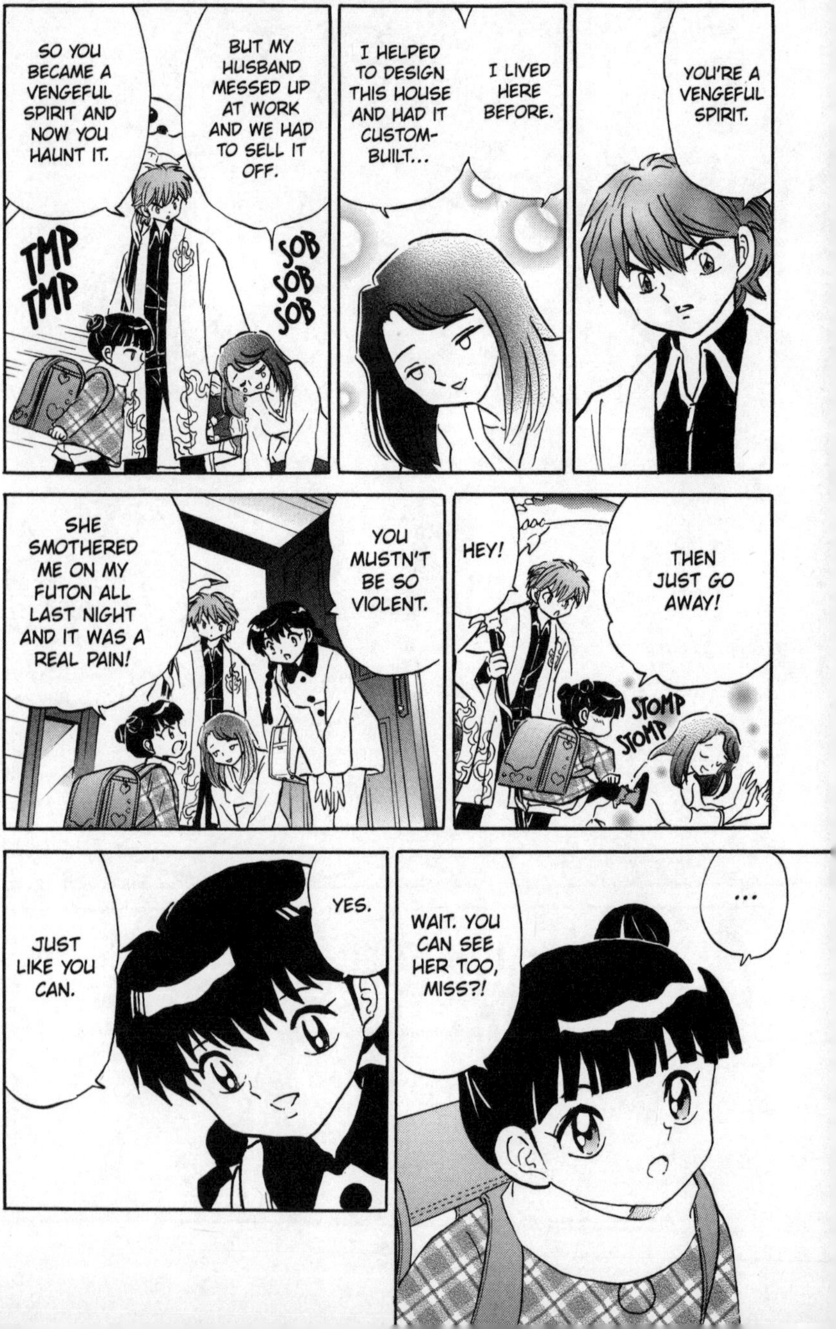
YOU'RE A VENGEFUL SPIRIT.
I LIVED HERE BEFORE.
I HELPED TO DESIGN THIS HOUSE AND HAD IT CUSTOM-BUILT...
BUT MY HUSBAND MESSED UP AT WORK AND WE HAD TO SELL IT OFF.
SOB SOB SOB
SO YOU BECAME A VENGEFUL SPIRIT AND NOW YOU HAUNT IT.
TMP TMP
THEN JUST GO AWAY!
HEY!
STOMP STOMP
YOU MUSTN'T BE SO VIOLENT.
SHE SMOTHERED ME ON MY FUTON ALL LAST NIGHT AND IT WAS A REAL PAIN!
...
WAIT. YOU CAN SEE HER TOO, MISS?!
YES.
JUST LIKE YOU CAN.

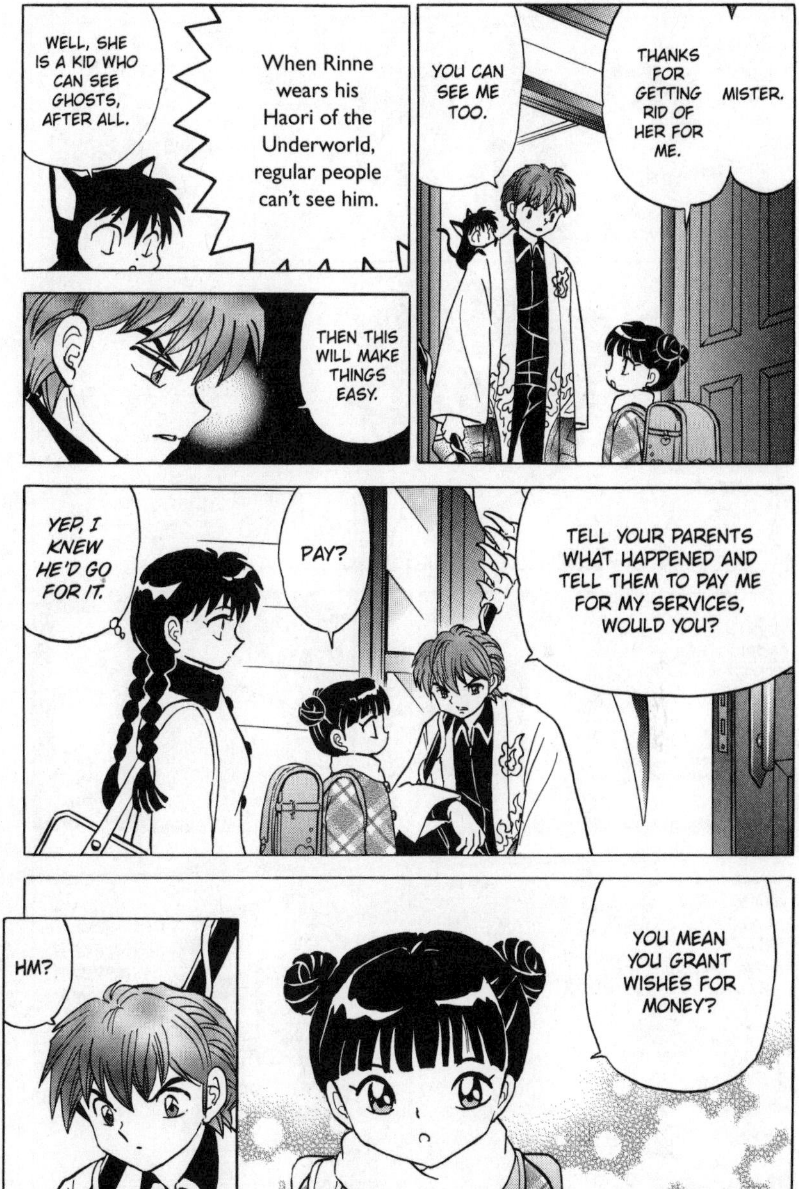
MISTER.
THANKS FOR GETTING RID OF HER FOR ME.
YOU CAN SEE ME TOO.
When Rinne wears his Haori of the Underworld, regular people can't see him.
WELL, SHE IS A KID WHO CAN SEE GHOSTS, AFTER ALL.
THEN THIS WILL MAKE THINGS EASY.
TELL YOUR PARENTS WHAT HAPPENED AND TELL THEM TO PAY ME FOR MY SERVICES, WOULD YOU?
PAY?
YEP, I KNEW HE'D GO FOR IT.
YOU MEAN YOU GRANT WISHES FOR MONEY?
HM?

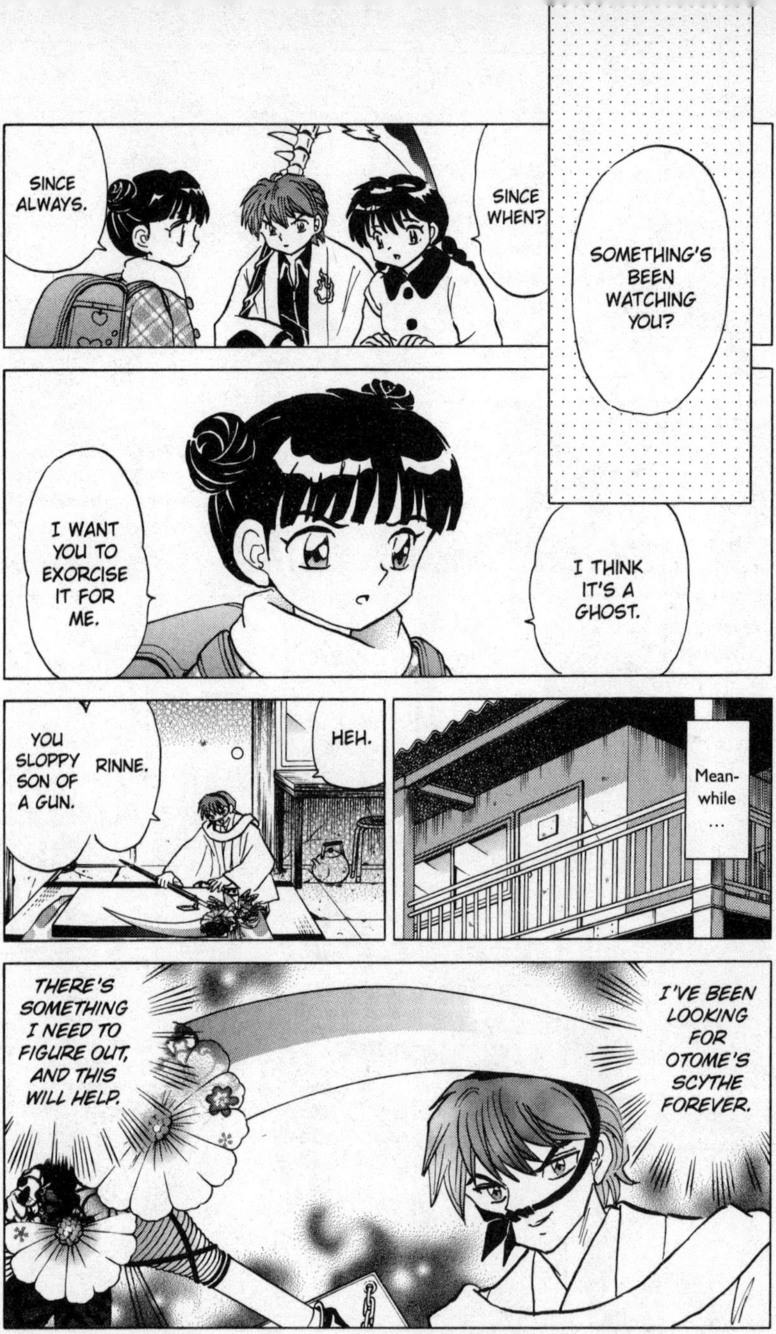
SOMETHING'S BEEN WATCHING YOU?
SINCE WHEN?
SINCE ALWAYS.
I THINK IT'S A GHOST.
I WANT YOU TO EXORCISE IT FOR ME.
Mean-while...
HEH.
RINNE.
YOU SLOPPY SON OF A GUN.
I'VE BEEN LOOKING FOR OTOME'S SCYTHE FOREVER.
THERE'S SOMETHING I NEED TO FIGURE OUT, AND THIS WILL HELP.

CHAPTER 314: SOMETHING'S WATCHING

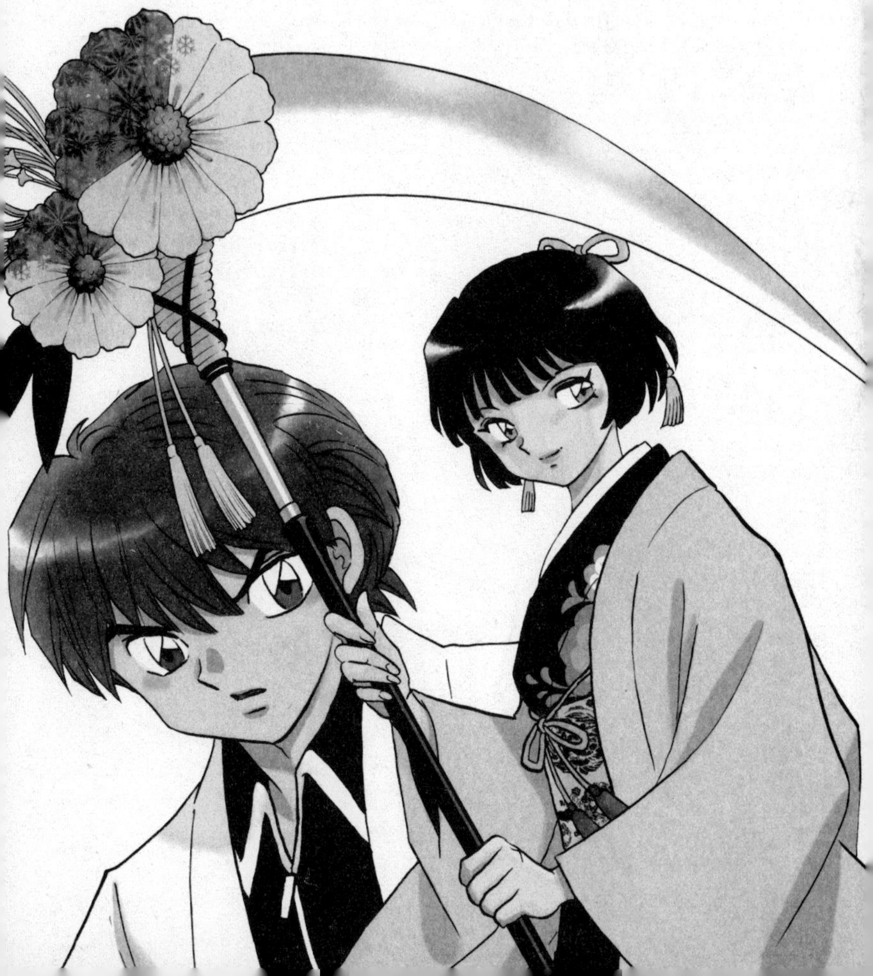

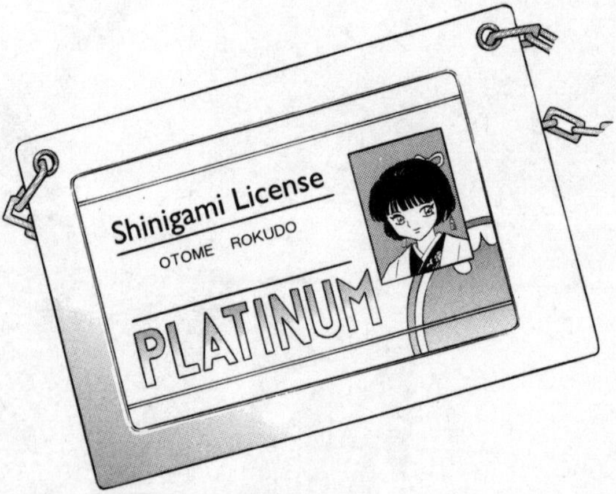
Shinigami License
OTOME ROKUDO
PLATINUM

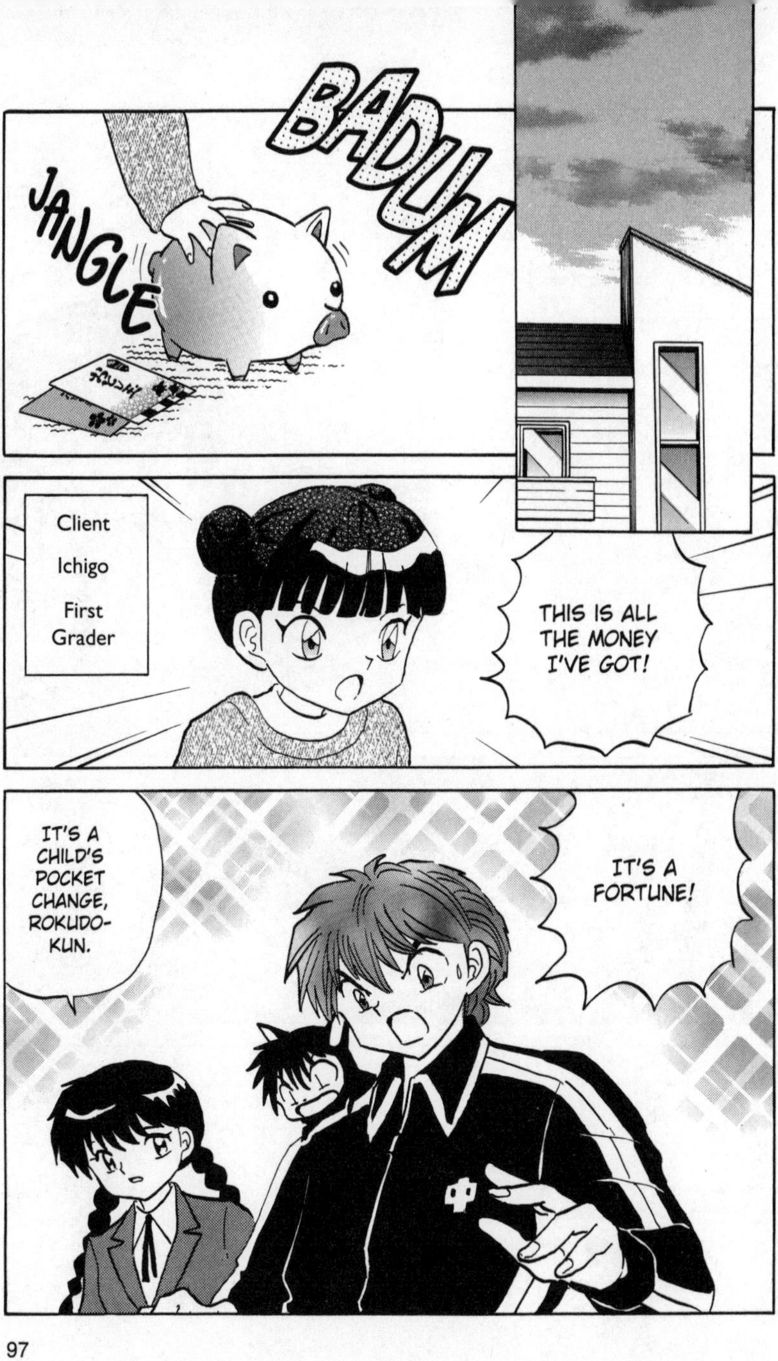
BADUM
JANGLE
THIS IS ALL THE MONEY I'VE GOT!
Client Ichigo First Grader
IT'S A FORTUNE!
IT'S A CHILD'S POCKET CHANGE, ROKUDO-KUN.

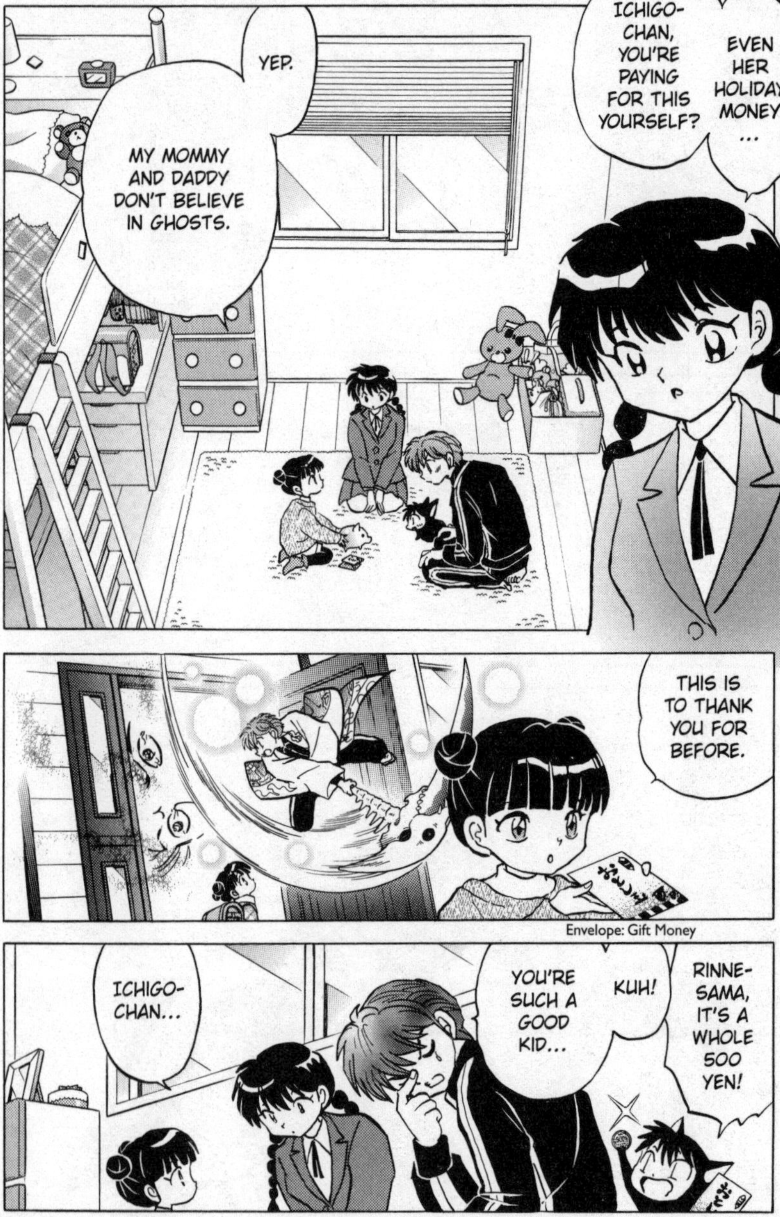

ICHIGO-CHAN, YOU'RE PAYING FOR THIS YOURSELF?
EVEN HER HOLIDAY MONEY ...
YEP.
MY MOMMY AND DADDY DON'T BELIEVE IN GHOSTS.
THIS IS TO THANK YOU FOR BEFORE.
Envelope: Gift Money
RINNE-SAMA, IT'S A WHOLE 500 YEN!
KUH!
YOU'RE SUCH A GOOD KID...
ICHIGO-CHAN...

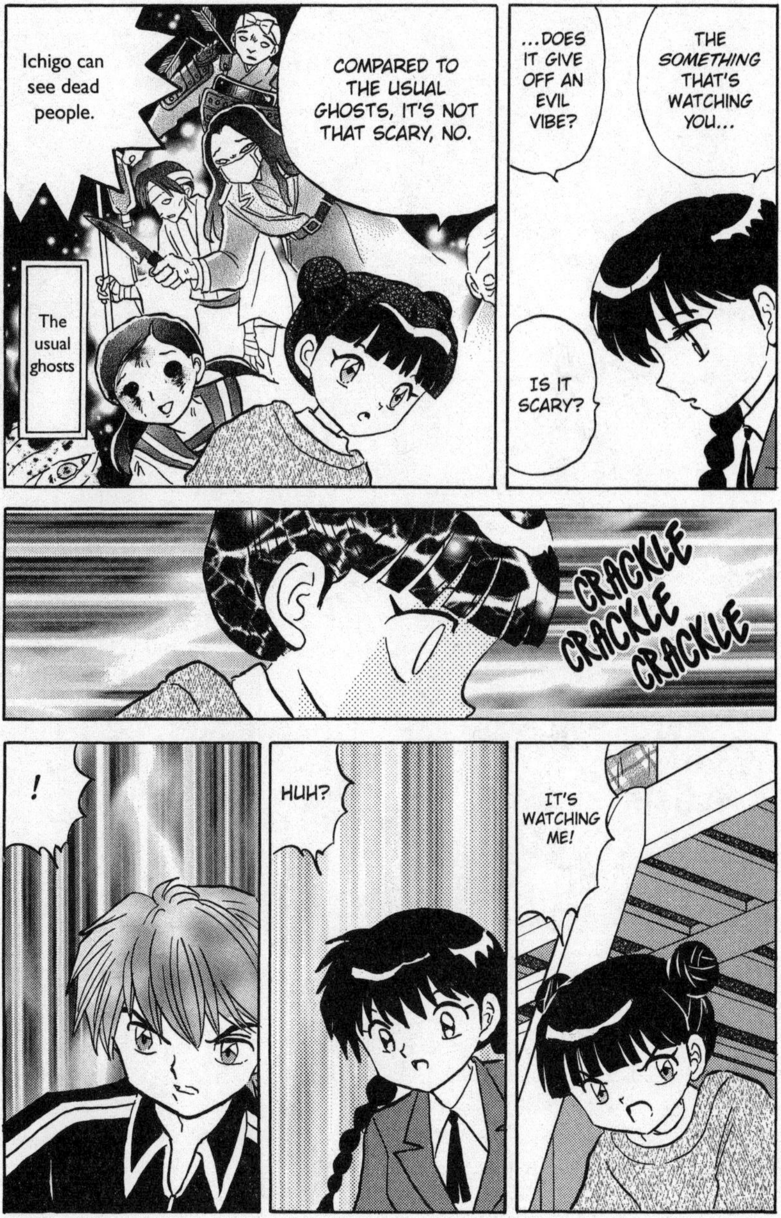
THE SOMETHING THAT'S WATCHING YOU...
...DOES IT GIVE OFF AN EVIL VIBE?
IS IT SCARY?
COMPARED TO THE USUAL GHOSTS, IT'S NOT THAT SCARY, NO.
Ichigo can see dead people.
The usual ghosts
CRACKLE CRACKLE CRACKLE CRACKLE
IT'S WATCHING ME!
HUH?
!

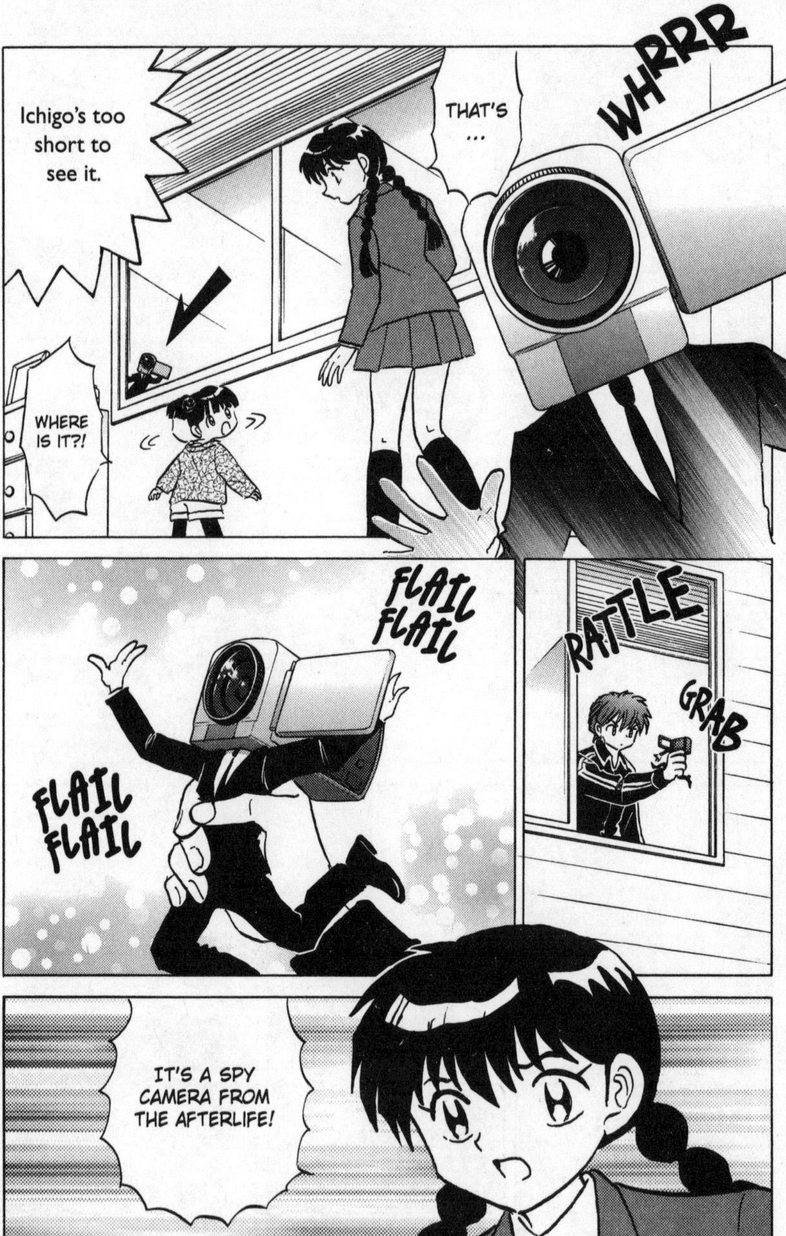
WHRRR
THAT'S ...
Ichigo's too short to see it.
WHERE IS IT?!
RATTLE
GRAB
FLAIL FLAIL
FLAIL FLAIL
IT'S A SPY CAMERA FROM THE AFTERLIFE!

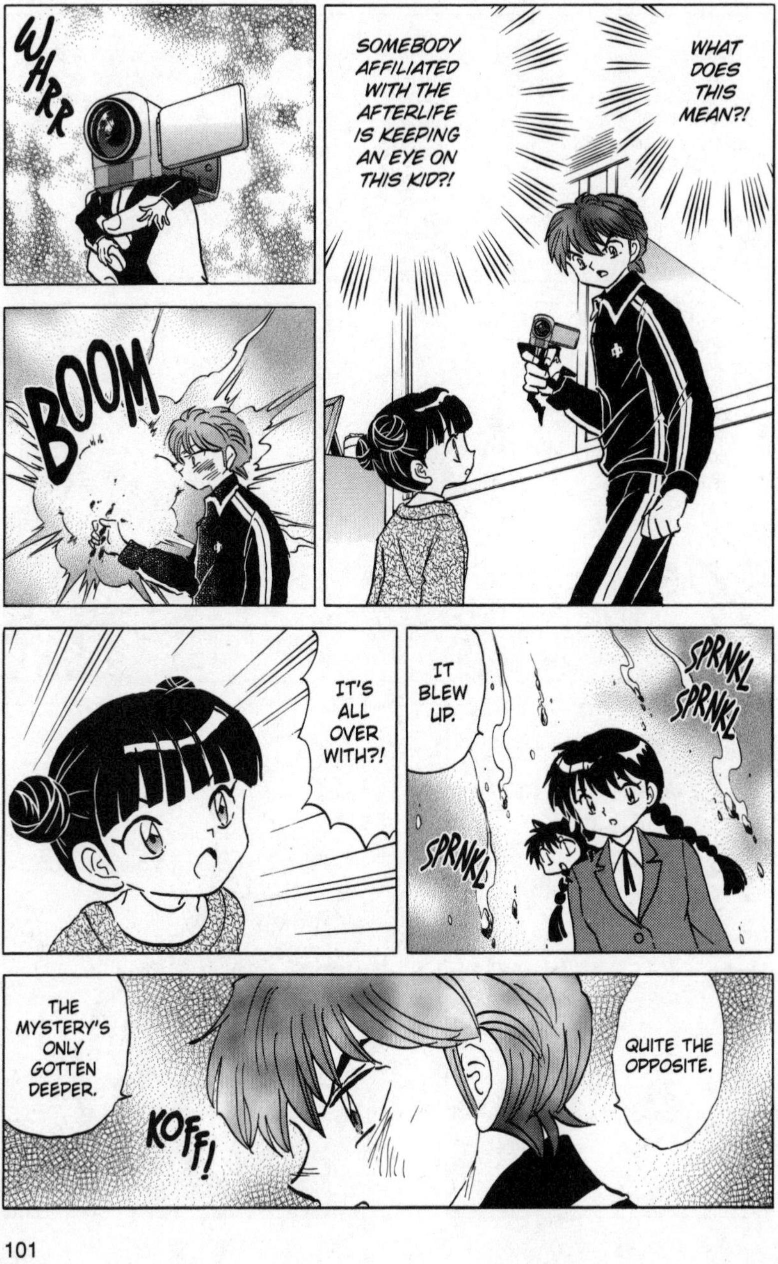
WHAT DOES THIS MEAN?!
SOMEBODY AFFILIATED WITH THE AFTERLIFE IS KEEPING AN EYE ON THIS KID?!
WHRR
BOOM
SPRNKL SPRNKL
IT BLEW UP.
SPRNKL
IT'S ALL OVER WITH?!
QUITE THE OPPOSITE.
THE MYSTERY'S ONLY GOTTEN DEEPER.
KOFF!

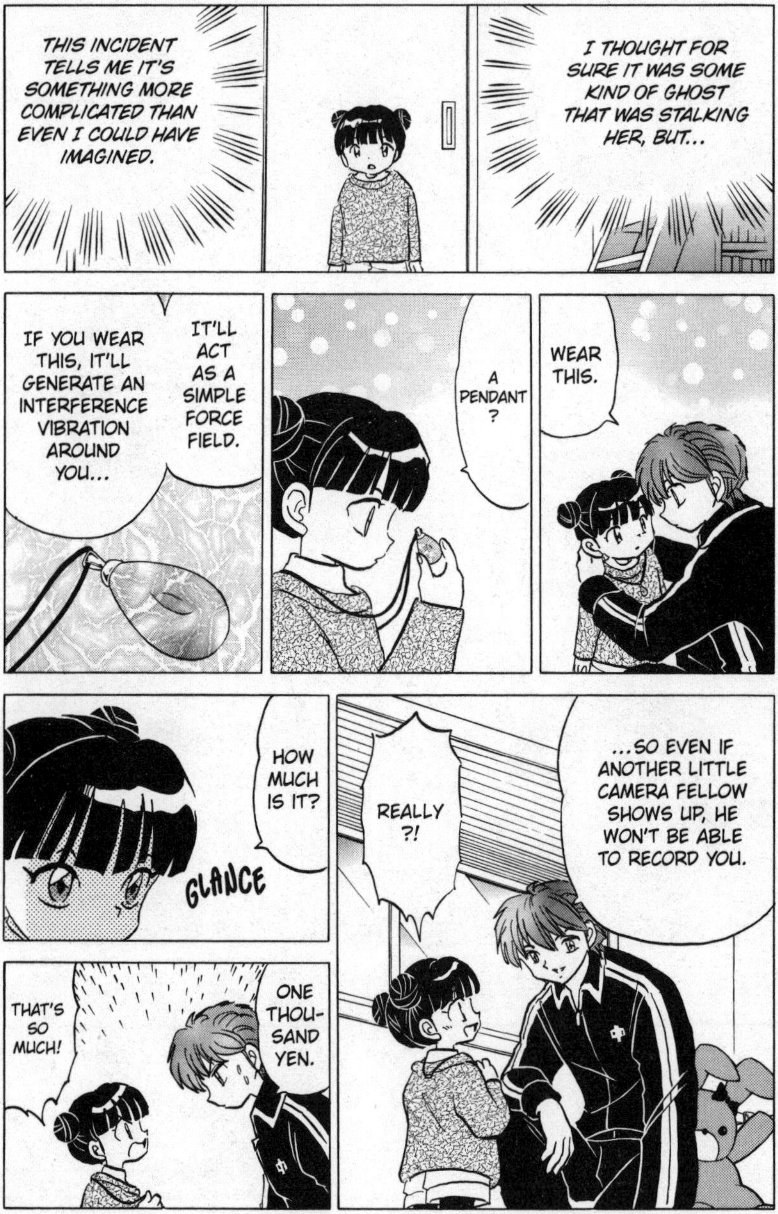
I THOUGHT FOR SURE IT WAS SOME KIND OF GHOST THAT WAS STALKING HER, BUT...
THIS INCIDENT TELLS ME IT'S SOMETHING MORE COMPLICATED THAN EVEN I COULD HAVE IMAGINED.
WEAR THIS.
A PENDANT?
IT'LL ACT AS A SIMPLE FORCE FIELD.
IF YOU WEAR THIS, IT'LL GENERATE AN INTERFERENCE VIBRATION AROUND YOU...
...SO EVEN IF ANOTHER LITTLE CAMERA FELLOW SHOWS UP, HE WON'T BE ABLE TO RECORD YOU.
REALLY?!
HOW MUCH IS IT?
GLANCE
ONE THOU-SAND YEN.
THAT'S SO MUCH!

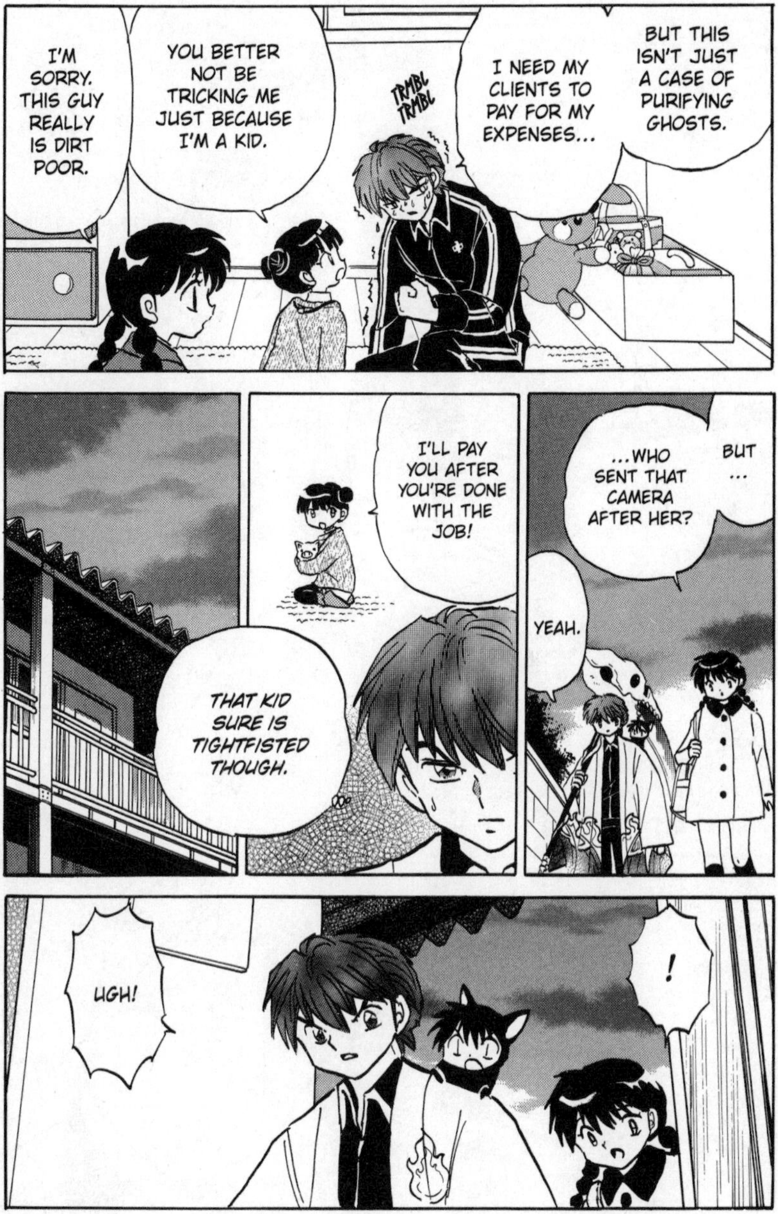
BUT THIS ISN'T JUST A CASE OF PURIFYING GHOSTS.
I NEED MY CLIENTS TO PAY FOR MY EXPENSES...
TRMBL TRMBL
YOU BETTER NOT BE TRICKING ME JUST BECAUSE I'M A KID.
I'M SORRY. THIS GUY REALLY IS DIRT POOR.
BUT...
...WHO SENT THAT CAMERA AFTER HER?
YEAH.
I'LL PAY YOU AFTER YOU'RE DONE WITH THE JOB!
THAT KID SURE IS TIGHTFISTED THOUGH.
!
UGH!

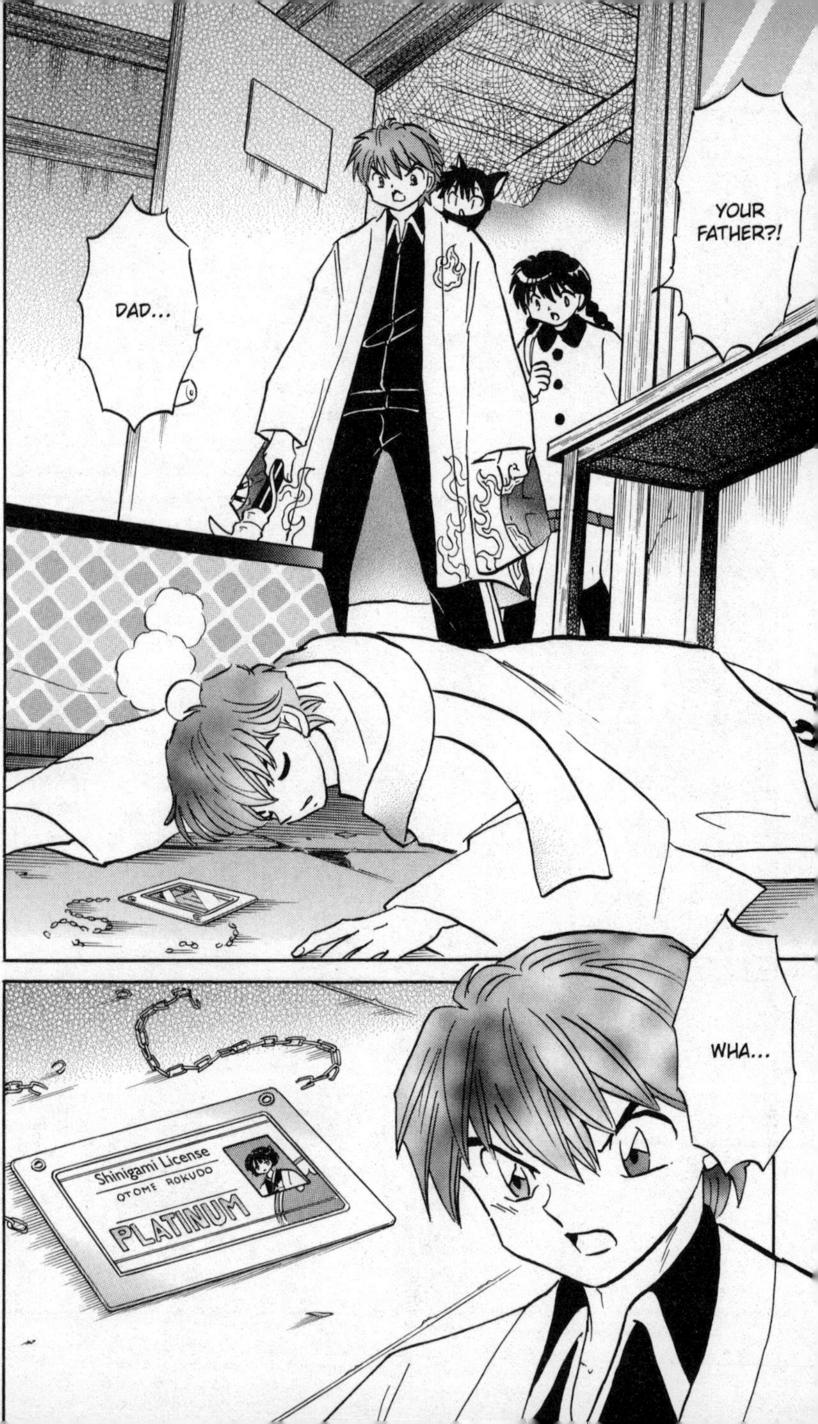
YOUR FATHER?!
DAD...
WHA...
Shinigami License
OTOME ROKUDO
PLATINUM

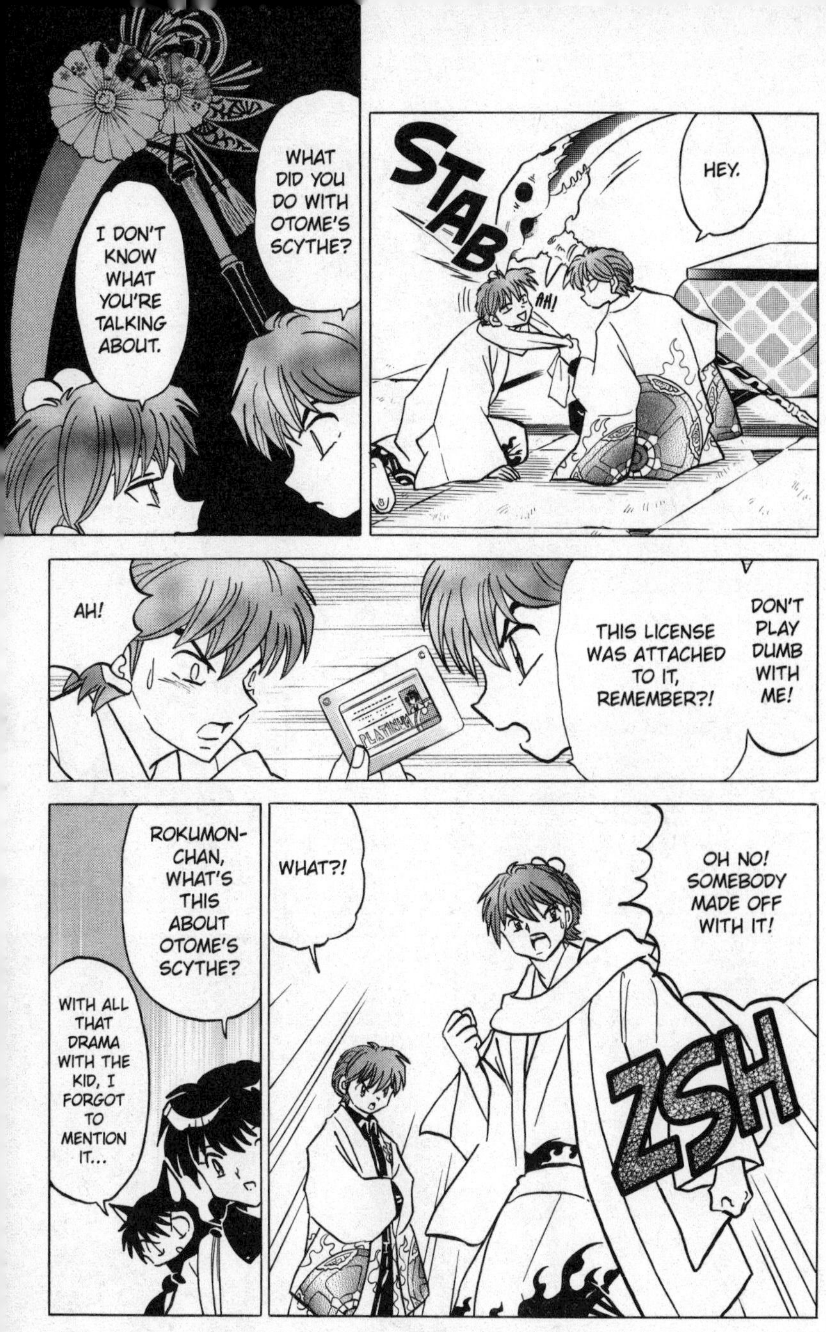
STAB
HEY.
AH!
WHAT DID YOU DO WITH OTOME'S SCYTHE?
I DON'T KNOW WHAT YOU'RE TALKING ABOUT.
DON'T PLAY DUMB WITH ME!
THIS LICENSE WAS ATTACHED TO IT, REMEMBER?!
PLATINUM
AH!
OH NO! SOMEBODY MADE OFF WITH IT!
ZSH
WHAT?!
ROKUMON-CHAN, WHAT'S THIS ABOUT OTOME'S SCYTHE?
WITH ALL THAT DRAMA WITH THE KID, I FORGOT TO MENTION IT...

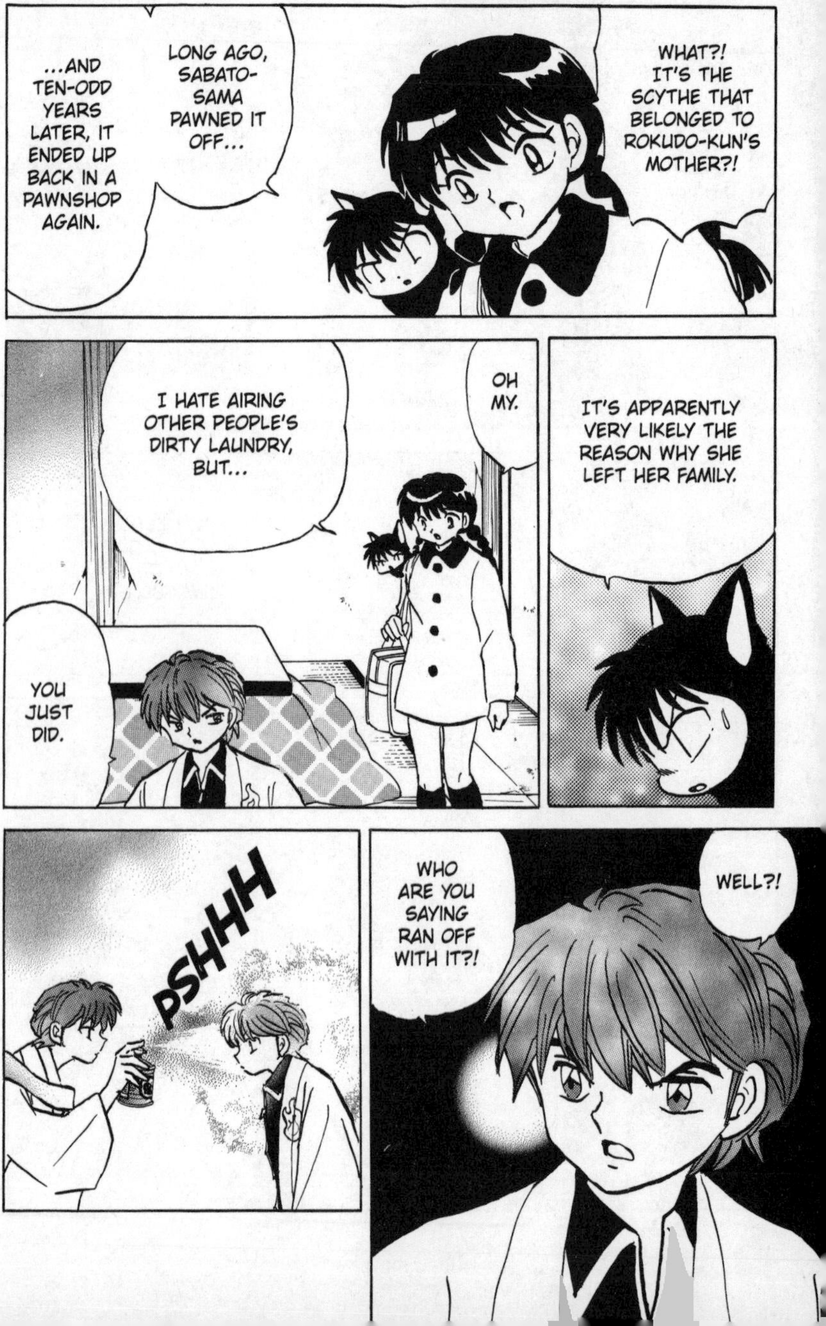
WHAT?! IT'S THE SCYTHE THAT BELONGED TO ROKUDO-KUN'S MOTHER?!
LONG AGO, SABATO-SAMA PAWNED IT OFF...
...AND TEN-ODD YEARS LATER, IT ENDED UP BACK IN A PAWNSHOP AGAIN.
IT'S APPARENTLY VERY LIKELY THE REASON WHY SHE LEFT HER FAMILY.
OH MY.
I HATE AIRING OTHER PEOPLE'S DIRTY LAUNDRY, BUT...
YOU JUST DID.
WELL?!
WHO ARE YOU SAYING RAN OFF WITH IT?!
PSHHH

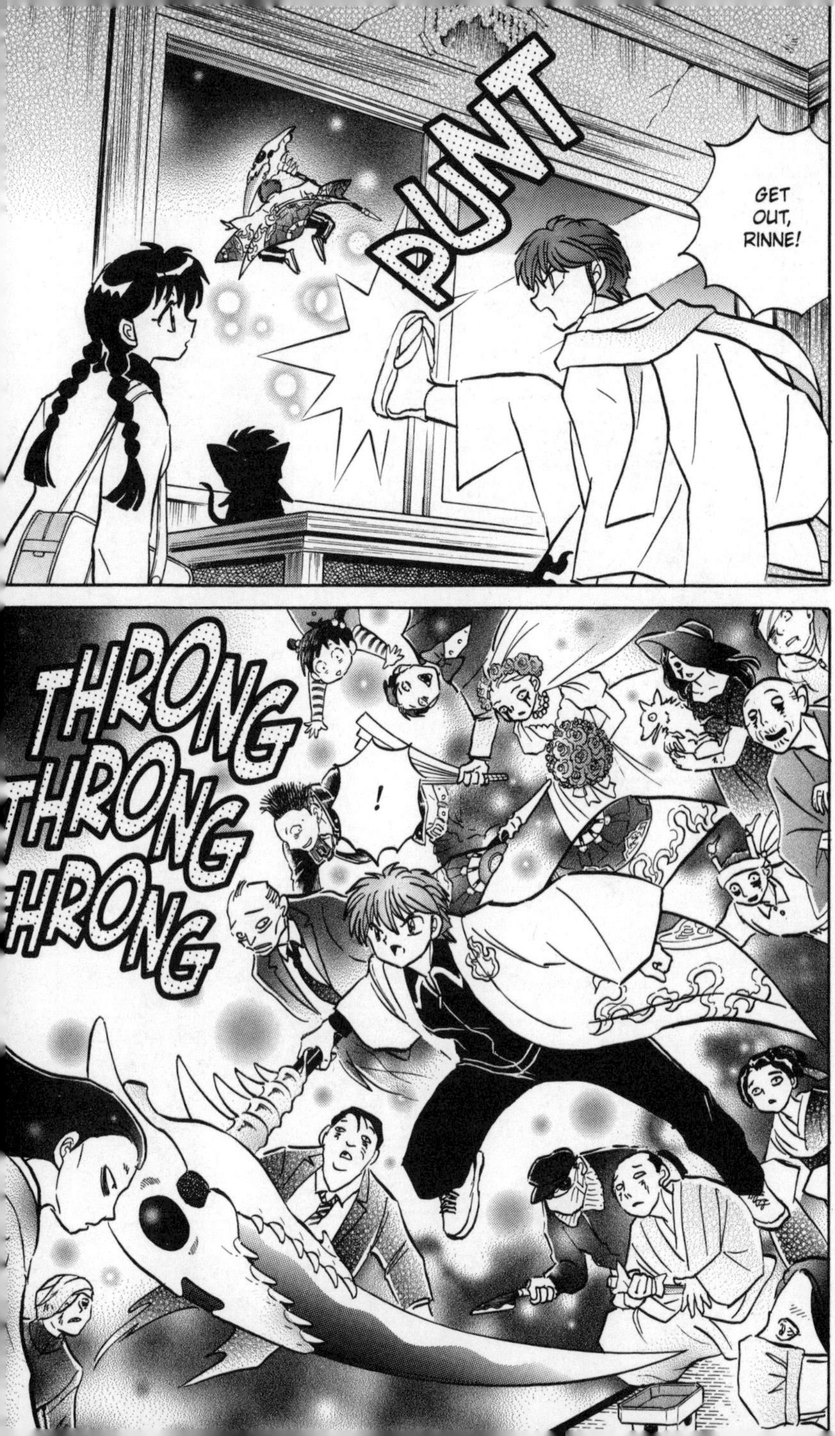

GET OUT, RINNE!
PUNT
THRONG THRONG THRONG THRONG
!

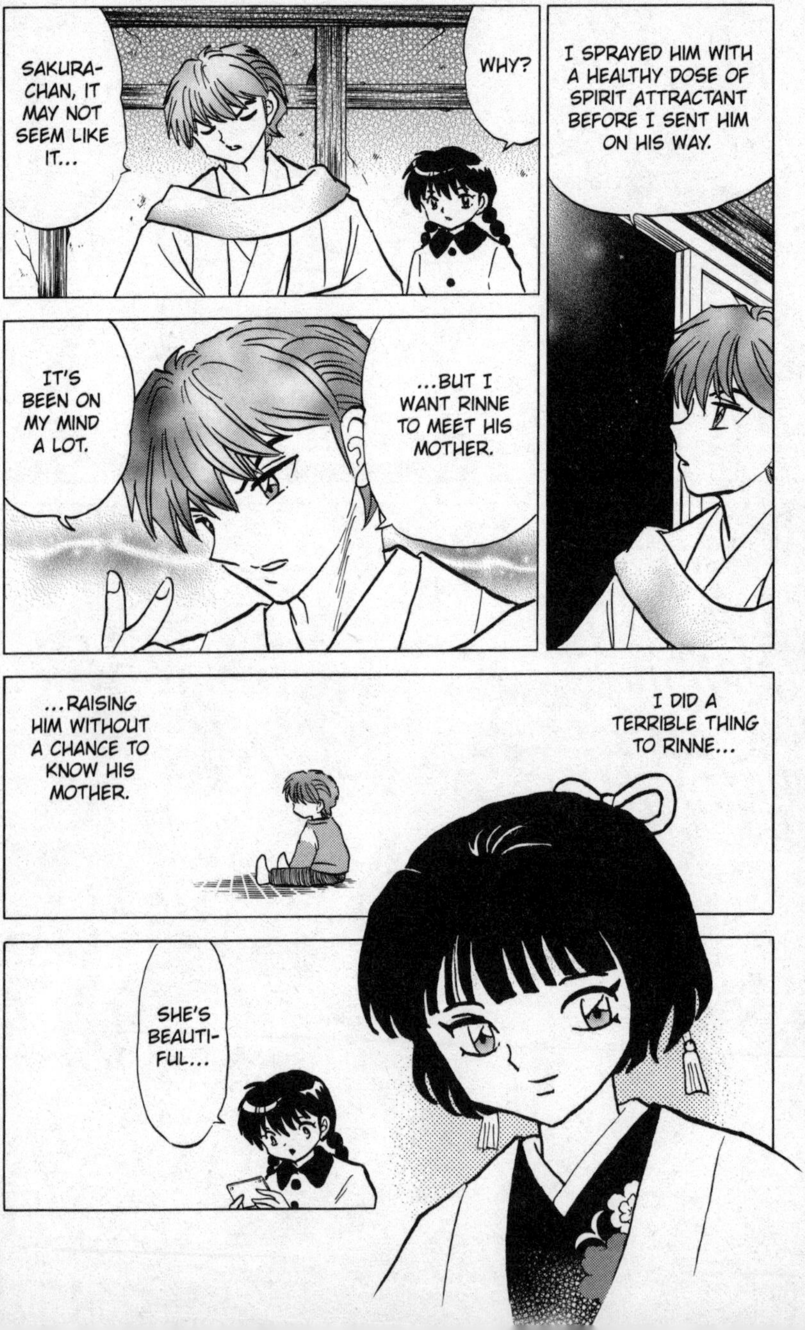
I SPRAYED HIM WITH A HEALTHY DOSE OF SPIRIT ATTRACTANT BEFORE I SENT HIM ON HIS WAY.
WHY?
SAKURA-CHAN, IT MAY NOT SEEM LIKE IT...
...BUT I WANT RINNE TO MEET HIS MOTHER.
IT'S BEEN ON MY MIND A LOT.
I DID A TERRIBLE THING TO RINNE...
...RAISING HIM WITHOUT A CHANCE TO KNOW HIS MOTHER.
SHE'S BEAUTI-FUL...

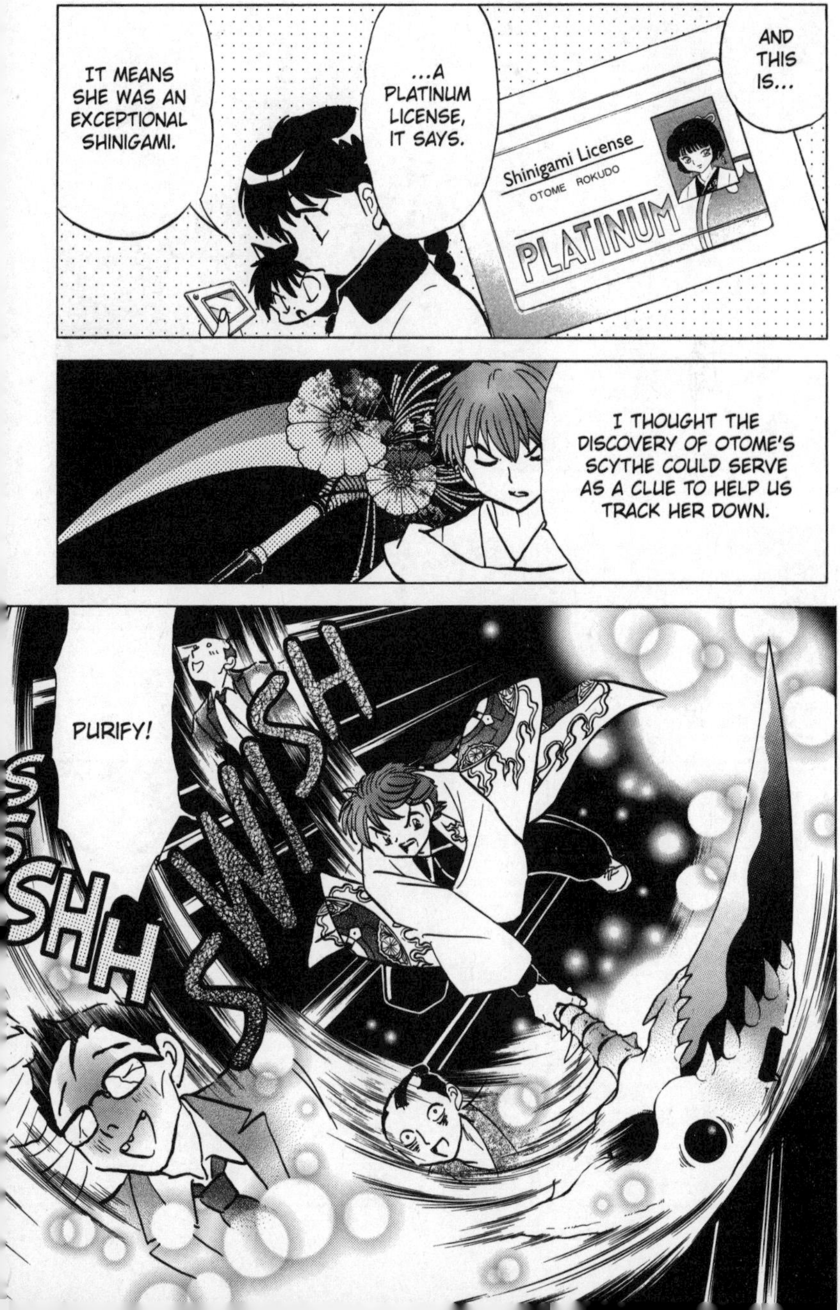
AND THIS IS...
Shinigami License
OTOME ROKUDO
PLATINUM
...A PLATINUM LICENSE, IT SAYS.
IT MEANS SHE WAS AN EXCEPTIONAL SHINIGAMI.
I THOUGHT THE DISCOVERY OF OTOME'S SCYTHE COULD SERVE AS A CLUE TO HELP US TRACK HER DOWN.
SWISH
PURIFY!
SWISHH

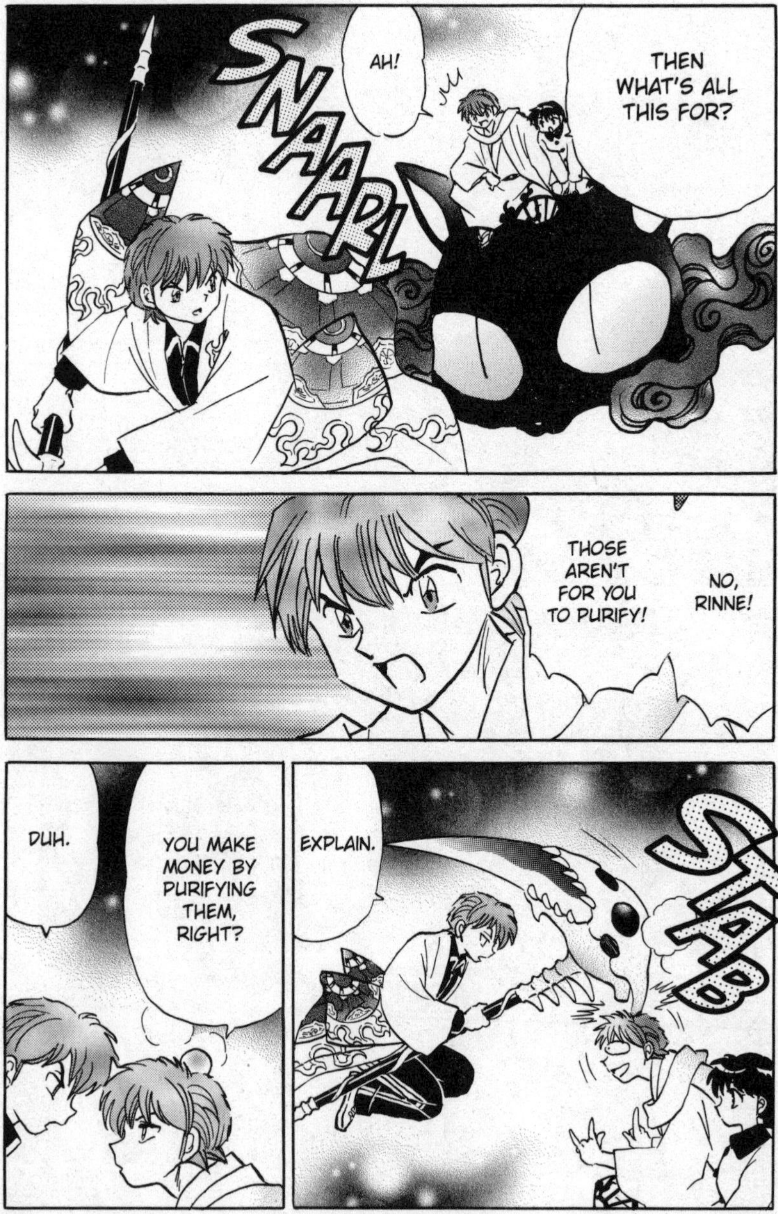
THEN WHAT'S ALL THIS FOR?
AH!
SNAARL
NO, RINNE!
THOSE AREN'T FOR YOU TO PURIFY!
STABB
EXPLAIN.
YOU MAKE MONEY BY PURIFYING THEM, RIGHT?
DUH.

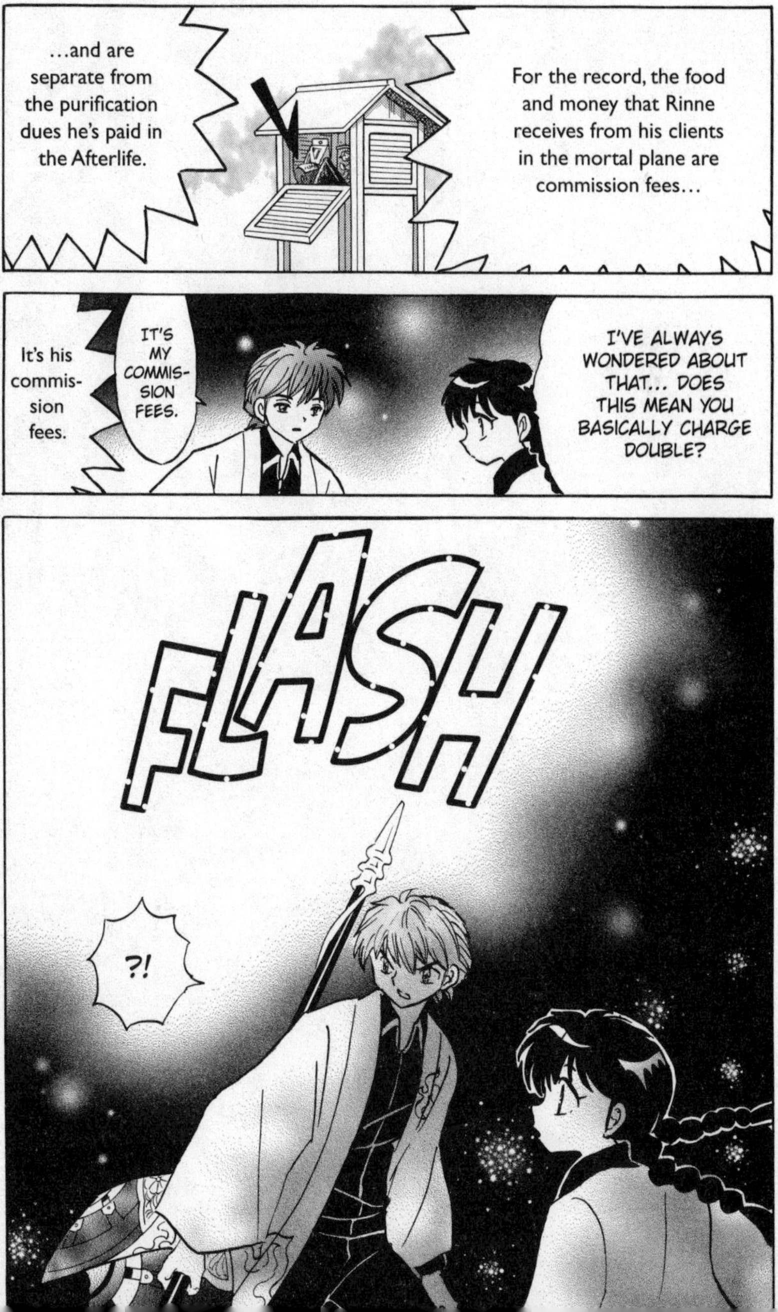
For the record, the food and money that Rinne receives from his clients in the mortal plane are commission fees...
...and are separate from the purification dues he's paid in the Afterlife.
I'VE ALWAYS WONDERED ABOUT THAT... DOES THIS MEAN YOU BASICALLY CHARGE DOUBLE?
IT'S MY COMMISSION FEES.
It's his commission fees.
FLASH
?!

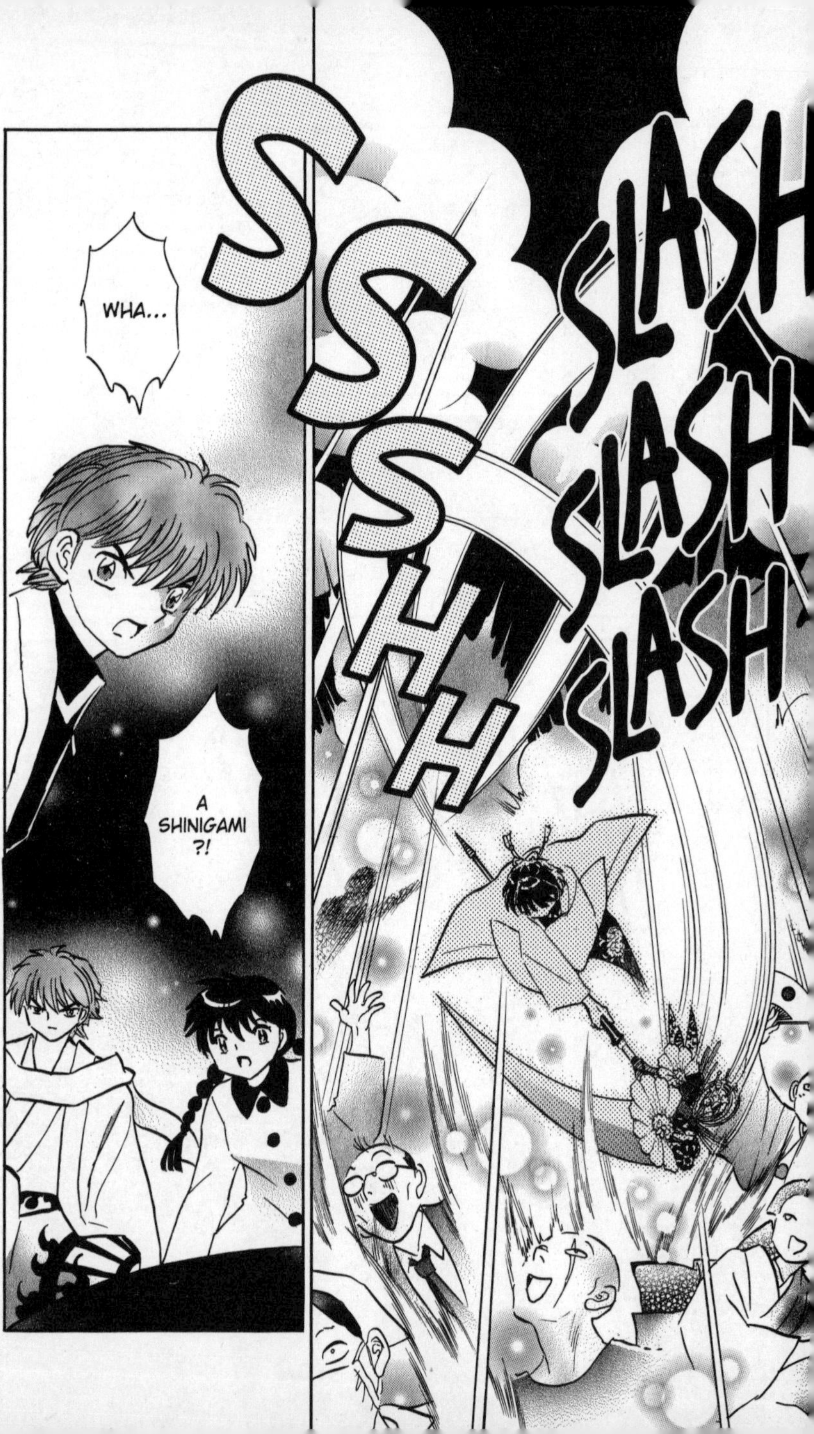
SLASH
SLASH
SLASH
SLASH
SSHHH
WHA...
A SHINIGAMI ?!

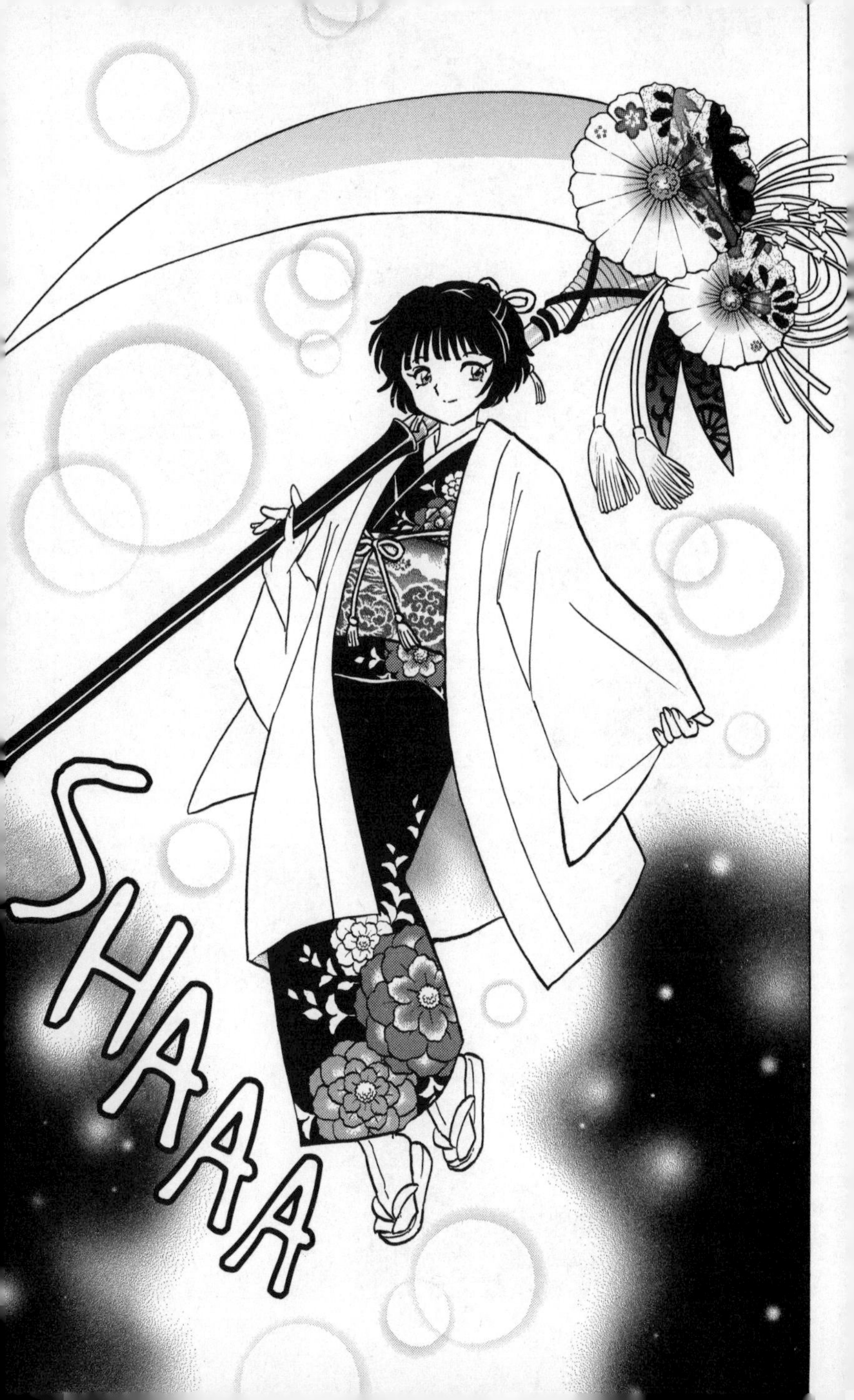
SHAAA

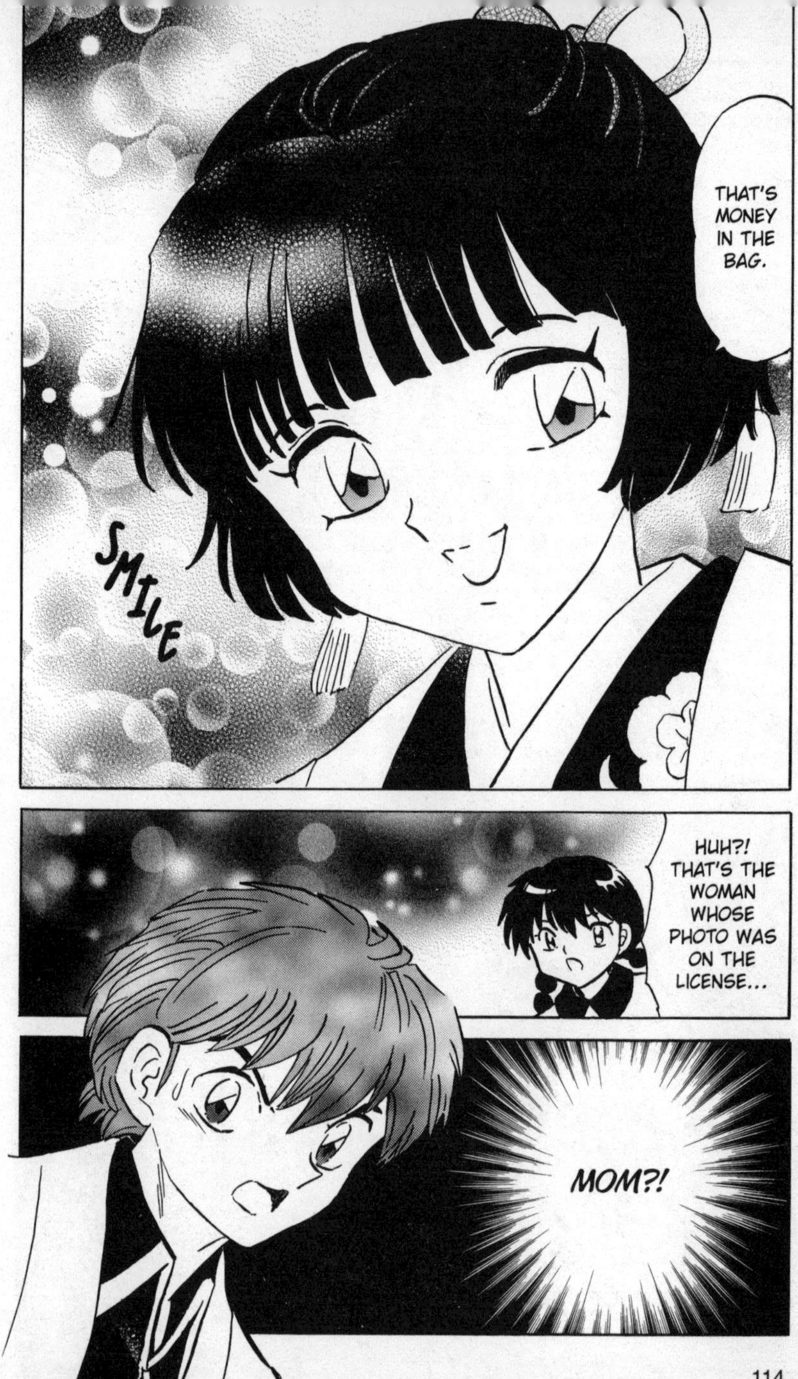
THAT'S MONEY IN THE BAG.
SMILE
HUH?! THAT'S THE WOMAN WHOSE PHOTO WAS ON THE LICENSE...
MOM?!

CHAPTER 315: OTOME'S MEMORIES

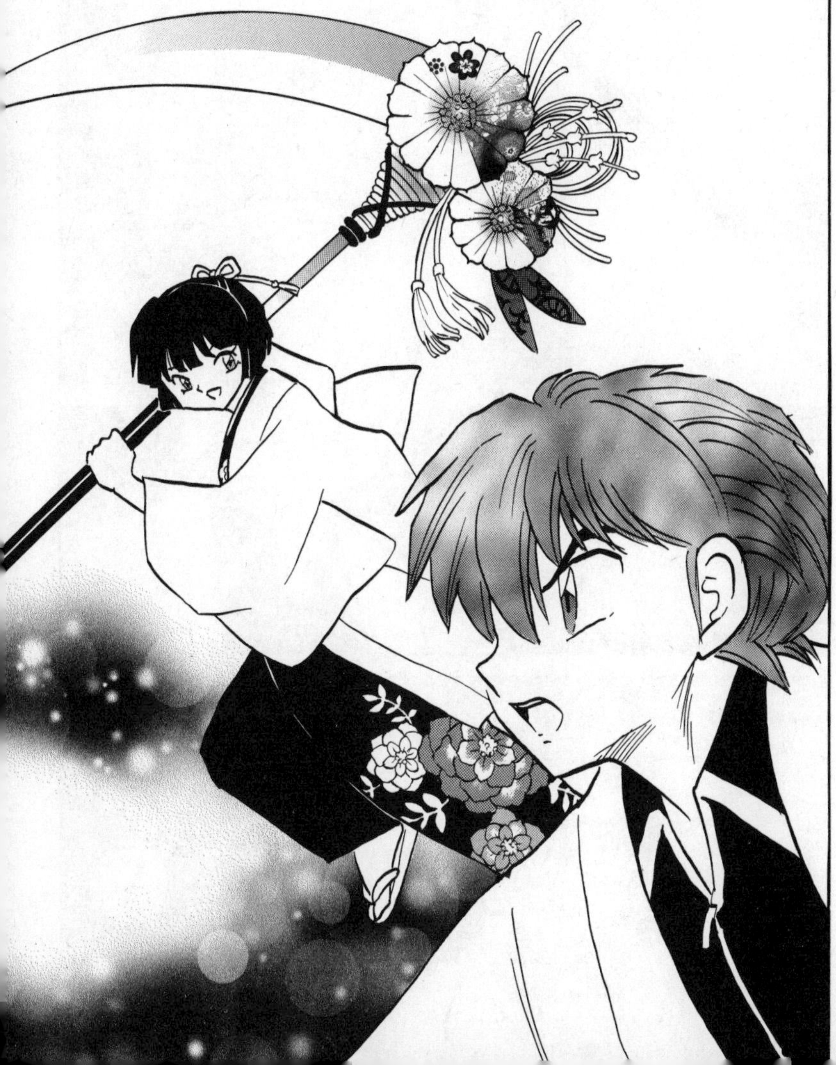

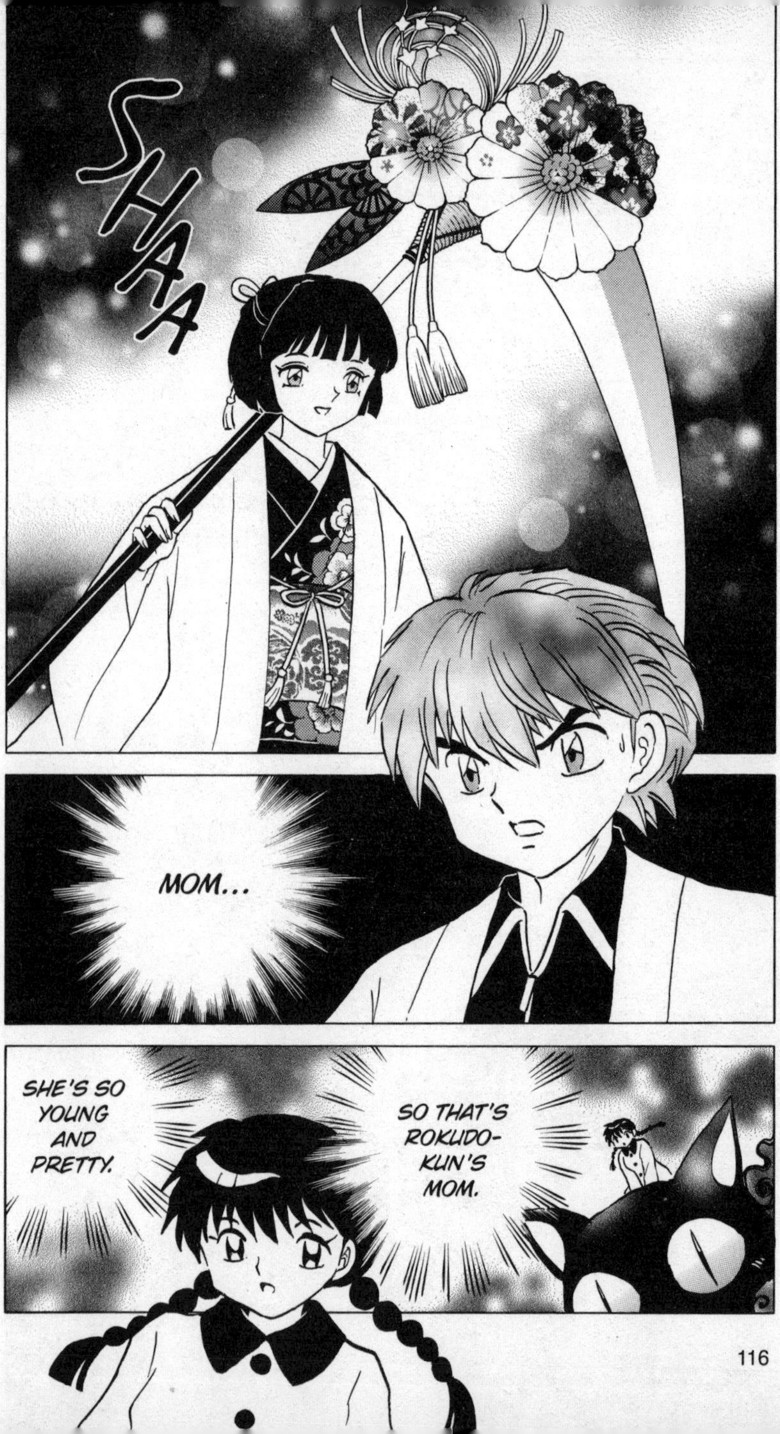
SHAA
MOM...
SO THAT'S ROKUDO-KUN'S MOM.
SHE'S SO YOUNG AND PRETTY.

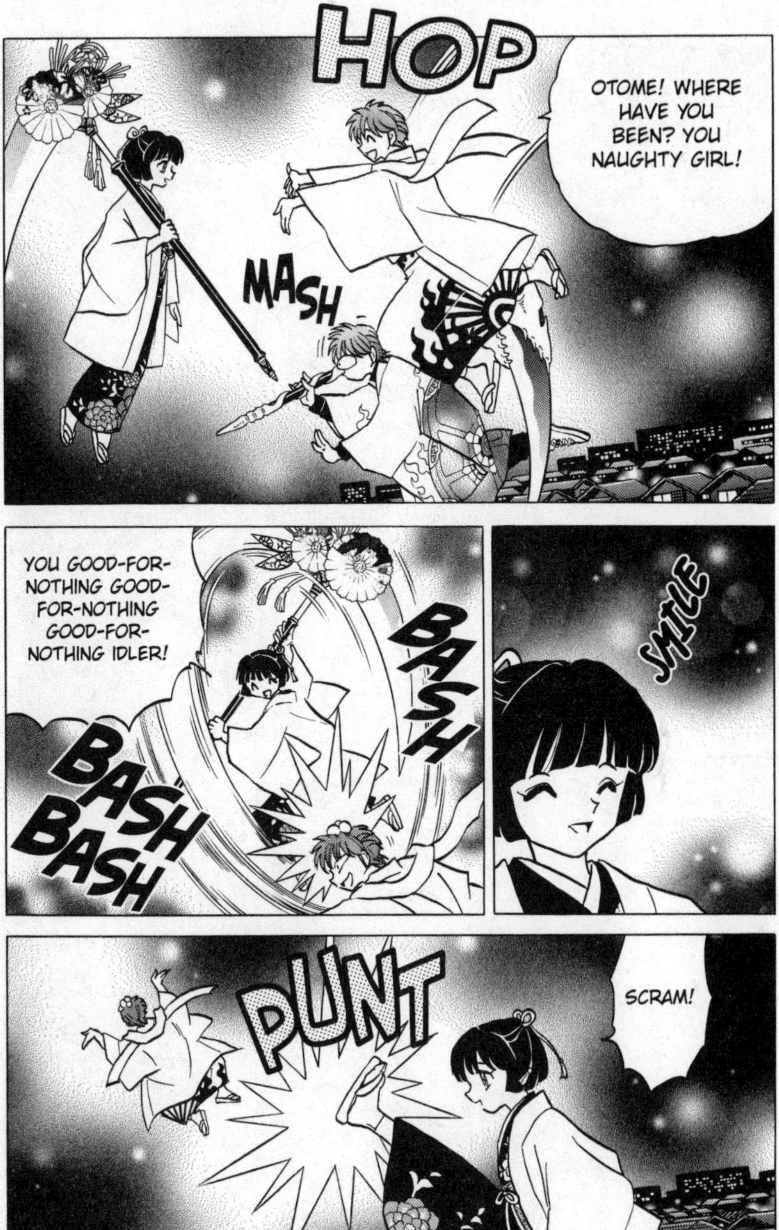
HOP
OTOME! WHERE HAVE YOU BEEN? YOU NAUGHTY GIRL!
MASH
SMILE
BASH
YOU GOOD-FOR-NOTHING GOOD-FOR-NOTHING GOOD-FOR-NOTHING IDLER!
BASH BASH
SCRAM!
PUNT

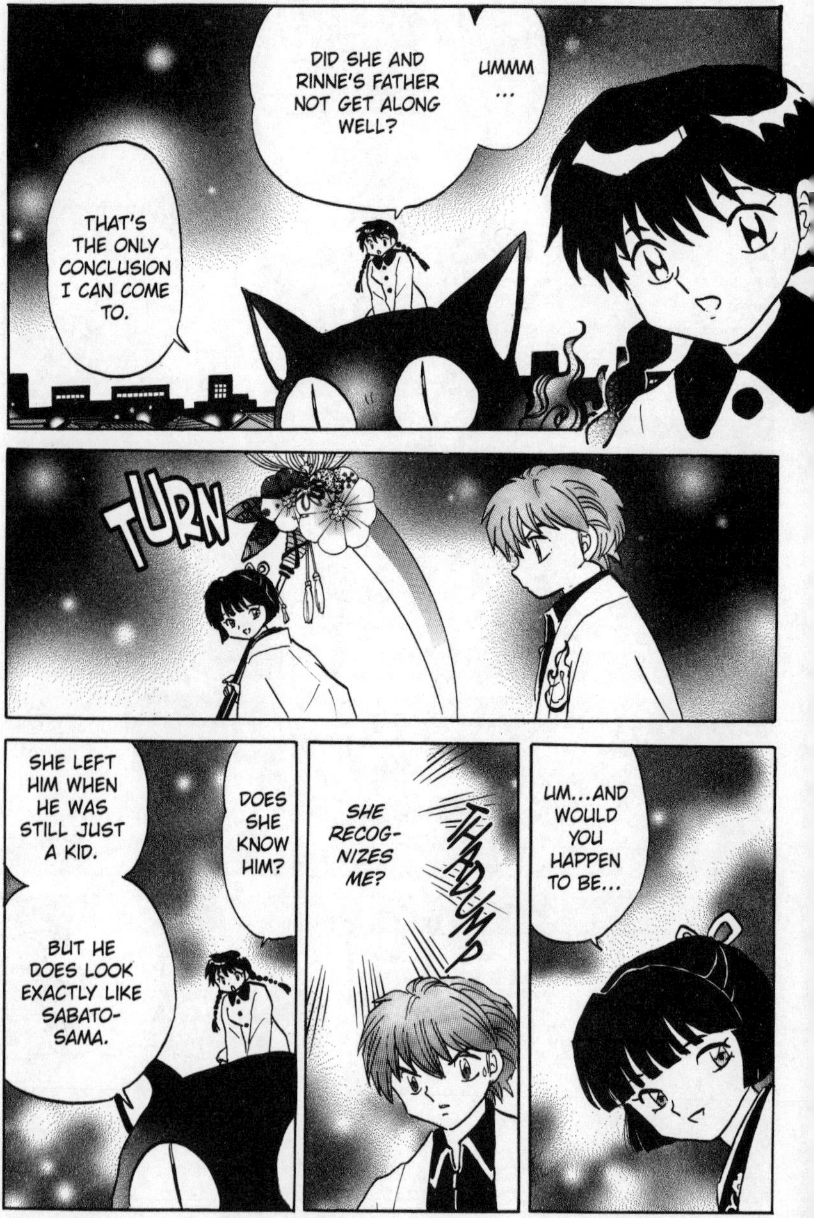
UMMM ...
DID SHE AND RINNE'S FATHER NOT GET ALONG WELL?
THAT'S THE ONLY CONCLUSION I CAN COME TO.
TURN
UM...AND WOULD YOU HAPPEN TO BE...
THADUMP
SHE RECOG-NIZES ME?
DOES SHE KNOW HIM?
SHE LEFT HIM WHEN HE WAS STILL JUST A KID.
BUT HE DOES LOOK EXACTLY LIKE SABATO-SAMA.

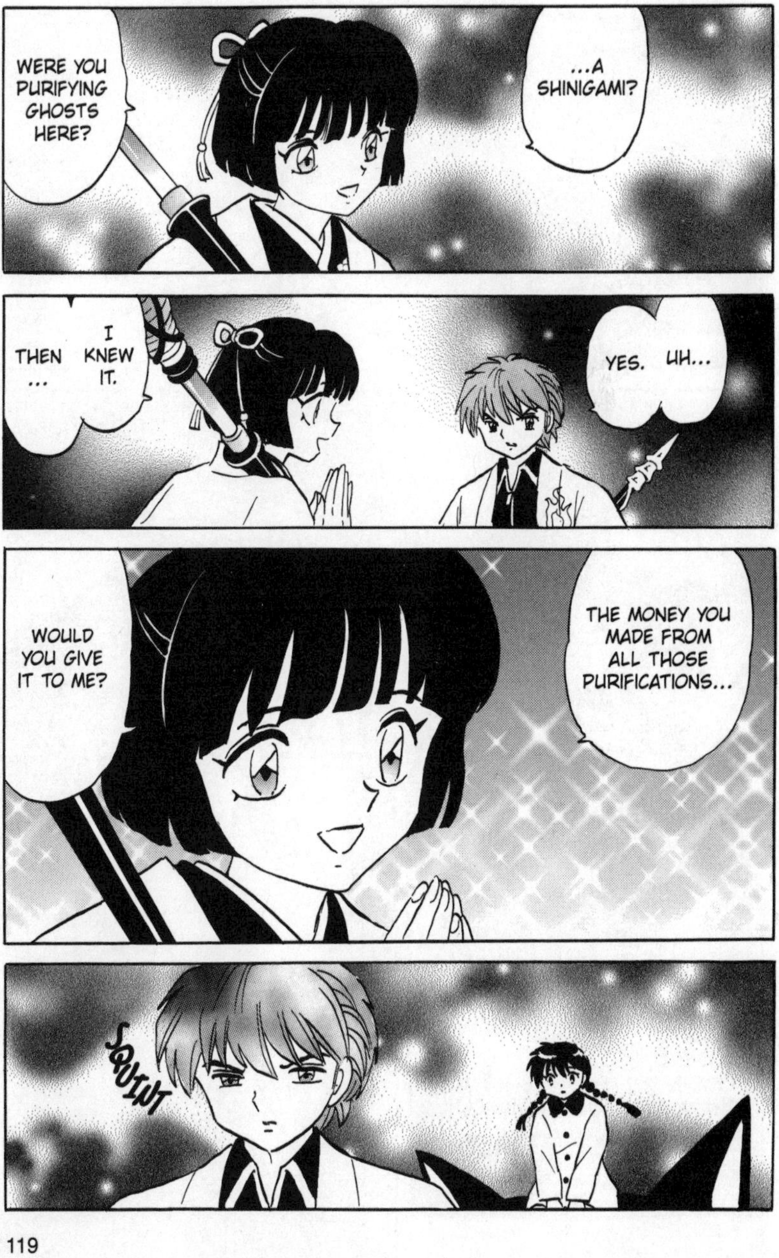
...A SHINIGAMI?
WERE YOU PURIFYING GHOSTS HERE?
YES. UH...
I KNEW IT.
THEN...
THE MONEY YOU MADE FROM ALL THOSE PURIFICATIONS...
WOULD YOU GIVE IT TO ME?
SQUINT

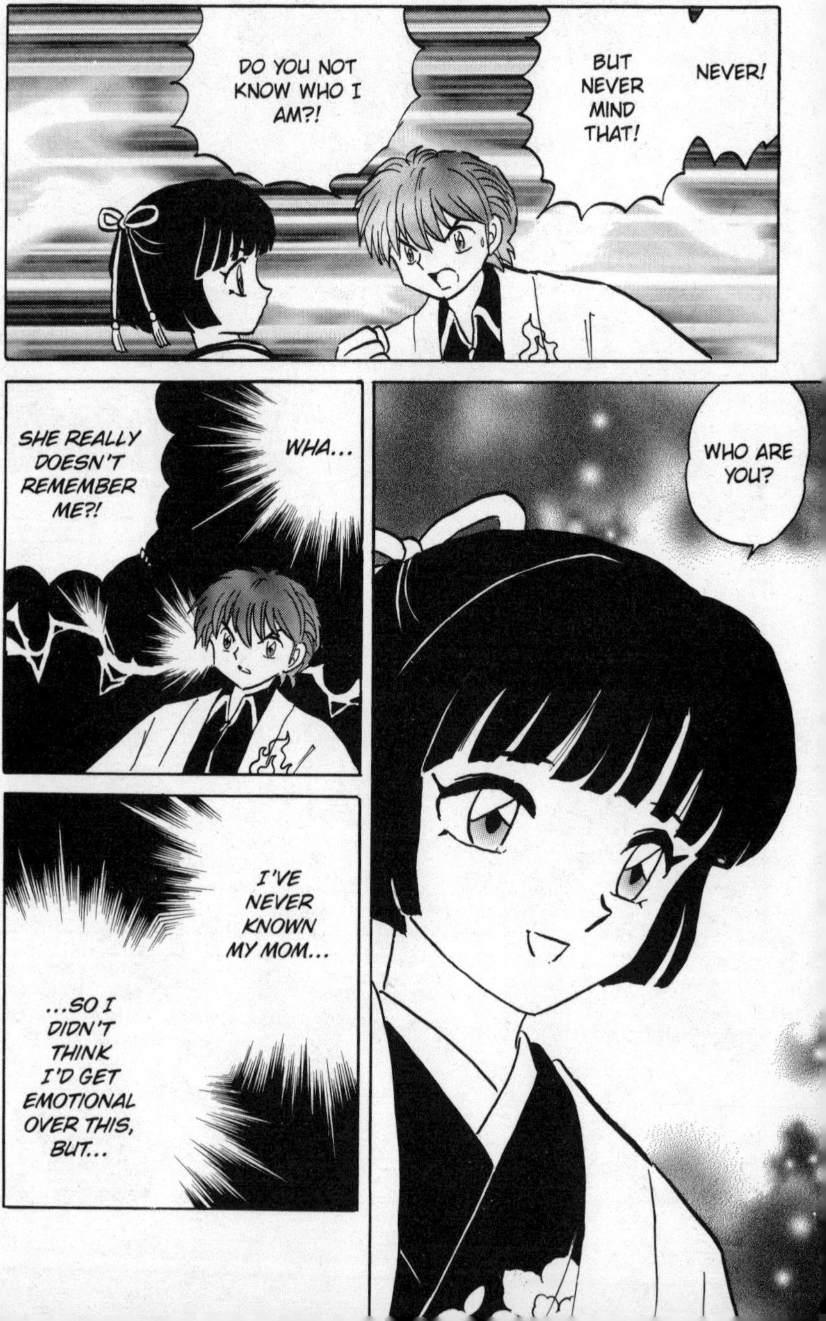
NEVER!
BUT NEVER MIND THAT!
DO YOU NOT KNOW WHO I AM?!
WHO ARE YOU?
WHA...
SHE REALLY DOESN'T REMEMBER ME?!
I'VE NEVER KNOWN MY MOM...
...SO I DIDN'T THINK I'D GET EMOTIONAL OVER THIS, BUT...

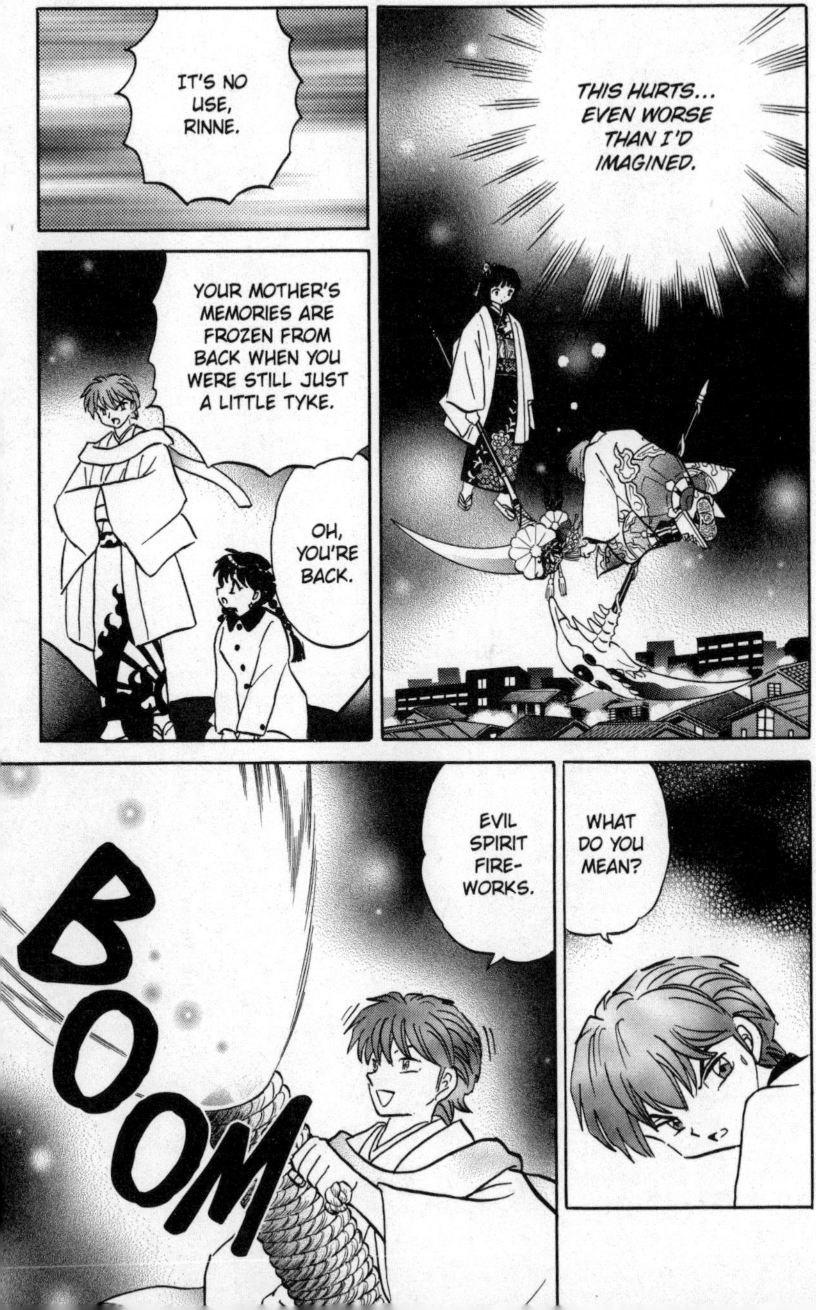
THIS HURTS... EVEN WORSE THAN I'D IMAGINED.
IT'S NO USE, RINNE.
YOUR MOTHER'S MEMORIES ARE FROZEN FROM BACK WHEN YOU WERE STILL JUST A LITTLE TYKE.
OH, YOU'RE BACK.
WHAT DO YOU MEAN?
EVIL SPIRIT FIRE-WORKS.
BOOM

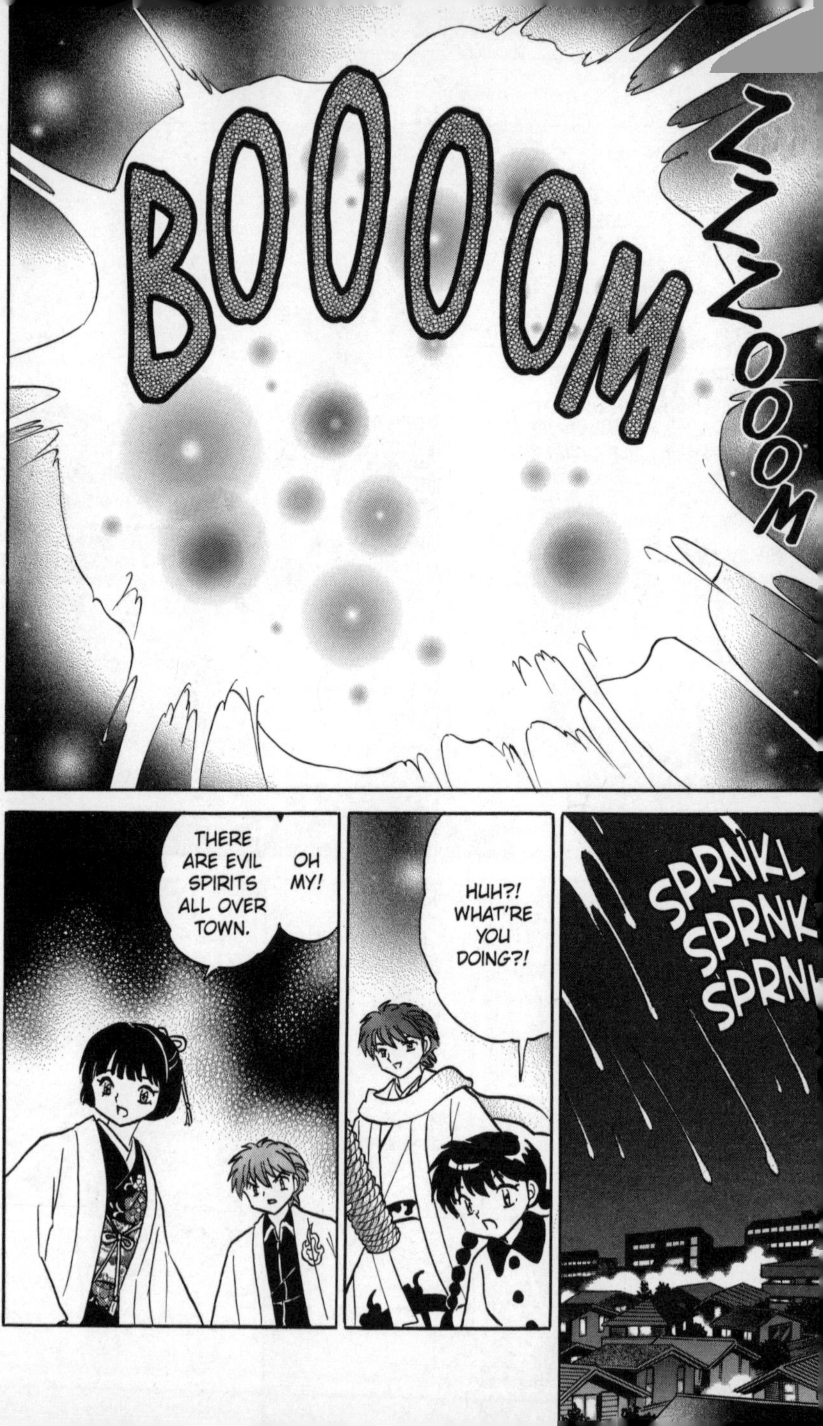

ZZZOOOM
BOOOOM
SPRNKL SPRNK SPRN
HUH?! WHAT'RE YOU DOING?!
OH MY!
THERE ARE EVIL SPIRITS ALL OVER TOWN.

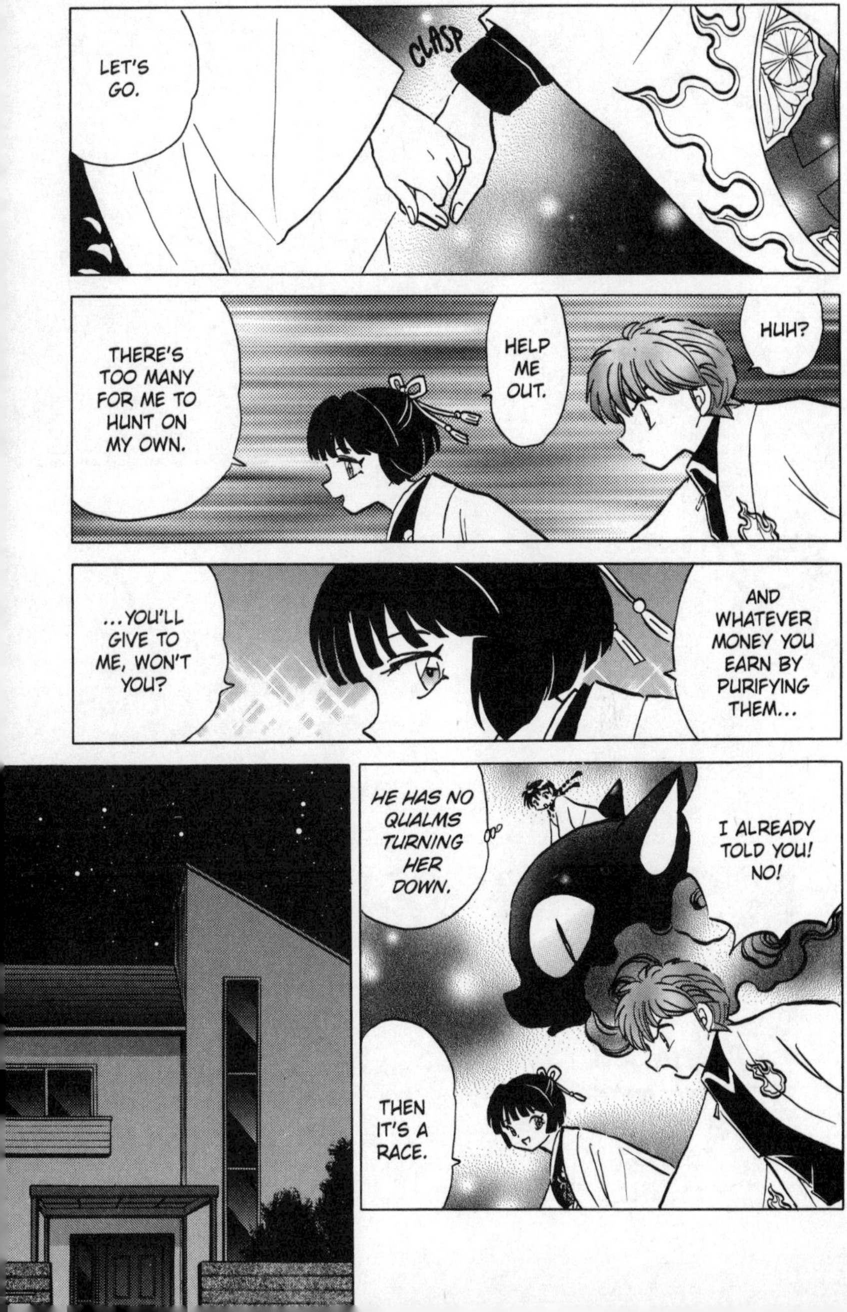
CLASP
LET'S GO.
HUH?
HELP ME OUT.
THERE'S TOO MANY FOR ME TO HUNT ON MY OWN.
AND WHATEVER MONEY YOU EARN BY PURIFYING THEM...
...YOU'LL GIVE TO ME, WON'T YOU?
I ALREADY TOLD YOU! NO!
HE HAS NO QUALMS TURNING HER DOWN.
THEN IT'S A RACE.

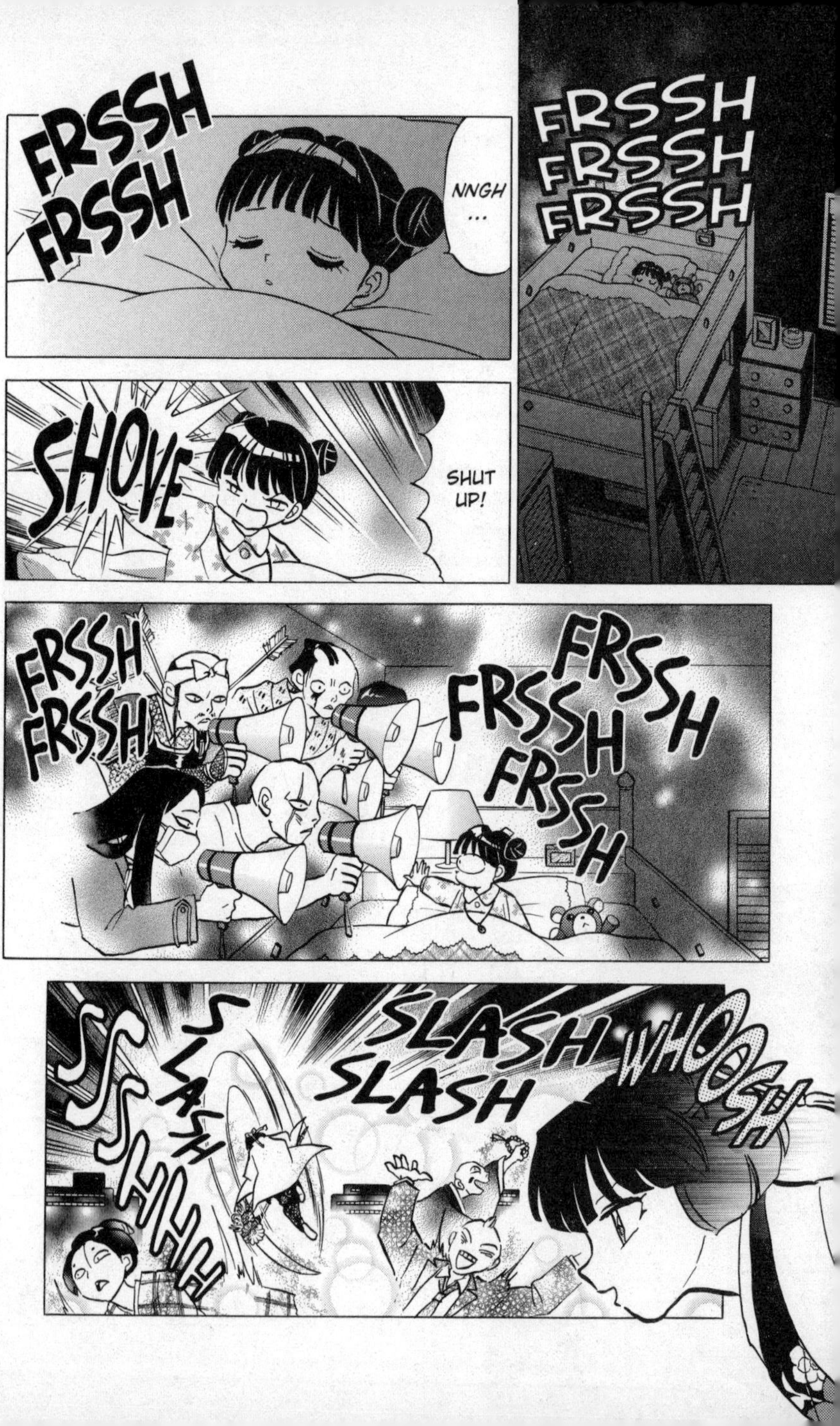
FRSSH
FRSSH
FRSSH
NNGH ...
FRSSH
FRSSH
SHUT UP!
SHOVE
FRSSH
FRSSH
FRSSH
FRSSH
FRSSH
FRSSH
WHOOSH
SLASH
SLASH
SLASH
SSSHHHH

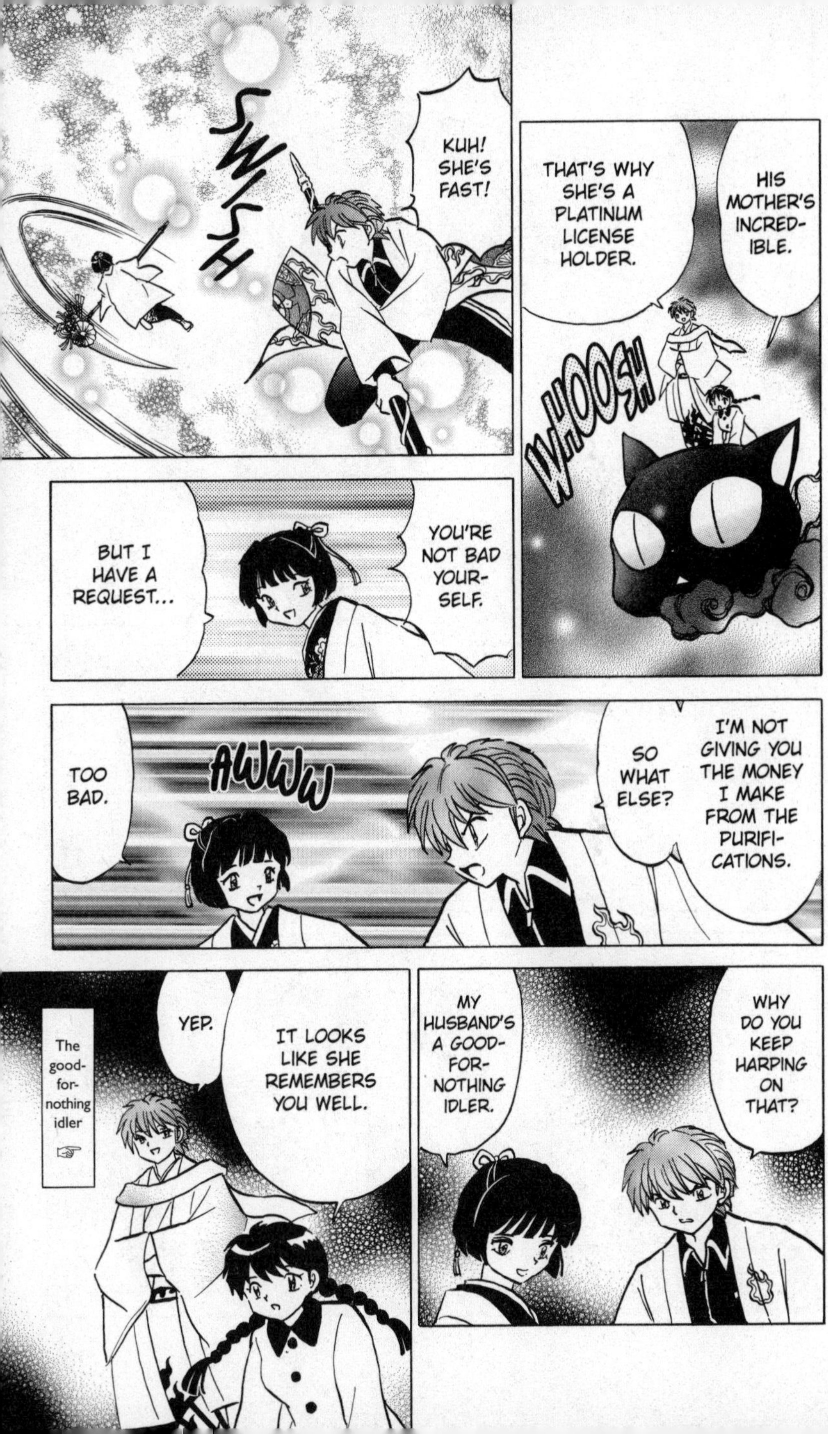
HIS MOTHER'S INCRED-IBLE.
THAT'S WHY SHE'S A PLATINUM LICENSE HOLDER.
WHOOSH
SWISH
KUH! SHE'S FAST!
YOU'RE NOT BAD YOUR-SELF.
BUT I HAVE A REQUEST...
I'M NOT GIVING YOU THE MONEY I MAKE FROM THE PURIFI-CATIONS.
SO WHAT ELSE?
AWWW
TOO BAD.
WHY DO YOU KEEP HARPING ON THAT?
MY HUSBAND'S A GOOD-FOR-NOTHING IDLER.
IT LOOKS LIKE SHE REMEMBERS YOU WELL.
YEP.
The good-for-nothing idler ☞

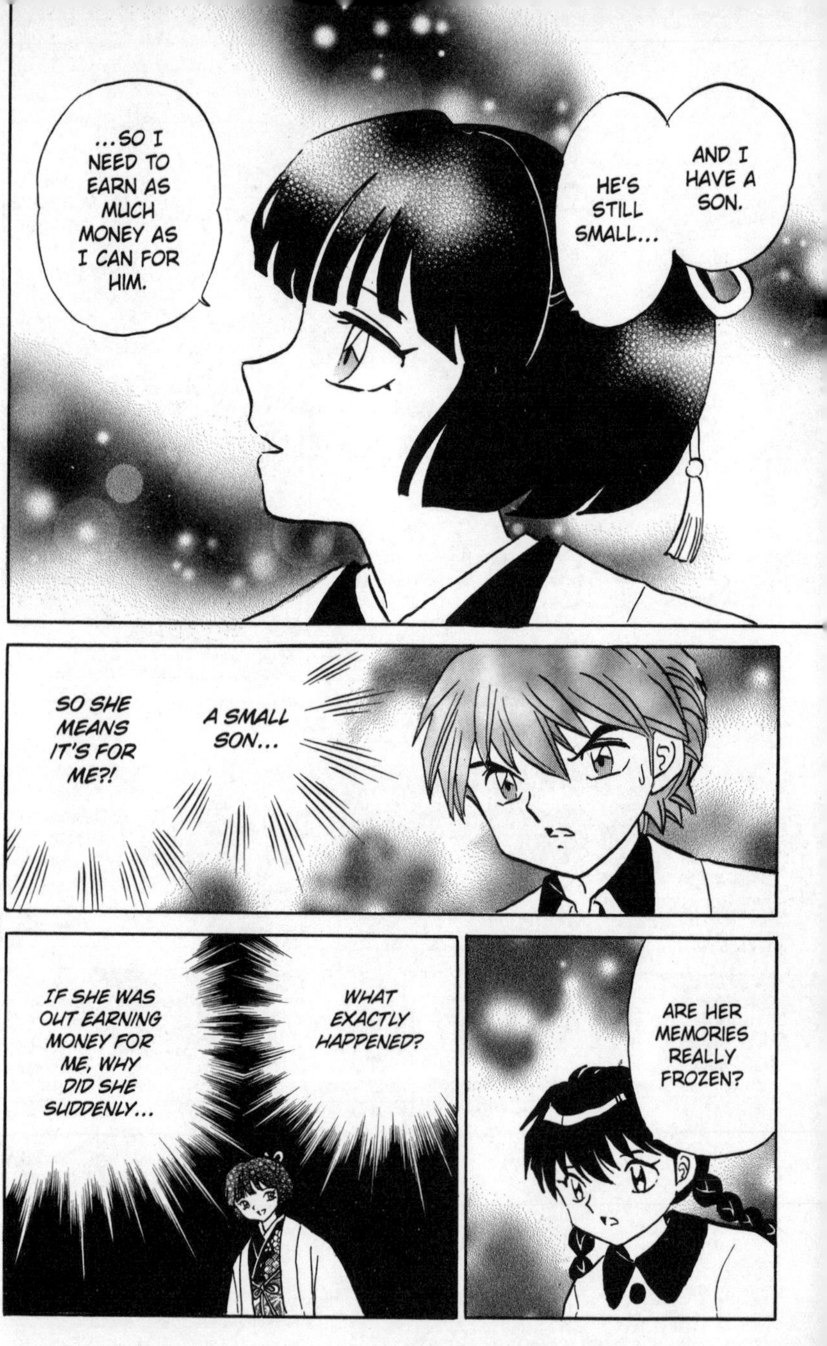
AND I HAVE A SON.
HE'S STILL SMALL...
...SO I NEED TO EARN AS MUCH MONEY AS I CAN FOR HIM.
A SMALL SON...
SO SHE MEANS IT'S FOR ME?!
ARE HER MEMORIES REALLY FROZEN?
WHAT EXACTLY HAPPENED?
IF SHE WAS OUT EARNING MONEY FOR ME, WHY DID SHE SUDDENLY...

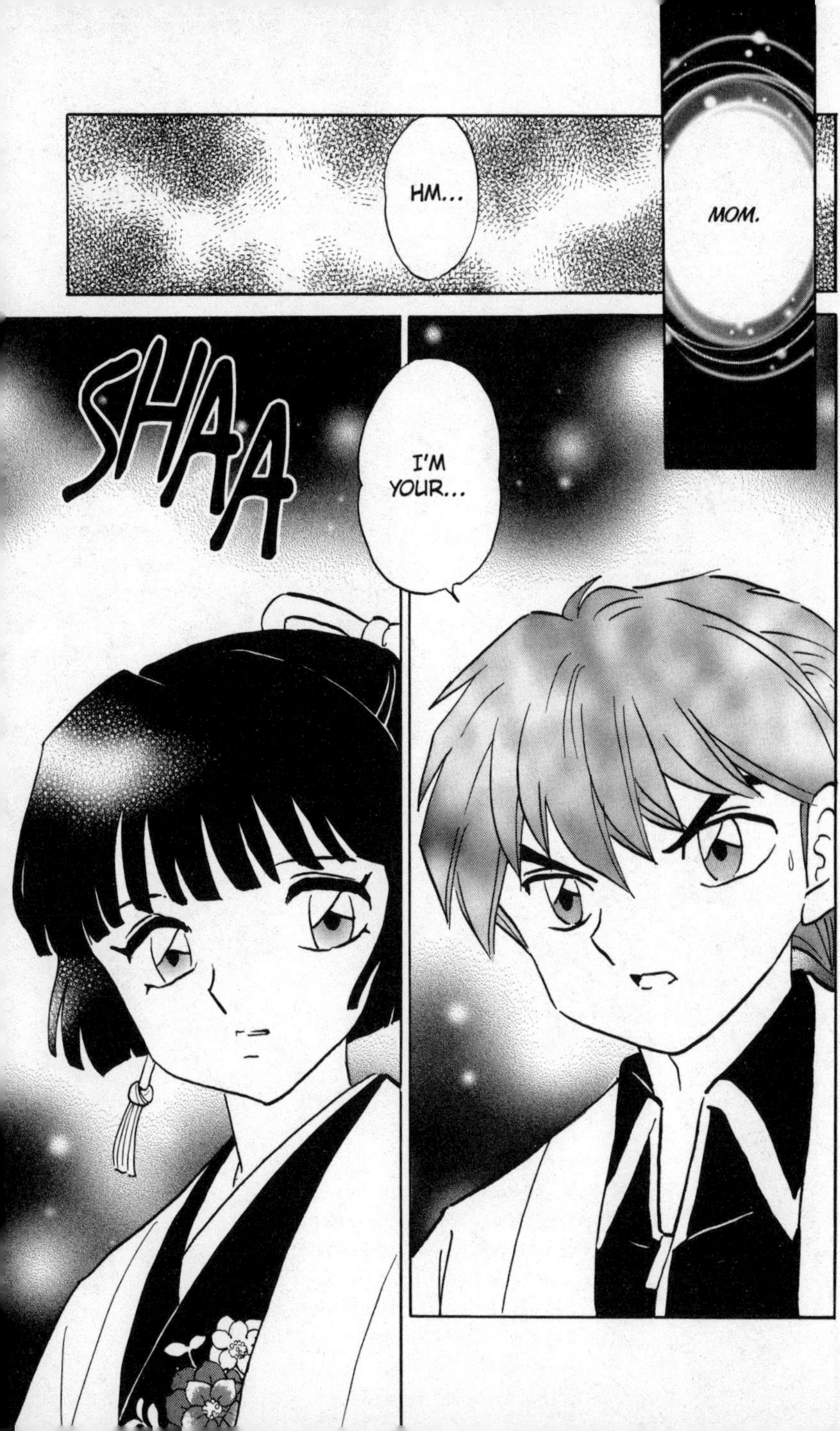
MOM.
HM...
I'M YOUR...
SHAA

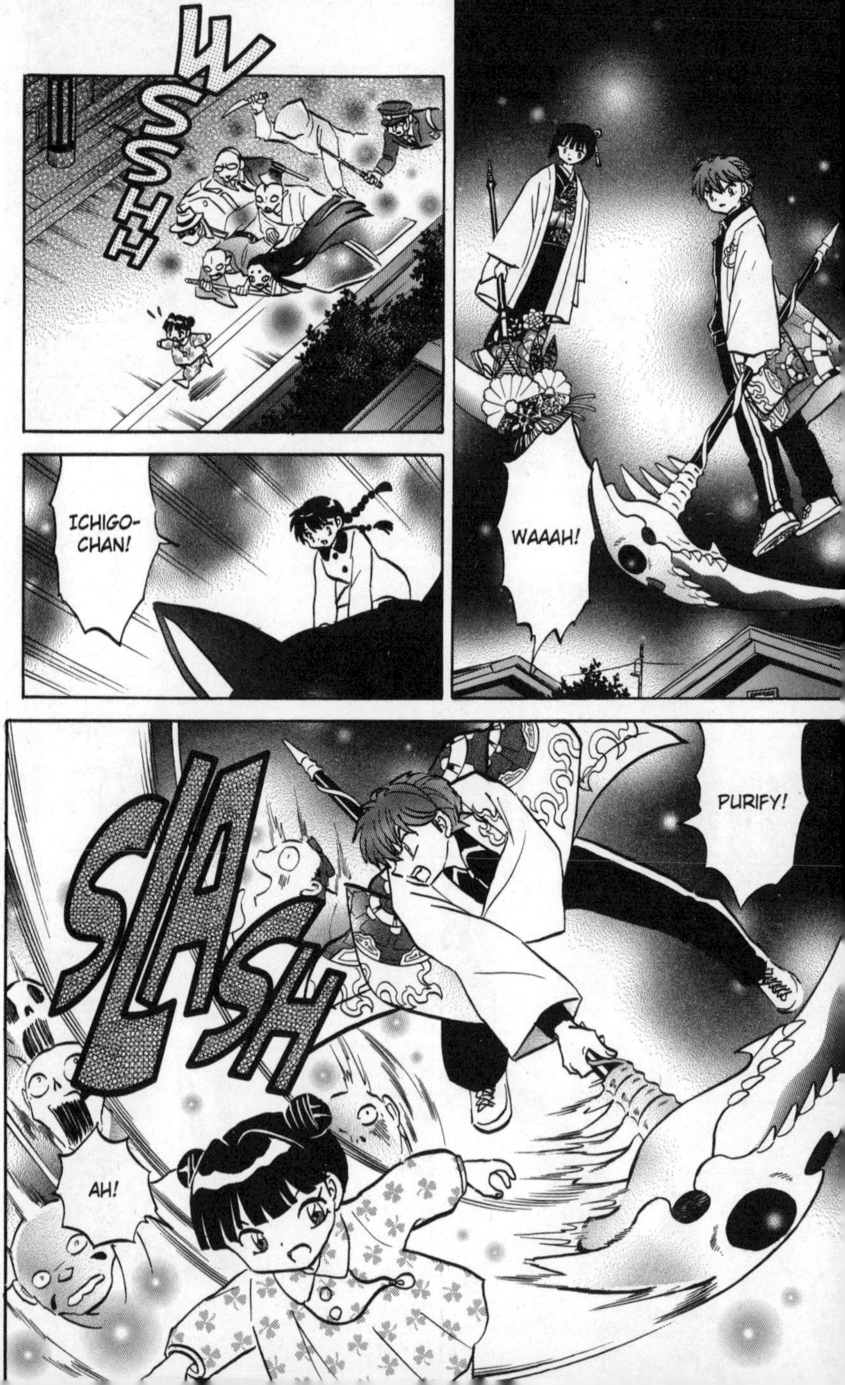
WAAAH!
WSSHHH
ICHIGO-CHAN!
PURIFY!
SLASH
AH!

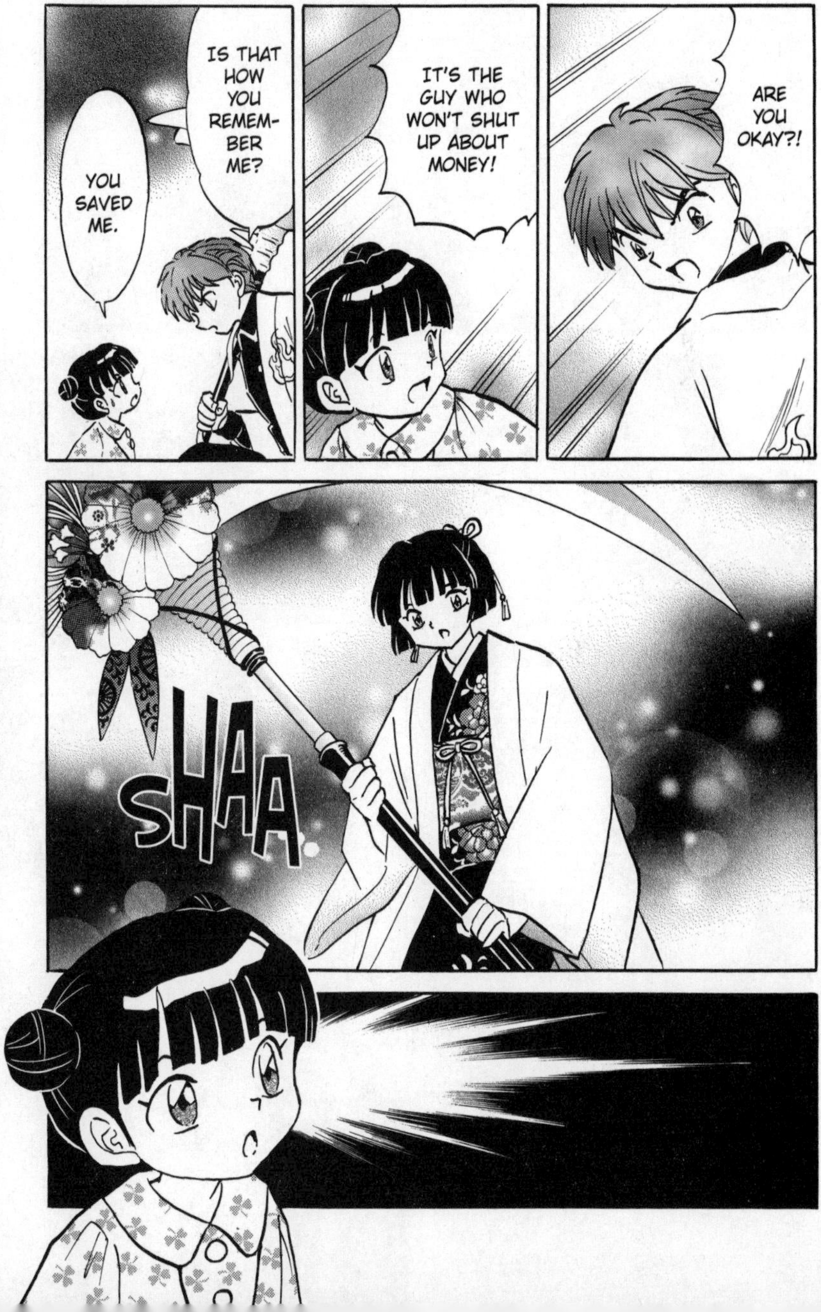
ARE YOU OKAY?!
IT'S THE GUY WHO WON'T SHUT UP ABOUT MONEY!
IS THAT HOW YOU REMEMBER ME?
YOU SAVED ME.
SHAA

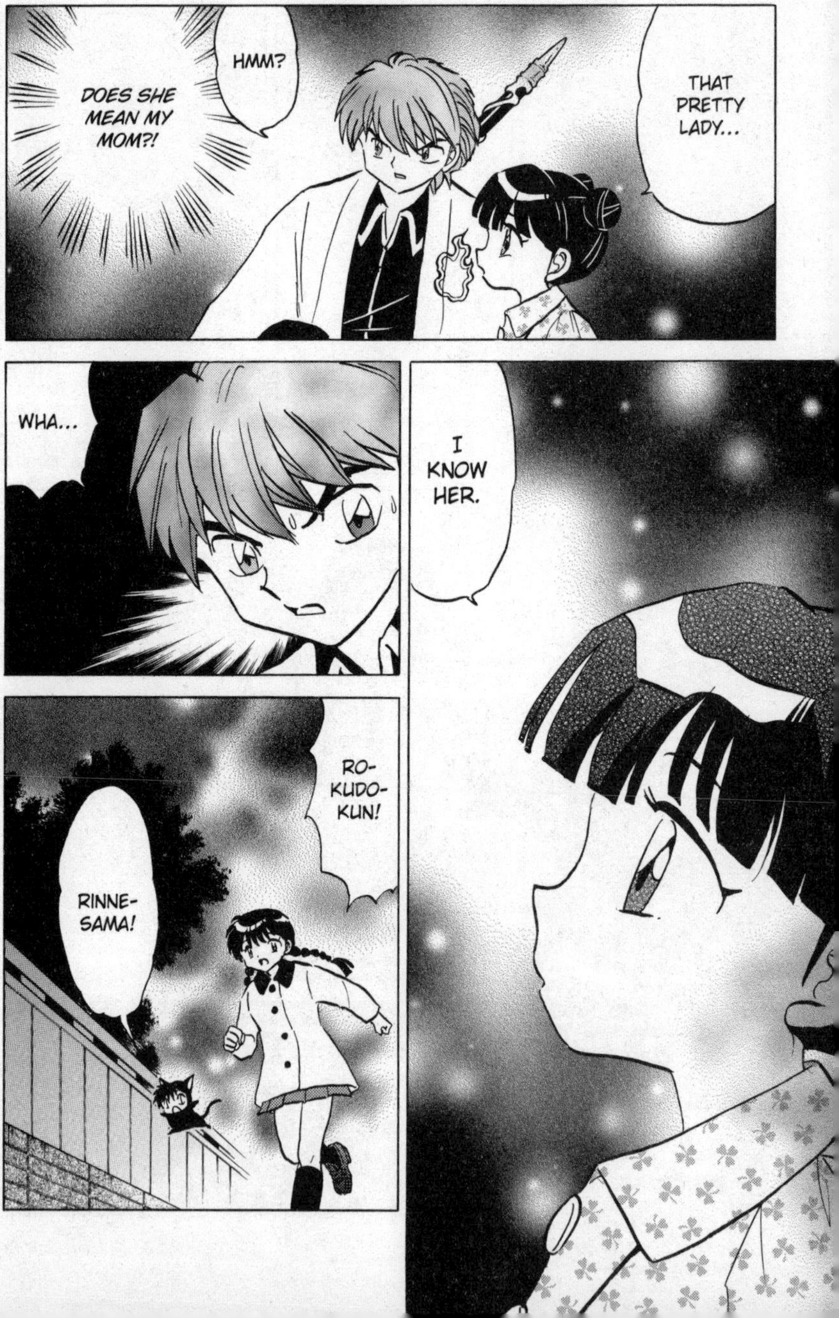
THAT PRETTY LADY...
HMM?
DOES SHE MEAN MY MOM?!
I KNOW HER.
WHA...
RO-KUDO-KUN!
RINNE-SAMA!

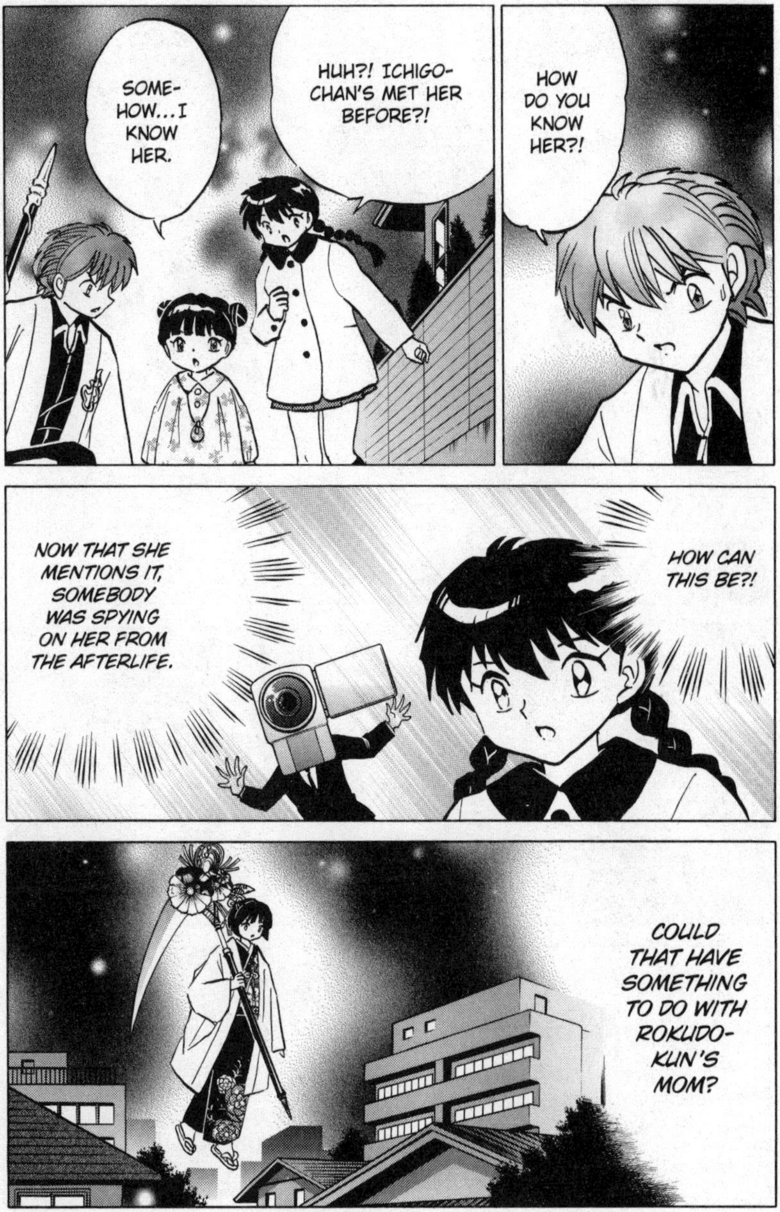
HOW DO YOU KNOW HER?!
HUH?! ICHIGO-CHAN'S MET HER BEFORE?!
SOME-HOW...I KNOW HER.
HOW CAN THIS BE?!
NOW THAT SHE MENTIONS IT, SOMEBODY WAS SPYING ON HER FROM THE AFTERLIFE.
COULD THAT HAVE SOMETHING TO DO WITH ROKUDO-KUN'S MOM?

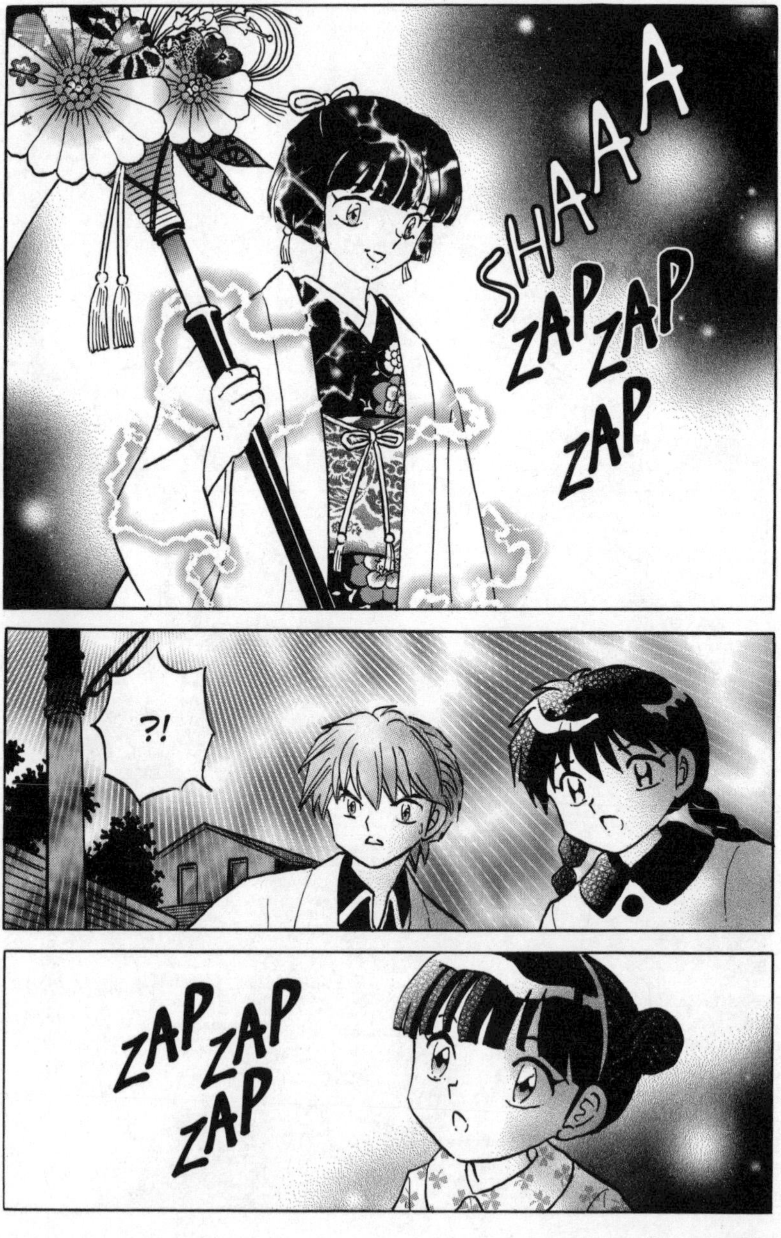
SHAAA
ZAP ZAP ZAP
?!
ZAP ZAP ZAP

CHAPTER 316: THE DETAILS OF HER DISAPPEARANCE

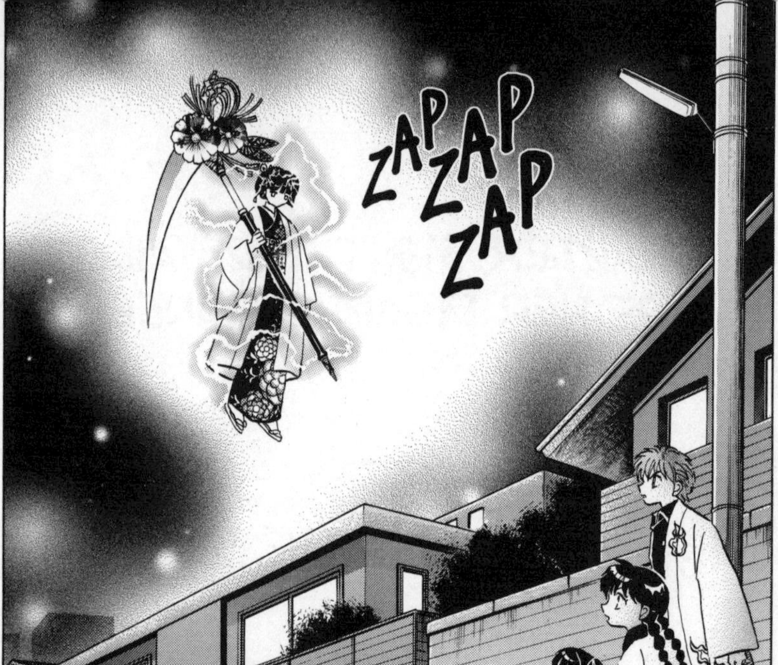
ZAP ZAP ZAP
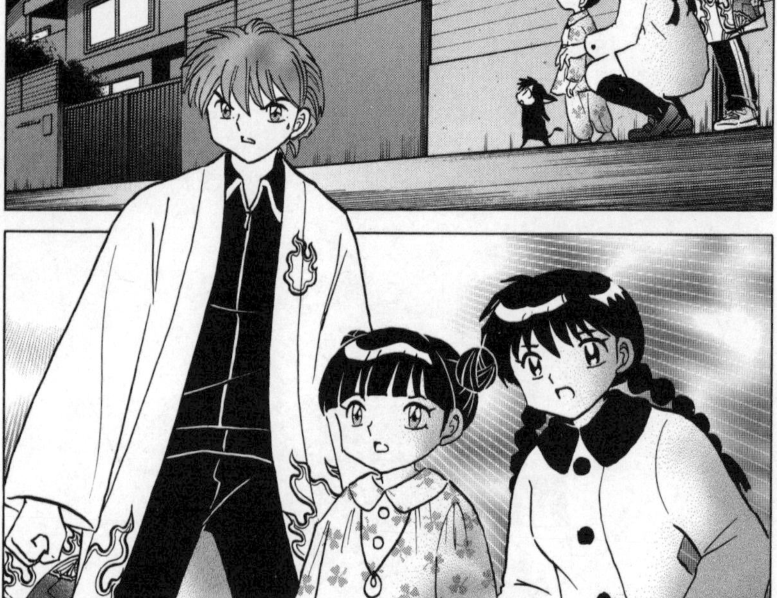

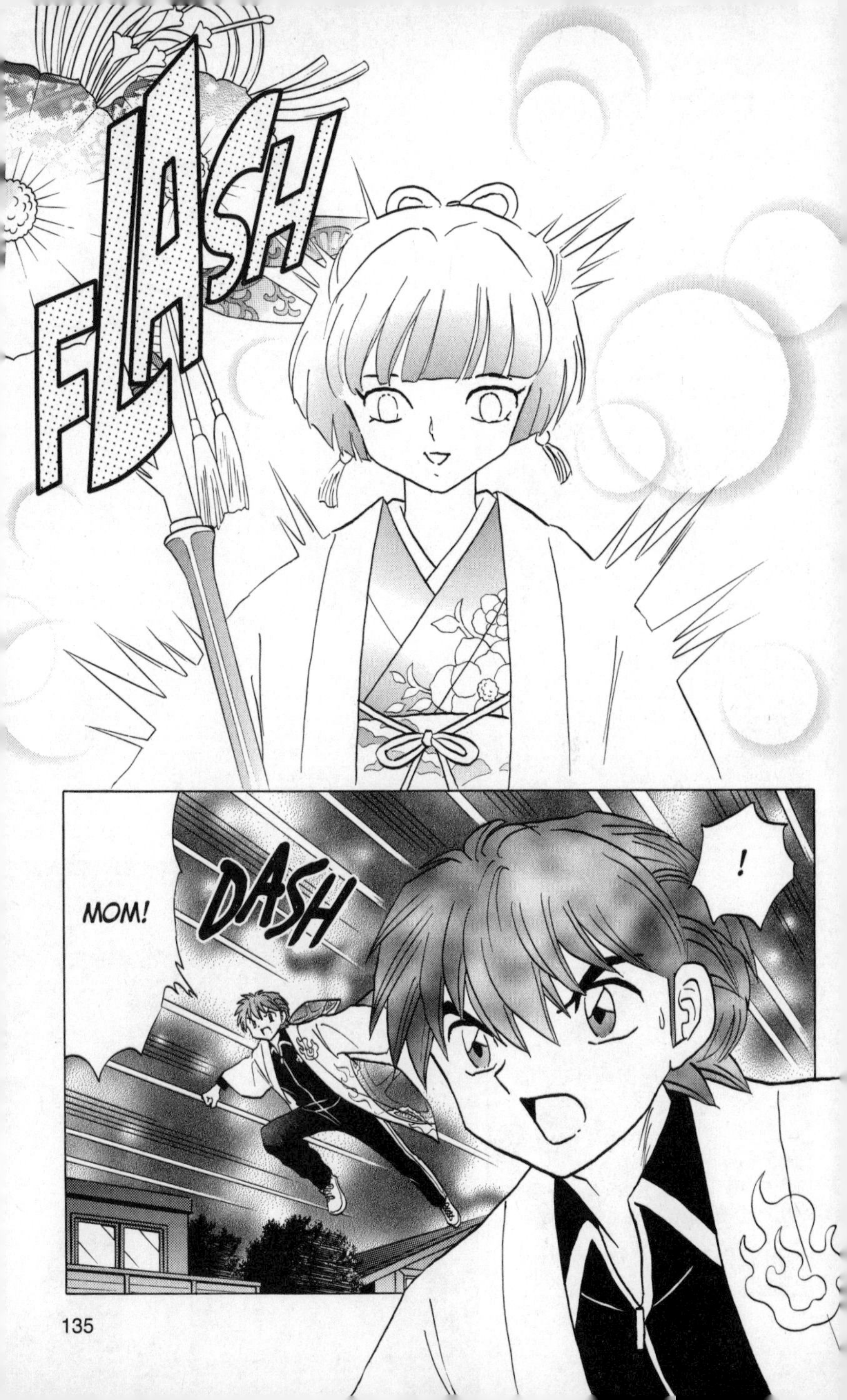
FLASH
!
DASH
MOM!

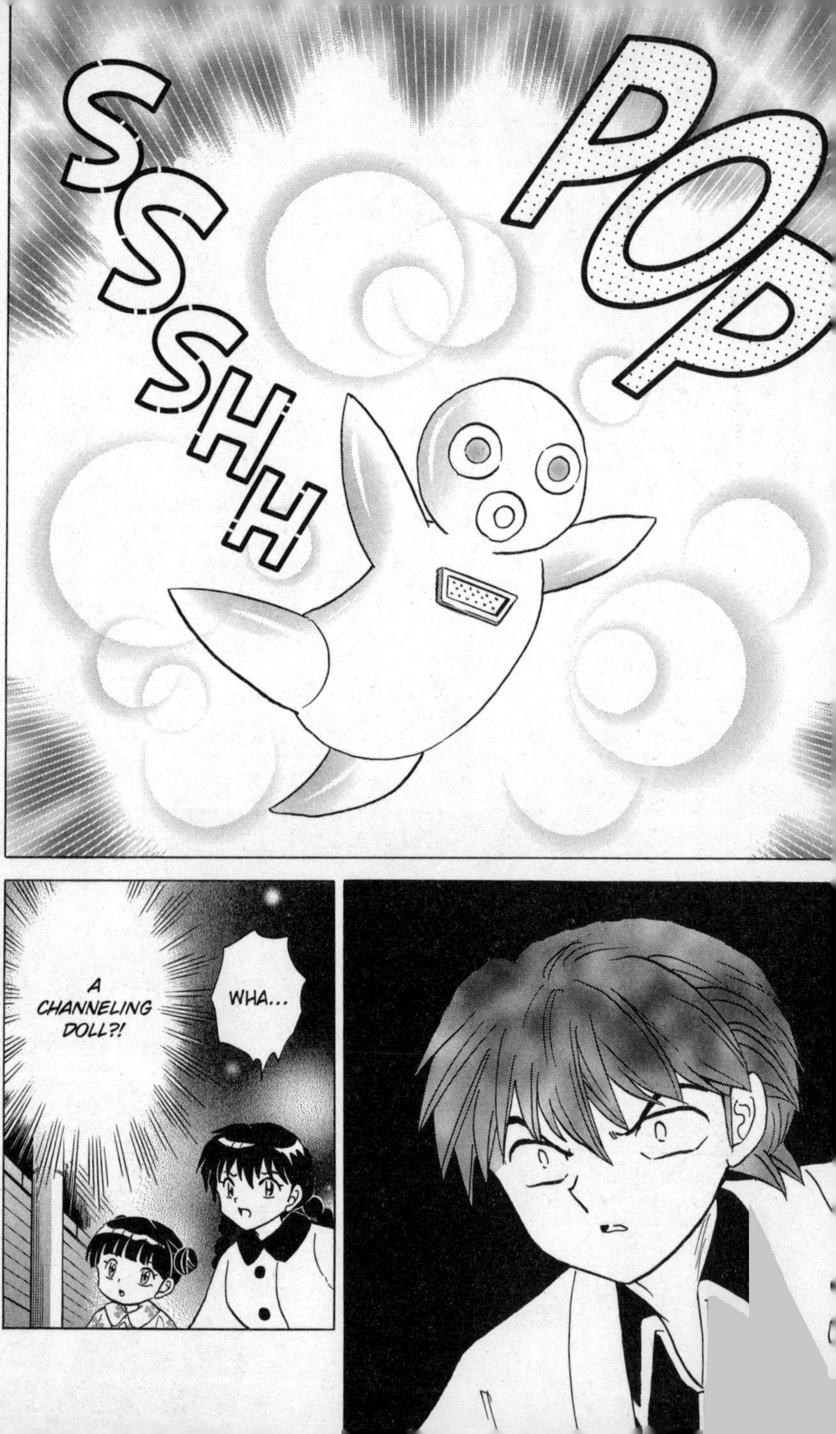
POP
SSSHHH
WHA...
A CHANNELING DOLL?!

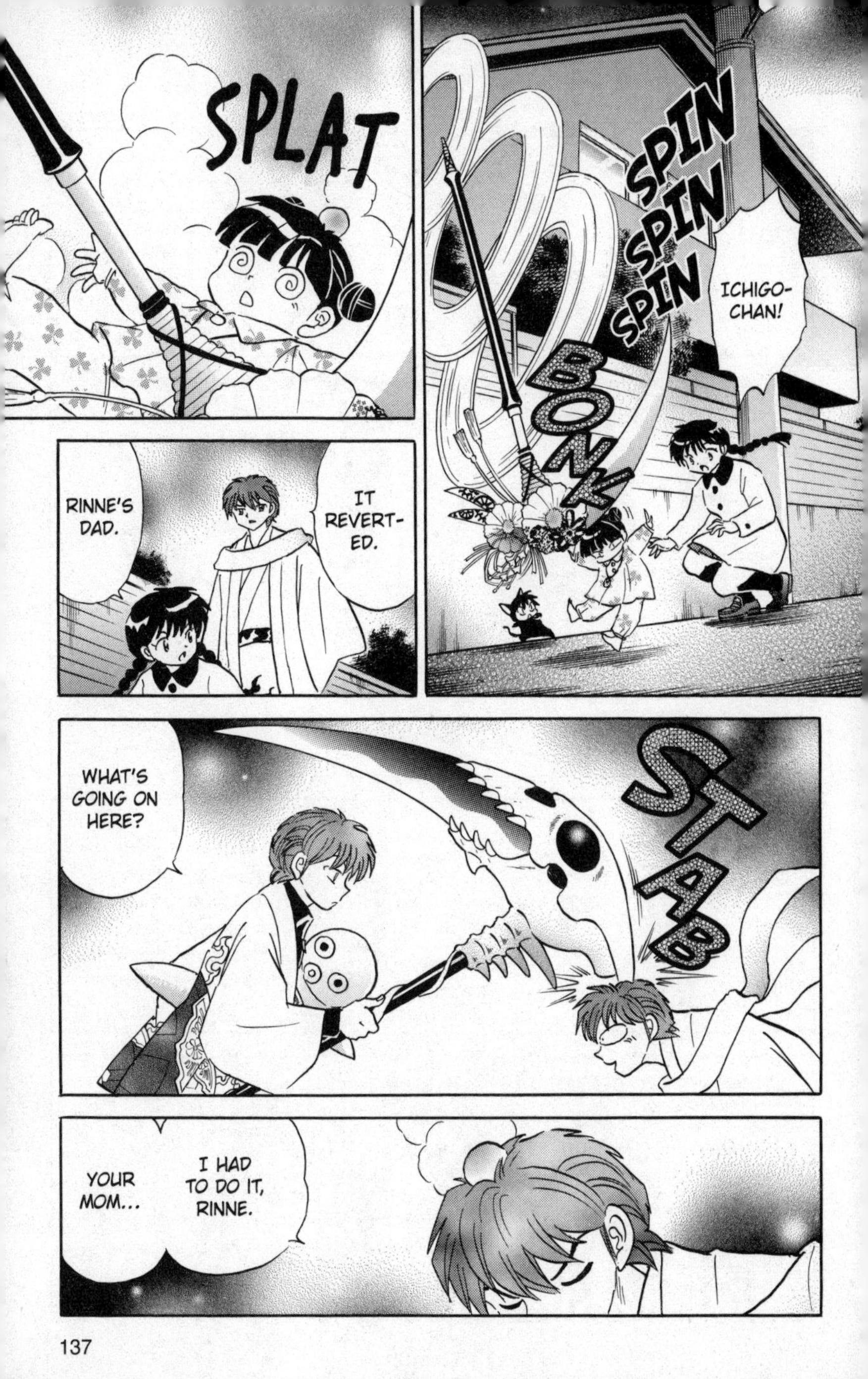
SPIN
SPIN
SPIN
ICHIGO-CHAN!
BONK
SPLAT
IT REVERT-ED.
RINNE'S DAD.
STAB
WHAT'S GOING ON HERE?
I HAD TO DO IT, RINNE.
YOUR MOM...

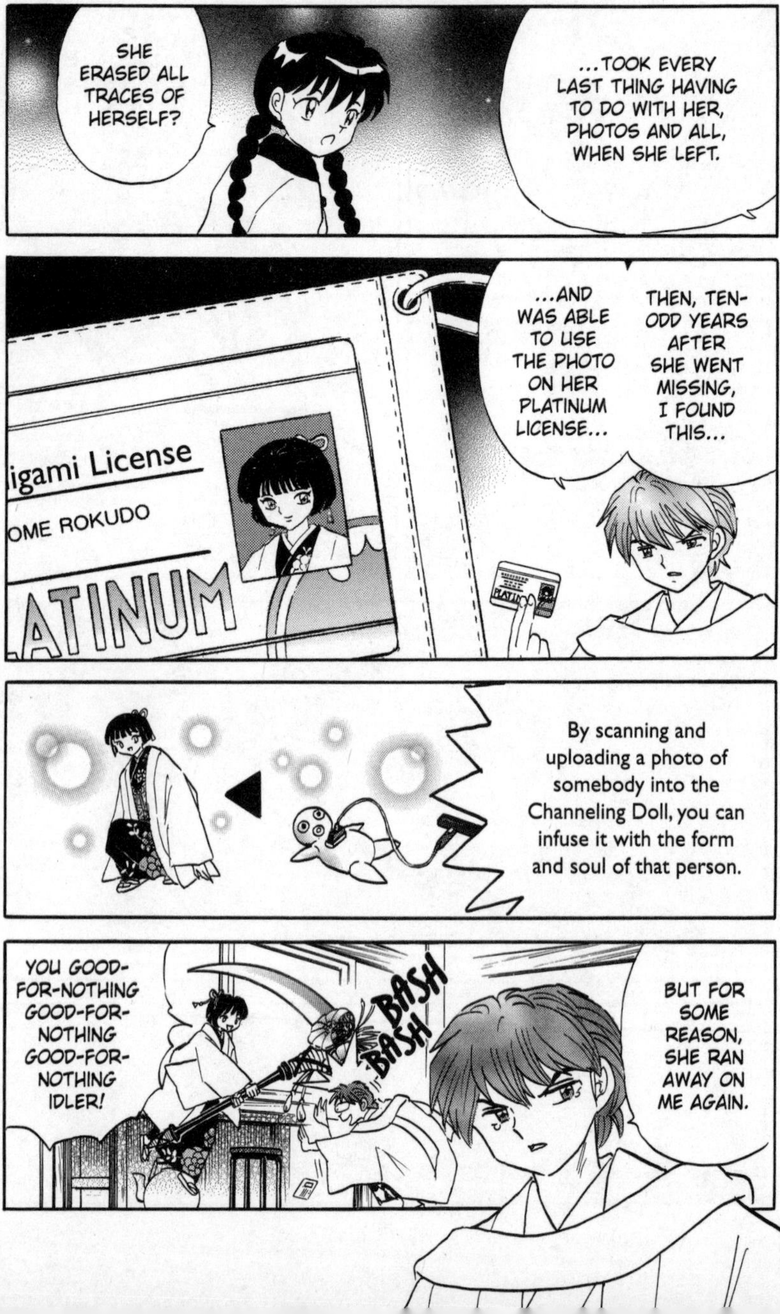
...TOOK EVERY LAST THING HAVING TO DO WITH HER, PHOTOS AND ALL, WHEN SHE LEFT.
SHE ERASED ALL TRACES OF HERSELF?
THEN, TEN-ODD YEARS AFTER SHE WENT MISSING, I FOUND THIS...
...AND WAS ABLE TO USE THE PHOTO ON HER PLATINUM LICENSE...
igami License
OME ROKUDO
ATINUM
By scanning and uploading a photo of somebody into the Channeling Doll, you can infuse it with the form and soul of that person.
BUT FOR SOME REASON, SHE RAN AWAY ON ME AGAIN.
BASH
BASH
YOU GOOD-FOR-NOTHING GOOD-FOR-NOTHING GOOD-FOR-NOTHING IDLER!

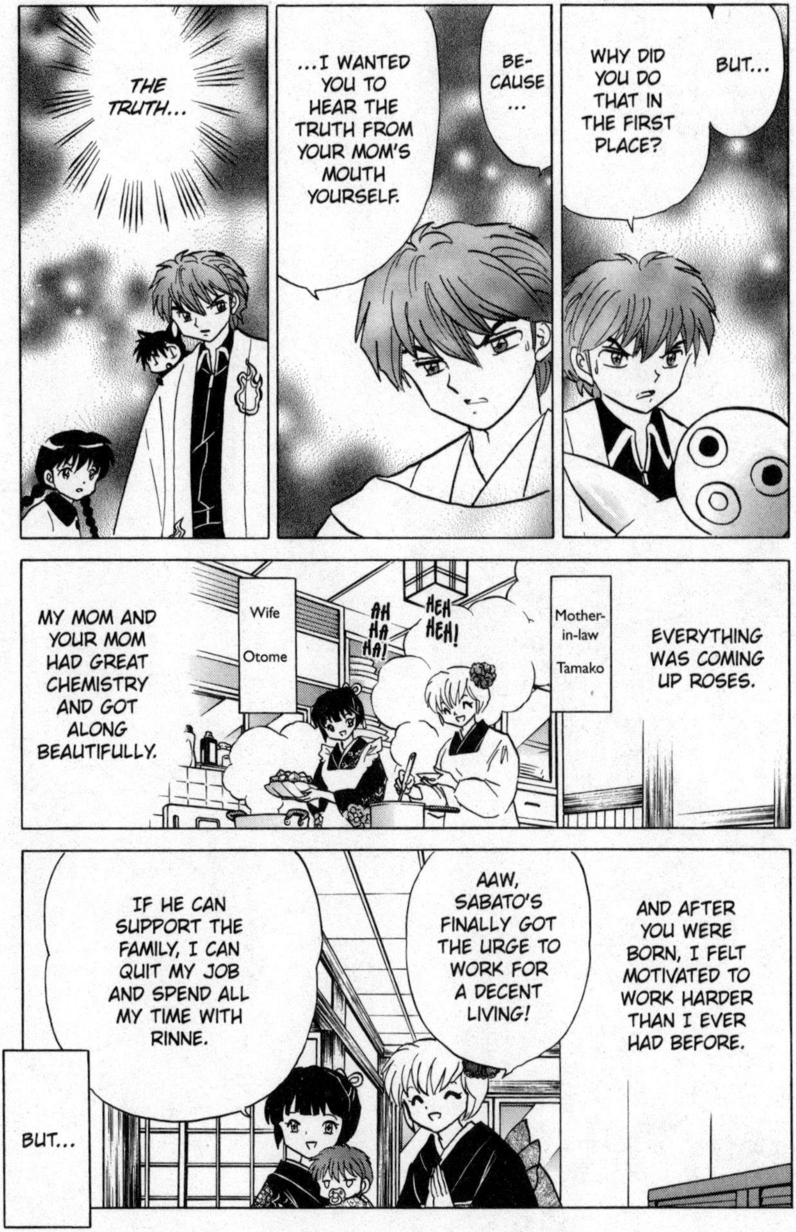
BUT...
WHY DID YOU DO THAT IN THE FIRST PLACE?
BE-CAUSE ...
...I WANTED YOU TO HEAR THE TRUTH FROM YOUR MOM'S MOUTH YOURSELF.
THE TRUTH...
EVERYTHING WAS COMING UP ROSES.
Mother-in-law Tamako
HEH HEH!
AH HA HA!
Wife Otome
MY MOM AND YOUR MOM HAD GREAT CHEMISTRY AND GOT ALONG BEAUTIFULLY.
AND AFTER YOU WERE BORN, I FELT MOTIVATED TO WORK HARDER THAN I EVER HAD BEFORE.
AAW, SABATO'S FINALLY GOT THE URGE TO WORK FOR A DECENT LIVING!
IF HE CAN SUPPORT THE FAMILY, I CAN QUIT MY JOB AND SPEND ALL MY TIME WITH RINNE.
BUT...

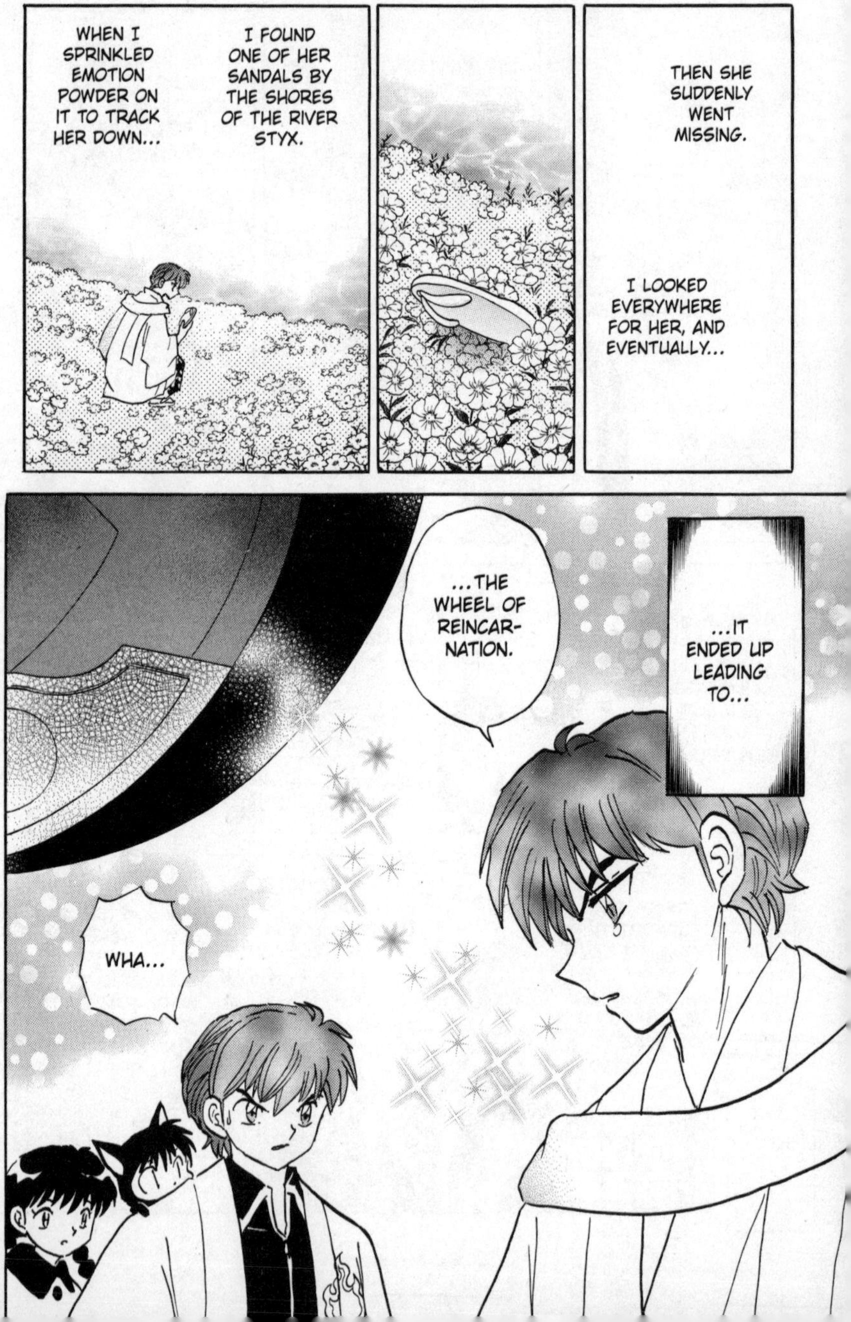
THEN SHE SUDDENLY WENT MISSING.
I LOOKED EVERYWHERE FOR HER, AND EVENTUALLY...
I FOUND ONE OF HER SANDALS BY THE SHORES OF THE RIVER STYX.
WHEN I SPRINKLED EMOTION POWDER ON IT TO TRACK HER DOWN...
...IT ENDED UP LEADING TO...
...THE WHEEL OF REINCAR-NATION.
WHA...

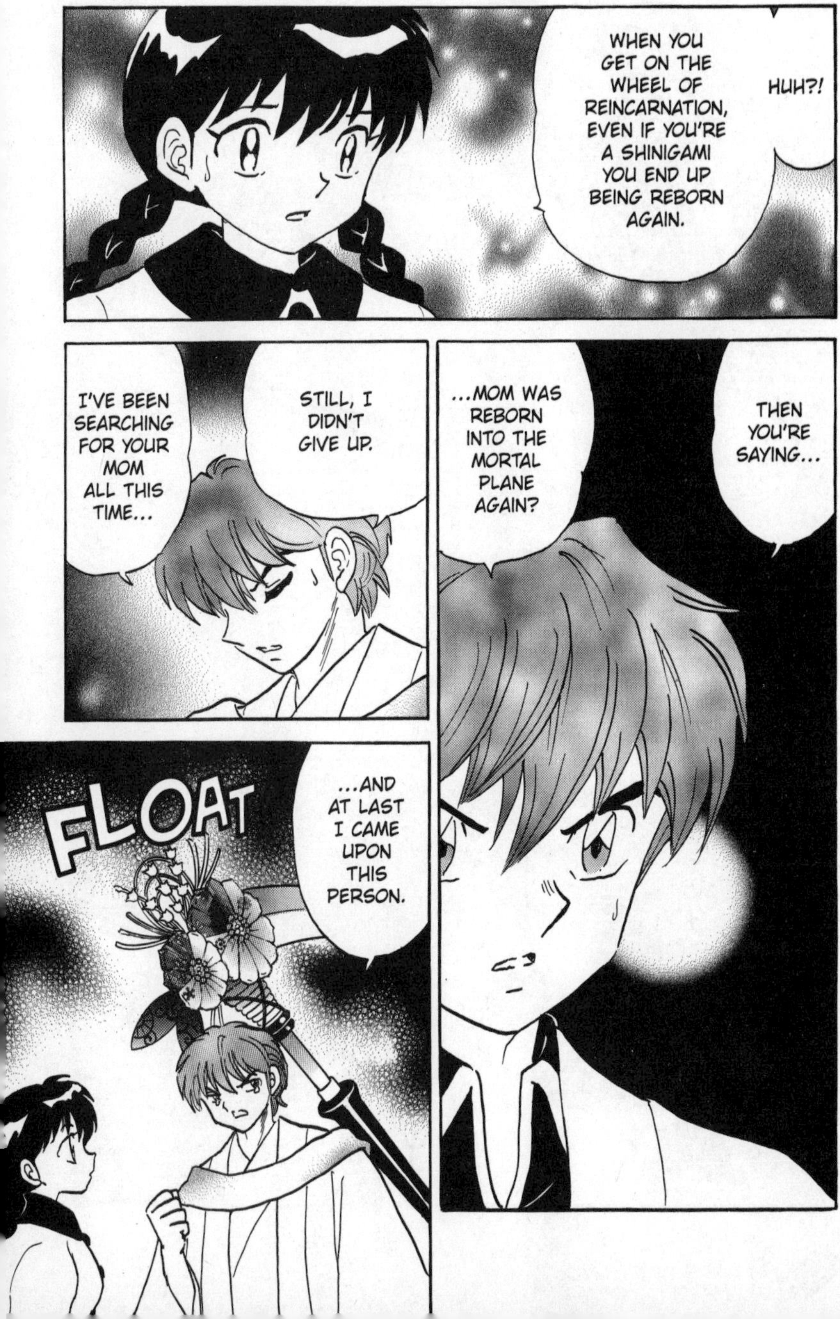
HUH?!
WHEN YOU GET ON THE WHEEL OF REINCARNATION, EVEN IF YOU'RE A SHINIGAMI YOU END UP BEING REBORN AGAIN.
THEN YOU'RE SAYING...
...MOM WAS REBORN INTO THE MORTAL PLANE AGAIN?
STILL, I DIDN'T GIVE UP.
I'VE BEEN SEARCHING FOR YOUR MOM ALL THIS TIME...
...AND AT LAST I CAME UPON THIS PERSON.
FLOAT

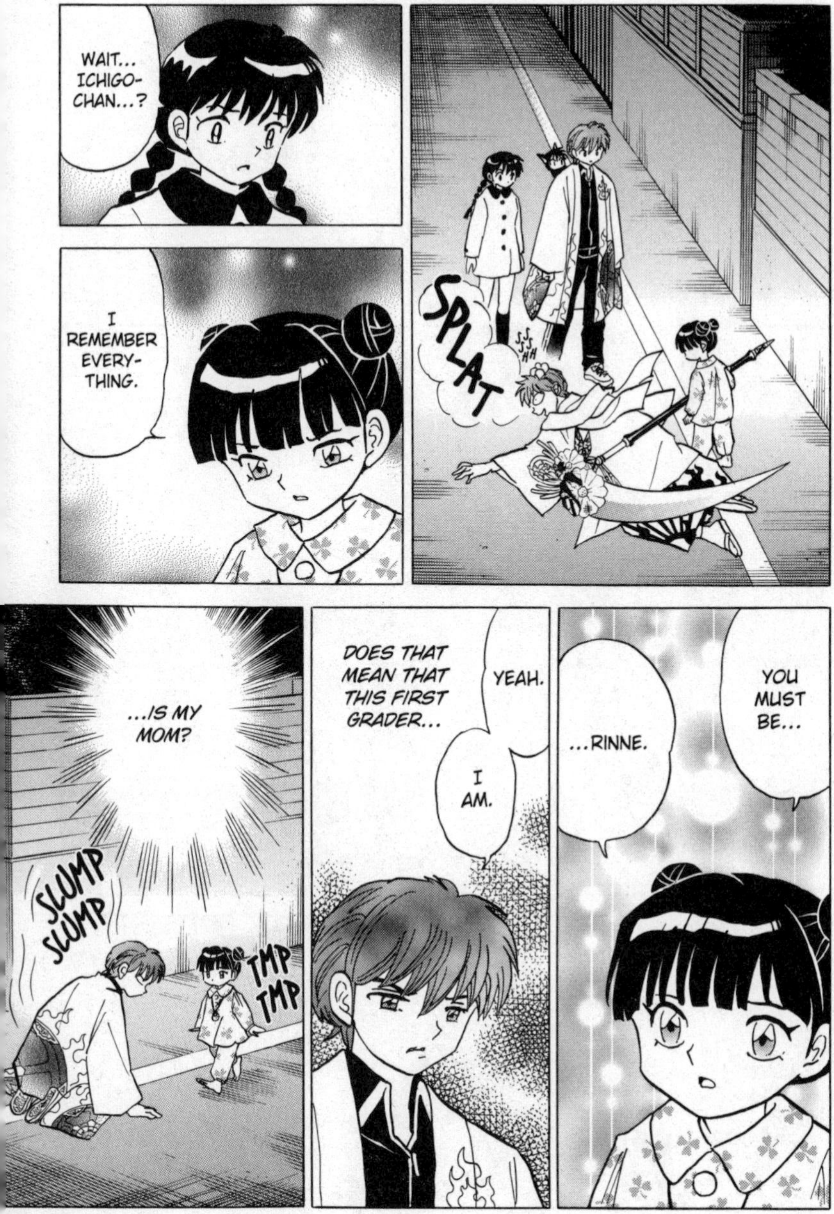
SPLAT
SSSHH
WAIT... ICHIGO-CHAN...?
I REMEMBER EVERY-THING.
YOU MUST BE...
...RINNE.
YEAH.
I AM.
DOES THAT MEAN THAT THIS FIRST GRADER...
...IS MY MOM?
SLUMP SLUMP
TMP TMP

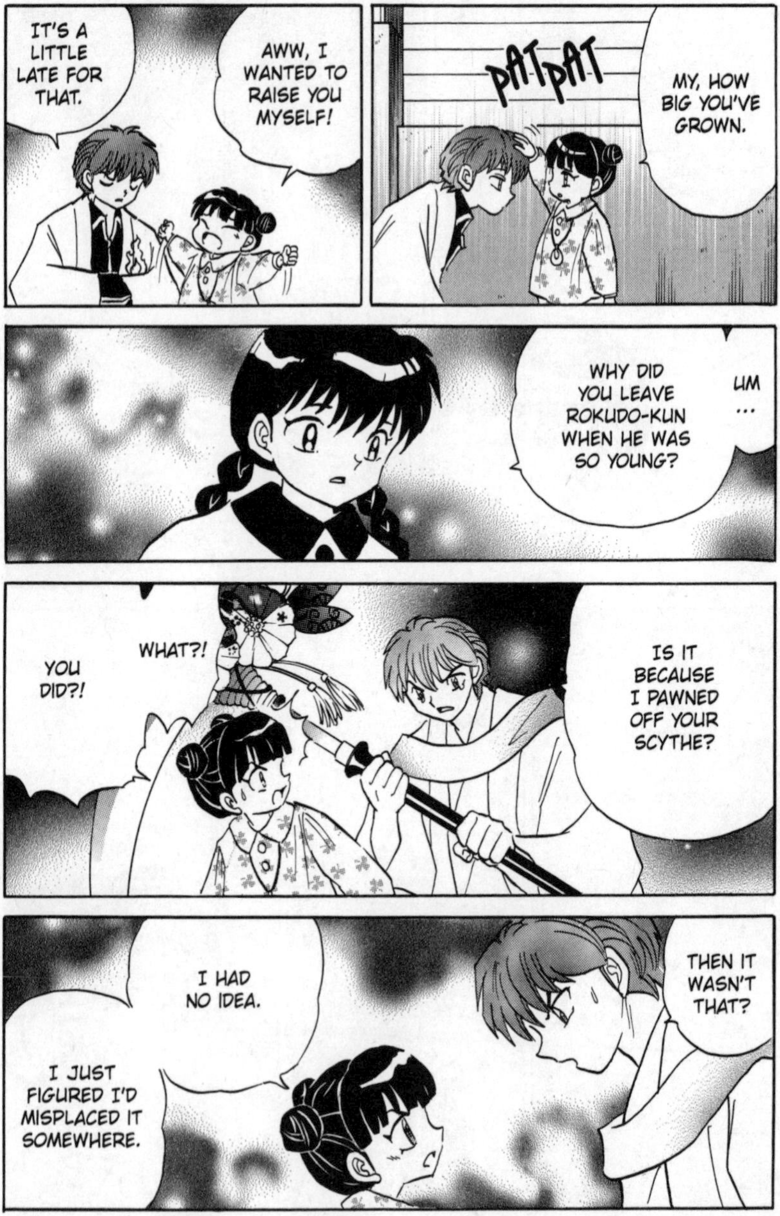
PAT PAT
MY, HOW BIG YOU'VE GROWN.
AWW, I WANTED TO RAISE YOU MYSELF!
IT'S A LITTLE LATE FOR THAT.
UM ...
WHY DID YOU LEAVE ROKUDO-KUN WHEN HE WAS SO YOUNG?
IS IT BECAUSE I PAWNED OFF YOUR SCYTHE?
WHAT?!
YOU DID?!
THEN IT WASN'T THAT?
I HAD NO IDEA.
I JUST FIGURED I'D MISPLACED IT SOMEWHERE.

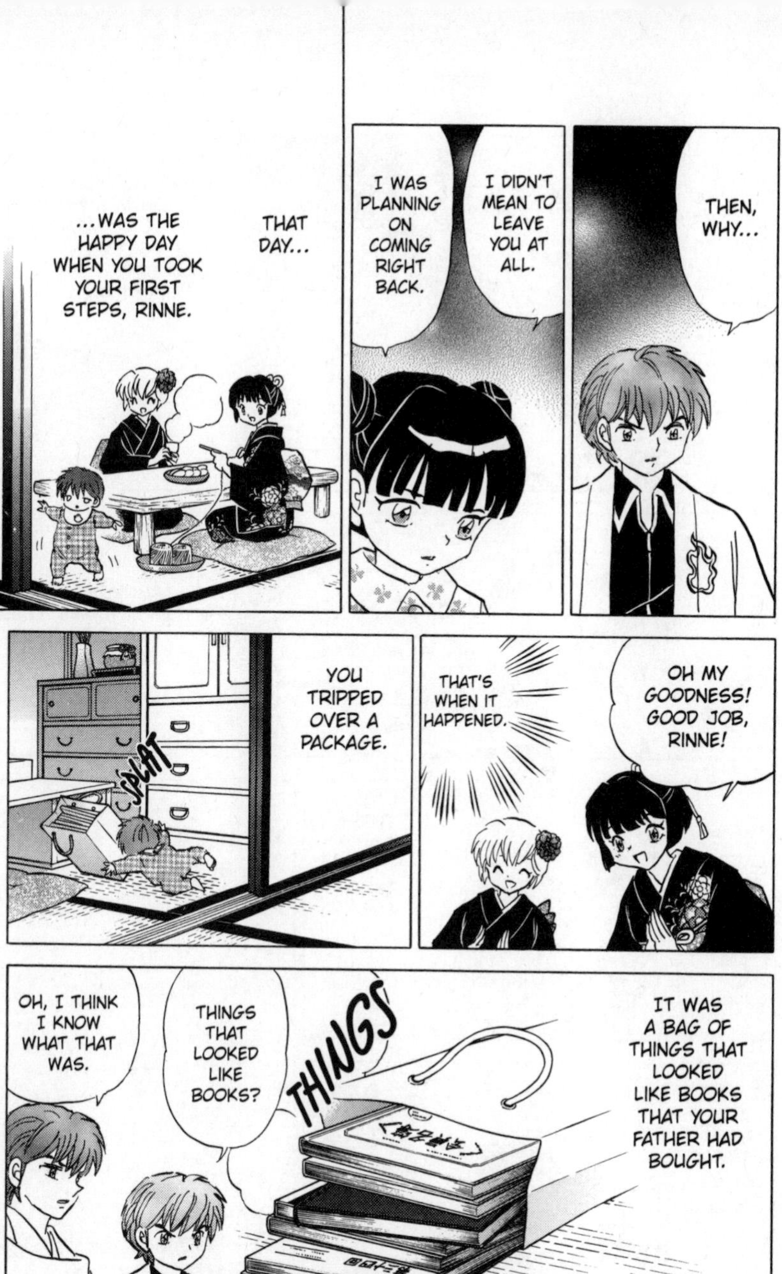
THEN, WHY...
I DIDN'T MEAN TO LEAVE YOU AT ALL.
I WAS PLANNING ON COMING RIGHT BACK.
THAT DAY...
...WAS THE HAPPY DAY WHEN YOU TOOK YOUR FIRST STEPS, RINNE.
OH MY GOODNESS! GOOD JOB, RINNE!
THAT'S WHEN IT HAPPENED.
YOU TRIPPED OVER A PACKAGE.
SPLAT
IT WAS A BAG OF THINGS THAT LOOKED LIKE BOOKS THAT YOUR FATHER HAD BOUGHT.
THINGS
THINGS THAT LOOKED LIKE BOOKS?
OH, I THINK I KNOW WHAT THAT WAS.

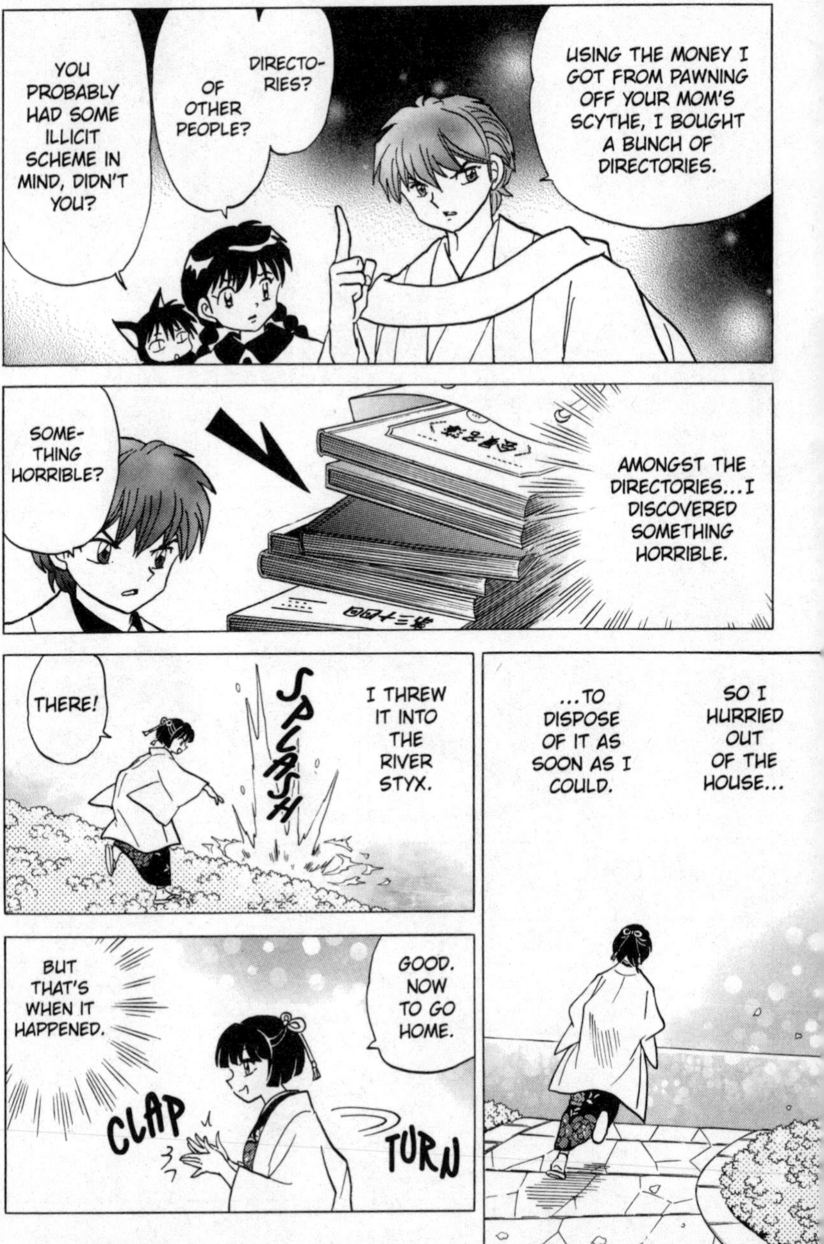
USING THE MONEY I GOT FROM PAWNING OFF YOUR MOM'S SCYTHE, I BOUGHT A BUNCH OF DIRECTORIES.
DIRECTORIES? OF OTHER PEOPLE?
YOU PROBABLY HAD SOME ILLICIT SCHEME IN MIND, DIDN'T YOU?
AMONGST THE DIRECTORIES...I DISCOVERED SOMETHING HORRIBLE.
SOMETHING HORRIBLE?
SO I HURRIED OUT OF THE HOUSE...
...TO DISPOSE OF IT AS SOON AS I COULD.
I THREW IT INTO THE RIVER STYX.
SPLASH
THERE!
GOOD. NOW TO GO HOME.
BUT THAT'S WHEN IT HAPPENED.
CLAP
TURN

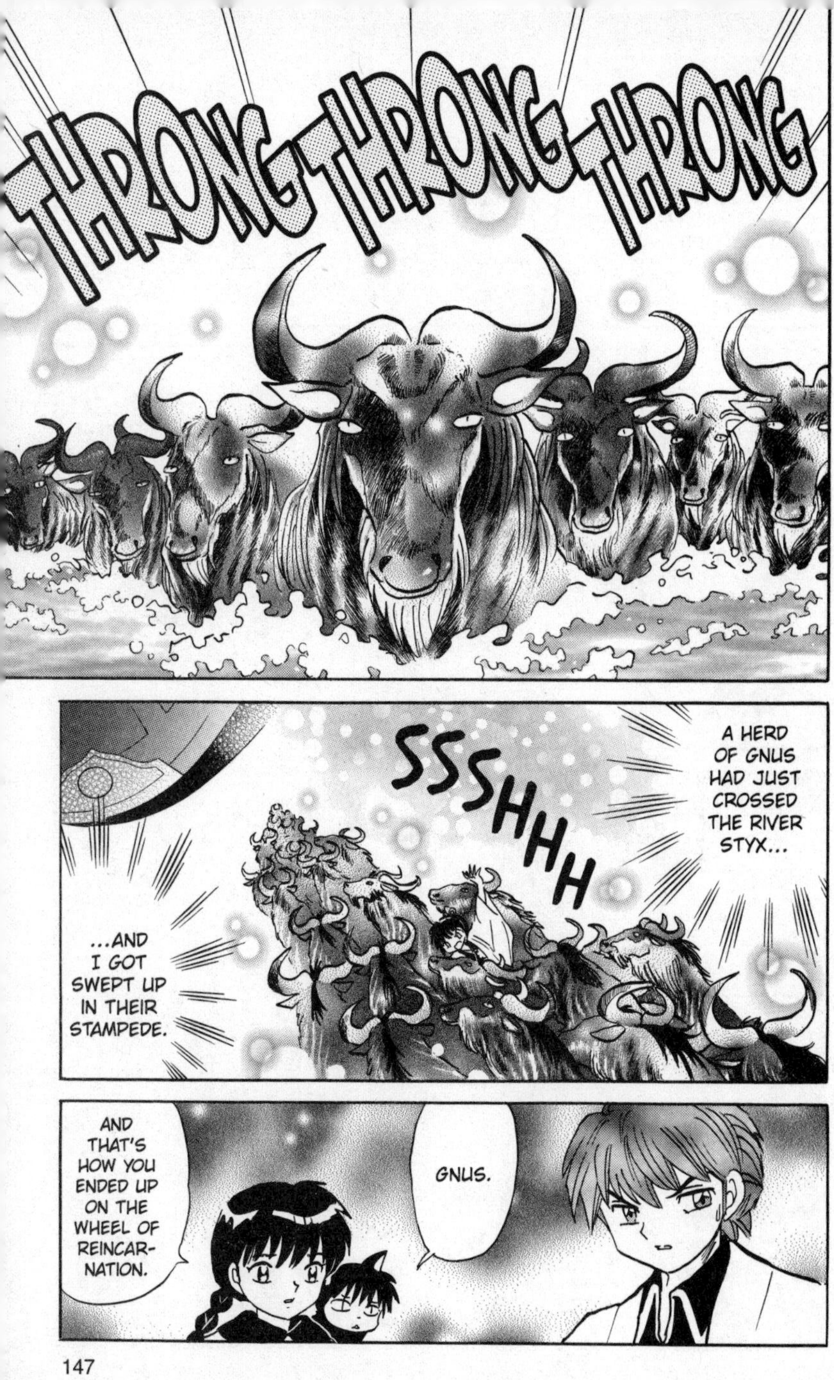
THRONG THRONG THRONG
A HERD OF GNUS HAD JUST CROSSED THE RIVER STYX...
SSSHHH
...AND I GOT SWEPT UP IN THEIR STAMPEDE.
GNUS.
AND THAT'S HOW YOU ENDED UP ON THE WHEEL OF REINCARNATION.

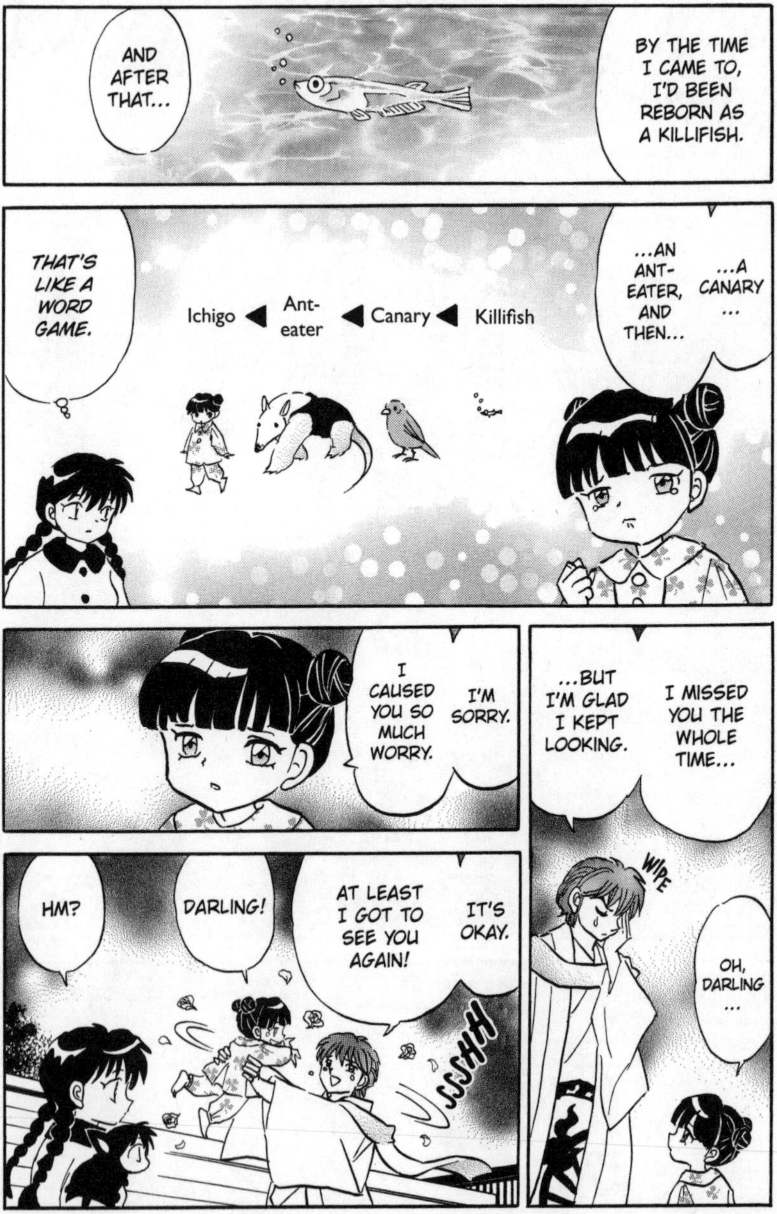
BY THE TIME I CAME TO, I'D BEEN REBORN AS A KILLIFISH.
AND AFTER THAT...
...A CANARY...
...AN ANT-EATER, AND THEN...
Ichigo ◀ Ant-eater ◀ Canary ◀ Killifish
THAT'S LIKE A WORD GAME.
I MISSED YOU THE WHOLE TIME...
...BUT I'M GLAD I KEPT LOOKING.
WIPE
OH, DARLING...
I'M SORRY.
I CAUSED YOU SO MUCH WORRY.
IT'S OKAY.
AT LEAST I GOT TO SEE YOU AGAIN!
DARLING!
HM?
SSHH

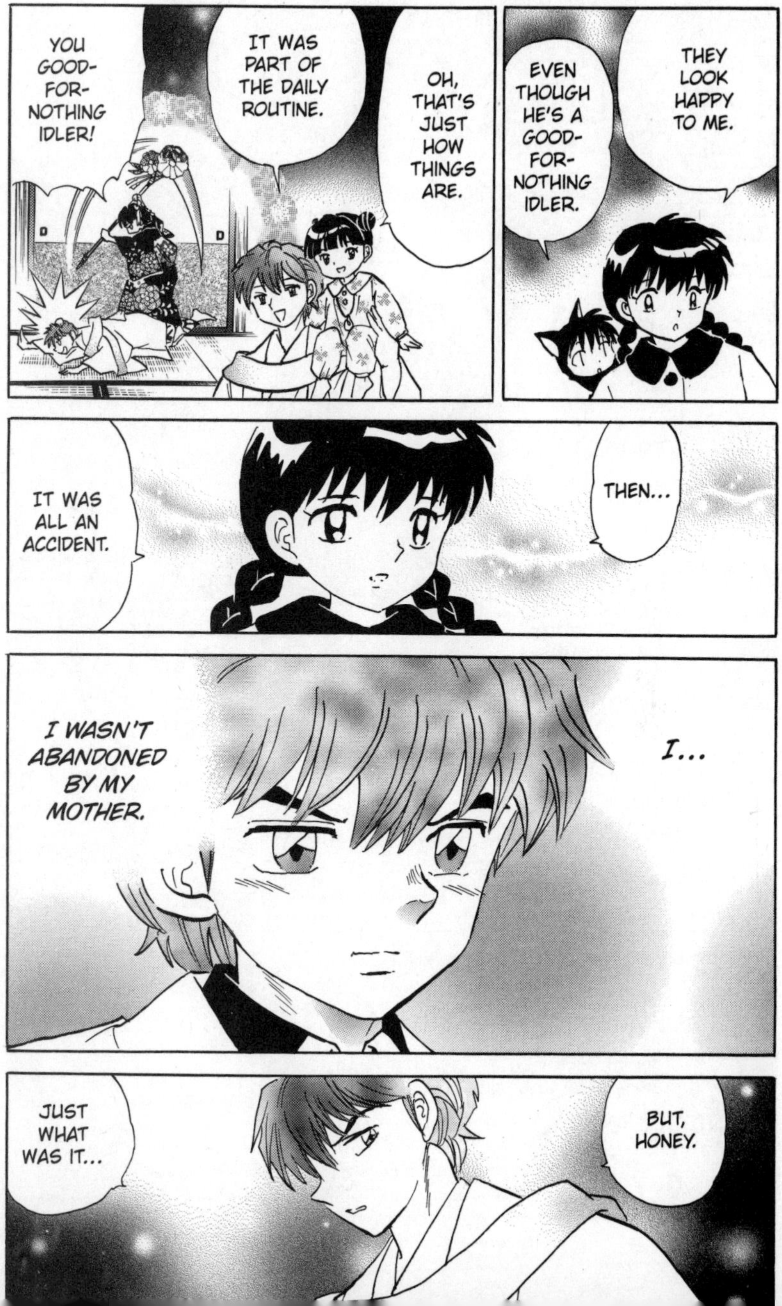
THEY LOOK HAPPY TO ME.
EVEN THOUGH HE'S A GOOD-FOR-NOTHING IDLER.
OH, THAT'S JUST HOW THINGS ARE.
IT WAS PART OF THE DAILY ROUTINE.
YOU GOOD-FOR-NOTHING IDLER!
THEN...
IT WAS ALL AN ACCIDENT.
I...
I WASN'T ABANDONED BY MY MOTHER.
BUT, HONEY.
JUST WHAT WAS IT...

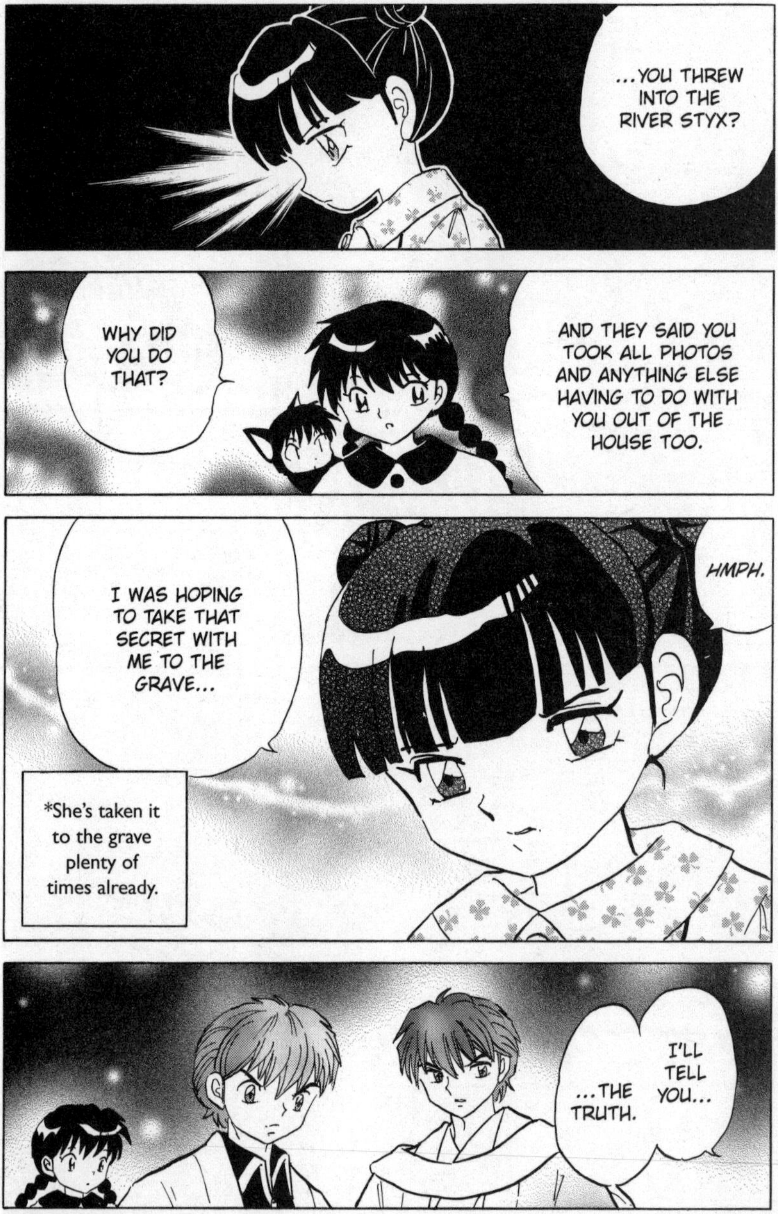
...YOU THREW INTO THE RIVER STYX?
AND THEY SAID YOU TOOK ALL PHOTOS AND ANYTHING ELSE HAVING TO DO WITH YOU OUT OF THE HOUSE TOO.
WHY DID YOU DO THAT?
HMPH.
I WAS HOPING TO TAKE THAT SECRET WITH ME TO THE GRAVE...
*She's taken it to the grave plenty of times already.
I'LL TELL YOU...
...THE TRUTH.

CHAPTER 317: TRUTH AND LIES!

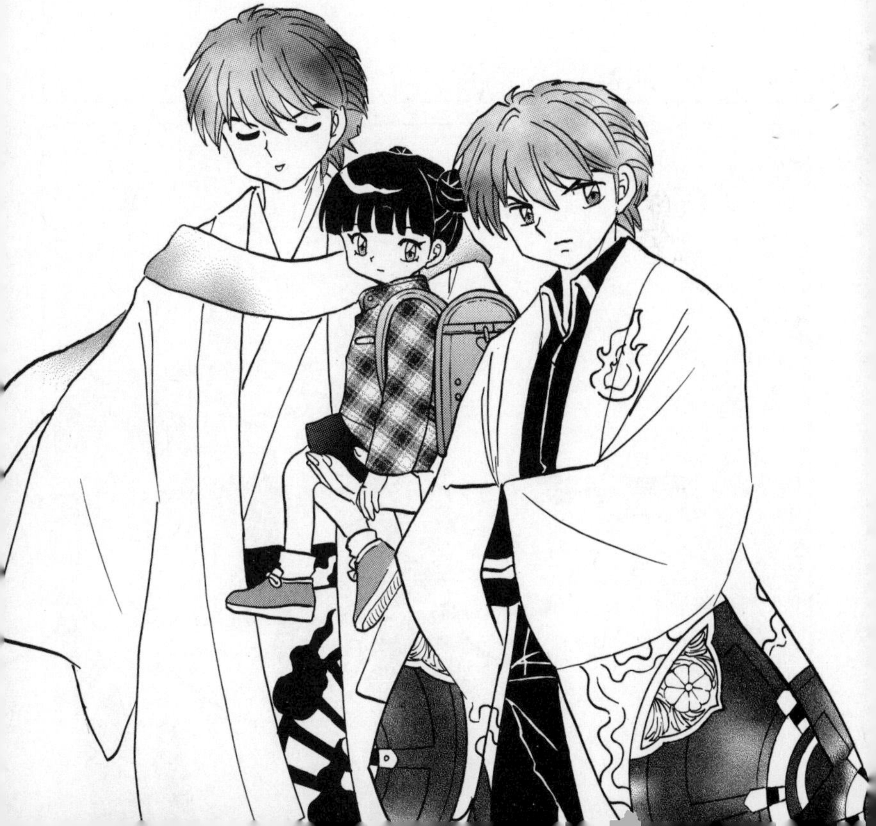

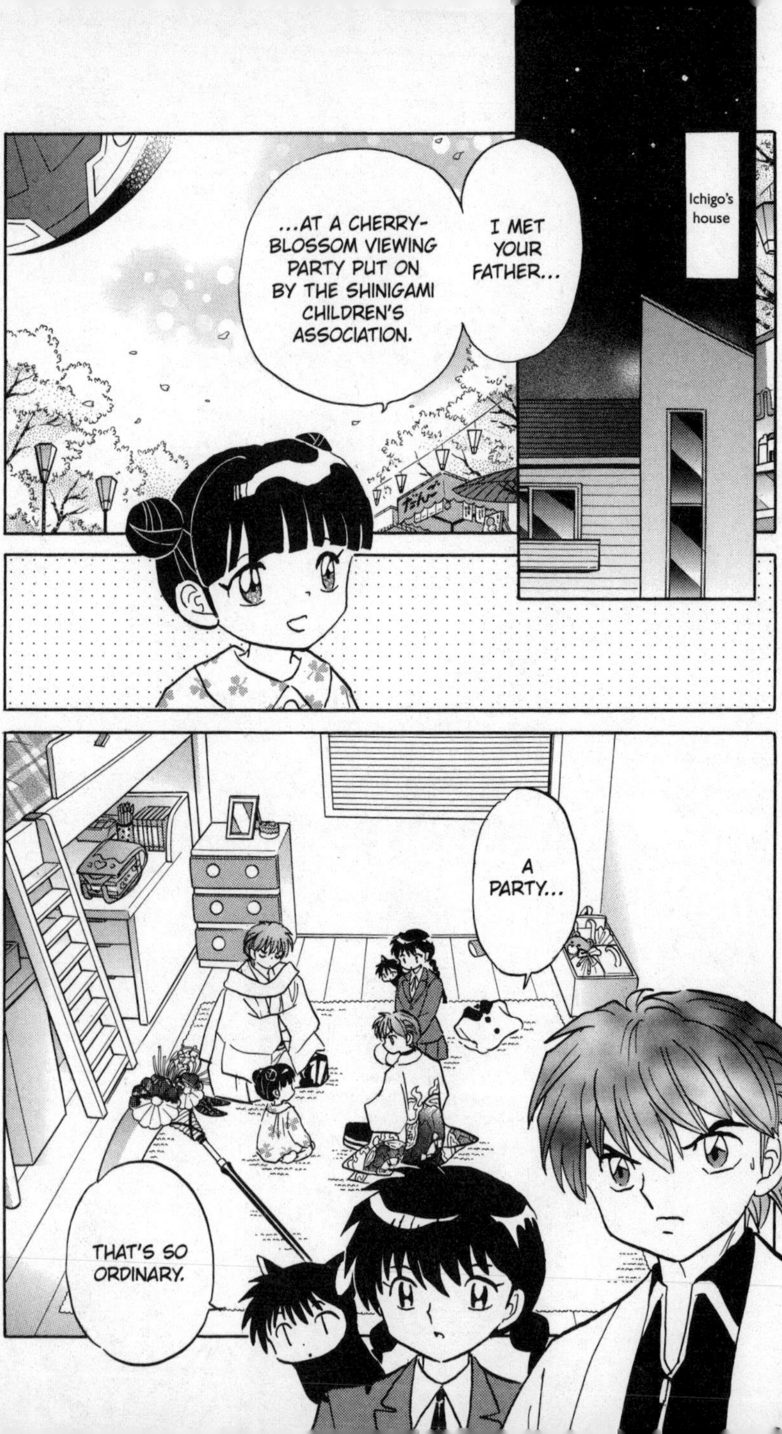
Ichigo's house
I MET YOUR FATHER...
...AT A CHERRY-BLOSSOM VIEWING PARTY PUT ON BY THE SHINIGAMI CHILDREN'S ASSOCIATION.
A PARTY...
THAT'S SO ORDINARY.

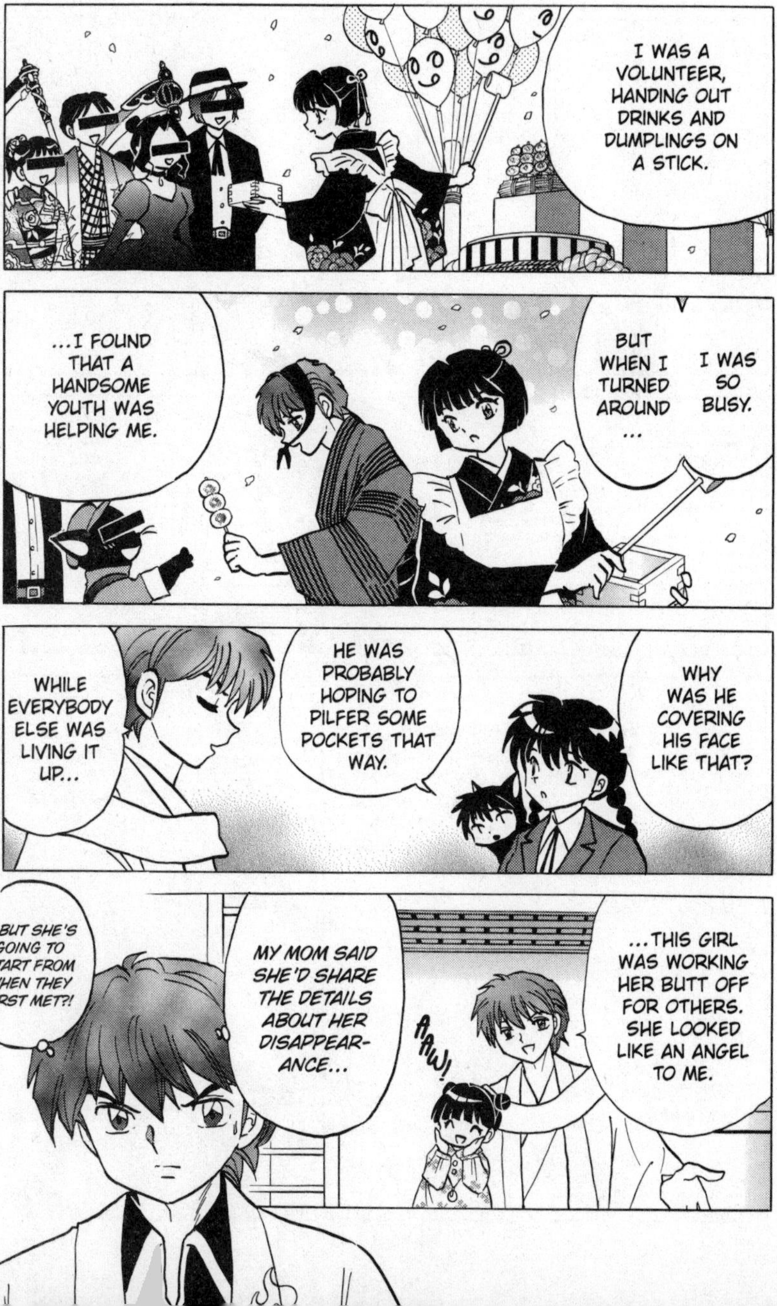
I WAS A VOLUNTEER, HANDING OUT DRINKS AND DUMPLINGS ON A STICK.
I WAS SO BUSY.
BUT WHEN I TURNED AROUND...
...I FOUND THAT A HANDSOME YOUTH WAS HELPING ME.
WHY WAS HE COVERING HIS FACE LIKE THAT?
HE WAS PROBABLY HOPING TO PILFER SOME POCKETS THAT WAY.
WHILE EVERYBODY ELSE WAS LIVING IT UP...
...THIS GIRL WAS WORKING HER BUTT OFF FOR OTHERS. SHE LOOKED LIKE AN ANGEL TO ME.
AAW!
MY MOM SAID SHE'D SHARE THE DETAILS ABOUT HER DISAPPEAR-ANCE...
...BUT SHE'S GOING TO START FROM WHEN THEY FIRST MET?!

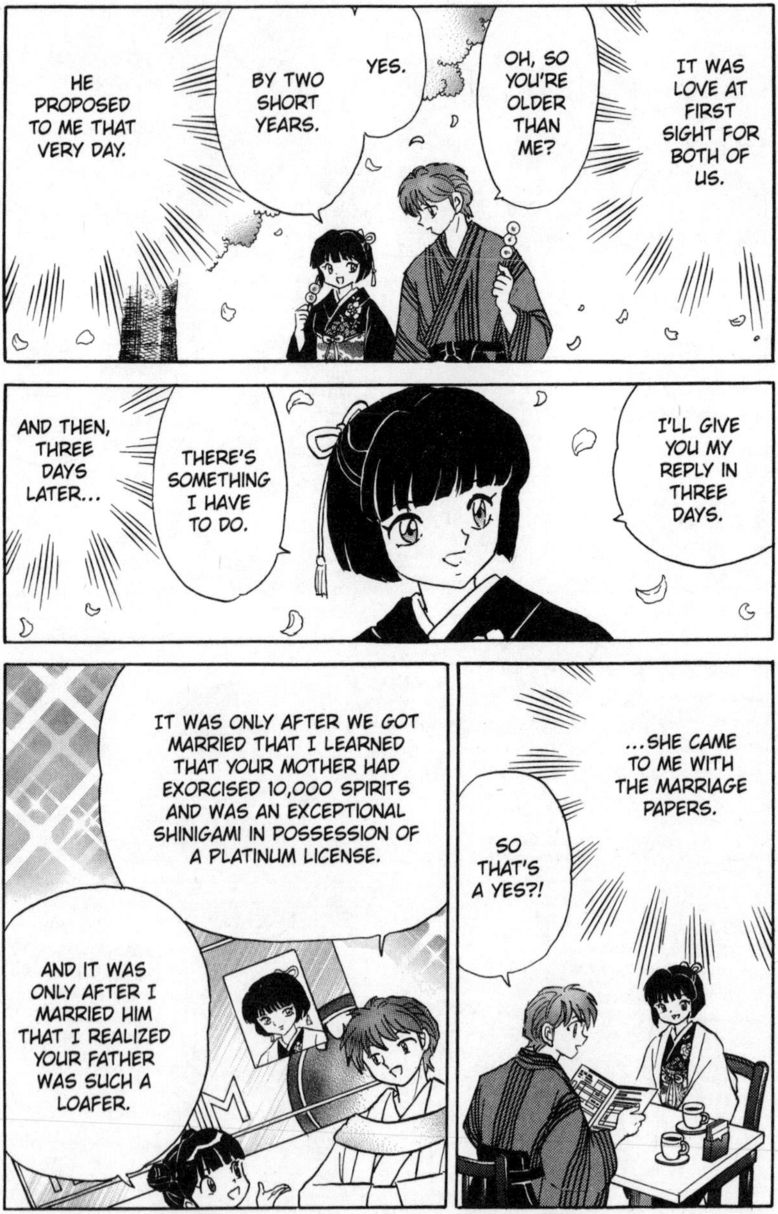
IT WAS LOVE AT FIRST SIGHT FOR BOTH OF US.
OH, SO YOU'RE OLDER THAN ME?
YES.
BY TWO SHORT YEARS.
HE PROPOSED TO ME THAT VERY DAY.
I'LL GIVE YOU MY REPLY IN THREE DAYS.
THERE'S SOMETHING I HAVE TO DO.
AND THEN, THREE DAYS LATER...
...SHE CAME TO ME WITH THE MARRIAGE PAPERS.
SO THAT'S A YES?!
IT WAS ONLY AFTER WE GOT MARRIED THAT I LEARNED THAT YOUR MOTHER HAD EXORCISED 10,000 SPIRITS AND WAS AN EXCEPTIONAL SHINIGAMI IN POSSESSION OF A PLATINUM LICENSE.
AND IT WAS ONLY AFTER I MARRIED HIM THAT I REALIZED YOUR FATHER WAS SUCH A LOAFER.

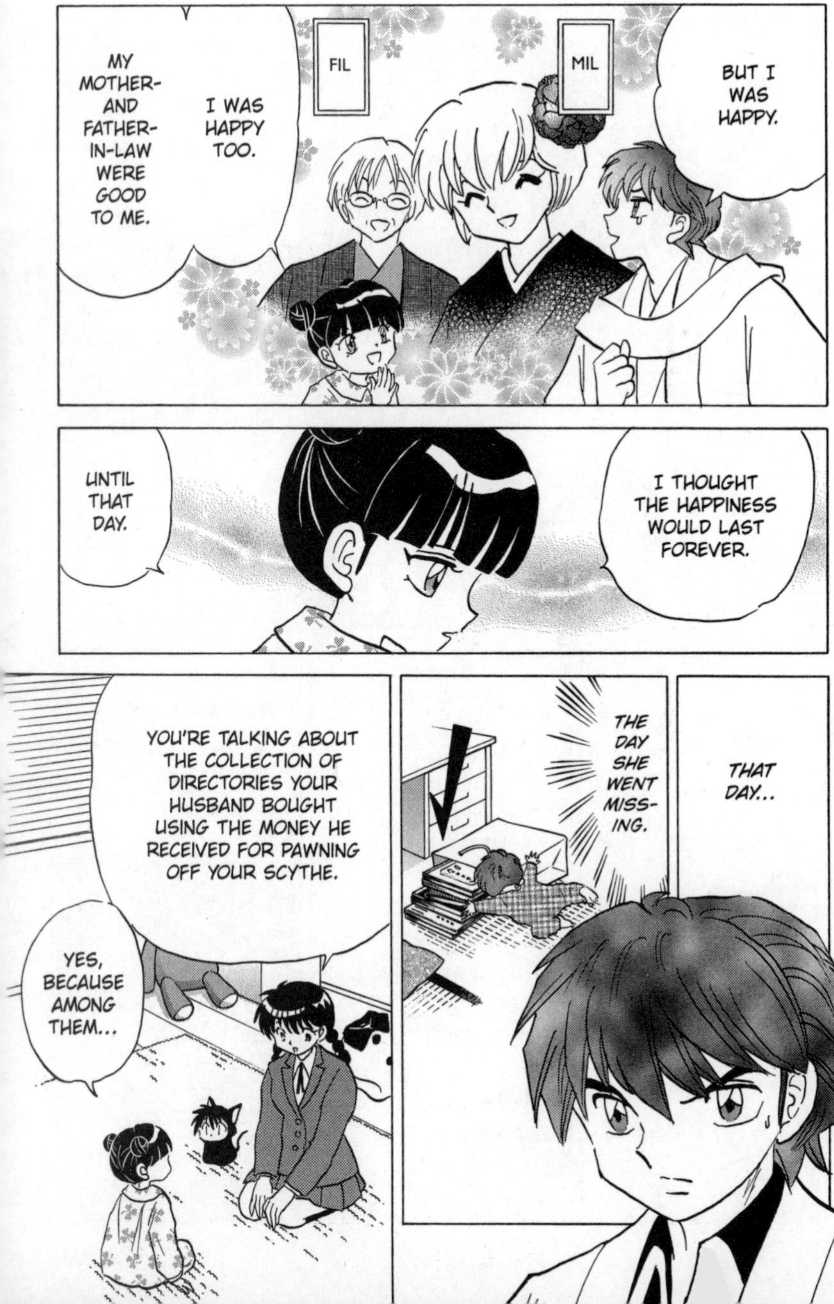
BUT I WAS HAPPY.
MIL
FIL
I WAS HAPPY TOO.
MY MOTHER-AND FATHER-IN-LAW WERE GOOD TO ME.
I THOUGHT THE HAPPINESS WOULD LAST FOREVER.
UNTIL THAT DAY.
THAT DAY...
THE DAY SHE WENT MISS-ING.
YOU'RE TALKING ABOUT THE COLLECTION OF DIRECTORIES YOUR HUSBAND BOUGHT USING THE MONEY HE RECEIVED FOR PAWNING OFF YOUR SCYTHE.
YES, BECAUSE AMONG THEM...

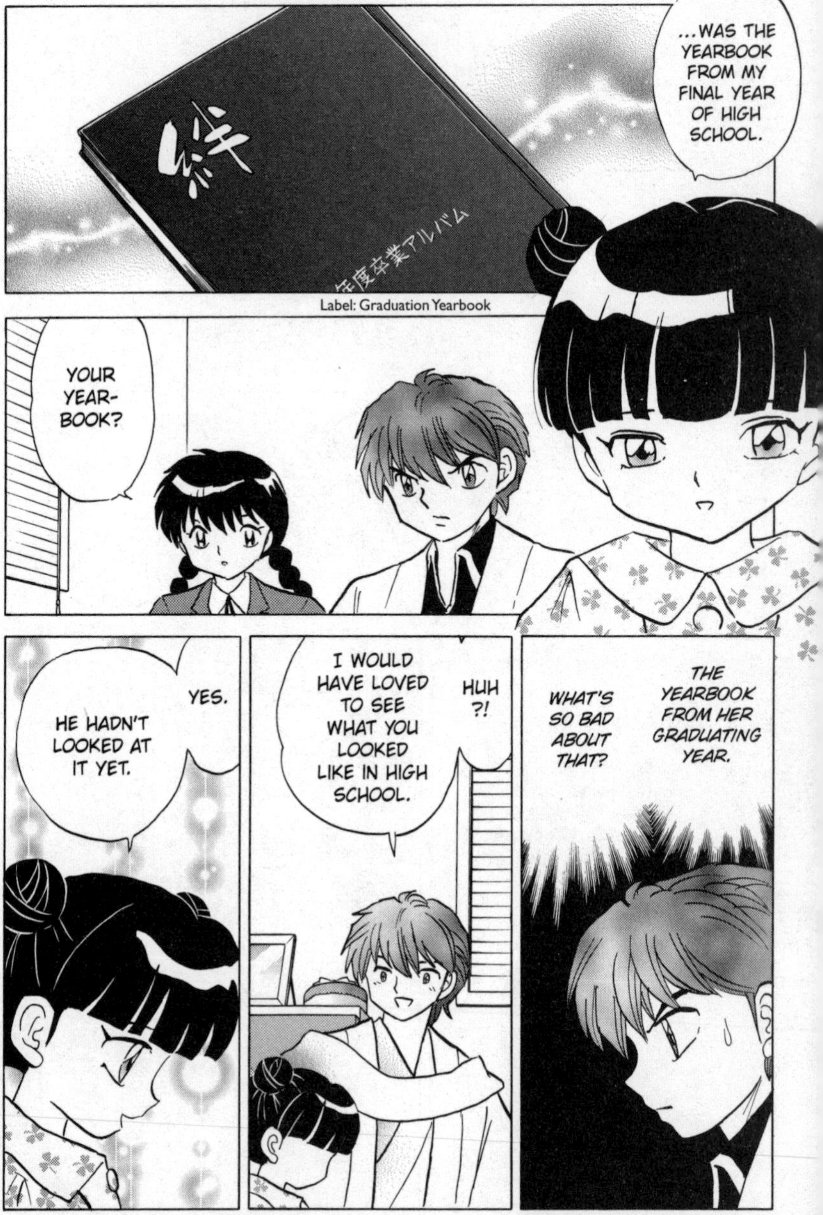
...WAS THE YEARBOOK FROM MY FINAL YEAR OF HIGH SCHOOL.
年度卒業アルバム
Label: Graduation Yearbook
YOUR YEAR-BOOK?
THE YEARBOOK FROM HER GRADUATING YEAR.
WHAT'S SO BAD ABOUT THAT?
HUH ?!
I WOULD HAVE LOVED TO SEE WHAT YOU LOOKED LIKE IN HIGH SCHOOL.
YES.
HE HADN'T LOOKED AT IT YET.

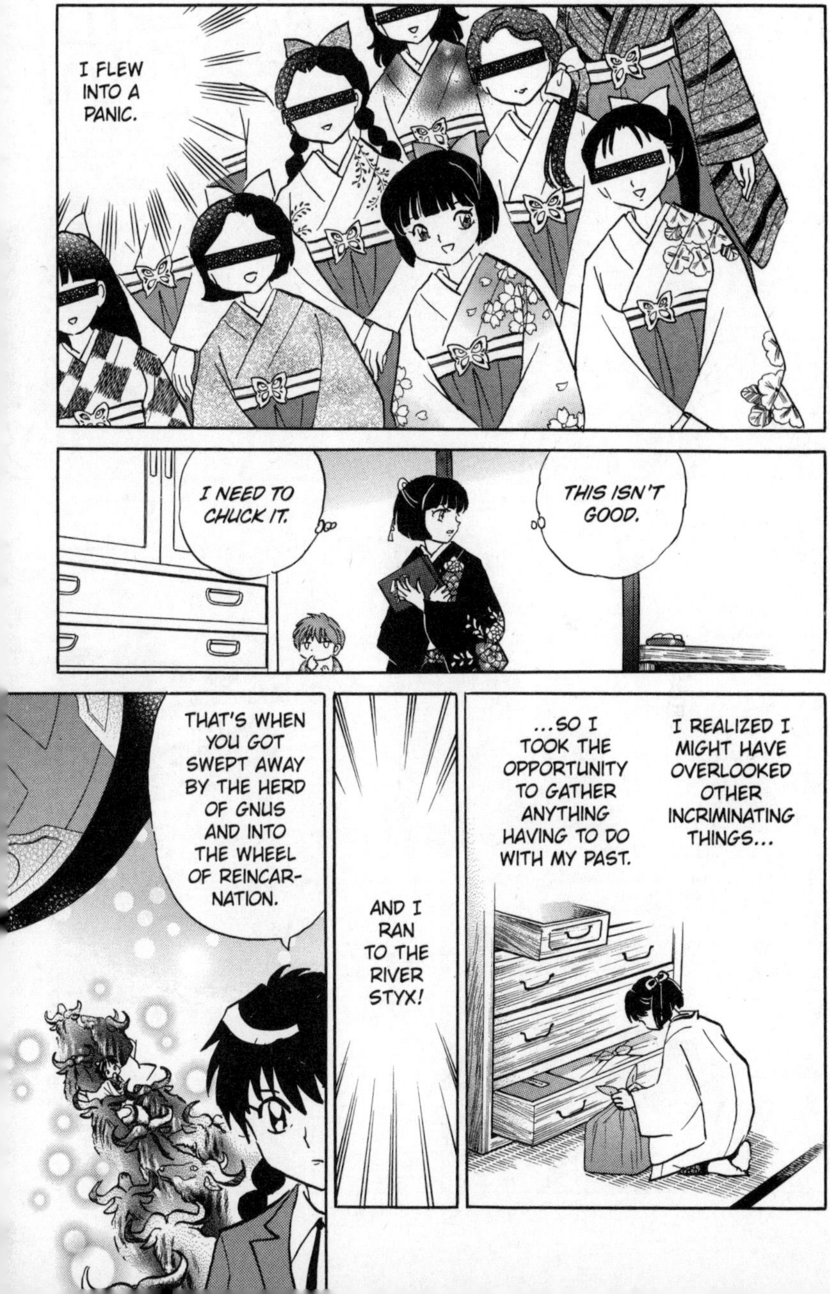
I FLEW INTO A PANIC.
THIS ISN'T GOOD.
I NEED TO CHUCK IT.
I REALIZED I MIGHT HAVE OVERLOOKED OTHER INCRIMINATING THINGS...
...SO I TOOK THE OPPORTUNITY TO GATHER ANYTHING HAVING TO DO WITH MY PAST.
AND I RAN TO THE RIVER STYX!
THAT'S WHEN YOU GOT SWEPT AWAY BY THE HERD OF GNUS AND INTO THE WHEEL OF REINCAR-NATION.

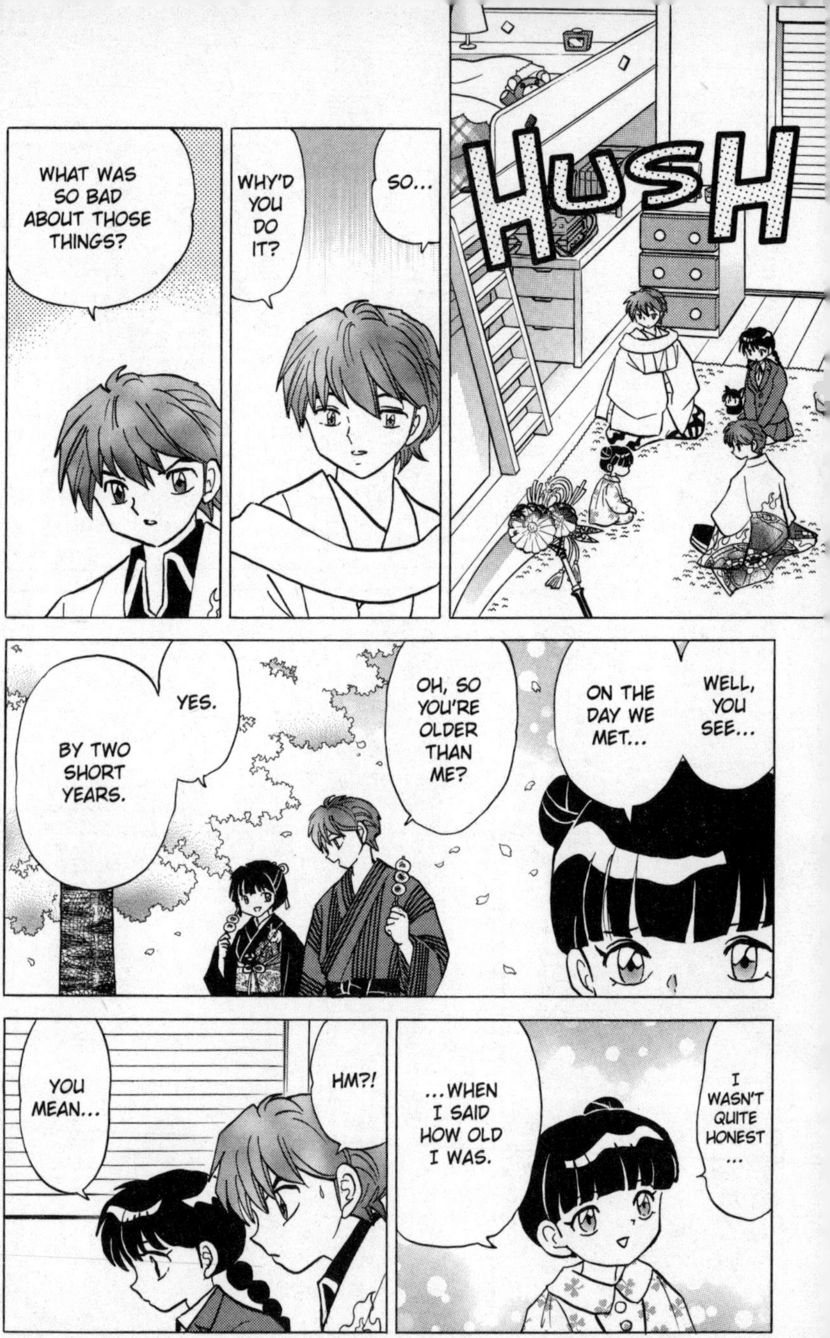
HUSH
SO...
WHY'D YOU DO IT?
WHAT WAS SO BAD ABOUT THOSE THINGS?
WELL, YOU SEE...
ON THE DAY WE MET...
OH, SO YOU'RE OLDER THAN ME?
YES.
BY TWO SHORT YEARS.
I WASN'T QUITE HONEST...
...WHEN I SAID HOW OLD I WAS.
HM?!
YOU MEAN...

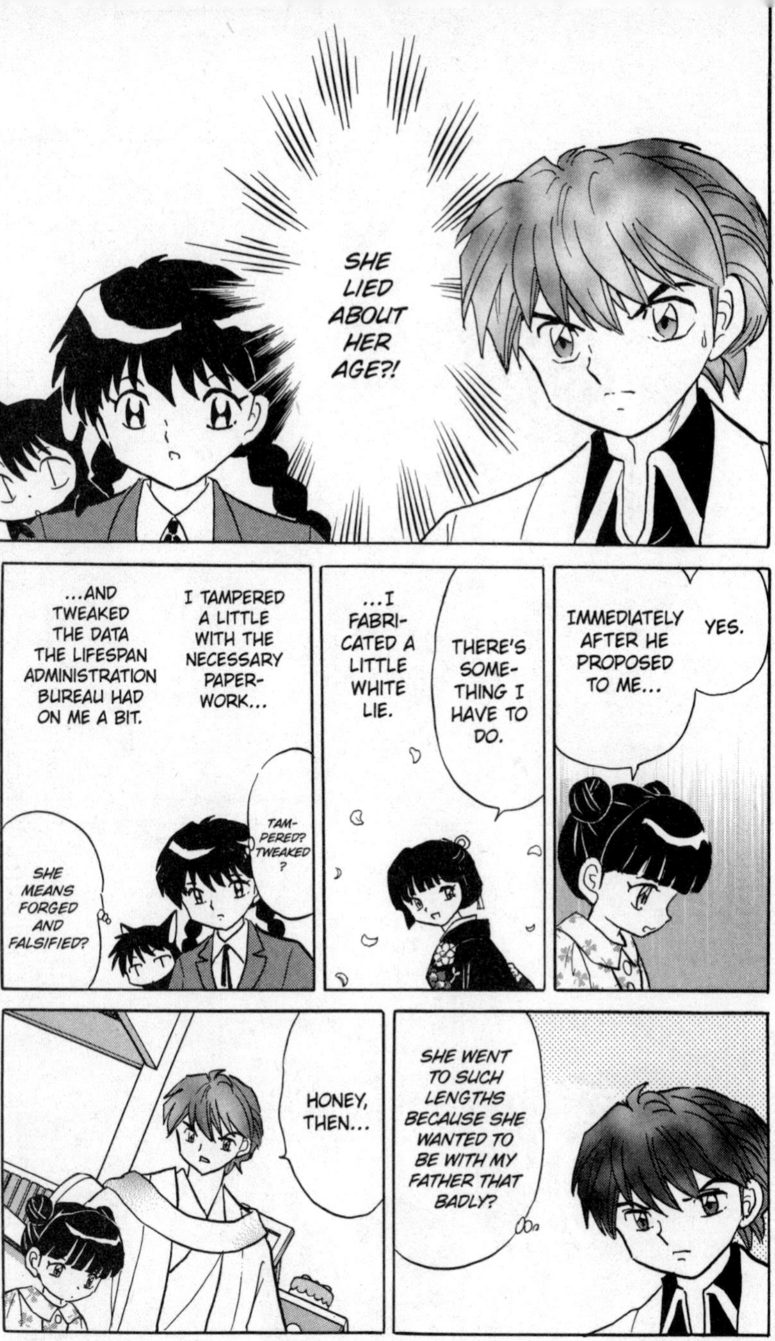
SHE LIED ABOUT HER AGE?!
YES.
IMMEDIATELY AFTER HE PROPOSED TO ME...
THERE'S SOMETHING I HAVE TO DO.
...I FABRICATED A LITTLE WHITE LIE.
I TAMPERED A LITTLE WITH THE NECESSARY PAPERWORK...
...AND TWEAKED THE DATA THE LIFESPAN ADMINISTRATION BUREAU HAD ON ME A BIT.
TAMPERED? TWEAKED?
SHE MEANS FORGED AND FALSIFIED?
SHE WENT TO SUCH LENGTHS BECAUSE SHE WANTED TO BE WITH MY FATHER THAT BADLY?
HONEY, THEN...

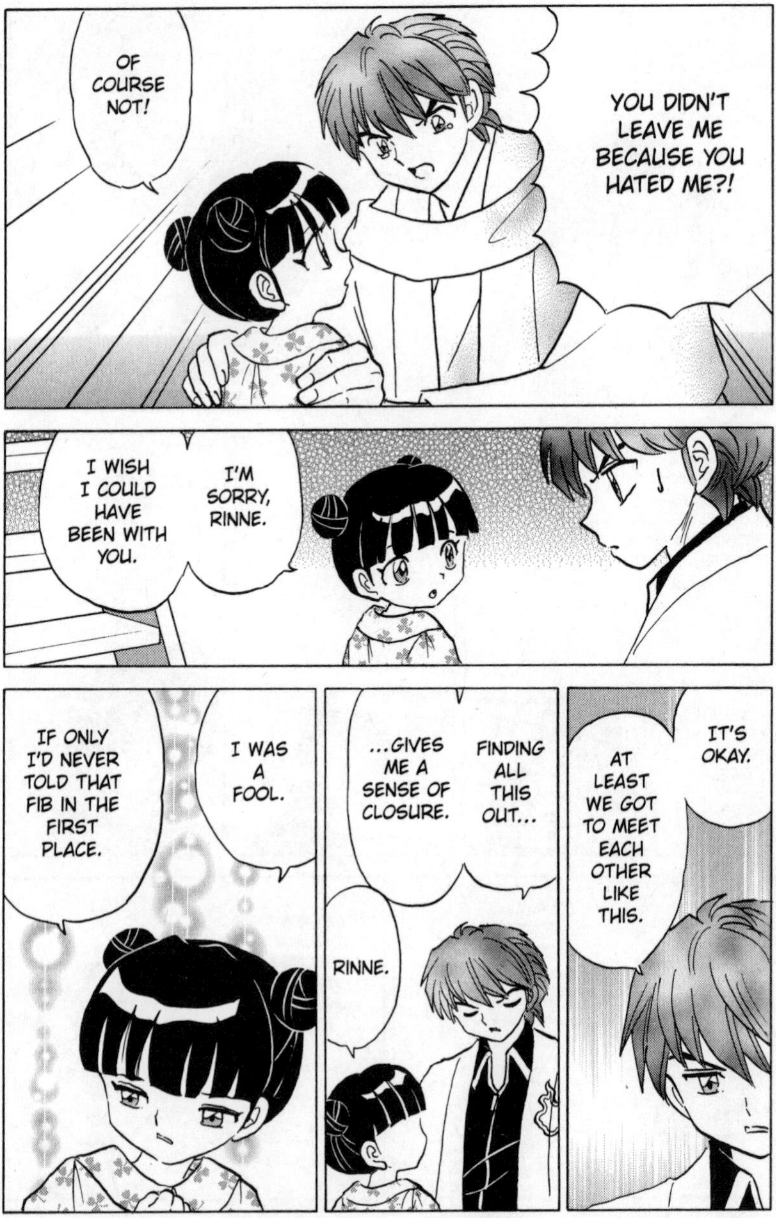
YOU DIDN'T LEAVE ME BECAUSE YOU HATED ME?!
OF COURSE NOT!
I'M SORRY, RINNE.
I WISH I COULD HAVE BEEN WITH YOU.
IT'S OKAY.
AT LEAST WE GOT TO MEET EACH OTHER LIKE THIS.
FINDING ALL THIS OUT...
...GIVES ME A SENSE OF CLOSURE.
RINNE.
I WAS A FOOL.
IF ONLY I'D NEVER TOLD THAT FIB IN THE FIRST PLACE.

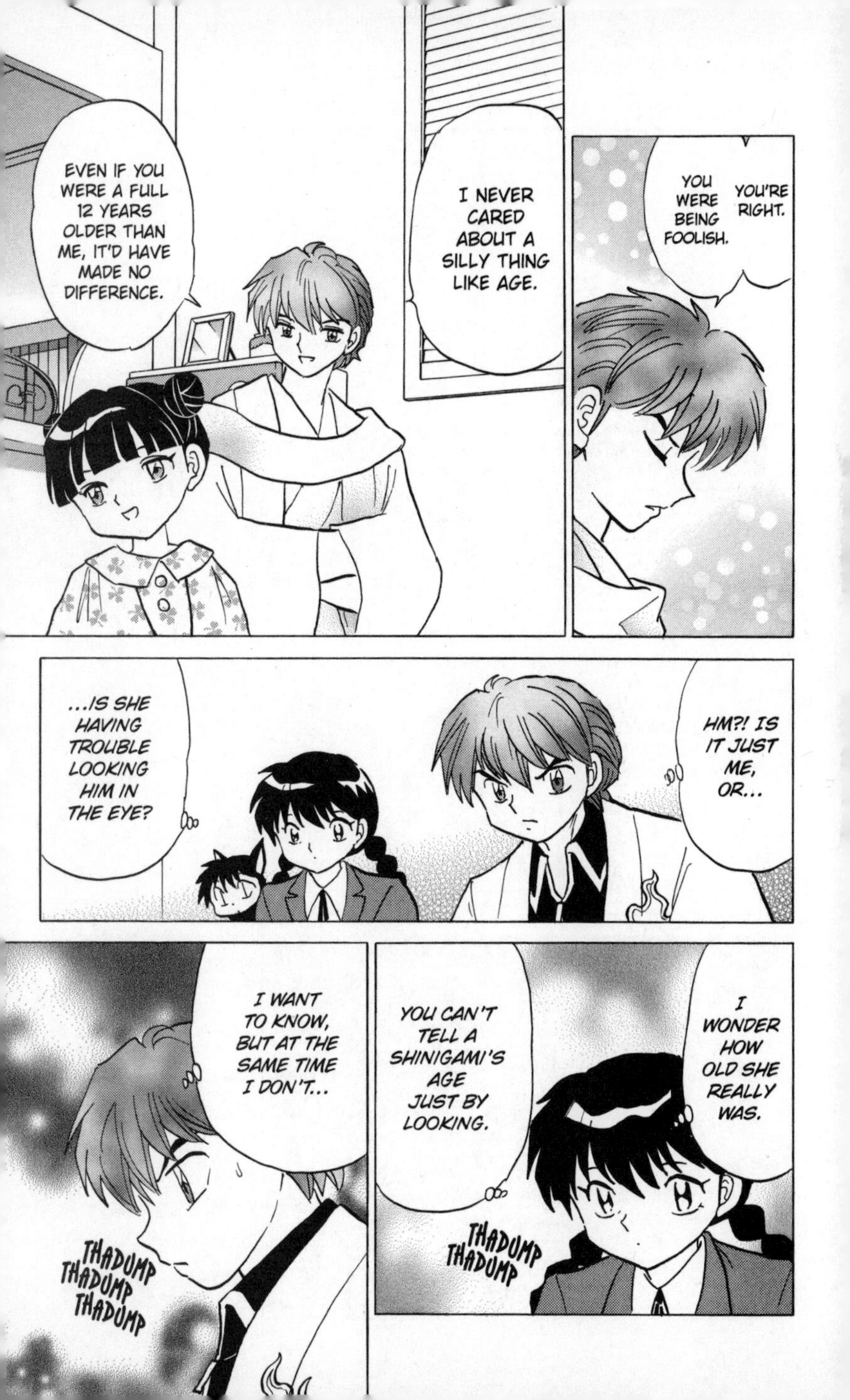
YOU'RE RIGHT.
YOU WERE BEING FOOLISH.
I NEVER CARED ABOUT A SILLY THING LIKE AGE.
EVEN IF YOU WERE A FULL 12 YEARS OLDER THAN ME, IT'D HAVE MADE NO DIFFERENCE.
HM?! IS IT JUST ME, OR...
...IS SHE HAVING TROUBLE LOOKING HIM IN THE EYE?
I WONDER HOW OLD SHE REALLY WAS.
YOU CAN'T TELL A SHINIGAMI'S AGE JUST BY LOOKING.
THADUMP THADUMP
I WANT TO KNOW, BUT AT THE SAME TIME I DON'T...
THADUMP THADUMP THADUMP

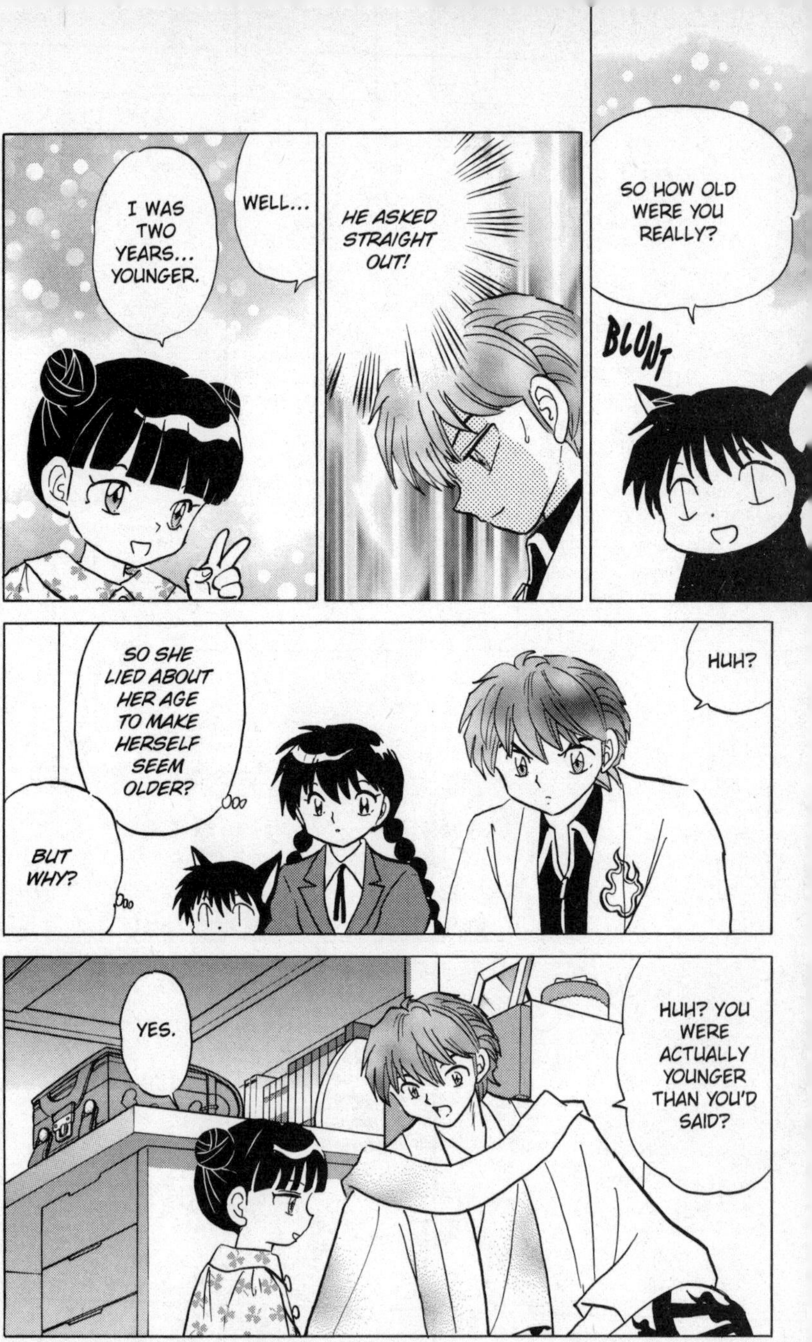
SO HOW OLD WERE YOU REALLY?
BLUNT
HE ASKED STRAIGHT OUT!
WELL...
I WAS TWO YEARS... YOUNGER.
HUH?
SO SHE LIED ABOUT HER AGE TO MAKE HERSELF SEEM OLDER?
BUT WHY?
HUH? YOU WERE ACTUALLY YOUNGER THAN YOU'D SAID?
YES.

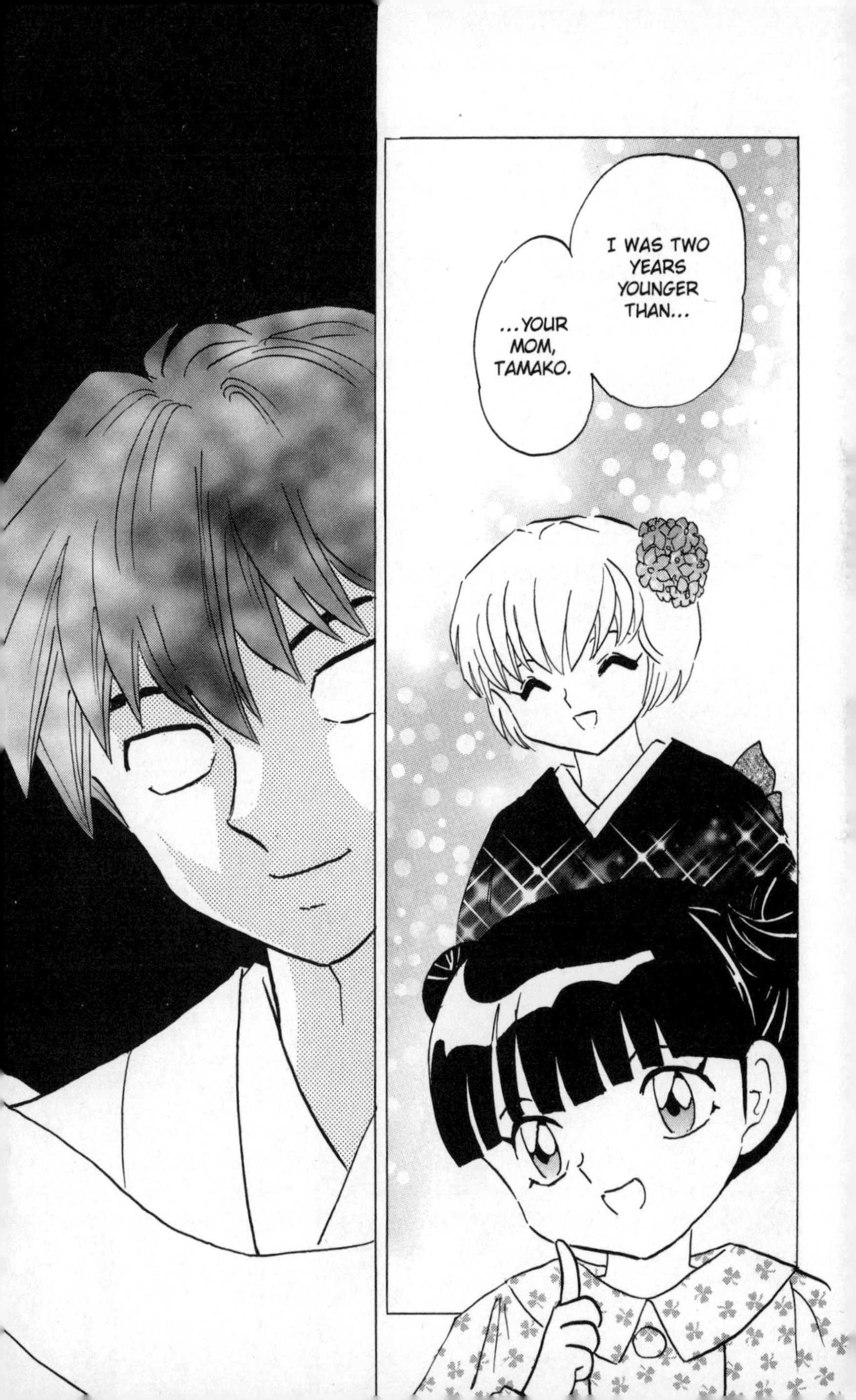
I WAS TWO YEARS YOUNGER THAN...
...YOUR MOM, TAMAKO.

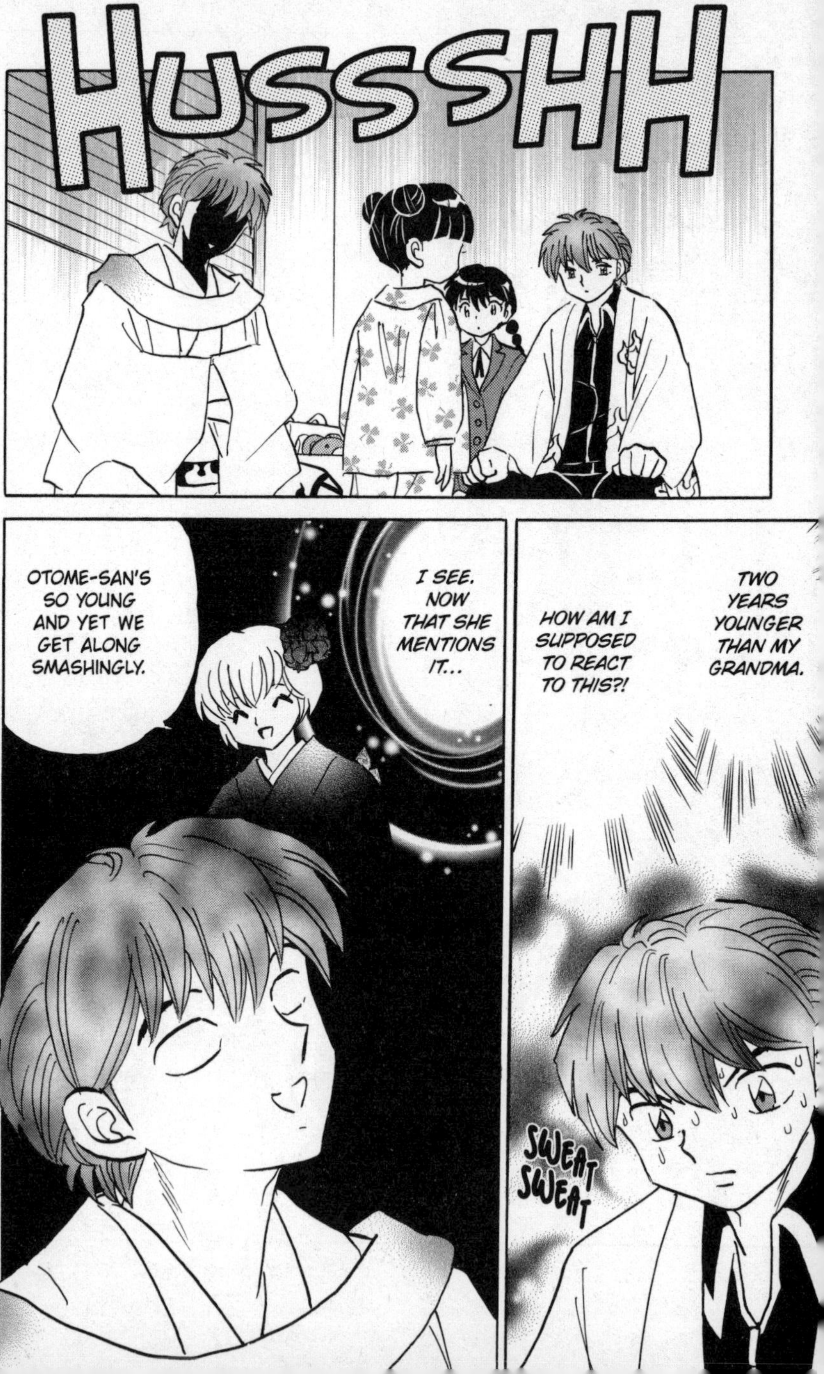
HUSSSHH
TWO YEARS YOUNGER THAN MY GRANDMA.
HOW AM I SUPPOSED TO REACT TO THIS?!
SWEAT SWEAT
I SEE. NOW THAT SHE MENTIONS IT...
OTOME-SAN'S SO YOUNG AND YET WE GET ALONG SMASHINGLY.

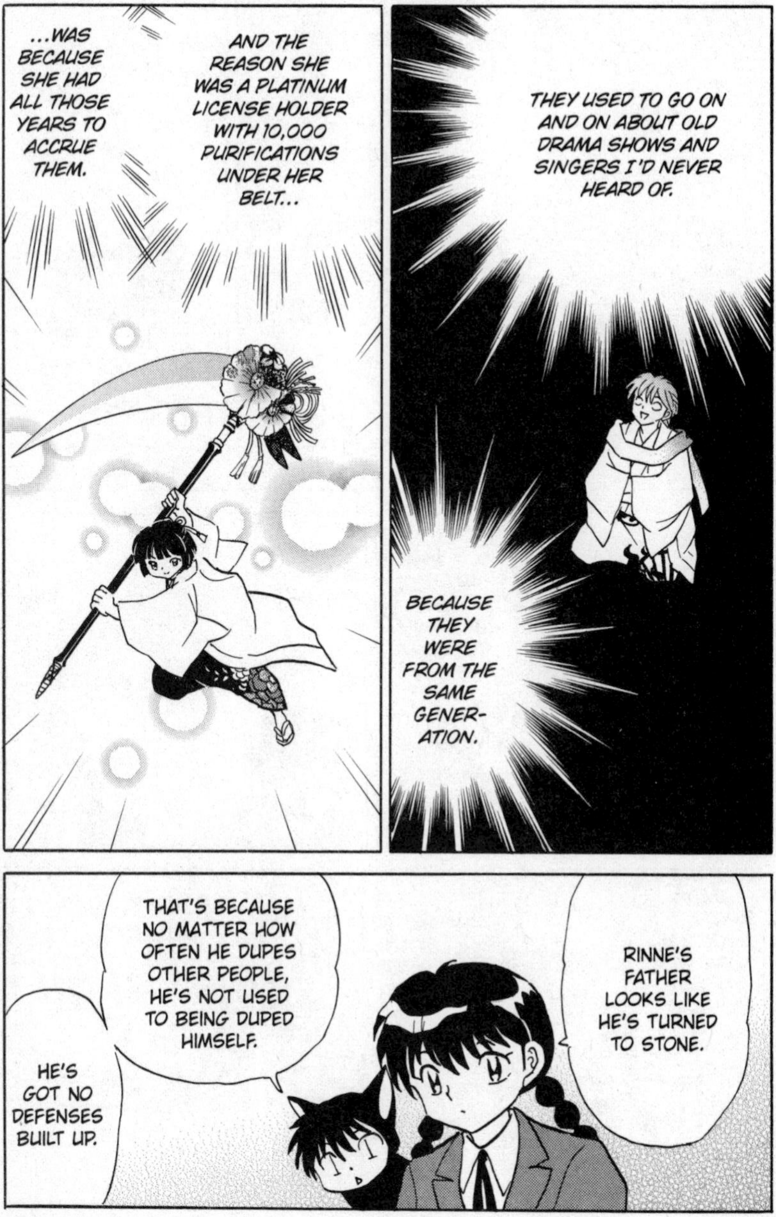
THEY USED TO GO ON AND ON ABOUT OLD DRAMA SHOWS AND SINGERS I'D NEVER HEARD OF.
BECAUSE THEY WERE FROM THE SAME GENER-ATION.
AND THE REASON SHE WAS A PLATINUM LICENSE HOLDER WITH 10,000 PURIFICATIONS UNDER HER BELT...
...WAS BECAUSE SHE HAD ALL THOSE YEARS TO ACCRUE THEM.
RINNE'S FATHER LOOKS LIKE HE'S TURNED TO STONE.
THAT'S BECAUSE NO MATTER HOW OFTEN HE DUPES OTHER PEOPLE, HE'S NOT USED TO BEING DUPED HIMSELF.
HE'S GOT NO DEFENSES BUILT UP.

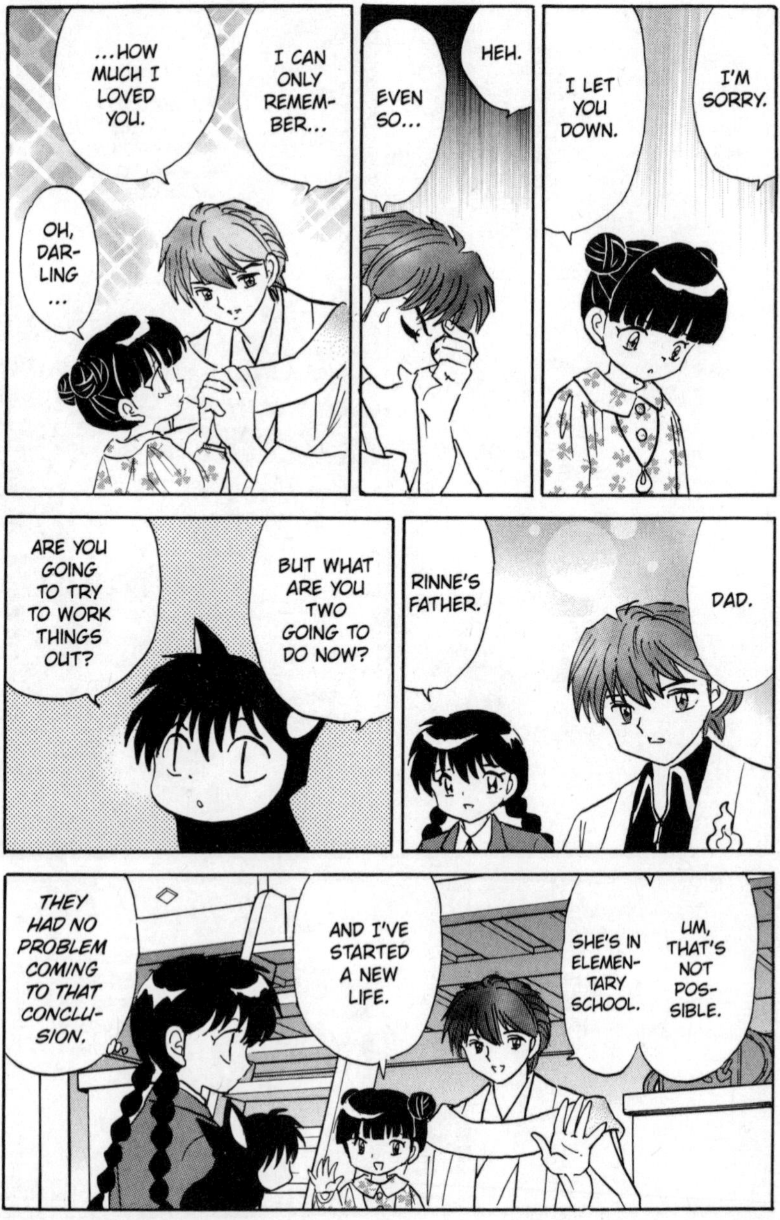
I'M SORRY.
I LET YOU DOWN.
HEH.
EVEN SO...
I CAN ONLY REMEMBER...
...HOW MUCH I LOVED YOU.
OH, DARLING...
DAD.
RINNE'S FATHER.
BUT WHAT ARE YOU TWO GOING TO DO NOW?
ARE YOU GOING TO TRY TO WORK THINGS OUT?
UM, THAT'S NOT POSSIBLE.
SHE'S IN ELEMENTARY SCHOOL.
AND I'VE STARTED A NEW LIFE.
THEY HAD NO PROBLEM COMING TO THAT CONCLUSION.

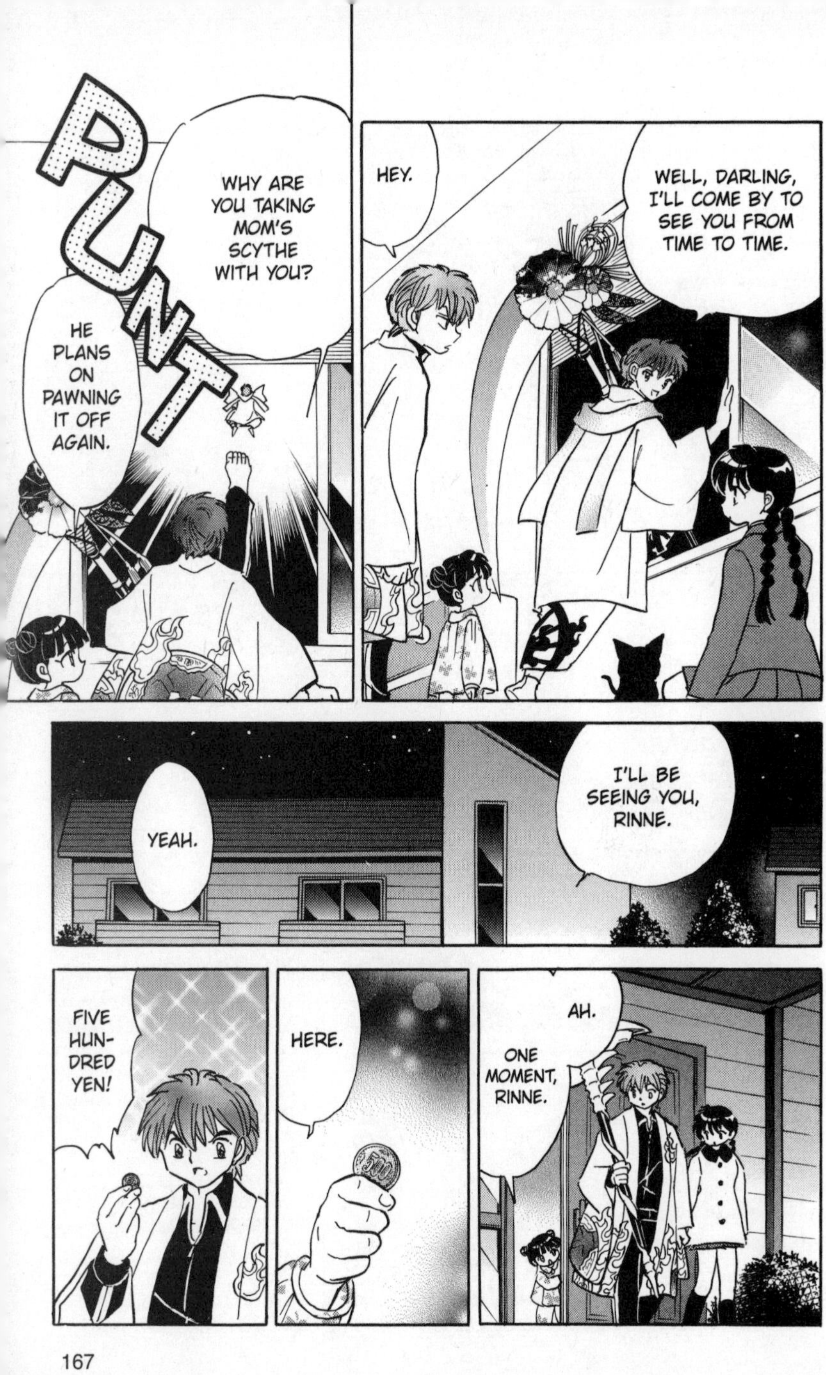
WELL, DARLING, I'LL COME BY TO SEE YOU FROM TIME TO TIME.
HEY.
WHY ARE YOU TAKING MOM'S SCYTHE WITH YOU?
PUNT
HE PLANS ON PAWNING IT OFF AGAIN.
I'LL BE SEEING YOU, RINNE.
YEAH.
AH.
ONE MOMENT, RINNE.
HERE.
FIVE HUN-DRED YEN!

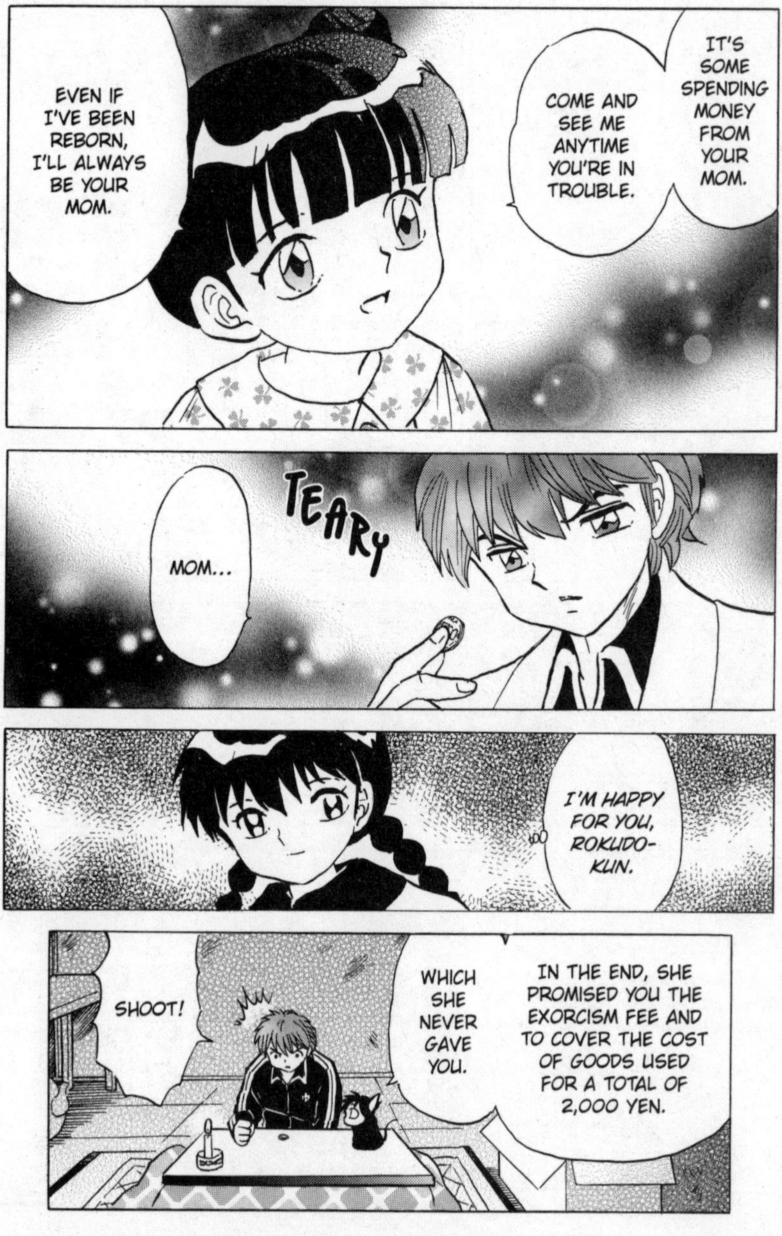
IT'S SOME SPENDING MONEY FROM YOUR MOM.
COME AND SEE ME ANYTIME YOU'RE IN TROUBLE.
EVEN IF I'VE BEEN REBORN, I'LL ALWAYS BE YOUR MOM.
TEARY
MOM...
I'M HAPPY FOR YOU, ROKUDO-KUN.
IN THE END, SHE PROMISED YOU THE EXORCISM FEE AND TO COVER THE COST OF GOODS USED FOR A TOTAL OF 2,000 YEN.
WHICH SHE NEVER GAVE YOU.
SHOOT!

CHAPTER 318: THE WHITE SPIRIT

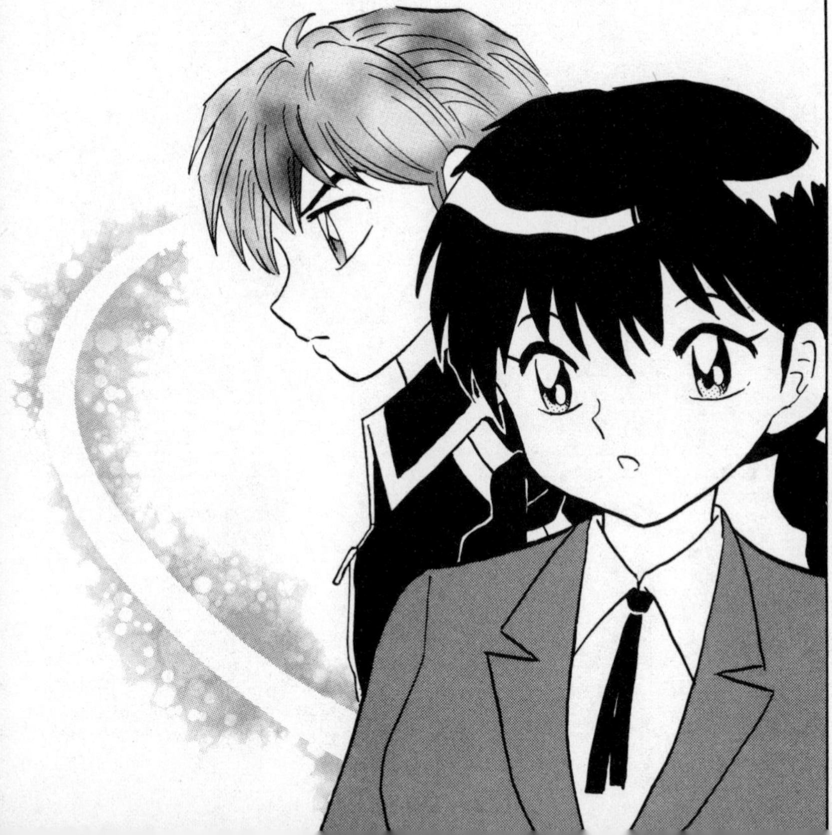

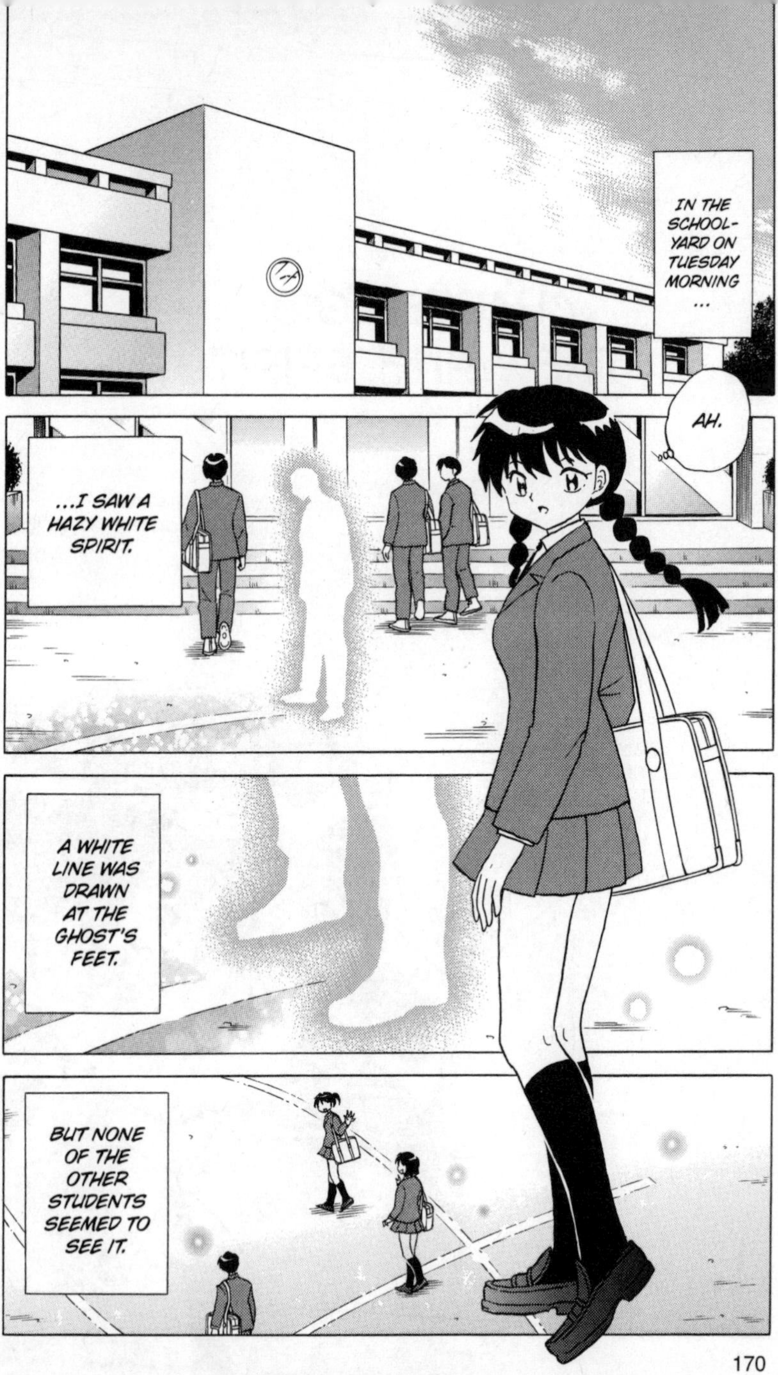
IN THE SCHOOL-YARD ON TUESDAY MORNING ...
AH.
...I SAW A HAZY WHITE SPIRIT.
A WHITE LINE WAS DRAWN AT THE GHOST'S FEET.
BUT NONE OF THE OTHER STUDENTS SEEMED TO SEE IT.

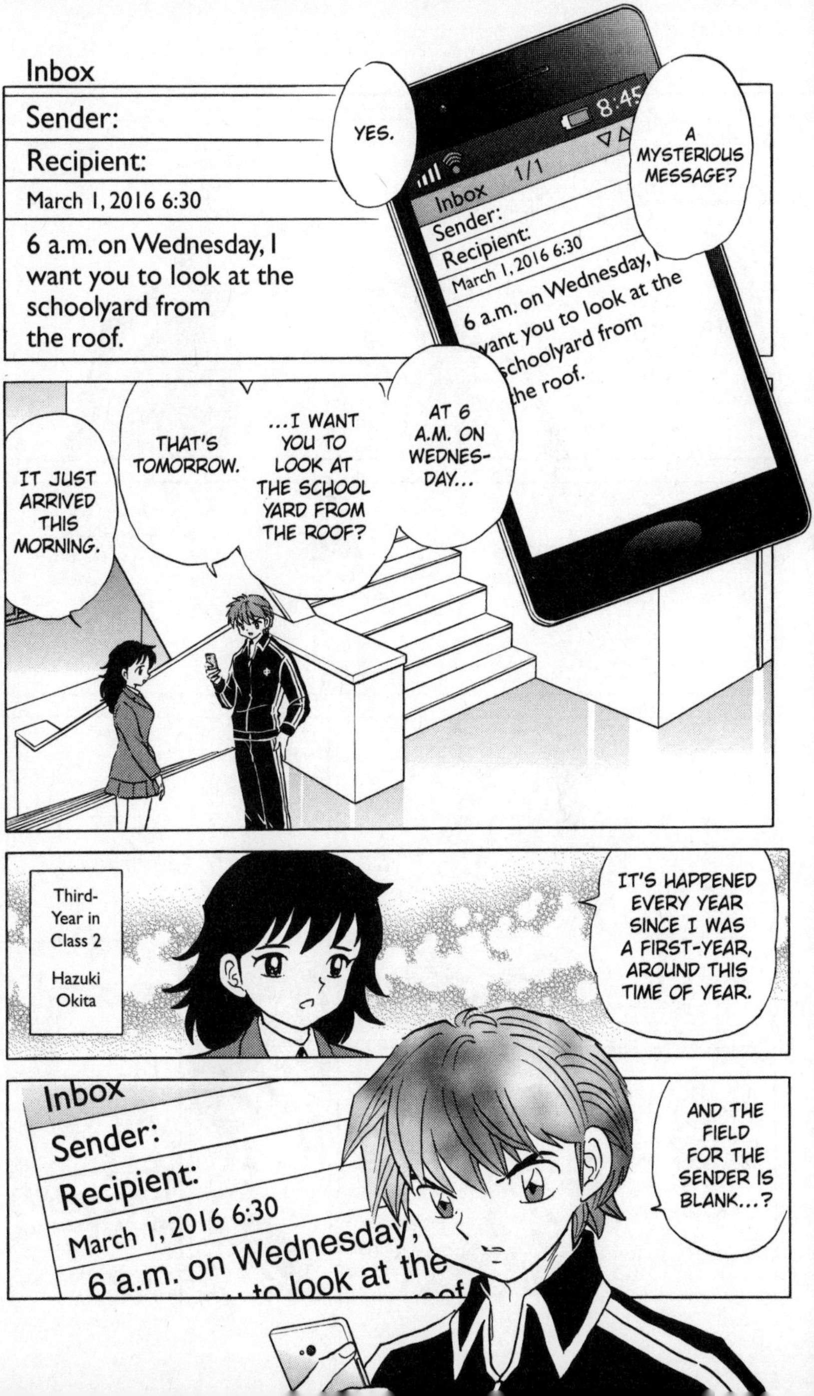
A MYSTERIOUS MESSAGE?
YES.
Inbox
Sender:
Recipient:
March 1, 2016 6:30
6 a.m. on Wednesday, I want you to look at the schoolyard from the roof.
8:45
AT 6 A.M. ON WEDNES-DAY...
...I WANT YOU TO LOOK AT THE SCHOOL YARD FROM THE ROOF?
THAT'S TOMORROW.
IT JUST ARRIVED THIS MORNING.
IT'S HAPPENED EVERY YEAR SINCE I WAS A FIRST-YEAR, AROUND THIS TIME OF YEAR.
Third-Year in Class 2
Hazuki Okita
AND THE FIELD FOR THE SENDER IS BLANK...?
Inbox
Sender:
Recipient:
March 1, 2016 6:30
6 a.m. on Wednesday,
look at the

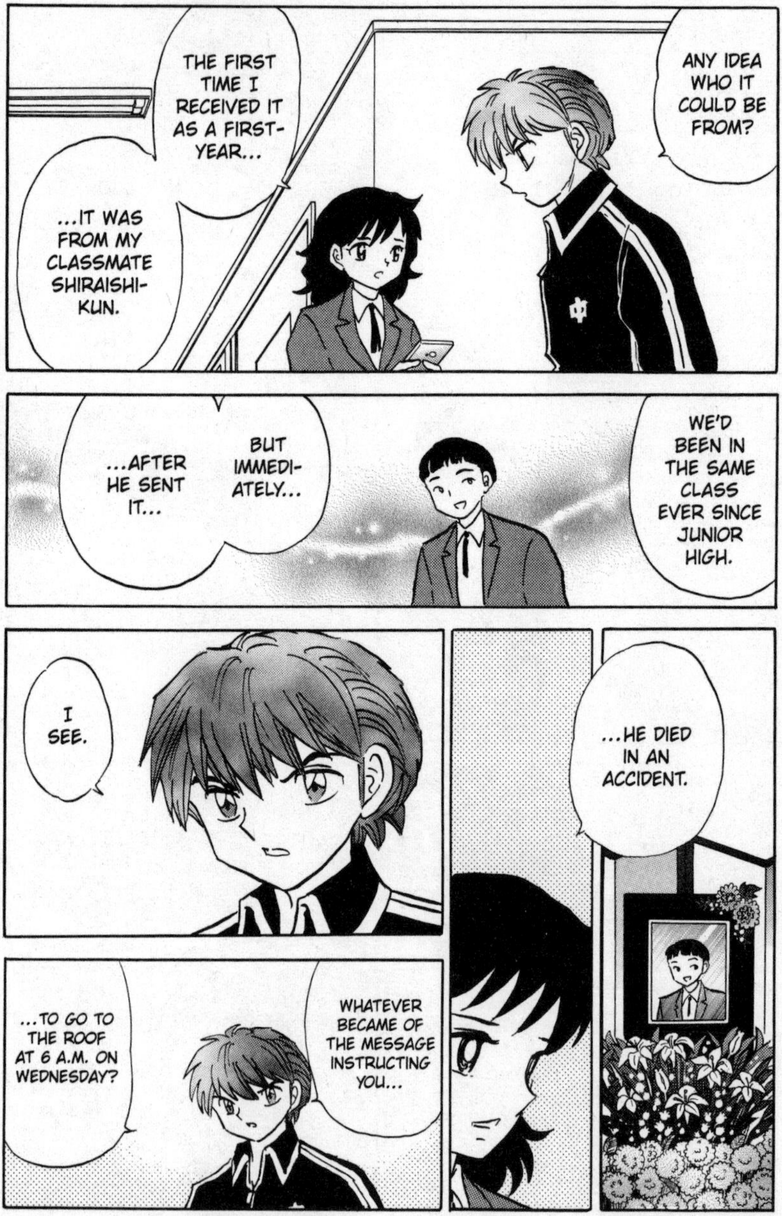
ANY IDEA WHO IT COULD BE FROM?
THE FIRST TIME I RECEIVED IT AS A FIRST-YEAR...
...IT WAS FROM MY CLASSMATE SHIRAISHI-KUN.
WE'D BEEN IN THE SAME CLASS EVER SINCE JUNIOR HIGH.
BUT IMMEDIATELY...
...AFTER HE SENT IT...
...HE DIED IN AN ACCIDENT.
I SEE.
WHATEVER BECAME OF THE MESSAGE INSTRUCTING YOU...
...TO GO TO THE ROOF AT 6 A.M. ON WEDNESDAY?

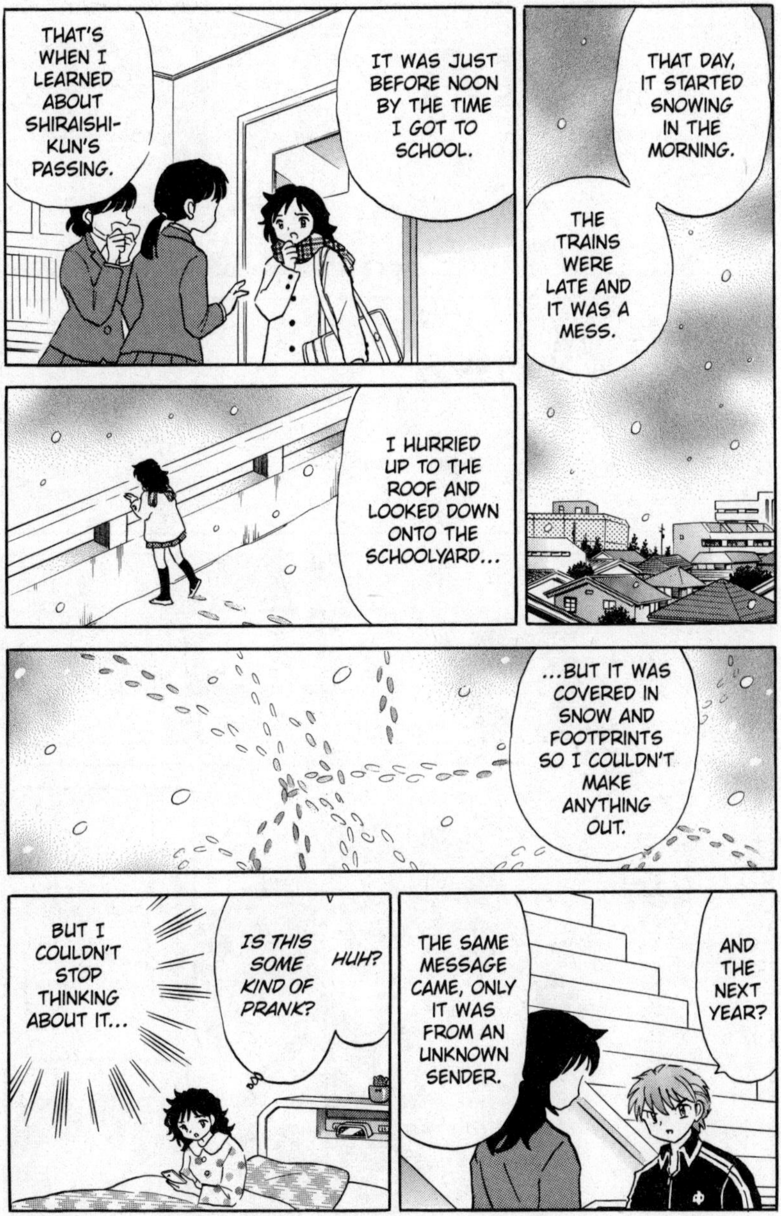
THAT DAY, IT STARTED SNOWING IN THE MORNING.
THE TRAINS WERE LATE AND IT WAS A MESS.
IT WAS JUST BEFORE NOON BY THE TIME I GOT TO SCHOOL.
THAT'S WHEN I LEARNED ABOUT SHIRAISHI-KUN'S PASSING.
I HURRIED UP TO THE ROOF AND LOOKED DOWN ONTO THE SCHOOLYARD...
...BUT IT WAS COVERED IN SNOW AND FOOTPRINTS SO I COULDN'T MAKE ANYTHING OUT.
AND THE NEXT YEAR?
THE SAME MESSAGE CAME, ONLY IT WAS FROM AN UNKNOWN SENDER.
HUH?
IS THIS SOME KIND OF PRANK?
BUT I COULDN'T STOP THINKING ABOUT IT...

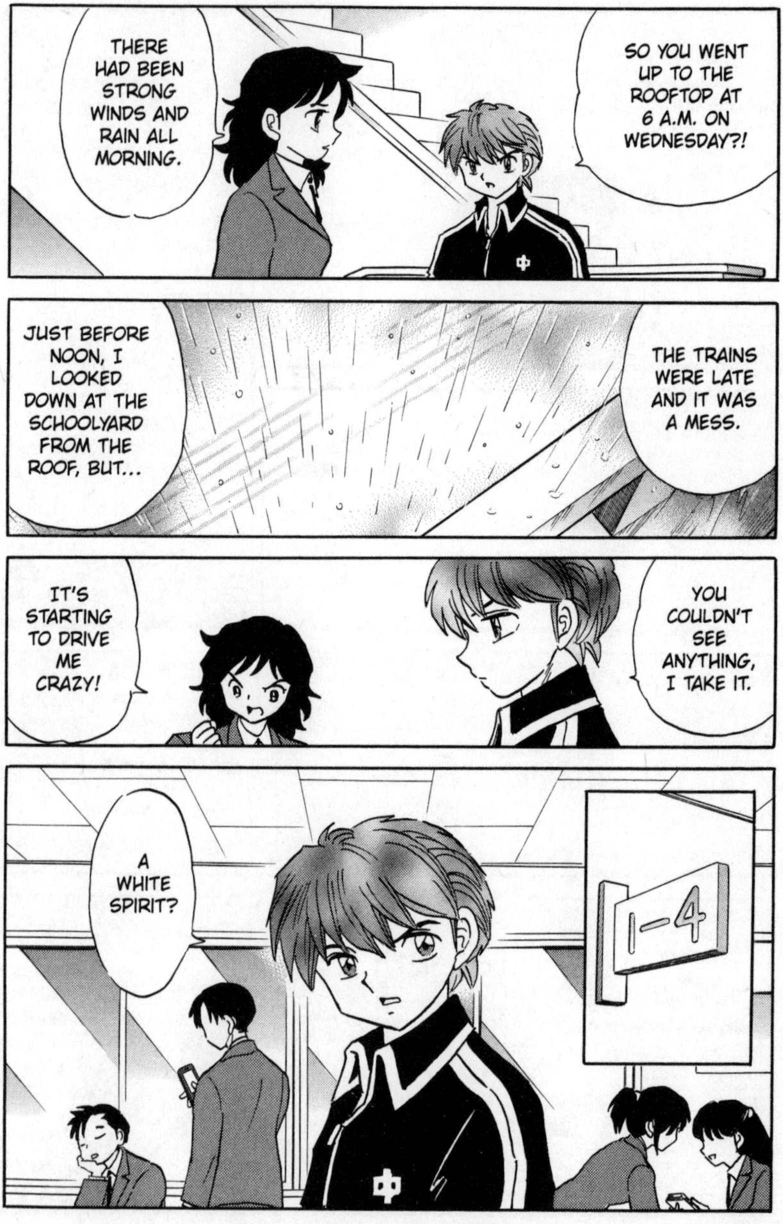
SO YOU WENT UP TO THE ROOFTOP AT 6 A.M. ON WEDNESDAY?!
THERE HAD BEEN STRONG WINDS AND RAIN ALL MORNING.
THE TRAINS WERE LATE AND IT WAS A MESS.
JUST BEFORE NOON, I LOOKED DOWN AT THE SCHOOLYARD FROM THE ROOF, BUT...
YOU COULDN'T SEE ANYTHING, I TAKE IT.
IT'S STARTING TO DRIVE ME CRAZY!
1-4
A WHITE SPIRIT?

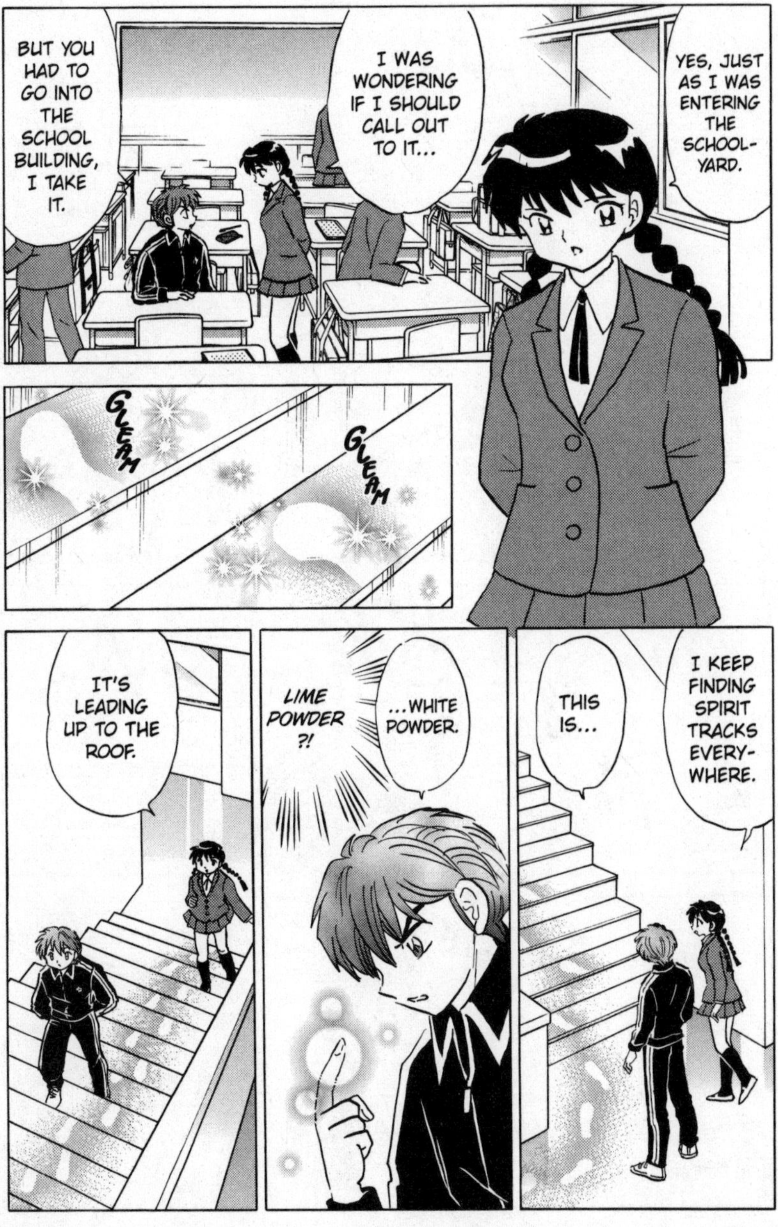
YES, JUST AS I WAS ENTERING THE SCHOOL-YARD.
I WAS WONDERING IF I SHOULD CALL OUT TO IT...
BUT YOU HAD TO GO INTO THE SCHOOL BUILDING, I TAKE IT.
GLEAM
GLEAM
I KEEP FINDING SPIRIT TRACKS EVERY-WHERE.
THIS IS...
...WHITE POWDER.
LIME POWDER ?!
IT'S LEADING UP TO THE ROOF.

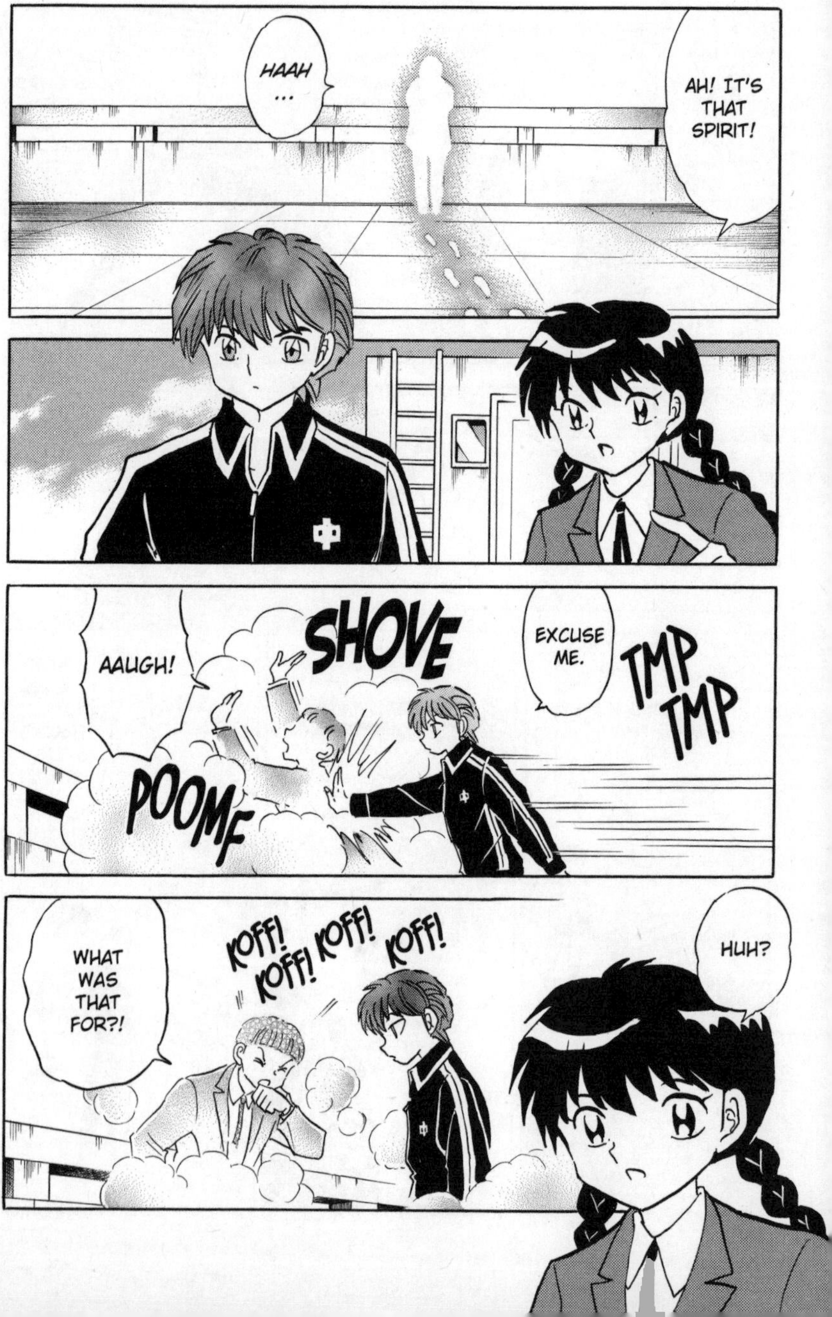
AH! IT'S THAT SPIRIT!
HAAH ...
TMP TMP
EXCUSE ME.
SHOVE
AAUGH!
POOMF
HUH?
KOFF!
KOFF! KOFF!
KOFF!
WHAT WAS THAT FOR?!

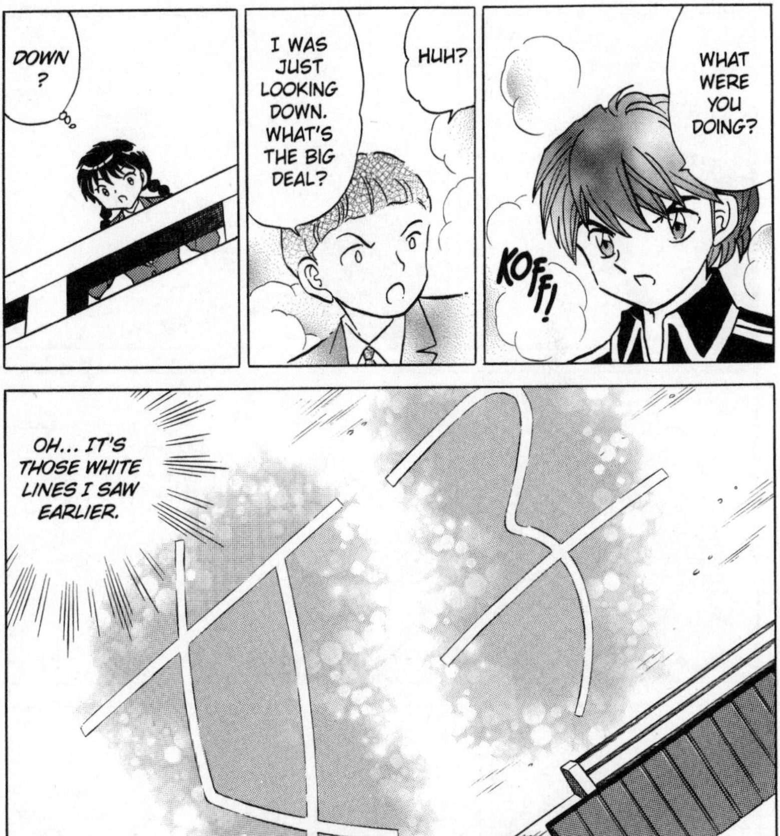
WHAT WERE YOU DOING?
KOFF!
HUH?
I WAS JUST LOOKING DOWN. WHAT'S THE BIG DEAL?
DOWN?
OH... IT'S THOSE WHITE LINES I SAW EARLIER.
Writing on ground: girl

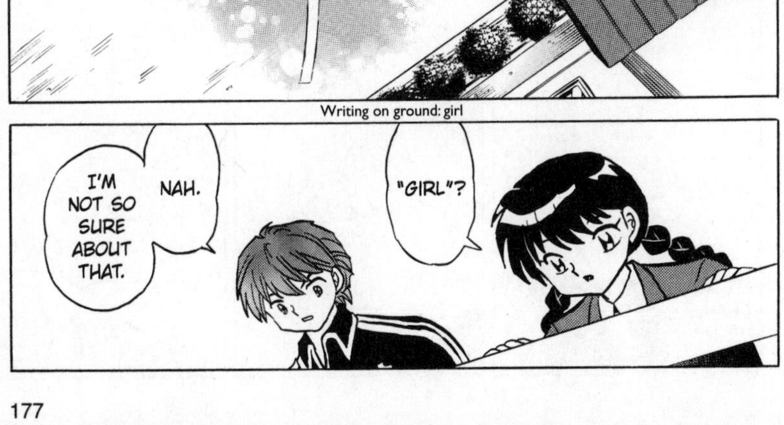
"GIRL"?
NAH.
I'M NOT SO SURE ABOUT THAT.

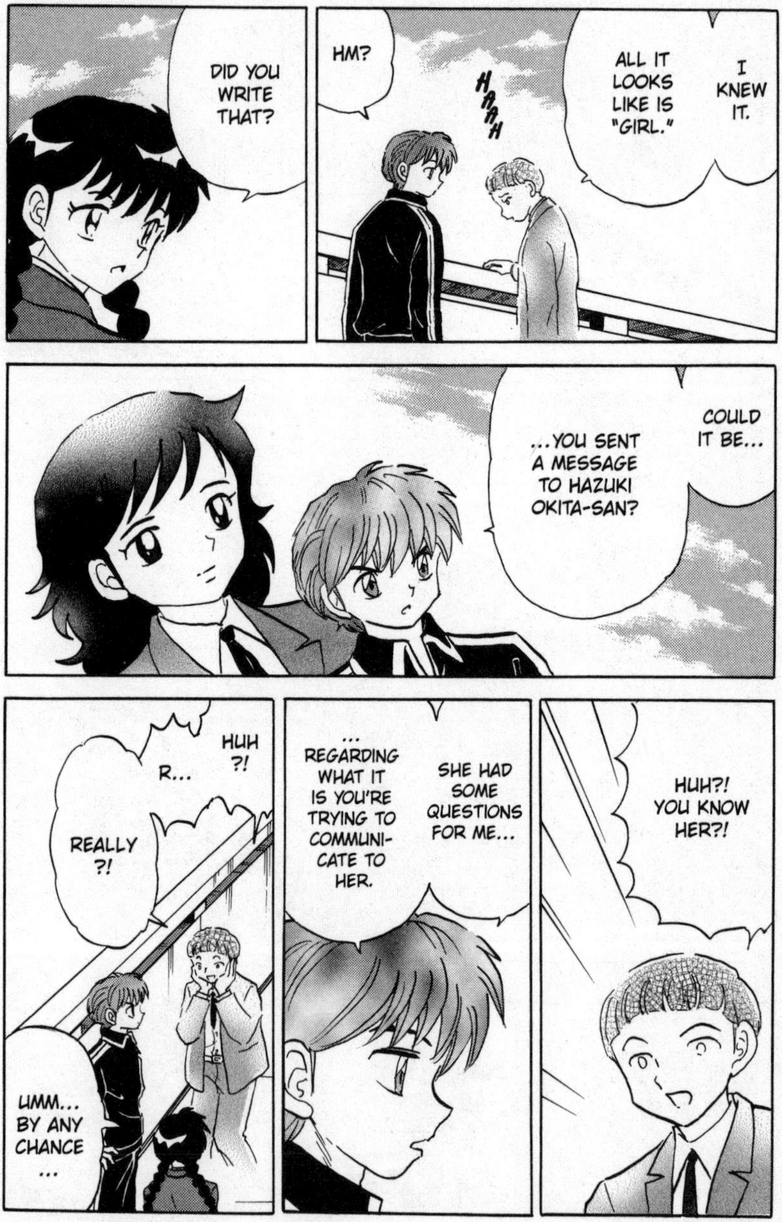
I KNEW IT.
ALL IT LOOKS LIKE IS "GIRL."
HAAH
HM?
DID YOU WRITE THAT?
COULD IT BE...
...YOU SENT A MESSAGE TO HAZUKI OKITA-SAN?
HUH?! YOU KNOW HER?!
SHE HAD SOME QUESTIONS FOR ME...
... REGARDING WHAT IT IS YOU'RE TRYING TO COMMUNICATE TO HER.
HUH ?!
R...
REALLY ?!
UMM... BY ANY CHANCE ...

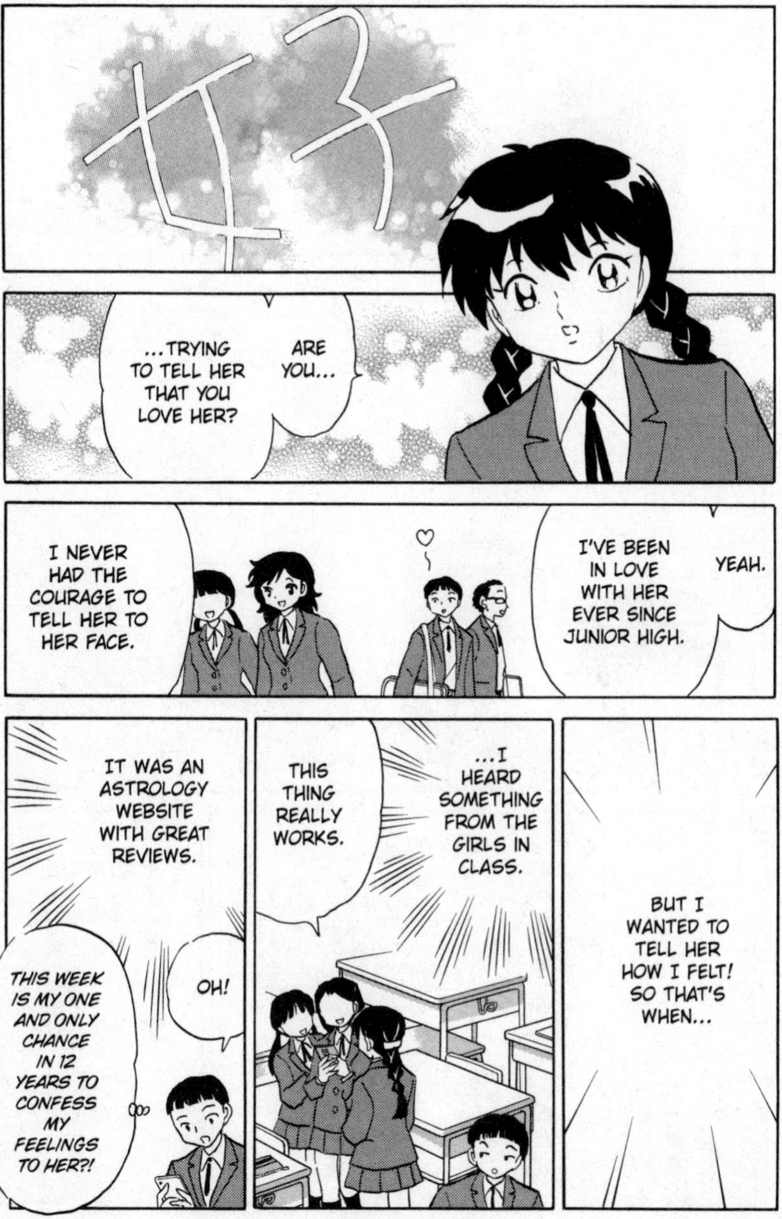
ARE YOU...
...TRYING TO TELL HER THAT YOU LOVE HER?
YEAH.
I'VE BEEN IN LOVE WITH HER EVER SINCE JUNIOR HIGH.
I NEVER HAD THE COURAGE TO TELL HER TO HER FACE.
BUT I WANTED TO TELL HER HOW I FELT! SO THAT'S WHEN...
...I HEARD SOMETHING FROM THE GIRLS IN CLASS.
THIS THING REALLY WORKS.
IT WAS AN ASTROLOGY WEBSITE WITH GREAT REVIEWS.
OH!
THIS WEEK IS MY ONE AND ONLY CHANCE IN 12 YEARS TO CONFESS MY FEELINGS TO HER?!

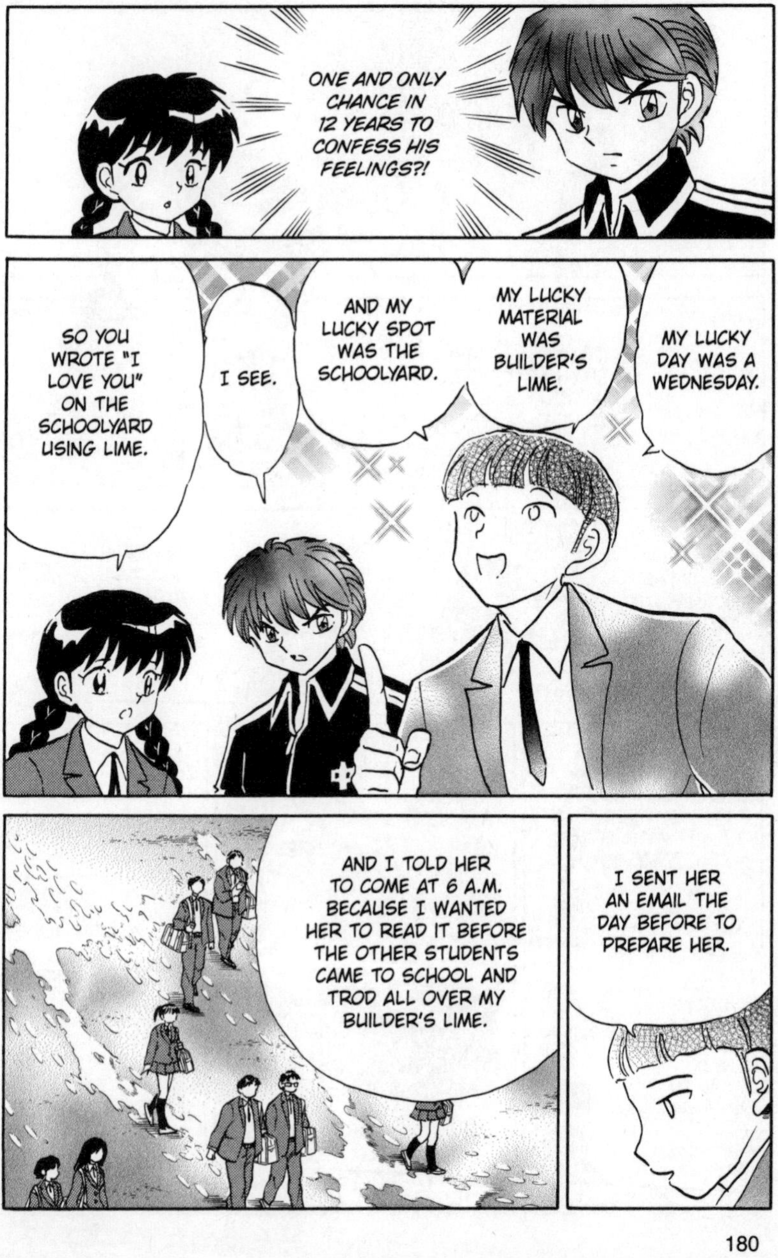
ONE AND ONLY CHANCE IN 12 YEARS TO CONFESS HIS FEELINGS?!
MY LUCKY DAY WAS A WEDNESDAY.
MY LUCKY MATERIAL WAS BUILDER'S LIME.
AND MY LUCKY SPOT WAS THE SCHOOLYARD.
I SEE.
SO YOU WROTE "I LOVE YOU" ON THE SCHOOLYARD USING LIME.
I SENT HER AN EMAIL THE DAY BEFORE TO PREPARE HER.
AND I TOLD HER TO COME AT 6 A.M. BECAUSE I WANTED HER TO READ IT BEFORE THE OTHER STUDENTS CAME TO SCHOOL AND TROD ALL OVER MY BUILDER'S LIME.

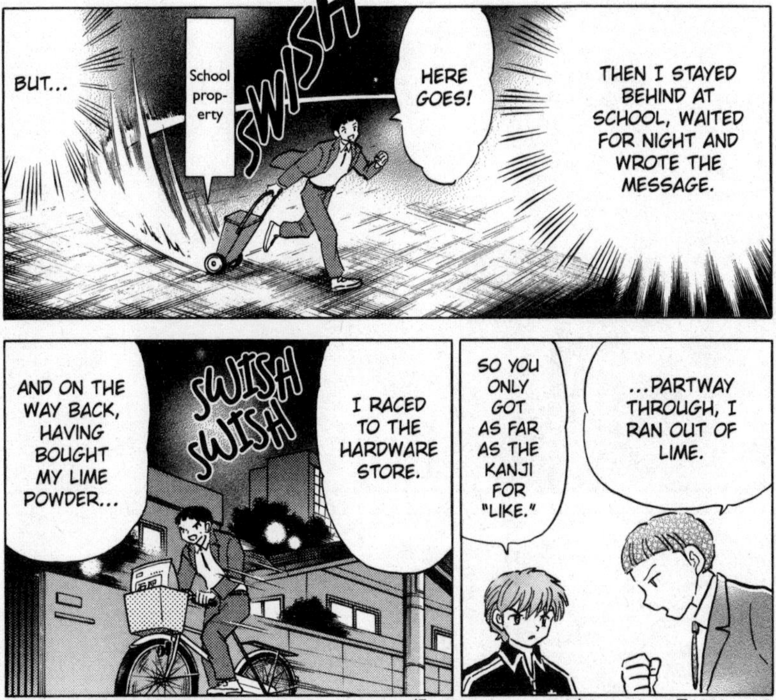
THEN I STAYED BEHIND AT SCHOOL, WAITED FOR NIGHT AND WROTE THE MESSAGE.
HERE GOES!
SWISH
School property
BUT...
...PARTWAY THROUGH, I RAN OUT OF LIME.
SO YOU ONLY GOT AS FAR AS THE KANJI FOR "LIKE."
I RACED TO THE HARDWARE STORE.
SWISH SWISH
AND ON THE WAY BACK, HAVING BOUGHT MY LIME POWDER...

The kanji that expresses the concept of like/love is 好, which is composed of 女(woman) and 子(child, or girl).

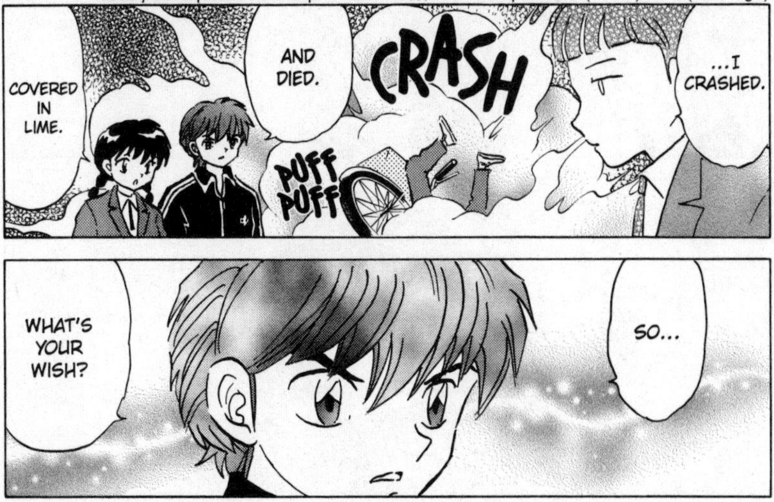
...I CRASHED.
CRASH
AND DIED.
PUFF PUFF
COVERED IN LIME.
SO...
WHAT'S YOUR WISH?

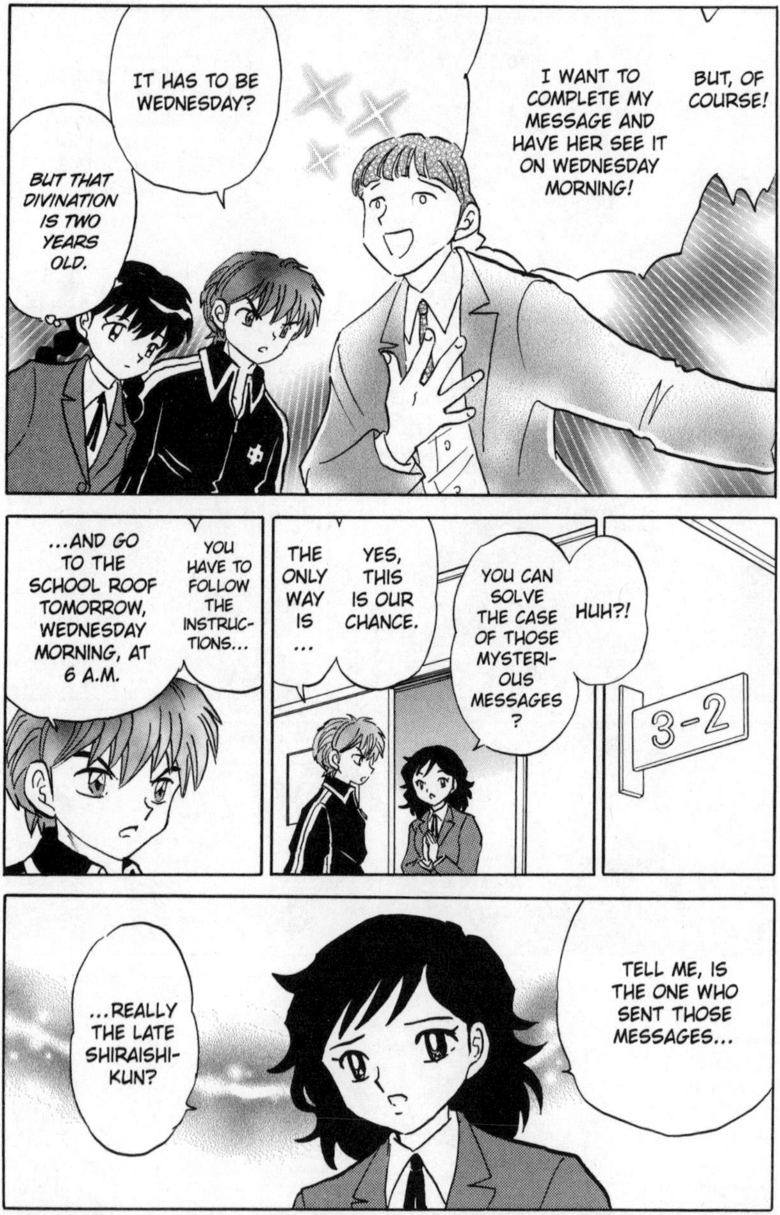
BUT, OF COURSE!
I WANT TO COMPLETE MY MESSAGE AND HAVE HER SEE IT ON WEDNESDAY MORNING!
IT HAS TO BE WEDNESDAY?
BUT THAT DIVINATION IS TWO YEARS OLD.
HUH?!
YOU CAN SOLVE THE CASE OF THOSE MYSTERIOUS MESSAGES?
YES, THIS IS OUR CHANCE.
THE ONLY WAY IS ...
YOU HAVE TO FOLLOW THE INSTRUCTIONS...
...AND GO TO THE SCHOOL ROOF TOMORROW, WEDNESDAY MORNING, AT 6 A.M.
3-2
TELL ME, IS THE ONE WHO SENT THOSE MESSAGES...
...REALLY THE LATE SHIRAISHI-KUN?

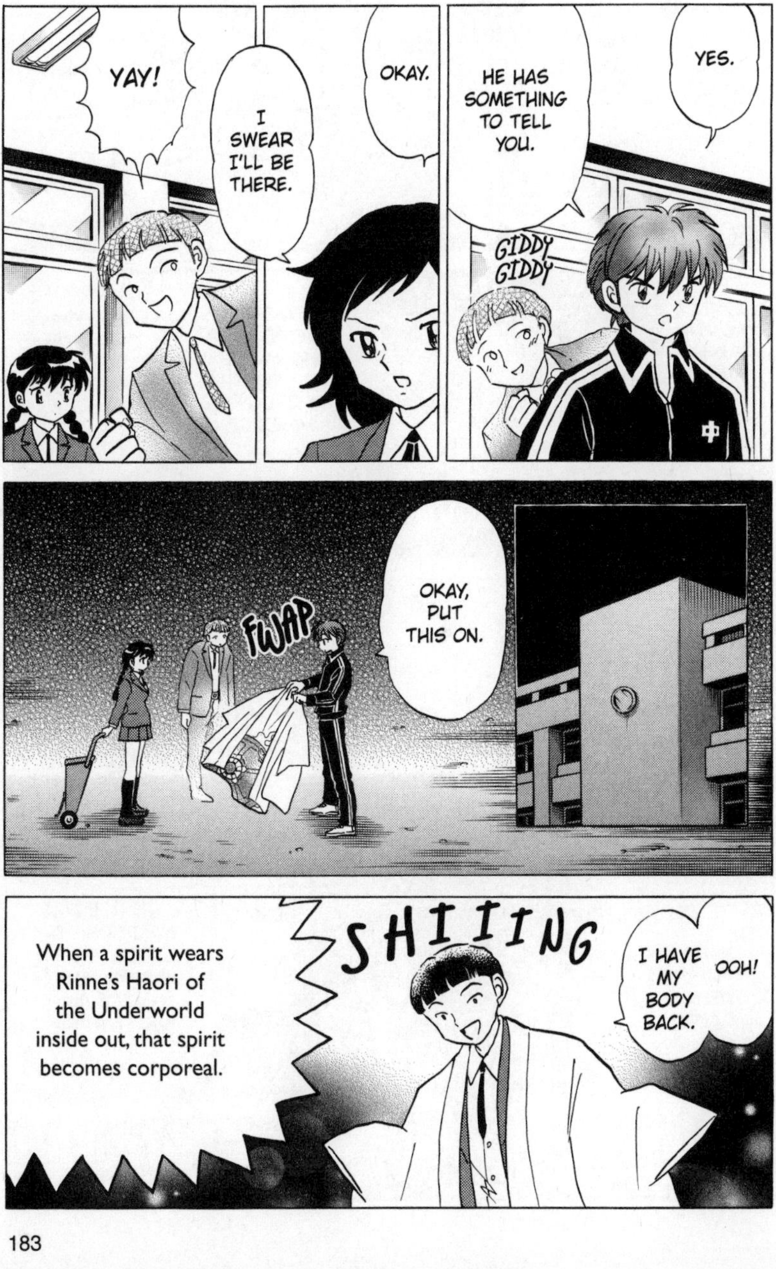
YES.
HE HAS SOMETHING TO TELL YOU.
GIDDY GIDDY
OKAY.
I SWEAR I'LL BE THERE.
YAY!
OKAY, PUT THIS ON.
FWAP
OOH!
I HAVE MY BODY BACK.
SHIIING
When a spirit wears Rinne's Haori of the Underworld inside out, that spirit becomes corporeal.

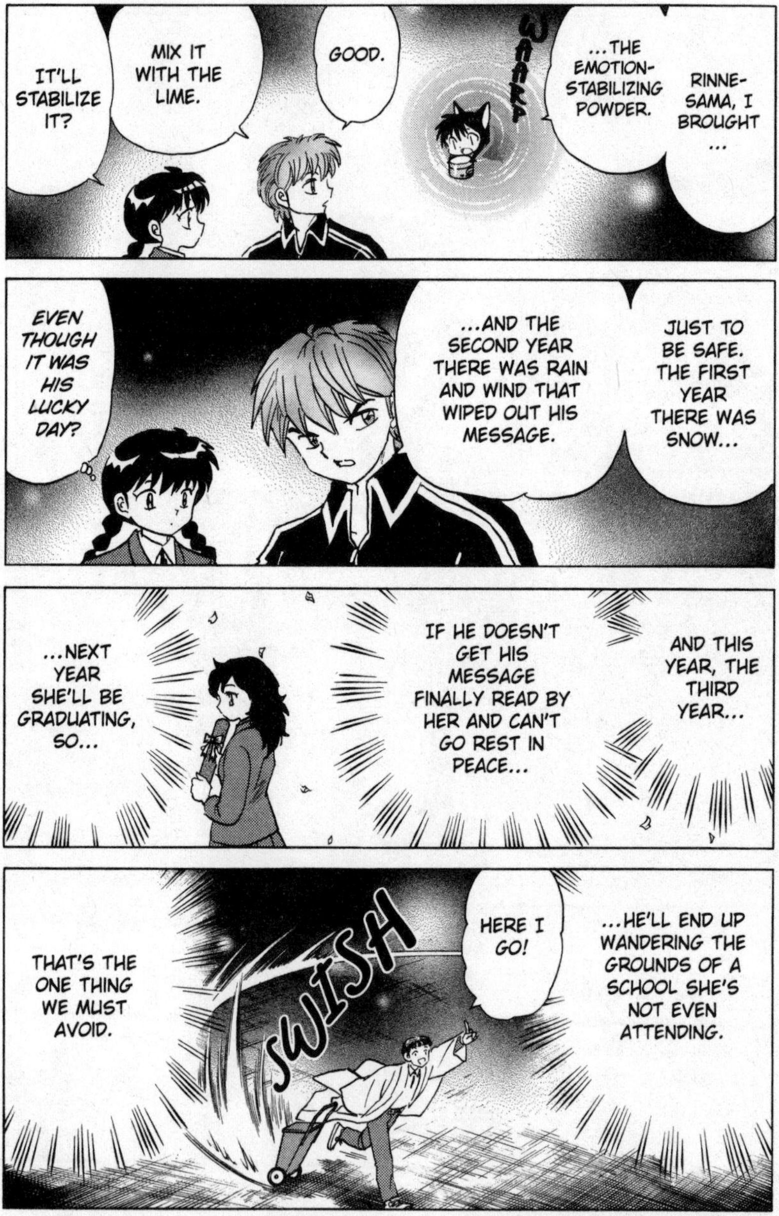
RINNE-SAMA, I BROUGHT...
...THE EMOTION-STABILIZING POWDER.
WAAARP
GOOD.
MIX IT WITH THE LIME.
IT'LL STABILIZE IT?
JUST TO BE SAFE. THE FIRST YEAR THERE WAS SNOW...
...AND THE SECOND YEAR THERE WAS RAIN AND WIND THAT WIPED OUT HIS MESSAGE.
EVEN THOUGH IT WAS HIS LUCKY DAY?
AND THIS YEAR, THE THIRD YEAR...
IF HE DOESN'T GET HIS MESSAGE FINALLY READ BY HER AND CAN'T GO REST IN PEACE...
...NEXT YEAR SHE'LL BE GRADUATING, SO...
...HE'LL END UP WANDERING THE GROUNDS OF A SCHOOL SHE'S NOT EVEN ATTENDING.
HERE I GO!
SWISH
THAT'S THE ONE THING WE MUST AVOID.

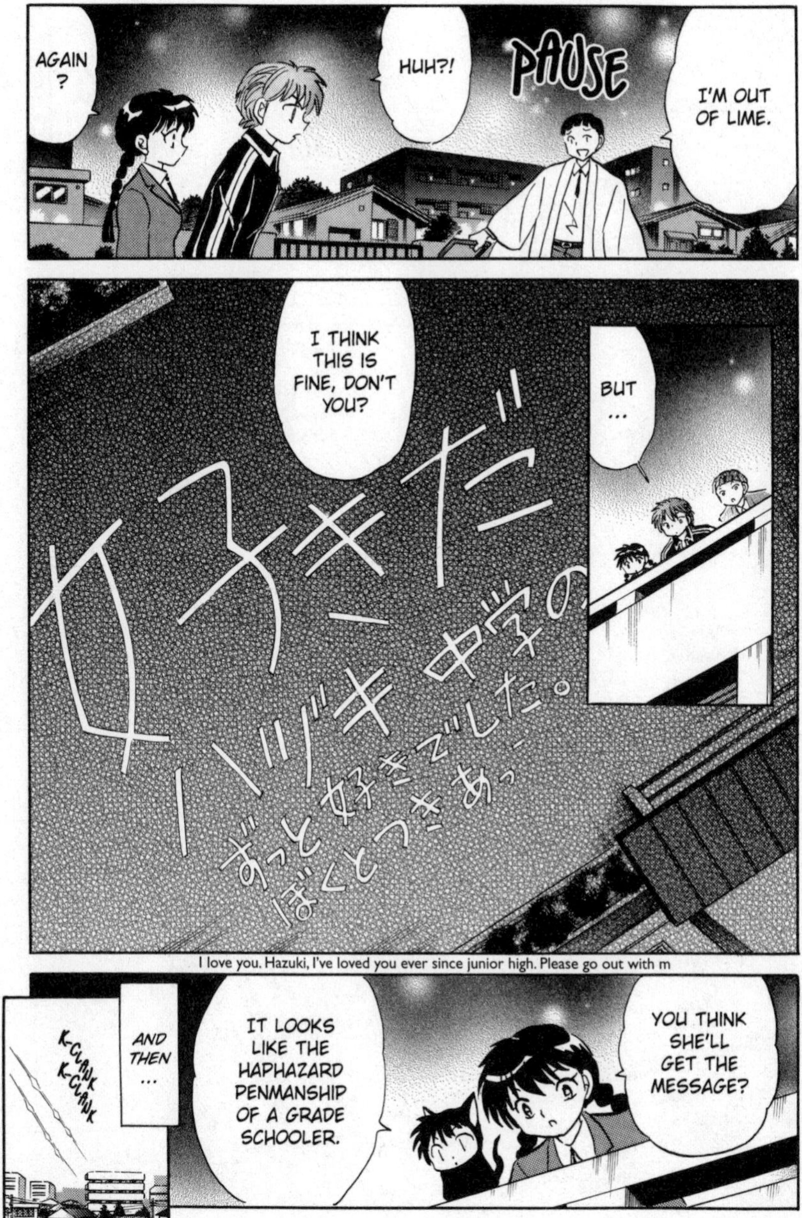
I'M OUT OF LIME.
PAUSE
HUH?!
AGAIN ?
BUT ...
I THINK THIS IS FINE, DON'T YOU?
好きだ
ハヅキ
中学の
ずっと好きでした。
ぼくとつきあっ
I love you. Hazuki, I've loved you ever since junior high. Please go out with m
YOU THINK SHE'LL GET THE MESSAGE?
IT LOOKS LIKE THE HAPHAZARD PENMANSHIP OF A GRADE SCHOOLER.
AND THEN ...
K-CLANK K-CLANK

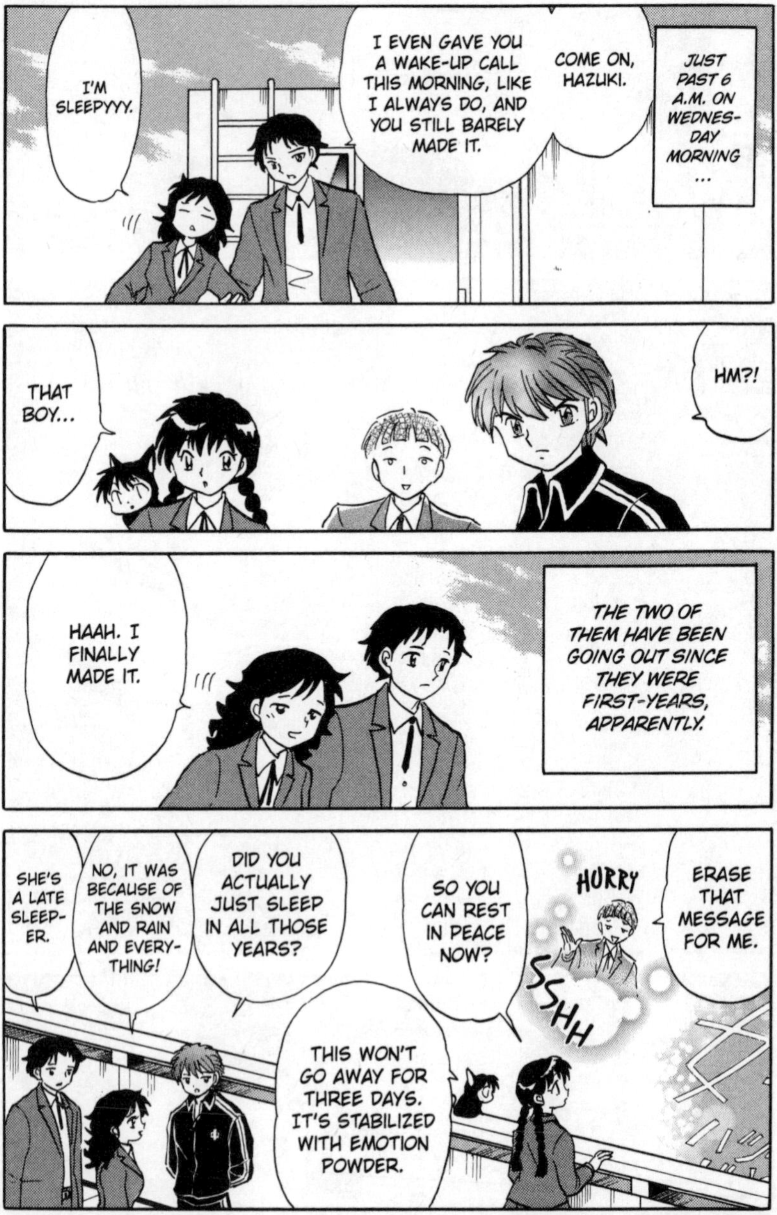
JUST PAST 6 A.M. ON WEDNES-DAY MORNING ...
COME ON, HAZUKI.
I EVEN GAVE YOU A WAKE-UP CALL THIS MORNING, LIKE I ALWAYS DO, AND YOU STILL BARELY MADE IT.
I'M SLEEPYYY.
HM?!
THAT BOY...
THE TWO OF THEM HAVE BEEN GOING OUT SINCE THEY WERE FIRST-YEARS, APPARENTLY.
HAAH. I FINALLY MADE IT.
ERASE THAT MESSAGE FOR ME.
HURRY
SSHH
SO YOU CAN REST IN PEACE NOW?
DID YOU ACTUALLY JUST SLEEP IN ALL THOSE YEARS?
THIS WON'T GO AWAY FOR THREE DAYS. IT'S STABILIZED WITH EMOTION POWDER.
NO, IT WAS BECAUSE OF THE SNOW AND RAIN AND EVERY-THING!
SHE'S A LATE SLEEP-ER.

RIN-NE VOLUME 32 - END -

Rumiko Takahashi

The spotlight on Rumiko Takahashi's career began in 1978 when she won an honorable mention in Shogakukan's prestigious New Comic Artist Contest for *Those Selfish Aliens*. Later that same year, her boy-meets-alien comedy series, *Urusei Yatsura*, was serialized in *Weekly Shonen Sunday*. This phenomenally successful manga series was adapted into anime format and spawned a TV series and half a dozen theatrical-release movies, all incredibly popular in their own right. Takahashi followed up the success of her debut series with one blockbuster hit after another—*Maison Ikkoku* ran from 1980 to 1987, *Ranma ½* from 1987 to 1996, and *Inuyasha* from 1996 to 2008. Other notable works include *Mermaid Saga*, *Rumic Theater*, and *One-Pound Gospel*.

Takahashi was inducted into the Will Eisner Comic Awards Hall of Fame in 2018. She won the prestigious Shogakukan Manga Award twice in her career, once for *Urusei Yatsura* in 1981 and the second time for *Inuyasha* in 2002. A majority of the Takahashi canon has been adapted into other media such as anime, live-action TV series, and film. Takahashi's manga, as well as the other formats her work has been adapted into, have continued to delight generations of fans around the world. Distinguished by her wonderfully endearing characters, Takahashi's work adeptly incorporates a wide variety of elements such as comedy, romance, fantasy, and martial arts. While her series are difficult to pin down into one simple genre, the signature style she has created has come to be known as the "Rumic World." Rumiko Takahashi is an artist who truly represents the very best from the world of manga.

RIN-NE
VOLUME 32
Shonen Sunday Edition

STORY AND ART BY
RUMIKO TAKAHASHI

KYOKAI NO RINNE Vol. 32
by Rumiko TAKAHASHI
© 2009 Rumiko TAKAHASHI
All rights reserved.
Original Japanese edition published by SHOGAKUKAN.
English translation rights in the United States of America,
Canada, the United Kingdom, Ireland, Australia and New
Zealand arranged with SHOGAKUKAN.

Translation/Christine Dashiell
Touch-up Art & Lettering/Evan Waldinger
Design/Yukiko Whitley
Editor/Megan Bates

Printed in the U.S.A.

Published by VIZ Media, LLC
P.O. Box 77010
San Francisco, CA 94107

10 9 8 7 6 5 4 3 2 1
First printing, March 2020

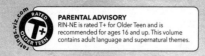

viz.com

shonensunday.com

Komi Can't Communicate

Story & Art by Tomohito Oda

The journey to a hundred friends begins with a single conversation.

Socially anxious high school student Shoko Komi's greatest dream is to make some friends, but everyone at school mistakes her crippling social anxiety for cool reserve. With the whole student body keeping its distance and Komi unable to utter a single word, friendship might be forever beyond her reach.

 VIZ

COMI-SAN WA, COMYUSHO DESU. © 2016 Tomohito ODA/SHOGAKUKAN

Kidnapped by the Demon King and imprisoned in his castle, Princess Syalis is...bored.

SLEEPY PRINCESS IN THE DEMON CASTLE

Story & Art by
KAGIJI KUMANOMATA

Captured princess Syalis decides to while away her hours in the Demon Castle by sleeping, but getting a good night's rest turns out to be a lot of work! She begins by fashioning a DIY pillow out of the fur of her Teddy Demon guards and an "air mattress" from the magical Shield of the Wind. Things go from bad to worse—for her captors—when some of Princess Syalis's schemes end in her untimely—if temporary—demise and she chooses the Forbidden Grimoire for her bedtime reading...

Hey! You're Reading in the Wrong Direction!

This is the end of this graphic novel!

To properly enjoy this VIZ graphic novel, please turn it around and begin reading from right to left. Unlike English, Japanese is read right to left, so Japanese comics are read in reverse order from the way English comics are typically read.

This book has been printed in the original Japanese format in order to preserve the orientation of the original artwork. Have fun with it!

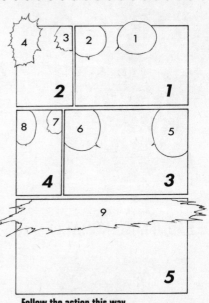

Follow the action this way